DRUMMING WITH DEAD CAN DANCE

AND PARALLEL ADVENTURES

DRUMMING WITH

DEAD CAN DANCE

AND PARALLEL ADVENTURES

PETER ULRICH

Red Hen Press | *Pasadena , CA*

Book layout by Mark E. Cull

Library of Congress Cataloging-in-Publication Data

Names: Ulrich, Peter, 1958– author.
Title: Drumming with Dead Can Dance and parallel adventures/Peter Ulrich.

Description: Pasadena, CA : Red Hen Press, 2022. | Includes index.
Identifiers: LCCN 2022016763 (print) | LCCN 2022016764 (ebook) | ISBN
    9781636280738 (hardcover) | ISBN 9781636280745 (ebook)
Subjects: LCSH: Ulrich, Peter, 1958– | Drummers (Musicians)—Biography. |
    Dead Can Dance (Musical group) | Darkwave (Music)—History and
    criticism. | LCGFT: Autobiographies.
Classification: LCC ML419.U474 A3 2022 (print) | LCC ML419.U474 (ebook) |
    DDC 782.42166092 [B]—dc23/eng/20220407
LC record available at https://lccn.loc.gov/2022016763
LC ebook record available at https://lccn.loc.gov/2022016764

Publication of this book has been made possible in part through the generous financial support of Ann Beman.

The National Endowment for the Arts, the Los Angeles County Arts Commission, the Ahmanson Foundation, the Dwight Stuart Youth Fund, the Max Factor Family Foundation, the Pasadena Tournament of Roses Foundation, the Pasadena Arts & Culture Commission and the City of Pasadena Cultural Affairs Division, the City of Los Angeles Department of Cultural Affairs, the Audrey & Sydney Irmas Charitable Foundation, the Meta & George Rosenberg Foundation, the Albert and Elaine Borchard Foundation, the Adams Family Foundation, Amazon Literary Partnership, the Sam Francis Foundation, and the Mara W. Breech Foundation partially support Red Hen Press.

First Edition
Published by Red Hen Press
www.redhen.org

ACKNOWLEDGEMENTS

I thank everyone who appears in this memoir, together with anyone I've inadvertently omitted, who all contributed to the thickening of the plot.

I thank everyone who helped proofread and check various versions and portions, including Brendan, Lisa, Nicki, Louise, my amazing Aunt Barbara (aka Carolyn Gray), Lisa Tenzin-Dolma, Trebor Lloyd, Jules Maxwell, and Jon Brahams. My thanks also to WHV for extensive support and for making the innocent enquiry which gave rise to my first Appendix.

I thank everyone who helped compile the illustrations – those whose credits appear alongside their pictures, and also Rich Walker at 4AD, Steve Webbon and Sadie Matthew at Beggars Banquet, Saskia Dommisse, Olivier Mellano, Alice Atkinson at Air-Edel, the team at Snappy Snaps in Norwich, Trebor and a bunch of members of the wonderful TPUC crew – Erin Hill, Anne Husick, Sharon Hochma-Hawk, and Tim Dark – who all went above and beyond, and especially Jeff Earp, who mined the vaults with unstinting resolve and unearthed some gems!

I thank everyone who helped with each push along the road to finding my publishing home, with a mention in dispatches for Stephen Davies and Jon Tregenna at Penderyn Distillery, Tom Mayer at W. W. Norton, Tim O'Donnell, and Graeme Milton at Helter Skelter.

I thank everyone at Red Hen Press for bringing this book into being, particularly Kate Gale and Mark E. Cull for taking it on, Natasha McClellan and Rebeccah Sanhueza for guiding it so carefully through production, and Tobi Harper, Monica Fernandez and Tansica Sunkamaneevongse for shouting its credentials from the rooftops.

I thank my nearest and dearest, particularly Nicki, Louise, and Ellie, for constant support and encouragement.

And, of course, I can never sufficiently thank Brendan and Lisa, not only for the wonderful music they create, the incredible opportunities they gave me, and their support for my music projects, but also for the enthusiasm they've shown for this written record of our adventures, and the huge help they've given me in bringing this all together.

And I thank the huge hand of fate.

Thank you all.

CONTENTS

FOREWORD

When I look back at the glazed paragraphs of the past, the stench of stale beer rotting back stage carpets, hunger, and grey London skies, they drift into a dissolving memory from which the poetry of our dreams rose and found unsensed significance, not only in our hearts, but also in the hearts of others.

—Lisa Gerrard

ONE

December 1982. I was working at Riverside Studios, a fringe theatre and arts centre in West London where I was Press and Publicity Officer. I should've been one of a team of six, but the promotions department had been whittled down to just me as the centre hurtled towards financial disaster. Finally the day came when those of us remaining on the skeleton staff were told that Riverside was going into 'administration' and we were being made redundant with immediate effect. Although we'd been expecting it, nobody quite knew how to react. Some vowed to work on for no wages in the hope that a financial saviour would swoop to the rescue, others started packing their things to leave.

I sat alone in my office contemplating a long list of outstanding tasks. If the theatre was about to 'go dark', what was the point in continuing to promote performances that would likely never take place? A couple of months earlier, I'd been offered the opportunity to jump ship and join the promotions team at the Lyric Theatre in Hammersmith – a larger and better funded setup just down the road. I'd been flattered, and tempted, but turned it down out of loyalty to Riverside, which would've been unable to appoint a replacement for me and left with no publicity staff at all. The position at the Lyric had since been filled, so that door was closed, and now here I was with no job and no idea what I'd do next.

The phone rang. The caller introduced himself as Brendan Perry and asked me – with impeccable timing of which he was entirely oblivious – if I had much on. He'd heard I was a drummer and asked if I'd be interested in auditioning for a band. It turned out he lived in an adjacent block of flats to mine on the Barkantine Estate in an area of East London colourfully called The Isle of Dogs. He'd been given my number by a friend from the estate.

The Barkantine is a 1960s-built public sector housing estate of dubious architectural merit, apparently designed to represent the layout of a sailing galleon if viewed aerially. Today this may be possible using a drone-cam, but back then you couldn't unless you cared to charter a plane and fly over it. Its most prominent feature is four, twenty-one-storey tower blocks – Topmast Point, Midship Point, Knighthead Point, and Bowsprit Point – around which various low-rise residential blocks plus a few shops are arranged in equally nautically named streets such as Tiller Road and The Quarterdeck.

Brendan had recently arrived in London from Australia where, by virtue of his father's local family roots, he'd been allocated a flat on the thirteenth floor of Bowsprit Point, together with Lisa Gerrard, Paul Erikson, Jeff Earp, and Jim Atkins. Brendan, Lisa, and Paul formed the nucleus of a band called 'Dead Can Dance', which they'd formed in Melbourne a couple of years earlier, and had now come to London in search of a recording deal. Their original drummer, Simon Munroe, had decided against the move and elected to stay in Melbourne. Jeff and Jim were friends from Melbourne, Jeff studying photography and film, Jim a sometime sound engineer and roadie for the band who now, due to insufficient rooms in the flat, inhabited a sizeable but windowless storage cupboard off the hallway and apparently lived off little other than variously prepared configurations of chickpeas.

I'd lived for almost two years in a flat on the sixth floor of Knighthead Point with my girlfriend, Nicki. We weren't originally from the area, both having grown up in West London, but my first job after graduating had been in the Public Relations office at Tower Hamlets Council, and I'd become eligible for a council flat in the borough as an employee. We moved in when Nicki completed her postgraduate teacher training, and she'd quickly found herself a job at nearby Cubitt Town School.

To the casual observer, the Barkantine Estate appeared drab and run-down, with the usual spattering of graffiti, litter flying around in the fierce drafts of wind which were channelled between the concrete monoliths, and a constant aroma of stale urine in the lifts and stair wells. But the flats themselves were bright, spacious and had truly spectacular views over the River Thames and central London skyline. In between Bowsprit and Knighthead lay a characterless, rectangular box of a community hall with anti-vandal wire grilles covering all the windows. The hall was available for hire by local residents, and for convenience's sake (particularly as none of us owned a car) this was the natural choice of venue for my audition.

My phone number had been given to Brendan by Tony Wright, another drummer who lived on the nineteenth floor of Knighthead. Tony had already auditioned, but it hadn't worked out so he suggested me. I wasn't sure what to make of this. Tony was about as different from me as possible – a cool, good-looking, charismatic Black guy who dressed sharply and specialised in slick soul drumming. He was always playing with four or five different bands at any given time and was desperate to break into the 'music biz' on a professional basis and quit his day job as a chef. Tony was technically a far better drummer than me, constantly studying the jazz greats and refining his skills. We'd borrow equipment off each other and, whenever I went up to his flat, he'd whisk out a flurry of vinyl recordings by the likes of Gene Krupa and Max Roach and have me checking out different beats and fills which were way beyond my capabilities. During his DCD audition, Tony had apparently kept time patiently to a few of Brendan, Lisa, and Paul's songs before suggesting that they might be better off trying something with a reggae vibe to lighten things up a bit. They fairly rapidly all came to the conclusion that Tony was not the drummer Dead Can Dance were looking for.

So there I was, setting up my battered old Premier Olympic drum kit under the watchful eyes of the three recent arrivals from the other side of the world, wondering what to expect. I realised I'd kind of 'met' Lisa before as she'd called at our flat a few weeks earlier selling houseplants door-to-door – I knew I hadn't bought one, but hoped I hadn't been rude. Initially just Brendan and Paul started playing guitar and bass, but I was immediately struck by two sensations. The first was wonderment at what I was hearing; the second bewilderment because I had no idea what to play to it. The music sounded amazing – all sorts of complexities going on between the two instruments, plus a barrage of effects, creating a brooding, mystical form which completely enveloped me and set the stark, featureless Barkantine Hall rattling and buzzing. I'd heard a few things vaguely like this before, but I'd never played anything like it. I was a pub band drummer who essentially played basic time-keeping to standards. On that level, I was quite competent, but here I was way out of my depth.

After a couple of fairly pathetic attempts at pitching myself into the sound, I shot Brendan a pleading look for help and he stopped playing and came over. Although he'd never learnt to play a drum kit, he had an ability to hear what he wanted in his head, then throw himself at the kit and hold the pattern for maybe three or four bars before he lost the necessary limb coordination to sustain it. This, then, was my time frame in which to take in what he was doing, and try to replicate it. We managed to figure out a couple of drum parts he wanted by this method and muddled through a couple of songs. We then enacted that most English of traditions and took a tea break. Although Paul was quiet, and seemingly quite shy, Brendan and Lisa were very open and friendly. We quickly discovered some shared tastes, including a love of Joy Division and a fascination with African drumming, and I was (I think) the first person they'd met since arriving in England who'd not only heard of, but actually owned an album by The Birthday Party, who they'd known on the club scene in Melbourne before Nick Cave & Co had moved to London ahead of them and signed to 4AD Records.

We played through the couple of songs again and I started feeling a little more comfortable. But by the time we packed up, I felt I'd been privileged to join in briefly with something that sounded so powerful, but that I'd proved myself hopelessly inadequate. I expected they'd thank me, we'd say goodbye, and I'd see them around and look out for their progress. Nothing much was said, and we started humping equipment back to the flats. Then, to my surprise, as we took a lift full of amps and guitars to the thirteenth floor in Bowsprit, Lisa turned to Brendan and said in a matter-of-fact way, but apparently completely genuinely and with a sigh of relief, 'Well, at least we've found a drummer now.' Brendan didn't reply, and I knew he hadn't reached the same conclusion, but his attitude towards me remained warm and I was asked along to the next rehearsal.

Fig. 1. Rehearsing in the Barkantine Hall, early 1983. Left to right: Lisa, Paul Erikson on bass, me on drums, and Brendan. Photo by Jeffrey Earp.

As far as I remember, I was never formally invited to join Dead Can Dance, but over the next few weeks I was just, sort of . . . absorbed. Probably the most important element of this was the friendship which quickly developed between us. Brendan had been forced to leave the bulk of his record collection back in Australia so his visits to my flat gave him the opportunity to rake through mine. In return, he'd bring over his few cherished cassette tapes to play to me – and these included a couple of the most striking things I'd ever heard.

One was a single song – the original recording which he and Lisa had made in Australia of a piece of music they'd written called 'Frontier'. Brendan had spontaneously created a driving rhythm on three old oil drums which had been hammered to create different notes, and using a pair of broken chair legs for drumsticks as they were the only things to hand. He had to record it in one take because the oil drums were disintegrating as he played. Over this rhythm, he'd recorded a low vocal part like a monastic chant, fed through a Roland Space Echo to create some atmospherics, and Lisa had then added a soaring, astonishingly powerful lead vocal in a mysterious, indecipherable language. The finishing touches were some occasional notes and flourishes played on an exotic Chinese instrument of Lisa's called a yang ch'in (a type of hammered dulcimer). It was a startling piece, like nothing I'd heard before, and I was overcome by an urge to take the tape and play it to everybody I could find, saying, 'You've got to hear this, just stop and listen to this!!'

The second was a well-worn cassette of an album by then New York-based Nigerian drummer Babatunde Olatunji called 'Drums of Passion'. All tracks are performed by a group of drummers and a vocal chorus. One song – Jin-Go-Lo-Ba (which, depending on your source, is either the album title, or means 'Don't worry' in the Yoruba language, or perhaps both?) – I knew by Santana's version, but hadn't previously realised theirs was a cover, and much as I liked Santana's, hearing the original now was a revelation. Olatunji's ensemble produced one of the most vibrant and exciting albums I'd ever come across – like a sound I'd been searching for but never previously found.

By this stage, I'd also heard more of Dead Can Dance's music, I'd experienced the extraordinary power that Brendan could drive out of his guitar, and I'd heard Lisa sing – enough said! I'd heard these things in the utterly uninspiring and acoustically awful surrounds of the Barkantine Hall, and yet they sounded phenomenal. Although I still felt out of my depth in their company, I knew I desperately wanted to be involved in making music with these people who both created and were inspired by these new sounds I was being exposed to.

I think this was Brendan's final test of my suitability for the DCD drum stool. He wanted to gauge my reaction to all he was laying before me, and fortunately my reaction was strong enough to allow him to feel settled that the decision was made – he could mould me and develop me as a drummer, provided I bought into his vision and commitment. In all probability, another critical factor in his decision was the discovery of our shared passion for football ('soccer' to those who think football is played by blokes in crash helmets using their hands). Much to Lisa's dismay and Paul's bemusement, breaks in rehearsals became regularly hijacked by the latest game analysis – something Brendan had clearly missed during his absence from England for the past few years (he'd been brought up in London until his family emigrated to New Zealand when he was fifteen). However, Lisa recognised this as a useful safety valve for Brendan, and graciously allowed the indulgence, only occasionally trying to switch the conversation to some odd concept called 'Aussie Rules'.

I learnt a little more of their backgrounds. Brendan's introduction to the guitar had come during his emigratory six-week voyage aboard an old Greek ship, the *Ellinis*. Learning the instrument became the foundation stone of his new life in New Zealand, and an expansion to playing bass paved his way into the punk scene in Auckland. After joining local band The Scavengers in late 1977, he also took over vocal duties, adopting a sneering delivery in a marked Johnny Rotten-style, and an alter ego of 'Ronnie Recent'. Frustrated by the lack of opportunity offered by the local scene, the band moved to Australia the following year, initially to Sydney, then to Melbourne where they changed name to Marching Girls. Ironically, having taken lengths to distance themselves, Marching Girls sneaked into the NZ singles charts in 1980 with the song 'True Love' (for which Brendan's writing contribution is attributed to 'R. Perry'). Brendan grew bored with the confines of repetitive punk formats and drifted away to explore more experimental musical climes with a broader range of influences. To free himself from the anchor role of bass guitarist, he found local bassist Paul and devised the name for his new project – 'Dead Can Dance' – for which he also recruited former Scavengers/Marching Girls drummer Simon Munroe (aka 'Des Truction' and 'Des Hefner').

Lisa had been born in Melbourne to an Irish father and English mother (opposite of Brendan – English father, Irish mother). She grew up in the suburb of Prahran with its large Greek community, the culture and particularly the music of which had a big influence in her formative years, as did exposure at home to a traditional form of Irish unaccompanied singing known as 'Sean-nós' which her father was particularly partial to. She was naturally drawn to performance and, as young as fourteen, was sneaking out to sing in notorious local bars with drunken brawls regularly flying around her. Her parents found out and whisked her off to the local operatic society in an attempt to rechannel her stage lust, but a brush with *Oklahoma* was too much for Lisa. She escaped to the post-punk 'Little Band' scene which was flourishing as the 1970s drew to a close in the neighbourhoods of Fitzroy and St Kilda, and was briefly in a duo called Junk Logic, then lead vocalist in a band called Microfilm which released one single, 'Centrefold', in 1980. Microfilm had another song, 'Summer House', included on the compilation album *From Belgravia with Love* released on American label Cleopatra in 1981, which also featured a song 'Mosaic' under Lisa's own name. But like Brendan, Lisa was uncomfortable in the constrictions of formulaic band and song structures and needed to find freedom of expression in her music. Armed with the unlikely duo of an old piano accordion and her yang ch'in, which she trundled around in a shopping trolley, she returned to solo performing and became increasingly experimental with her vocal style, singing either somewhat skewed lyrics or in an entirely made-up language, and pounding frenetically at one or other of her accompanying instruments. She'd play pretty much anywhere that would have her, and secured a residency at the Rising Sun Hotel in Richmond where she recalls establishing her first fan club – three stalwarts who would turn up for her every appearance.

It was as witness to such a performance, and with Lisa singing about finding a man in the park and asking her mother's permission to bring him home and keep him in her wardrobe, that Brendan first encountered her, and he confesses to have found her terrifying! Nevertheless, he saw a quality in what she was doing that, if he could just bring it within the framework of his own emerging musical vision without clipping its wings, they could have something truly unique and inspiring. So Lisa and Brendan got to know each other, fell in love with each other's music, and with each other. Lisa joined the nascent Dead Can Dance and on 24 October 1981 they made their debut at the Carlton Community Centre in Melbourne. The gig was compèred by local celebrity Ron Rude who, as well as having been the prime mover behind Microfilm and the *Belgravia* compilation, was a pioneer of indie/DIY recording (having self-released his first album in 1979) and a figure of some notoriety for staging a hunger strike in a record shop window demanding that a local radio station play his music and threatening to drown himself in a bucket of water if they refused!

A week later DCD's second gig was secured at the venue which was central to their musical world at the time – the Seaview Hotel in St Kilda. The Seaview not only hosted indigenous bands including Boys Next Door/The Birthday Party, The Go-Betweens, Midnight Oil, INXS, and Hunters & Collectors, but also rising international acts of the era including The Cure, Simple Minds, Magazine, The Stranglers, XTC, Dead Kennedys, and Iggy Pop. In all the Seaview Ballroom crops up eleven times in the schedule of DCD's early Australian appearances, making it to this day DCD's most-played venue by some distance:

Melbourne, Australia:
1981
Saturday, 24 October, Carlton Community Centre
Saturday, 31 October, St Kilda, Seaview Ballroom
Saturday, 7 November, Richmond, Royal Oak Hotel Tiger Lounge
Saturday, 21 November, St Kilda, Seaview Ballroom
Thursday, 26 November, Caulfield Technical Institute
Friday, 4 December, St Kilda, Seaview Ballroom
Saturday, 5 December, Collingwood, Jump Club
Tuesday, 8 December, St Kilda, Seaview Ballroom
Thursday, 31 December, St Kilda, Seaview Ballroom

1982
Saturday, 9 January, St Kilda, Seaview Ballroom
Thursday, 14 January, Richmond, Central Club
Saturday, 23 January, St Kilda, Seaview Ballroom
Thursday, 28 January, Richmond, Central Club
Saturday, 20 February, St Kilda, Seaview Ballroom
Saturday, 13 March, St Kilda, Seaview Ballroom
Friday, 19 March, St Kilda, Seaview Ballroom
Saturday, 20 March, East Prahran, Mount Erica Hotel
Saturday, 27 March, Carlton North, Stockade Hotel
Friday, 2 April, St Kilda, Seaview Ballroom

The above gigs were performed with a set of around ten original DCD songs. They ranged from sharing an unlikely looking bill with People With Chairs Up Their Noses and the Beaumaris Tennis Club Quartet (Caulfield, 26 November 1981), via headlining the downstairs bar at the Seaview before Simple Minds (on their inaugural tour of Australia) played the main ballroom stage (8 December 1981), playing the Seaview with The Birthday Party who were making a return appearance after their move to London in 1980 (20 February 1982), to sharing bills with The Go-Betweens, The Moodists, Plays with Marionettes, and Hunters & Collectors. After the performance at Collingwood's Jump Club on 5 December 1981, promoter Laurie Richards, who operated many of Melbourne's music venues around this time, pronounced DCD the worst band he'd ever seen . . . well, everyone needs their Beatles' 'Dick Rowe' (I know, he denied it, please don't write in).

While this tight-knit corner of the Melbourne club scene had proved ideal to cut DCD's teeth, Brendan's vision was already demanding a bigger stage. His family had recently returned from New Zealand to London, and now his own return was calling. He and Lisa packed their bags, boarded a flight and headed for the other hemisphere. On first arrival they moved into the modest council flat which Brendan's family had been allocated in Poplar. Together with Ma and Pa Perry, sister Dawn and brother Robert, they now numbered six – one short of the local council's official definition of 'overcrowded'. A friend from Melbourne, Jeff Earp, also recently arrived in London, was commandeered to become an honorary Perry cousin and given a berth on the sofa until the council inspector called by to confirm too many sardines in the tin. The flat in Bowsprit Point was awarded, which Jeff recalls was 'minus a good deal of window glass and just about everything else'.

Fig. 2. The Barkantine Estate, Isle of Dogs, early 1983: the inspirational (?) setting for DCD's output in those early years. Photo by Jeffrey Earp.

While Lisa did her best to furnish their new home on a virtually nonexistent budget from the local secondhand shop 'Treasure Island' (I kid you not!), Brendan summoned the other half of Dead Can Dance only to be met with stubborn resistance to leave Oz. Eventually, he managed to persuade bassist Paul to take the plunge, but drummer Des (Simon) wouldn't budge. A first batch of demo tapes, which Brendan cobbled together with some cheap cases acquired from Chrisp Street Market and hand-delivered by bicycle tour around London-based indie record labels Cherry Red, Mute, Rough Trade, and 4AD, had failed to elicit any response, and now Lisa and Paul's first experience of a grey and bitter London winter set in.

The contrast to what they'd left behind was both harsh and extreme. They were no longer in the heart of a vibrant musical community, they were no longer by the sea, they knew virtually nobody and they were marooned in one of the world's great capital cities with no money, only their dream of an elusive record deal. Their lives had changed dramatically, and now they changed the course of mine. In a few short weeks straddling Christmas 1982 I went from being a redundant theatre press officer to the drummer of Dead Can Dance, an ambition that had never previously crossed my mind.

TWO

Perhaps there were signs I might have a musical destiny. My birth on the exact same day as Michael Jackson (29 August 1958) and my shared surname with Metallica drummer Lars Ulrich are no doubt pure coincidence. But there is music in my family.

A great-aunt Alice (father's side) was a piano teacher, and great-aunt Marjorie reputedly the first woman to publicly play the mighty organ in London's Royal Albert Hall. My paternal grandparents met through amateur operatics, and my aunt Barbara (father's sister) was a professional singer who appeared in musicals and light operas in London's theatreland. She even had a stage name – Carolyn Gray – which was considered a very exotic thing. As a child I loved outings to see her in big productions such as *The Sound of Music, Mame* with Ginger Rogers, and *The Great Waltz*, being taken backstage afterwards to meet members of the cast and visiting her flat in Kensington where the toilet walls were painted dark red and covered with posters and programmes from her shows. On my mother's side too it had been the norm for families to have a piano and for all children to take lessons as a matter of course. Somewhere amongst the nth cousins so many times removed was a lad called Bobby Crush (genuinely his name – not a stage name) who won the 'Opportunity Knocks' TV talent contest in 1972 and went on to become a renowned pianist and entertainer, appearing in productions of *Rocky Horror Show* and *Chicago* and touring with Gene Pitney.

And so my parents dutifully installed an upright piano and when I was about seven I started lessons. My first teacher was Miss West, a spinster (presumably) of advancing years whose demeanour was a curious blend of warmth and sternness. Lessons were conducted in her home music room, so full of voluminous houseplants it seemed like stepping into a jungle, giving a distinctly surreal edge to suburban scale learning. It was soon apparent that I wasn't a natural – progress was laboured and I found practising the basics very tedious. The only way I could derive any enjoyment from learning piano was by trying to write things myself. So, armed with the most basic grasp of musical notation, I composed my first piece of music. It was only a few bars, and more of a trumpet line just in the treble clef, but it seemed to impress Miss West, and to my parents it attained Mozart-like child prodigy status. However, I was frustrated by my technical limitations and progress remained slow. My three years of formal piano tuition straddled a move of house from Harrow to Eastcote – one northwest London suburb to another nearby – and a consequent change of piano teacher to Mr Scott, a younger guy who also taught guitar, and whose tuition I should have found more stimulating, but didn't.

Fig. 3. That's me in 1960, coming up to two years old and showing more interest in transportation than anything musical at this point. Photo from family archive (probably taken by my dad).

I finally convinced my parents that the piano and me were not destined for marital bliss. I'd achieved two examination grades without any distinction, which was of no real consequence, but I did come away with a basic grasp of musical notation and scores which has proved very useful to me and, for this, I'm indebted to my parents for pressing me to persist as long as I did. Around this time, as I turned ten years old, came the musical experience which really did inspire me – my first close encounter with a drum.

My maternal grandfather, Bill Rowell, used a redundancy payment from losing his job as a docker in the 1920s to acquire a grocery shop. Having tried a couple of locations, he settled on a premises on the Isle of Dogs (the very place where I later met Brendan and Lisa). He and my grandmother, Charlotte, worked tirelessly through the following decades, raising three children (of which my mother was the middle) while expanding the business to an empire of six stores around 'The Island'. When they eventually retired, they rewarded themselves with a series of lengthy cruises on the world's most prestigious passenger liners of the day, including the SS *Canberra*, and travelled the seven seas. They'd return bearing gifts for the grandchildren and, on this particular occasion, the three male grandchildren (me and my cousins Simon and David) each received a pair of bongo drums they'd bought during a stopover in Acapulco, Mexico. The bowls of the drums were hand-thrown clay pots and the skins were, I think, calf. They were rough and earthy, the type of simple drums you might now be offered by wandering hawkers on beaches almost anywhere in the world, but in 1968 it was like receiving an unimaginable gift from another planet. Initially, at least, I was probably more fascinated by the look, touch, and smell of them than by the sound they produced – but I certainly fell in love with them.

The arrival of the bongos coincided with my musical awakenings. My parents listened to a lot of music – mainly light classics with a smattering of 'pop'. We had a clunky, mono record player and the vinyl collection included a couple of singles by The Beatles and Elvis, but that was about the limit of their dabblings in contemporary music. Now, however, I was starting to take notice of TV shows featuring groups like The Rolling Stones and Manfred Man – and The Beatles, of course. I was hearing things that started to arouse emotions in me and set my pulse racing – making me want to hear more, and making me actively want to play music for the first time. And I was hooked on the TV series featuring The Monkees, which gave a 'behind-the-scenes' view of a pop group's life, no matter how artificial!

In 1969 I bought my first single – 'I'm the Urban Spaceman' by The Bonzo Dog Doo Dah Band. I still have the record and am still pretty chuffed with my choice. My first album also, I think, remains a good call – a singles compilation by The Move including such classics as 'Blackberry Way', 'Fire Brigade', and 'Flowers in the Rain'. I was soon buying stuff by T. Rex and Simon & Garfunkel, and my musical foundations were being laid. Also in 1969, I formed my first band. It was called The Vibrations – the name plundered from the title of The Beach Boys' 'Good Vibrations'. The lineup of this groundbreaking unit was Martin Shepherdly on an untunable plastic toy 'Beatles' guitar (a past gift from my aunt Barbara) and Nigel Dallas on the bongos (neither of whom could play, but who participated under my direction as an occasional alternative to playing football, riding bikes, or climbing trees), with me singing into a fake microphone fashioned out of the cardboard tube from a loo roll, adding a hint of 'reverb'. A typical plan of action would be to rehearse in my bedroom for about ten minutes, then hurtle downstairs for an impromptu performance to my long-suffering parents. Although The Vibrations had no merit in performance, I was at least singing original songs I'd written. There must've been a few, but only two stick in my mind. One was called 'Cuckoo Hill' – a love song about meeting a girl in the eponymous location which was melodically a total rip-off of the Donovan song 'Jennifer'. The other was called 'Suncamp' – a high-speed thrash number on just two chords which, with hindsight, might possibly have been the first punk song ever written.

The other major event of 1969 for me was starting secondary school (high school) – at John Lyon in Harrow, just down the hill from the famous Harrow School. I've no recollection of music being included in the curriculum in my primary schools (other than singing hymns in assemblies), but John Lyon actually had a purpose-built 'Music School' and we now had a weekly music lesson plus extracurricular musical activities. The school had a renowned 'motet' choir which performed at festivals overseas and made the occasional recording which would be cut on vinyl and flogged to doting parents. I auditioned and failed, so that was the end of that.

Music lessons in the first couple of years tended to focus heavily on learning to play the recorder. I don't know if this is a very English thing, but being an enforced member of a mass recorder ensemble during childhood seems to be integral to our national heritage. While most kids hate learning recorder, I loved it. I found it relatively easy to play, I could quickly progress to being able to play a tune (which I never could with the piano), and I adored the sound (even of the cheap plastic student recorders). Unfortunately, few of the other kids took it seriously, and the music teacher struggled to achieve any semblance of cohesion when we played together in lessons.

Fig. 4. A 10-year-old me playing youth football (soccer); this would be just around the time I was given my first set of bongo drums, setting me on my musical path. Photo from family archive (probably taken by my dad).

Recorder was compulsory for the first two high school years, and these efforts culminated in an evening performance to parents of a selection of songs from *West Side Story* which was sounding passable in final rehearsals. One lad – Andrew French – who had no empathy with the instrument and whose participation unsettled the group, had been pulled out by the teacher and 'promoted' to conductor. French had achieved some kind of legendary status for coming to school one Monday and, when we were all required to hand in our weekend homework, his was customarily unavailable. Our teacher, patience now gossamer thin, asked for his latest excuse and received the answer that French had done his homework, but his father had been decorating and accidentally pasted his completed work sheets to the wall behind the wallpaper. As the class dissolved into hysterics, the teacher couldn't keep a straight face and let French off the usual punishment in acknowledgement of his creativity and originality.

So here now was French, standing on the conductor's podium with his baton raised in the air like the Statue of Liberty, awaiting the music teacher's cue to launch us into Bernstein's 'I like to be in America'. Having been instructed to tap his music stand lightly with the baton as our cue, French brought the thin stick down with such over-exuberance that it shattered into several pieces and left him standing frozen in full spotlight holding just the stump of the handle with a bemused grin on his face. Realising that our starting signal was no longer going to arrive, all we performers started playing in our own time, all sniggering into our recorders, producing a strange staccato wave effect. We gradually floated into synchronisation, the song settled down and, while French stood waving his arms like a human windmill before us, we turned in a pretty fair performance.

Recorders were never touched again after that. Music lessons ceased to be practical, with the emphasis shifting to analysis and 'appreciation' of some of the great composers. All I remember of this is spending so many weeks (maybe months) dissecting Mozart's 'Eine Kleine Nachtmusik' that I struggle to listen to it to this day. Meanwhile, my own tastes passed through an infatuation with Ziggy Stardust–era Bowie and another with Slade. I also used to spend a couple of hours each night ducked under my bedclothes clutching a small transistor radio tuned to pirate station Radio Luxembourg. I particularly liked that you'd hear songs on Luxembourg some weeks before they were picked up by the licensed UK radio stations, so you could keep ahead of what was coming through and be the first to own new records before most people heard of them. Unknown to me at the time, I was following a practice with impressive heritage – a letter written in the early 1960s by Paul McCartney to Beatles photographer and stylist Astrid Kirchherr included the recommendation: 'Gerry and the Pacemakers have just made a record – it's quite good, so listen to Luxembourg and you may hear it.'

My bongo drums remained a prized possession throughout all this, and I continued to play them a little from time to time, without really having any direction or influences. Apart from Mickey Finn in T. Rex, I don't remember anyone playing bongos as part of any of the music I was listening to. Then, as so often happens, a new influence arrived from a surprising source. Throughout my youth I remained a Scout – going from Cubs to Scouts to Ventures. I wasn't fond of the uniform and parading, but loved the outdoor adventure. The group

I belonged to – Fourth Eastcote – had some good camping and canoeing equipment, as well as being another outlet for sports, and I had some great times and made some good friends. I loved campfire sessions singing rounds of 'Ging Gang Goolie' and 'Kumbaya', and we had a leader called Graham who played acoustic guitar and would dip into the American folk songbook. I was particularly smitten with his rambling version of Arlo Guthrie's 'Alice's Restaurant' which had innumerable verses and allowed us all to join in the addictive chorus each time round. When I was older and we were sneaking out to pubs in the evening, a group of us had an unforgettable experience when invited to stay for an after-hours lock-in at a pub near Llyswen in the beautiful Wye Valley in central Wales as the assembled locals suddenly began an impromptu male voice choir session which was stunning.

The Scout Group would organise 'jumble sales' to raise funds which gave me and my mates the opportunity to rake through the paperback books in search of anything with titillating sexual content. One time I was first to lay hands on a book called *Voodoo Slave* which I squirrelled away to read. While it provided the craved dose of sex and violence, it also contained an account of a ceremony in which drummers (playing hand drums) worked themselves into a trance which enabled them to continue playing nonstop for several hours, building to an ecstatic frenzy which left their hands broken and bloodied. I was intrigued and made a couple of forlorn attempts to recreate the scenario in my bedroom with my bongos, but I wanted to know more about tribal and ritual drumming.

In 1973 my paternal grandmother, Eleanor, died. She was a religious woman who'd been born into a strict churchgoing family in Saundersfoot, near Tenby in South Wales, and retained her devotion throughout her life. I'd only ever really known her as a widow – grandfather Sidney having died when I was a young child – during much of which time she worked as a housekeeper to the Minister of a Baptist Church in the Cricklewood area of London. After retiring, she lived frugally on a meagre pension and had virtually no estate to leave when she died, but in her will she left a sum of twenty-five pounds to me to be used 'for his education'. My parents asked me what I'd like to buy – thinking books, stationery or such like – but I replied that I wanted a drum kit. They weren't against the idea, but we all very much doubted that twenty-five quid would be anywhere near sufficient, and a trip to the local music shop confirmed my in-heritance to be way off the mark. Not so easily defeated, I put word around and, lo and behold, found a tatty beginner's kit (Beverley brand), comprising only a bass (kick) drum, snare, and hi-hat, being offered second-hand for bang-on twenty-five pounds. My parents approved the 'educational' expense, and the 'kit' was installed in my bedroom.

It never occurred to me there might be teachers of kit drumming. Even if it had, my earlier experience of formal piano lessons would've dissuaded me, but still I needed to learn some basics. Around this time, all the boys at my school were offered the opportunity to join the Army Cadet Corps – a formal military corps affiliated to the national army, the joining of which required a signed-up commitment for at least two years. The big attraction for most of the kids was to access the school's armoury and go shooting real guns. This wasn't my scene, but the Corps had its own bugle and drum band in which I'd be able to learn to play military snare. I excitedly signed up, only to be told there were no places available in the band and that I was being assigned to the Motor Transport section along with a bunch of geeks who spent all their time dismantling and rebuilding the Corp's sole item of motorised transport – a clapped-out BSA Bantam motorbike. I was bitterly disappointed, but managed to enjoy some of the camping and expeditions before escaping as soon as my two years were up.

Meanwhile, I had to set about teaching myself drums. I made regular weekend trips into central London to the big music stores along Shaftesbury Avenue. I'd hang out in the drum departments, earwigging conversations about techniques, collecting catalogues, learning about all the latest gear, and generally absorbing everything to do with drums. Back at home, I taught myself the basic limb coordination for a simple rhythm on kick, snare and hi-hat, and used a practice pad (a circle of rubber mounted on a door wedge-shaped block of wood) to quietly practice rolls and other snare techniques at times when it was antisocial to play my kit. Although it was no bad thing to learn the basics on a small setup, I soon craved a bigger range. Rock music in the midseventies saw the traditional four- or five-drum kit displaced by double bass drum kits with racks of tom-toms. Iconic drummers of the time like Ginger Baker and John Bonham performed engulfed by huge kits, and then Karl Palmer eclipsed them all with his gargantuan drum/percussion set which required a full-length articulated lorry to transport it. I managed to gather together the immense sum of seventy pounds to buy another second-hand kit – a four-drum Premier Olympic kit with a couple of cymbals. By combining this with my original setup (fortunately both had white shells, similarly faded), and somehow acquiring some additional bits, I was able to assemble a kit with the requisite two bass drums, snare, three toms (two mounted, one floor), hi-hat and an array of cymbals.

One or two groups were forming at school, but not from amongst my closer friends. Then a group developed out of the ranks of my Scout group, but a good mate – Tim Turan, who also played drums – was more ready for the opportunity and was in the lineup before I knew it was happening. Tim was a great character and practical joker. One of his party tricks was to blow up a rubber washing up glove, just breathing out from his lungs, as one would blow up a balloon. The resultant inflation is huge, and one of my weirdest life experiences was being pinned to a kitchen cupboard together with several other hysterical and mildly inebriated party attendees by one of his rubber orbs. Tim had a part-time job at the 'Slush Puppy' factory in Wembley where he claimed to work alongside the father of Rolling Stones drummer Charlie Watts. Charlie's dad apparently told Tim that his world-famous son pressed him to give up work and would pay for everything he needed to enjoy his life, but the dad was happier down at the factory each day stirring great vats of 'Slush' flavoured ice! Tim went on to play drums for an outfit called Paul Jensen and the Car Thieves, who made a single with the actor Bob Hoskins on guest vocal, of which he proudly presented me with a cassette copy, but I'm not sure it ever saw the light of day.

Meanwhile, with no outlet for my drumming, I became a bit despondent and reacted by saving money from my Saturday job at the local hardware store and buying an acoustic guitar. Now I had to start from scratch, learning another instrument. Again I shunned formal lessons in favour of buying a basic tutor book and shutting myself in my bedroom. From this I learnt the standard tuning and three chords which would supposedly enable me to play 'The Grand Old Duke of York'. I never bothered with the nursery rhyme, preferring to use the three chords to start writing songs of my own again. I can only recall one song from this period – 'Time and a Word' – which remained in my subconscious to resurface years later, and which bears no relation to the Yes song of the same name which I was entirely unaware of when I wrote it.

By now I was around fifteen or sixteen and my tastes were moving on. I'd been gorging on Deep Purple albums, but preferred the more contemplative side of their music, especially the track 'Child in Time', and I was getting heavily into the 'progressive rock' scene. I loved Genesis (strictly Peter Gabriel era), Pink Floyd, and King Crimson, and I liked some of the stuff by ELP and Jethro Tull. There were also some European bands doing interesting things which were pushing the boundaries a bit – Can and Faust in Germany, and Focus from Holland whose 'Hocus Pocus' track sent my peer group into yodeling raptures. And then there was *Tubular Bells*. Regardless of whether or not you like it, Mike Oldfield's record was undoubtedly groundbreaking and influential. The unusual sounds, the spread of instrumentation, the structure, the multilayering. Perhaps there are musicians grounded in avant-garde jazz or 'contemporary classical' (if that's a thing) who would argue that *Tubular Bells* really contained nothing new and had all been done before, but no composition like it had ever reached my ears before, nor those, apparently, of the masses. And like him or loathe him, it's apparent that Richard Branson alone had the commercial vision to launch *Tubular Bells*. At the time of release, Branson was only twenty-three and Oldfield just turned twenty. Their big break came with the licensing of the album's opening theme to horror film *The Exorcist* after which sales mushroomed, and it's quite extraordinary that the entire global Virgin empire was effectively seeded in Branson's decision to back his instincts and finance that release.

A school friend, Nigel Gibson, had an older sister who frequented all the trendiest London clubs and venues on the 'prog' circuit, and through Nigel, I revelled in being introduced to her latest discoveries. Outstanding amongst these were two bands that became central to my listening at this time – Man and Nektar. Man had a fluid lineup drawn from a collective of musicians who frequented the Rockpile Studios in South Wales, made famous by Dave Edmunds. The principal figure throughout much of their history was guitarist Deke Leonard, while their regular drummer of that era was Terry Williams, who later joined Dire Straits. Nektar was a combination of two Englishmen and two Welshmen, though it was often mistaken for a German band as they'd based themselves in the land of 'Krautrock'. I particularly loved Nektar, and eagerly devoured every recording they issued, despite somewhat dodgy titles like 'A Tab in the Ocean'!

A secondhand record stall called 'Sellanby' opened in the railway arches market in South Harrow, about ten minutes' walk from my school, and I spent lunchtimes browsing the racks of their ever-changing stock, buying as many vinyl albums as I could afford. I broadened my musical horizons into the American scene, collecting recordings by the likes of Mahavishnu Orchestra, Allman Brothers Band, Joe Walsh, Jesse Colin Young, Mountain, and Jefferson Starship. Sellanby prospered and took a shop in the main high street, attracting a wider range of secondhand music into their racks, and I started to discover rock fusions with Latin and African music by Santana and Osibisa in which I loved the sound of the drum kit being augmented by the rattling accompaniment and explosive bursts of their exotic percussion sections.

Also around this time I started going to gigs, principally making Sunday pilgrimages to the Roundhouse in Chalk Farm – a wonderful, magical venue.

I'd seen many concert broadcasts from there on *The Old Grey Whistle Test* – the compulsory BBC TV programme of the era for the contemporary rock scene, presented by 'whispering' Bob Harris – and now I was finally in the audience myself. The Roundhouse is an old railway turning shed just north of Camden Town which had been converted into a music venue, and there was a show every Sunday which would start at 3.30, 5.30, or 7.30 p.m. depending on whether four, three, or just two bands were playing. I didn't check who was on in advance – I'd go whenever I managed to get all my school homework done in time and could negotiate clearance from my Mum. Shows were always popular, but usually I could get a ticket on the door. Sometimes, if there was a big-name band on, I would arrive to find the 'Sold Out' signs up. On these occasions, the procedure was to go 'round the side to 'Emergency Exit door two' and keep knocking until the security guard/bouncer opened it. This particular guard was a huge Black guy who towered over me. I would nervously ask if he could let me in and he would put out an enormous hand for three or four pound notes to be pressed into. He'd then produce a thick roll of notes from his inside pocket, brandish them under my nose, and slowly wrap my payment round. The wad would be replaced in his pocket and he'd say 'Wait' and disappear back inside. Next time the coast was clear, the door would reopen and I'd be ushered in. He never smiled, was never friendly, but he never turned me over, and he was the lifeline at sold-out gigs – for me and many others. Judging by the size of his wad of notes and the squash inside, that guy must have regularly sneaked another couple of hundred people into a venue which was only supposed to hold about a thousand.

I saw headline acts there such as Curved Air, Steve Marriott and the All Stars, Man, and UFO, and amongst the support acts I made discoveries like Fruupp, A Band Called O, Alkatraz, and AFT. The music was consistently good, and the atmosphere was always great. The air hung so thickly with hash smoke you'd get high just being in there. And then there was 'Jesus' – the famous character of the Roundhouse. 'Jesus' because he dressed and wore his hair like the traditional image of Jesus, and in the intervals between bands he'd go around preaching the gospel. But when the bands were on, he was always right down the front, dancing with abandon and pounding away at his tambourine. I don't think I ever went to the Roundhouse when Jesus wasn't there, and you could often see him in the footage on *Whistle Test*. The bands all knew him, and some would pull him up on stage to dance alongside them. The only time I ever saw Jesus outside the Roundhouse was at a Nektar show at the New Victoria Theatre – all the audience was seated, except for Jesus who was dancing around the aisles, nimbly evading the ushers who were trying to capture and reseat him.

Another of my favourite bands around this time was Caravan – one of the bands to come out of the so-called 'Canterbury scene'. Their mix of rock, psychedelia, folkiness, and electronica appealed to me, as did Pye Hastings's staunchly English delivery, refusing to bow to the rock cliché of adopting a mock American accent. They had a big influence on my musical leanings, and my record collection acquired more quirky titles including *For Girls Who Grow Plump in the Night* and *Blind Dog at St. Dunstans*. At one of their London shows I discovered Renaissance (who were supporting) fronted by opera singer Annie Haslam. I went to concerts by Hawkwind, Camel, Can, and John McLaughlin's post-Mahavishnu group Shakti, and venues including London's famous old Rainbow Theatre with its lush red carpets, sweeping brass-banistered staircases, and vast chandeliers. I saw Genesis in their post-Gabriel incarnation and kicked myself for not having seen them live before his departure. I was also at The Who's show at Charlton Football Club's 'The Valley' stadium in 1976 (with The Sensational Alex Harvey Band, Little Feat, Outlaws, and Streetwalkers) which held the world record for loudest concert for the next eight years.

Finally, when I was seventeen and in my last year of school, I got together with a few friends and formed a band. It was a halfhearted notion, an idea concocted on the spur of the moment one evening in the Black Horse pub in Old Eastcote, a couple of miles down the road from the Northwood Hills pub where Elton John (as Reg Dwight) first began entertaining the locals. I was with some of the lads I knew through the Scout group, amongst whose ranks we had a couple of decent singers and guitarists, and somebody suggested it. We spent most of the evening choosing the name 'Latin Edge' – a total misnomer as the band would have no Latin edge whatsoever, and only chosen as the phonetic reversal of the word 'genital' (doubtless very amusing to a bunch of adolescents). It wasn't even an original concept – the local band I'd missed out on to my mate Tim Turan was called 'Llamedos', a reversal of 'sod 'em all', a name given fame some years later by Terry Pratchett in his Discworld series.

Latin Edge managed two or three rehearsals in a cavernous recording studio in Mill Hill, North London, performing covers of rock standards like Free's 'Alright Now', before disintegrating through sheer lack of interest. From around this time, I have a rough recording made on a portable cassette player of myself (on bongos), Anton Jungreuthmayer (a guitarist/singer in Latin Edge), and Duncan Sykes (a good singer who'd been wise enough to steer clear of Latin Edge) performing a version of Peter Gabriel's 'Biko'. We possibly had the nucleus of something worthy of development between the three of us, but it came too close to a point of change in our lives where we went in different directions. In September 1976 I left home to start a three-year degree course at Hatfield Polytechnic, just north of London. I had a brilliant time at Hatfield, getting involved in student magazines (planning that I'd become a journalist), and helping out when bands came to play. The first of these was Mungo Jerry, and the highlight a Rag Ball show by crazy group Albertos y Los Trios Paranoias, while my huge disappointment was returning to Hatfield one September for the start of the new academic year to discover that Peter Gabriel had played a secret warm-up show a week earlier in preparation for his new tour. I was devastated to have missed that! In February 1979, towards the end of my final year, The Police did a televised performance at Hatfield for the BBC's *Rock Goes to College* series in their very early days when they'd just released 'Roxanne' – I think I've spotted myself in the audience in reruns of the TV footage, but I might be fantasising.

One or two student bands were forming and, although I wasn't actively looking for an opportunity, a friend of mine, Phil Hynes, decided we should form one. Phil played guitar and was a fan of Rod Stewart and The Faces. I'd never been much into their music, but Phil introduced me to some of the Small Faces material and the solo output of Ronnie Lane, which I really liked. I summoned my parents to deliver my long-dormant drum kit, and we booked one of the college halls and invited a few other alleged musicians along. The inaugural rehearsal turned out to be the last. The music was shambolic, not least because the various guitarists and the bassist failed to sort out the sound imbalances or overcome the feedback problems. The star of the show was a guy called Eddie who turned up to perform vocal duties, had clearly put great effort into cloning himself as Robert Plant, and was determined to give it his best shot regardless of the surrounding chaos.

Another close college friend, Bob Bridges, played acoustic guitar and was heavily into the rock/folk/blues troubadours. He was a big Dylan fan, but was primarily responsible for getting me into Neil Young. His favourite artist was eccentric English rogue Kevin Coyne, and he'd drag me along to the occasional concert. Bob and I made a few home recordings together – covers of songs by Dylan, Young, Coyne, and Roy Harper, interspersed with one or two of Bob's own works which were heavily derivative of his influences. We also hitched down to Blackbush for a big open-air concert headlined by Dylan, supported by Eric Clapton as well as the very fine Graham Parker and the Rumour.

I joined a summer trip with some old friends in the Scout group (from which we could still borrow camping equipment). We set off to hike the Ridgeway Path, an ancient ley line across England from the Avebury stones to Ivinghoe Beacon in the Chiltern Hills. About two-thirds along, we camped at a farm near Aylesbury belonging to the family of one of our group, intending to stop a couple of days, but got so comfortable we took root. The main attraction was the local pub, where we became overnight celebrities. We had a number of musicians amongst us and somehow managed to lay hands on two or three acoustic guitars, while I improvised a percussion set out of 'billy' cans and cooking utensils. We turned up at the local pub one night and asked if we could play. There were few customers in so the landlord, seeing the chance to keep the group of us in the pub drinking, agreed. We played a set of folk/rock standards, and the few people in the audience enjoyed it sufficiently for the landlord to ask us if we'd play again the following evening. Turning up next day, we were amazed – word had spread around the local farms and the place was heaving. We were initially a bit alarmed, but the landlord brought over a tray of free beers for 'the band', and we ploughed into our set again. The response was enthusiastic, the free beers continued to roll, and we had a great night. I embraced my complimentary beer supply, discovering next morning that I'd collapsed unconscious at closing time and been shoulder-carried back to the campsite by four of my mates – a rather inauspicious end to what I guess must have constituted my first public gig.

On returning to Hatfield for my second year, I moved into a shared student house in the Fleetville district of St Albans. One of my housemates was a guy called Paddy Smith who ran our weekly college rock disco (at which I could have been spotted brandishing my air guitar rather too regularly), and was notorious for boiling his socks in one of our communal kitchen saucepans (who the hell boils socks??). Far more importantly, with due respect to Paddy, another resident was a girl called Nicola Arundell. Nicki was taking the same degree as me so I already knew her vaguely from around the college. She was very attractive and, when her preexisting relationship broke up, we began going out for the occasional drink together. We got on really easily, my clowning around made her laugh, and gradually friendship evolved into something more. Nicki and I liked a lot of the same music. Her record collection introduced me to Leonard Cohen and to Lou Reed's *Transformer* album from which I'd only previously heard the single 'Walk on the Wild Side'. This, in turn, led me back into Velvet Underground territory which I now appreciated more. We were also both motivated by issues of social and political injustice – and shared a particular hatred of racism. The musical manifestation of this was a developing interest in reggae. The only really mainstream reggae artist then was Bob Marley, and Nicki already had the *Exodus* album, but we started to discover some of the highly politicised British reggae bands. I bought Steel Pulse's potent *Handsworth Revolution* album, and the wonderful *Hulet* by Aswad (years before they started releasing bouncy pop-reggae). Then came the powerful and brilliant albums by Linton Kwesi Johnson. And on the lighter side, we were into the lover's rock of the 'Cool Ruler', Gregory Isaacs.

Fig. 5. Me aged around 19 or 20 during college days (circa 1978), clinging on to the last throes of psychedelia and prog rock in the face of the rise of punk and new wave. Photo from family archive (possibly taken by Nicki, but our memories fail us).

In 1978, we joined coachloads of fellow students being bussed into London for a huge public march and demonstration under the banner 'Rock Against Racism'. Following the rally and political speeches, the march ended in Victoria Park, East London, where a big concert was staged. We'd been excited to see Steel Pulse perform, but were way back in the march and by the time we reached the Park, we couldn't get near the main stage. When Steel Pulse came on, we found ourselves stuck in a position where their sound was being sucked into a maelstrom with the sound of another band playing on the back of a truck somewhere behind us. As we had no hope of getting nearer the main stage, we gave up on Steel Pulse and went to check out the band behind which was gathering a small but highly appreciative audience. The disappointment of missing Steel Pulse diminished as we became hooked in, and the band turned out to be Misty In Roots. We subsequently bought their debut album and followed their progress.

This time was also, of course, the advent of punk. We had albums by The Sex Pistols, The Clash, The Stranglers, Siouxsie and the Banshees, and others, but tended not to go to the concerts because we weren't punks and would've been out of place. I remained wedded to my long hair and had no wish to discard my lingering hippy image; plus, the idea of going to gigs and coming out covered in other people's spittle curiously failed to entice us, but a lot of the music was good. Punk performed a truly great service by breaking down the overblown pomposity that had come to blight prog-rock, and by encouraging so many people to pick up an instrument, form a band, and get out on stage. Three or four guitar chords, a basic 4/4 drumbeat, heaps of attitude, and you were on! And this was also the Stiff/Two-Tone/ska era from which emerged The Specials, The Beat, Madness, The Selecter, Elvis Costello, et al. We liked a lot of the music and gathered various albums, but again tended not to go to gigs as it was also such a heavily fashion-linked scene. We did venture along to see Madness at the Hammersmith Palais a few years later, which was an enjoyable show apart from the faction of 'Sieg Heil'-ing skinheads in the audience which Madness long struggled to alienate.

I wanted to discover an ever more diverse range of music. A college friend, Christine Stewart, got me listening to Barclay James Harvest, and I went to see The Strawbs at The Forum in Hatfield. Nicki and I saw Jonathan Richman and the Modern Lovers in Dunstable, The Tubes at Hammersmith Odeon at the height of their 'White Punks on Dope' notoriety, and Springsteen with the E Street Band (Clarence on sax) at Wembley. And I went with Bob and another college friend, Graham Tinsley, to the Music Machine in Camden for a curious bill with Nico supporting The Adverts. Nico was performing solo – singing and playing harmonium. Graham was a huge Nico fan and had been thrilled at the prospect of seeing his idol. Sadly, the billing proved to be a disaster as the punks who turned up to see The Adverts couldn't wait to get down to some serious pogoing and bottled the legendary singer off stage before she'd completed three songs.

Nicki and I fell into the habit of going to The Horn of Plenty pub in St Albans on Monday nights where a local band had a residency which, while the rest of the city was generally pretty quiet on a Monday, always pulled a fair crowd. They were called Streetband, and the focus of attention was their singer, who had a great voice and a terrific rapport with the audience. This was Paul Young, and we knew we were seeing someone destined for a bigger stage. Streetband picked up a recording deal, released the single 'Toast' and hit the charts. They were soon gone from the local pub, but did return to play a show at Hatfield Poly (and would later morph into Q-Tips).

While at Hatfield, I returned a couple of times to the Chalk Farm Roundhouse. First, I went to two of the three nights of Man's farewell party in December 1976. There was a strange atmosphere at these. We all knew Man wouldn't really split up and disappear forever. It wasn't so much the end of the band, but rather the end of the peak of their popularity. But the shows were enjoyable, and they spawned the *All's Well That Ends Well* album. On the second occasion, it was to see Ian Dury and the Blockheads. Wow! I'd experienced the Roundhouse packed plenty of times, but this was totally rammed, and when Ian and the gang hit the stage, the place erupted. I'd worked my way into the middle of the unseated auditorium and, without my doing anything, was physically lifted off my feet and carried for several yards in either direction as the mass pogoing rolled from side to side. The performance was terrific and I came out drenched in sweat and thoroughly elated!

After graduating I got my first job – a trainee in the Public Relations Office at Tower Hamlets Council in the east end of London with a haircut and suit – while Nicki went to do a postgraduate teacher training course at Bristol Polytechnic. I returned to live at home with my parents, and as often as possible at weekends took the train to Bristol to see Nicki. There was a good club scene, and one of our favourite places was The Dugout which played a mix of indie rock tunes and a few chart hits. On one occasion, together with a couple of other friends from Hatfield who'd gravitated to Bristol, we ventured into the St Paul's district to a reggae club. With hindsight, we were naïve as four whites to walk into such a club at a time when racial tensions were volatile, but we were lucky that night and no one hassled us or gave us any trouble as we huddled in a corner, swaying to the thunderous bass sounds which shook the hall to its foundations.

Nicki came back to London after completing her course and in January 1981 we got our first home together – the flat in Knighthead Point on the Isle of Dogs. One day not long after, I was changing buses at Limehouse and noticed a handwritten advert in a newsagent's window – a local soul/blues band looking for a drummer. I phoned the number and was introduced to the bassist/vocalist of the group, Peter Hicks. A few days later, I was packing my drum kit (now scaled down to a regular four drums, hi-hat, and ride and crash cymbals) to head for a rehearsal as the new drummer of 'Mischief'. Rehearsals took place in a room over a pub on the east side of the Isle of Dogs called The Gun, which the landlord and landlady allowed us to use free of charge provided we drank plenty of (paid for) beer while we rehearsed, and that we played for free whenever they had a function or party night. The Gun is an old pub with a colourful history, and our rehearsal room was reputedly a regular location for Lord Nelson's clandestine liaisons with Lady Hamilton back in the eighteenth century. The other two members of Mischief were Con Maloney (guitar/vocals) and Chris Lambert (saxophone). We rehearsed twice a week and put together a set of classic covers including 'Sea Cruise', 'My Girl' (The Temptations' song), 'How Sweet It Is' (Junior Walker & The All Stars), 'The Sky Is Crying', 'It Must Be Love' (closer to the Madness version than Labi Siffre's), Tom Petty's 'Breakdown', and 'Blue Beat and Ska'.

We became a competent, tight unit and started gigging. We were excited to secure a Wednesday residency at another local pub – The Blackwall Arms – until on our first night we played to just the bar staff as not a single customer came in all evening. The new licensee had no existing clientele and had expected us to bring an audience, so we quickly organised some publicity and managed to get about twenty people in the following week. Word started to spread, a review appeared in the East End News (written by my old friend Bob Bridges, who also somehow ended up moving to the Isle of Dogs after Hatfield), and we eventually drew a reasonable crowd.

We went on to play the Half Moon Theatre on Mile End Road as part of the East End Festival, and then got our first private booking – a Saturday night function at a social club in Wapping. The event was well attended but the organisers asked us to play during the buffet meal and we were nearing the end of our set just as people started to give us some response and get up and dance. After a quick word with the organisers, it was agreed our fee would be increased and we'd play a second set. As we'd never previously played anywhere for more than free beer, this was 'big time'. While we took a break, an annoyingly cocky kid kept pestering us, telling us how good he was on drums, and pressing to show what he could do. Eventually we relented, just to shut him up, and he got on the kit and banged around fairly aimlessly. Egged on by some of my friends, I then did something I've never done before or since – I got up on stage and played a drum solo. I never much liked drum solos at gigs – the only two I ever vaguely enjoyed were by Jon Hiseman (at a Colosseum show), incorporating some impressive stick juggling, and the Albertos y Los Trios Paranoias drummer's kit-dismantling comic turn. I couldn't perform tricks, and had no particular routine worked out, but I had a few decent techniques, sufficient to put cocky-boy in his place and grab the audience's attention. My solo got a standing ovation and, seizing the moment, my bandmates jumped on stage and we plunged into a ripping version of 'Johnny B Goode'. Within seconds, just about everyone was dancing and it seemed to go on for hours. We were busking, playing requests (as best we could remember them), and having a great time.

This was the high spot for Mischief. We should've gone on from that to at least become a major force on the East London club and pub circuit, but somehow we didn't. It went the other way, and Mischief fizzled out. Peter went on to become rhythm guitarist/vocalist in another local band called Risky Bizness, which he formed with brothers Arthur and John White and Con's brother Tony. Arthur was the perfect pop front man – classically handsome, full of cockney attitude and pouty poses, and a good voice. His brother John was a brilliant natural bass player. I sat in on drums with them a few times until they found a regular drummer, and it was great playing with John – his playing was so fluid and we locked together easily. The problem was he was always completely bombed. Half the time he could barely hold a conversation, and when we weren't actually playing, he'd often be slumped in a corner, but when we played, he was bang on, fingers skipping effortlessly up and down the neck of his bass. The Risky boys were writing their own songs, craved commercial success, and got themselves a manager . . . and 'Freddy' was a walking caricature of a wannabe showbiz manager. By day he was a car-phone salesman back when cell-phones were the size and weight of house bricks (before they became 'mobiles'); by night he was a self-proclaimed Mr Big – big physically, big hair perm, big attitude, and big ambition. He was going to take Risky to the stars, but sadly it never quite happened.

All this while, my musical tastes were expanding, largely influenced by becoming a regular listener to the John Peel Show on BBC Radio. I shared his enthusiasm for The Undertones, and eagerly lapped up each of their albums on release. I discovered The Fall, The Birthday Party, Cocteau Twins, The Cure, Japan, Danse Society, Sisters of Mercy, Dead Kennedys, and so on. I also discovered Joy Division through John Peel, but sadly only on the release of *Closer* and thus just after the death of Ian Curtis, so I never saw them live. Joy Division's music became very important and influential to me (along with so many others). Years later reading the memoirs, I was greatly surprised to find a photo in Deborah Curtis's book *Touching from a Distance* of Ian sporting a Nektar T-shirt, while in his book *Unknown Pleasures*, Hooky cites *Nantucket Sleighride* by Mountain as a favourite. I was intrigued that they also had these influences in their backgrounds. The dark broodiness of much of this music I was now discovering held a particular attraction for me, and I found it curiously uplifting rather than depressive (as it's often portrayed). I immersed myself in listening to it, but never really considered playing it, simply because I didn't know any other musicians who were into it.

I worked at Tower Hamlets Council for two and a half years, based in the Town Hall in Bethnal Green. Good friends I made there included Nik Samson, a trained journalist who took me under her wing and taught me the basics of journalistic writing, proofreading, and editing. I joined the National Union of Journalists and for a while held an official Press Card. Another colleague and friend was Bernard Saltmarsh, who was Senior Press Officer and the main contact for the local newspapers. One of the journalists he got to know on the East London Advertiser at the time had his own band, and Bernard discovered he was looking for a drummer. He took me to a local pub one lunchtime to introduce me to this guy who turned out to be Ed Ka-Spel, the pivotal force of the Legendary Pink Dots. We discussed the possibility of me trying out on drums for them. I was interested and Ed seemed into it, but somehow the idea faded and nothing came of it.

By early 1982, I'd decided I wanted to work in theatre. I applied for a job at the Half Moon in Mile End Road, where I'd previously performed with Mischief, but then saw the Press Officer job at Riverside Studios advertised. Although Riverside was in Hammersmith, less conveniently the other side of London, it had a reputation as a thriving general arts centre, with some music included in its programming. I never found out how many applied for the Riverside job – apparently my predecessor, on secondment from the National Theatre, had lasted just three months before having a nervous breakdown, and better qualified insiders on the London arts circuit probably knew to steer clear. Certainly I was under-experienced for the post, and was surprised to be invited to interview, let alone get the job. The six months I worked there constituted the most gruelling and high-pressure period I've ever been through, but it was also hugely rewarding as I got to work with some incredible visiting theatre companies.

Riverside ran a wildly ambitious (if financially unsustainable) programme under Artistic Director David Gothard. During my time there we had *Woza Albert!* from South Africa – a riveting performance by actors Percy Mtwa and Mbongeni Ngema, Tadeusz Kantor's company from Poland, *Macunaima* from Brazil, and *Mabou Mines* from New York – two musical shows from director Lee Breuer, a 'Doo-Wop Opera' called *Sister Suzie Cinema*, and an Oedipus adaptation called *The Gospel at Colonus*. These were performed by a cappella quintet Fourteen Karat Soul, musical director Robert Otis Telson, and Ben Halley Jr – big guy with a heart-warming smile, and a gloriously rich voice in the Southern States Black gospel tradition. Then there were theatre workshops by Dario Fo and Franca Rame, and the UK's powerful company of actors with disabilities Graeae, along with dance from Bill T Jones and Arnie Zane, and Michael Clark. Riverside also had a gallery, which hosted a ground-breaking Mayakovsky exhibition and a couple of photographic shows, a cinema which showed a rolling programme of rare and arthouse films, and its own theatre design school.

Alongside the centre's own programme, studio space was hired out to TV companies and other media groups. It was the venue for the BBC's short-lived *Riverside Show*, and I snuck into the recording session featuring Bauhaus playing their 'Ziggy Stardust' cover when Daniel Ash messed up the final chord, smashed his guitar into his amp and stormed off in disgust – at least, I think that's what happened. I was also taken by surprise one day when I got an internal call from Front of House asking me to come down and show a couple of visitors round who were thinking of booking the venue for a showcase – the visitors turned out to be Demis Roussos – complete with trademark voluminous white costume – and Vangelis. There were always interesting people around Riverside. David Leveaux was an in-house director there at the time, and has since gone on to become a well-established director in London and New York. Peter Gill, one of the directors from the National Theatre, was a trustee and a regular visitor who took a particular liking to a Fairisle pullover knitted by my mother. Hanif Kureshi – whose novel *The Buddha of Suburbia* is one of my all-time favourites – ran a writers' group and frequented the cafe/bar, where Michael Clark was another regular just to hang out.

I continued expanding my musical horizons and an album released in the summer of 1982 made a particular impact on me. This was the benefit album released to coincide with the first WOMAD (World of Music Arts and Dance) festival in the UK. Although I didn't go to the festival itself, I was attracted to buy the album because of Peter Gabriel's deep involvement. The album featured a track by Gabriel, one by another of my favourite artists – David Byrne (taken from his brilliant score for Twyla Tharp's ballet *The Catherine Wheel*), and contributions from other high profile 'Western' artists such as Pete Townshend, The Beat, and XTC. But critically, nestled amongst these were tracks by Nusrat Fateh Ali Khan, the Burundi Drummers, and folk artists from Bali, Malawi, Ghana, and Senegambia. The album was a feast of amazing sounds and rhythms, and it set me on my path of exploring sounds and collecting instruments from around the world. The album closes with the sumptuously beautiful 'Persian Love' by Holger Czukay with fellow Can member Jaki Liebezeit – if you've never heard this, please . . .

Suddenly, it seemed, all the UK record labels were 'discovering' Africa, bringing a deluge of new sounds into high street shops. I bought albums by King Sunny Ade (on Island) and Orchestra Makassy (on Virgin), a compilation of songs from Mali, Cameroun, Central African Republic, Congo, and Zaire under the banner 'Sound D'Afrique' (Island), and another compilation of raw, gritty, passionate songs from the Apartheid-era South African townships called 'Soweto' (Rough Trade) – the latter being championed by John Peel in his ever-boundary-pushing radio broadcasts. I was also lucky enough to acquire a relatively obscure set of recordings – a set of six vinyl albums under the series title 'Music in the World of Islam' (Tangent) and with individual focuses on the voice, lutes, strings, flutes and trumpets, reeds and bagpipes, and drums and rhythms. This comprised field recordings made by music anthropologists travelling through northern Africa and the Middle East in the early 1970s. It was my first experience of hearing such recordings of music from daily life in these regions and cultures, not in any way written, edited, remixed, or produced to appeal to a 'Western' audience – a truly life-enhancing discovery.

It was with a mixture of these global sounds on the one hand, and Joy Division/John Peel's playlist on the other, floating around my consciousness, that I encountered Dead Can Dance. The hand of fate was on my shoulder. I don't know why Mischief faded, or why the opportunity to join the Legendary Pink Dots never materialised, but it meant I had no commitment to any other music project when I met Brendan and Lisa. And had Riverside struggled on a little longer, or I'd taken the job at the Lyric theatre a couple of months earlier, or had I been in any form of full-time employment when I'd taken that phone call from Brendan, I'm not at all sure I would have risked giving up the perceived security to commit to such a change of direction and such a wildly unpredictable 'profession'. But my circumstances dictated that I could find no good reason not to commit to Dead Can Dance, and I entered 1983 with that as my sole focus.

THREE

March 1983. I was sitting quietly on one side of the living room in my flat in Knighthead Point watching Brendan lying on the carpet dubbing his lead vocal onto a new Dead Can Dance song called 'A Passage in Time' using my Tensai two-track recorder. We'd known each other for three months now, much of which had been spent writing, rehearsing, recording, and doing a lot of talking – finding out about one another and making big plans for the future. I was well and truly absorbed into the DCD mindset, and was making my own small impression on the world that Brendan and Lisa were creating. They were pleased to discover my organisational and promotional skills, and I was currently overseeing the finalisation and issue of a new batch of demo tapes to record labels.

In Brendan and Lisa, I'd made far greater discoveries. I was working with two extraordinary people, either of whom on their own would have created a very special band, but both together in the same musical unit still had me reeling from the possibilities. The relationship between the two of them was highly volatile, which took some getting used to. It was intense on every level – working, social, and romantic – and neither believed in compromise. Arguments were frequent and explosive, and Paul and I quickly became compatriots in taking cover when tempers boiled over, trying to broker peace at opportune moments. It was uncomfortable at times, but somehow we were all aware that out of these tensions, these battles, the strongest music was born.

One thing I soon learnt about both Brendan and Lisa was that their response to everything (certainly in relation to their music) was only ever at one or other end of the spectrum. Everything we did was either 'brilliant' or 'absolute shit' – nothing was ever 'OK' or 'not bad'. There was no middle ground. This was a shock to my system. I was used to getting through a song and someone saying something like, 'That's starting to sound all right, we'll have that ready for the next gig.' But now I was working with two people who, until everything clicked and the passage of music we were working on would really gel, appeared physically sickened and distraught at its failings. In all my years with DCD, I must confess I never really got to grips with this, but it was inherent to the process, so had to be dealt with.

Brendan and Lisa's creative processes were very different. Lisa wrote and performed in an almost trancelike state. Everything came from deep within her – spontaneous and straight from the heart or soul. Brendan was meticulous and analytical in his study of music and in his composition. He also wrote and performed with great passion and intensity, but always controlling it, while Lisa's performances were like an out-of-body experience, like she was astral travelling on another plane. In those early days of rehearsals, I was frequently struck by the bizarre juxtaposition of our drab, grey surroundings in the Barkantine Hall in a bleak London winter with this soaring, glorious music enveloping me.

Fig. 6. Barkantine Hall rehearsal, 1983. Lisa's early percussion set-up, with small hand drum, African barrel drum, 'pang' cymbal, and her yang ch'in on the table behind; Paul, me and Brendan in the background. Photo by Jeffrey Earp.

While Lisa's contribution to the material and sound of Dead Can Dance was both huge and essential, it was Brendan who ultimately directed everything, honed the elements that were good, discarded the elements that weren't working, moulded the musical shapes and generally made everything work. Lisa didn't find it easy to be pinned down into structures, but she understood the necessity of it in order to arrive at a set of songs which were feasible for recording and re-peat performance, so ultimately she would put her trust in Brendan. Paul and I, meanwhile, were entirely directed by Brendan. He would possibly have enjoyed more creative input from both of us, but he was simply too far out of our league. We both made suggestions, and some were used as starting points. Brendan was always ready to consider any ideas we put to him, but would extract what he liked, work his magic, and turn them into something special and very much his own.

I could see no room existed within DCD for another creative force in addition to Brendan and Lisa – that zone was already bursting at the seams. So I embraced learning from both of them. Lisa's influence was more conceptual. I particularly remember her telling me: 'Look for the space in music, feel the space.' It's great advice – too many drummers overfill songs and don't give the other instruments sufficient space to breathe, and I've since tried not to do that. Brendan's direction followed as a practical manifestation of Lisa's mantra, and he quickly had me improving as a musician in leaps and bounds. The first thing he did was to break me of all my lazy habits. There was no room in DCD's music for a single drum beat or cymbal hit which didn't serve a purpose. There was no room for inserting a 'fill' in clichéd rock style every time a song went into or out of a chorus. There was no room for any tricks or stunts which would draw the listener's attention away from the overall sound and emotion of the piece. And there was certainly no room for drumming which merely kept time rather than performing an active role in shaping the music.

The next thing I discovered was that DCD songs were frequently written 'upside down'. Previously, I'd only ever worked with, or been aware of, writers or arrangers who came along to rehearsal with the basis of a song – i.e. the main melody(ies) – already worked out on a lead instrument such as guitar or keyboard, to which the rhythm section – bass and drums – then added complementary parts. Brendan had figured that this method of working regularly had two undesirable results. Firstly, songwriters who created their basic themes with guitar or keyboard would typically write a lot of songs with a similar feel because they always tended to fall into their natural style without having other influences to draw them out of their comfort zone. Secondly, the rhythm section would then naturally fall into standards and clichés, as they were merely adding their parts to a melodic structure which had already been created.

With DCD, we would often start by writing a drum pattern – looking for something that created an interesting and unusual rhythmic feel. The bass line would be written next, but not just something that sat comfortably on top of the drum pattern – rather a challenging bass line which would work off the drums, perhaps veering off in unsuspecting directions and then suddenly coming back into sync to create a climactic moment. We spent many rehearsals purely working on drum and bass interaction, with Brendan directing, showing us what he wanted, and urging Paul and I to master techniques alien to us. Brendan is an excellent bass player, with all his experience from the Scavengers/Marching Girls era, and was never satisfied playing standard bass lines. He was always an innovator, and appreciated other bassists – such as Peter Hook (Joy Division/New Order) – who took the instrument away from conventionality. We even had one song written in those early days – 'Fortune' – in which the bass was the only melodic instrument. Alongside Paul's bass, I played bass drum and toms, Brendan sang and played 'pang' cymbal, and Lisa played some additional percussion. I always felt that was the song in which we sounded closest to Joy Division.

Our first set of material included two songs written and previously performed in Australia – 'Frontier' and 'East of Eden' – so from my point of view, these presented a relatively straightforward task of learning the drum parts already written. Of course, nothing was ever quite that straightforward. For 'Frontier' we had to find some empty metal oil drums to try to replicate the effect Brendan had created on the original recording. This involved rummaging through local rubbish tips and factory waste sites, hopefully avoiding any that had stored toxic materials, and trying to gather a set that had at least some natural pitch variation as there was a limit to what the hammer could achieve. They then had to be mounted on a stand, and thereafter replaced periodically when they got beaten too far out of shape and/or tune.

'East of Eden' used a drum pattern played on bass/kick drum, tom-toms, and hi-hat – the snare drum being used with the 'snare' springs flicked off. Although generally a straightforward pattern to play, it did incorporate a 'flam' (two hits played almost simultaneously, but with a very slight yet discernible gap) between the bass drum and floor tom in each bar which was critical to the feel of the song. There was nothing particularly complex about playing this flam, but it wasn't a technique I'd used before and, while I was getting used to it, during any full run-through of the song there would tend to be two or three occasions on which I would either leave too big a gap between the beats, or I'd run them together – either way, losing the flam effect. It was during rehearsals of 'East of Eden' that I discovered the concept we came to know as 'Perry Ear'. It was an extraordinary thing that when Brendan was playing – even though he might be singing and simultaneously playing a busy guitar part – he would still be acutely aware of every note and beat played by every other member of the band. And if I put a single beat out of place (or de-flammed my flam), or Paul dropped a bass note, you could actually detect a slight twitch of Brendan's ear, and you knew he'd noticed the error and had been affected by it in his performance. This created a tension which could be either constructive or destructive, depending on how it was handled by the musician concerned. It certainly focused the concentration.

Another song to survive the migration from Australia was an instrumental called 'The Fatal Impact' which had been written and recorded with a particular drum machine whose sound we were unable to replicate. Brendan briefly toyed with the possibility of rearranging it, but decided it wouldn't work, so although the original recording from Australia was subsequently used, the piece was never rerecorded and never featured in our live sets.

The first new song written in the *Barkantine Hall Sessions* was 'The Trial' – a dark and aggressive song with Kafka-inspired lyrics which exemplified DCD's roots in the post-punk era. It's a good example of a song written 'upside down' – starting with the drums over which Brendan set a bass line which works in different length cycles to the drum pattern, immediately creating a tension. Over this he worked a counterpoint of vocal and driving guitar. Towards the end of the song, the drums change to a pattern in which the traditional relationship between bass drum and snare is reversed – known as the 'Motown backbeat' as it can be heard on numerous classic Motown recordings. I'd never have thought of transposing this backbeat into a song like 'The Trial', but Brendan did think of trying things like that, and it worked perfectly, powering the song to its conclusion with extra urgency. The other curious feature of 'The Trial,' particularly given its nature, is that most of it (before the beat changes at the end) is in a 3/4 time scale – meaning that, in classical definitions, it's a waltz!

The one percussion instrument which Brendan and Lisa had when I met them was an African tribal barrel drum – a drum the size and shape of a conga, with a shell of two-tone wood strips bound with iron hoops and a skin tensioned on protruding wooden pegs. Once Brendan, Paul, and I had 'The Trial' working, Lisa was asked to come in on the barrel drum in the end section to add to the drama of the climax. I couldn't imagine Lisa playing this drum. Although I knew she possessed an incredibly powerful voice and a strong will, she was nevertheless physically thin and frail-looking, and I was sceptical about what she was going to contribute. When her cue came, she attacked the barrel drum with such ferocity that she all but drowned out the sound I was making on the considerably more powerful kit. I had to up my game – and Brendan had engineered exactly the result he wanted. I came to enjoy seeing audiences react to Lisa's aggressive drumming with similar astonishment to my first encounter. It was, once again, an outburst of pure passion from her. Whereas I was concentrating on technically performing my part, she simply allowed herself to be seized by what was happening in the music around her and responded on gut instinct. The same phenomenon was present in another of our new songs – 'Threshold' – in which Lisa would suddenly switch from singing to pounding out intensifying rhythms on one of the steel oil drums, a moment during gigs when I would regularly see jaws drop in the front row of the audience.

It was apparent from the outset that, although we were essentially a guitar/bass/drums outfit with both male and female vocals, DCD would never sit within such limits. Brendan was always looking not only for different ways to use our basic instruments, but also for any other sounds we could incorporate. Lisa's yang ch'in added an important dimension, and the barrel drum and oil drums had been incorporated. For another new song called 'Ocean', for which Brendan had written the guitar and bass interplay but couldn't settle on a pattern for the drum kit, I found myself playing a 'tuned percussion' part with a hammer on a set of three metal pipes made from cut lengths of scaffold pole.

My Tensai two-track cassette machine, which at the time was the most sophisticated piece of recording equipment we possessed, also boasted a built in 'rhythm box'. This comprised eight different preset rhythms, including rumba, bossa nova, and cha-cha-cha. Brendan began experimenting and found that these preset rhythms could be combined if someone operated the machine, manually holding down various combinations of buttons, and that changes between the different presets could be effected quite seamlessly, provided the operator was sufficiently nimble of finger. Brendan used the Tensai to write two songs to the accompaniment of 'arrangements' of its preset rhythms – an instrumental piece, which was untitled at that stage, and 'Labour of Love' – hence my next assignment was to master 'performing' the Tensai rhythm box in that much-neglected genre: post-punk bossa nova!

So, now, as Brendan added his vocals to a live recording of 'A Passage in Time' from one of our Barkantine Hall rehearsals, we were close to finalising our first UK demo tape. As I watched him, it occurred to me that there was a striking and highly significant difference between Brendan and other people I'd encountered so far in my musical pursuits. Brendan totally, 100 percent, believed that his future lay in music. He wasn't doing another job and hoping for a break, he wasn't doing music as a hobby thinking it would be nice if it could ever become a career. He simply WAS a musician – that is what he'd been put on the earth to do. He was completely focused, and had instilled the same conviction in Lisa. He had absolute confidence that DCD's music would be recognised as something important and would make an impact. His journey had begun, and whoever was around who could help him and who was in for the ride was welcome.

Fig. 7. Mugshot sequences from our first photo session, 1983: taken in Brendan and Lisa's flat in Bowsprit Point, Barkantine Estate. By row: Brendan, Lisa, me. Photos by Jeffrey Earp.

On 25 March 1983, I issued a 'News Release' to announce very grandly that Dead Can Dance were in London working on new material and preparing for a 'British debut performance'. The News Release was accompanied by our demo cassette which comprised four tracks:

Side one, track one: Labour of Love 3:32

Side one, track two: A Passage in Time 4:20
Side two, track one: Frontier 2:57
(the original recording from Belgrave Studios, Melbourne)
Side two, track two: The Fatal Impact 2:28
(version from Fast Forward cassette magazine 008/9 issue)

This package was sent to a select few of the most prominent independent record labels of the day – Rough Trade, Cherry Red, Mute, 4AD, and Factory. It elicited just one response – from Ivo Watts-Russell, the head of 4AD Records and, coincidentally, the first label to have given an outlet to Nick Cave and The Birthday Party when they'd previously arrived in London from Melbourne on the same mission. Ivo's initial response was ambivalent. On the one hand, he'd clearly heard something that grabbed him in order to have responded, but on the other, he was at pains to stress that he didn't have the finance available to sign a new artist at that point. But our demo gnawed away at him, and a few weeks later he contacted us again. He wanted to see us play live and was offering us the opportunity to support one of 4AD's leading bands at the time – Xmal Deutschland – in a couple of forthcoming London dates.

The first of these was at a venue called The Ace, a former cinema in the centre of Brixton, south London, on 23 June. There was another band on the bill called The Box, playing between us and Xmal, featuring a couple of guys formerly with Clock DVA. We were well rehearsed, and I was really excited about the gig, but when the day came I couldn't believe how nervous I suddenly felt. It had been well over a year since I'd last played a live gig, and that would've been a relatively lowkey local gig with Mischief. Now I was going to play my first live show with Dead Can Dance, in a venue with a capacity of five or six hundred, to a paying audience, and with a record deal possibly hanging on our performance. My stomach was churning, I was mildly trembling, and the palms of my hands were sweating – not ideal for keeping a grip on the drumsticks.

We lugged our gear into the venue and waited to be called for our soundcheck. When we were summoned to the stage, I found that my kit was to be put on a drum riser (a raised platform higher than the rest of the stage) and that individual microphones were to be positioned for every drum and cymbal. Brendan, Lisa, and Paul had all taken it for granted that I was aware of this, but I simply hadn't given it a thought. Of course, I'd been to many shows where I'd have seen this type of setup, but I'd never experienced it myself before. I'd only ever been tucked away at the back of a cramped stage with the kit unmic'ed – I'd never been exposed like this, raised up, with spotlights on me, and my drum sounds going through the 'PA' system.

I set my kit up and then stood aside while the stage crew fixed up the mics. My little drum kit now looked huge, and my nervousness was morphing into full-scale panic. I was called to start soundchecking the drums. I sat at the kit, tapped the bass drum pedal and an explosion of sound boomed around the auditorium. I almost fell off the drum stool with shock. A voice in my head was screaming, 'That's what it's going to sound like every time you hit the bass drum – oh fuck!' I had to struggle to get a grip on myself at first, but as the soundcheck went on, I started to settle down a bit. Once we'd done all the individual instruments and mics, we played a warmup number to check the balance of levels and I started enjoying being enveloped by this enormous sound. I was back in control, telling myself I knew the songs, I was comfortable with my parts, I just needed to play like in rehearsals.

A friend of Brendan's from his time in New Zealand and Australia – James Pinker – had shown up during the soundcheck. Jim had been a member of industrial band SPK back in Sydney, but was now living in Vauxhall, just down the road from Brixton. While I was engrossed in my personal issues, Brendan was concerned about making sure the sound was right out front. He organised for Jim to work with 4AD/Xmal engineer Ray Conroy on the main PA mixing desk as Jim knew the DCD sound from back in Australia. Being last to soundcheck and first on stage, there wasn't long to wait until we were due on to play, but I still managed to fit in about half a dozen visits to the loo as the nerves came back with a vengeance. The Xmal girls were swanning around backstage, looking very relaxed. I presume Ivo had told them he'd put us on the bill to check us out, and they were really nice and wished us luck. I was thinking how the venue would soon be full of people who idolised these girls, and here we were chatting with them backstage.

It's amazing when you go on stage and the adrenalin is really pumping – you feel so sharp, so alive. If you can learn to channel them right, the nerves and adrenalin actually help greatly to raise your performance level. We launched into 'The Trial' and, although my playing was a bit rigid, I got through it. The response was good, and there were a fair few people in already, even though we were complete unknowns. I relaxed a little and started to take in more of what was going on around me. I realised that the majority of the audience had their gaze fixed on Lisa. I was used to seeing her around home and rehearsals with just a little makeup and ordinary day clothes, but tonight her look was utterly captivating. She had very white makeup, dark red lipstick, hair piled high, and a flowing formal dress. She'd floated serenely onto the stage, but then startled the audience with her sudden burst of ferocious drumming at the end of 'The Trial'. And now, she started to sing.

I had, of course, heard Lisa sing in rehearsals, and knew she had a wonderful voice, but now, on stage, it was something else altogether. The power was breath-taking. Some of the audience were open-mouthed as they watched – maybe I was myself. Her notes reached every nook and crevice of the hall and hung there, quivering, until the next arrived. Doors at the back of the hall flew open and people streamed through from the bars in search of the source of this ex-traordinary sound. Lisa's performance seemed to heighten Brendan's, and his voice became richer and more passionate than I'd heard it before. The atmo-sphere was electric and I was buzzing, my heart pumping like mad. I was ham-mering into my drums, now completely absorbed in the music and the moment until, a little way into 'Fortune', I suddenly lost the beat. I panicked, paused very briefly, and tried to come back in. I missed the beat and had to check and go for it again. Missed again, and only on the third attempt did I finally pick it up and pull the drums into line again. I felt devastated. I really thought I'd bro-ken the spell that Brendan and Lisa had been creating. I thought the entire au-dience must be thinking, 'Good band, but the drummer screwed up.' I couldn't get it out of my head, and for the rest of the set I went through the motions and saw the performance out. I slouched off stage to face the criticism, despite the enthusiastic reception we were receiving.

To my utter amazement, it seemed nobody (apart from Brendan, of course) had noticed. Nobody said anything about it. All I heard were people saying how brilliant we'd been. I went to seek out Jim at the mixing desk in the auditorium to ask him how obvious my cock-up had been. He hadn't noticed either – and he was a drummer. At first I couldn't believe it, but then I realised that everyone had been so transfixed by Brendan and Lisa's performances, nobody was paying any attention to what I was doing, or at least, not any kind of analytical attention. Sheer relief flooded over me. I grabbed a beer and started to relax. Brendan and Lisa were talking to Ivo. He confessed that it had been primarily Lisa's voice on our demo tape which had interested him, and seeing and hearing her perform live had been a revelation. But he was also marvelling over what Brendan could play on guitar whilst singing simultaneously. He wasn't being at all guarded – he'd clearly loved it. I went backstage again and bumped into Xmal's drummer, Manuela. She congratulated me and I thanked her. Wow – was all this really happening? We packed up our gear and waited around to see The Box and then Xmal. The Box were a bit disappointing for me as the elements I'd liked in Clock DVA seemed absent. Then Xmal came on and the place erupted into the wild romp the audience had come for. But DCD had made an impression on many of these people. We were up and running.

We had to wait a couple of weeks for the second of our two gigs while Xmal went off touring round the country before returning to London. It was a shame. I wanted more of this and would have loved to be out on stage again the following night. But the time soon passed, 7 July arrived, and we set off for the Clarendon Hotel in Hammersmith, West London. I'd been to this venue once before, a few years earlier, to see the band Chelsea – but that had been in a downstairs cellar bar, while Xmal's show was to be in a larger hall on the first floor of the building.

When our call came to go on stage this time, we emerged to find the hall almost empty. It was still early enough for daylight to be intruding and countering the effect of the stage lighting. The few members of the audience were either sat on the floor well away from the stage or huddled against the walls. Without sufficient bodies in the hall to soak up the sound, there was far too much natural reverb and the sound became a real mess. We were also struggling with severe problems in the onstage monitoring, particularly with feedback. At one point, shortly after I'd started playing the oil drums for 'Frontier', it became ear-splitting. I couldn't hear anything apart from the screaming feedback and I stopped playing and turned away. Brendan spun round and went mad at me, and after we came offstage he told me never to stop playing once a song was underway. He was right. I had to cope with stage problems and perform through it. I was learning fast.

Although I have no recollection of this, Brendan assures me that Gene Loves Jezebel played that night between us and Xmal. I liked GLJ and would have been eager to see them, but I was so despondent about the way our performance had gone that I packed up my gear and sought out the nearest pub where I could sulk quietly over a few pints. So I missed GLJ and I missed the last show of Xmal's tour, and never saw either play again. However, I soon learnt another lesson about not judging how an audience perceives a performance by your own perception of it. A review of the Clarendon show appeared in *Sounds* – one of the three big national weekly music papers in the UK at the time (along with *Melody Maker* and the *NME*). It was written by a reviewer called Robin Gibson – and we'd found the first person to champion the DCD cause in the media. His review mentioned that we struggled with sound problems, but went on to include the following description of our performance:

> It's a stunning musical landscape, a panorama sometimes of soft-hued ten-
> derness, sometimes of almost claustrophobic power. Whatever, nothing
> is ever lacking in depth or clarity . . . The pure scope contained in one set like
> this is staggering. It's a succession of changing, strikingly differing emotions
> and structures.

More importantly, Ivo remained enthusiastic. He wanted to meet up and talk
with us. Surely this had to be good? If he didn't want to pursue anything with
us, he'd just tell us politely by phone or letter. But he wanted to see us, and so
he was invited to dinner one evening at Brendan and Lisa's flat, together with
his girlfriend, Debbie, who ran the 4AD label with him. This was the cue for
Lisa and me to go into action on the culinary front. Brendan and Lisa had both
worked for a while in a Lebanese restaurant back in Melbourne and, although
they were only doing menial tasks, Lisa in particular had picked up some good
recipes and cooking techniques, including the assembly of a particularly fine
'baba ghannouj'. I've loved cooking since my student days and had discovered
some fantastic Bangladeshi restaurants in the nearby Brick Lane area of Whitechapel. I'd been studying various dishes, talking to restaurateurs, and acquiring a couple of Asian cookery books.

Our kitchens were small, and cooking facilities were limited, so we decided
to split the food preparation between us. I'd make some of the dishes in my flat,
while Lisa would prepare others in hers, then Nicki and I would run across with
our contributions once Ivo and Debbie arrived. Everything went more or less
to plan, despite Nicki and I getting some strange looks from some locals as we
carted steaming pots between tower blocks. The food was good, plenty of drink
was consumed and we had a grand evening. It was only after Ivo and Debbie
had gone I realised we hadn't discussed the recording deal at all. We'd talked
about all sorts of things – mostly music- and arts-related, a bit of philosophy
and politics thrown in for good measure – but had avoided 'business'. It had
been a social occasion simply to get to know each other, for Ivo to assess us as
people and decide if he wanted to work with us. I came to realise the importance
of this. Ivo wasn't a businessman working in the music industry and looking
for the next artist with commercial potential to sign. 4AD was very personal
to him, and it was essential that he surrounded himself with musicians whose
work he loved, but who he also felt comfortable with.

Ivo decided he did want to work with us and that 4AD would finance an
album. The budget was tight and we were to be given two weeks in Blackwing
Studios in South London where most of the 4AD artists recorded at the time.

Furthermore, a slot was free immediately and we were booked to start on 18 July. For me, this was all happening very fast. But for Brendan, Lisa, and Paul, it had been a tough and sacrificial struggle to reach this holy grail of recording a debut album. Their reaction was very much one of palpable relief, while mine was child-on-Christmas-Eve excitement.

The Blackwing studio complex had been developed in a decommissioned church in the Borough area of South London. It was the height of summer when we arrived and the tranquil, well-maintained gardens surrounding the old church were bathed in sunshine, in stark contrast to the dark and claustrophobic studio interior. Blackwing belonged to a guy called Eric Radcliffe who looked like the archetypal roadie and whose whereabouts were constantly revealed by the clanking of an enormous bunch of keys which always hung from his belt. Part of the building was occupied on an ongoing basis by Vince Clark, post-Yazoo and just around the time when he was reemerging as The Assembly. The Yazoo album title *Upstairs at Eric's* is a reference to it having been recorded at Blackwing. Clark had just taken delivery of a Fairlight computer which, at the time, was THE ultimate music composer system. They cost around forty thousand pounds and he and Peter Gabriel reputedly had the only two in the UK. Clark and Radcliffe were amusing themselves by running a Stylophone (anyone remember them?) through the Fairlight, and during the entire two weeks we spent recording our album, we only ever heard the same brief segment of a melody line drifting out of Clark's studio which became like a mounting torture every time we emerged from our confinement hoping to give our brains a break. Elsewhere in the complex, former Jam drummer Rick Buckler was rehearsing with his new band in preparation for a tour. I never actually encountered Buckler, and I only glimpsed Clark a couple of times, but the mere fact I was here in a recording studio at the expense of an established label, sandwiched between such high-profile musicians, was hard to grasp given that less than nine months earlier I wasn't even in a band and had no ambitions in this direction whatsoever.

The pressure was on from the outset. Brendan knew that we (or rather, he) needed to preserve as much of the allocated studio time as possible for the mixing and production, so we needed to get the actual recording done quickly. 'A Passage in Time' was chosen as the first song to record, and the drums were to be laid down first (with Brendan and Paul playing 'guide' parts on guitar and bass). This was analogue recording onto two-inch tape – there was no digital recording and computerised editing then. 'Passage' should have been straightforward. It has two distinct parts to the song, the first of which features a relatively standard drum pattern by DCD standards. However, the bass (kick) drum part involves playing on every beat of the bar, so the bass drum is pumping away all through, really driving the piece along.

At the time, still as a throwback to my days of playing laid-back blues and soul drums, my foot pedal technique was to keep my whole foot on the pedal and play using the heel as a pivot – the traditional jazz method which allows more controlled variation of the force of the kick beats. As we started recording I was presented with another set of unfamiliar circumstances. I'd never been in a studio before, playing with headphones on, and with my fellow musicians playing in segregated areas, and with the whole process being orchestrated from a glass-partitioned control room. In the back of my mind, I knew the clock was ticking and that every second of studio time was costing a lot of money. The nervousness kicked in again and I could feel myself tensing up. Suddenly, this bass drum part that I'd played for months in rehearsals, and had played in both the live shows without a second thought, became a problem and the muscles in my shin started to seize up. On the first take, I got about a minute and a half into the piece, and I was in agony. I couldn't continue, and had to stop. Take two . . . the muscles seized up even quicker. Take three . . . worse still. I was given a break for a couple of minutes, and then we tried again. Same problem.

Frustrated at the time being wasted, Brendan decided to try playing it himself. After a couple of practice runs, he went for a take and nailed it. However, halfway through the song, the rhythm changes to a drum pattern which Brendan couldn't play, but which I was much more comfortable with. So I went back behind the kit and studio engineer John Fryer had to do a very accurate 'drop in' on the tape where Brendan's part finished and I took over playing. Fortunately it worked. So the recording you hear on DCD's first album of 'A Passage in Time' features Brendan on drums in the first part, and me in the second. I subsequently retrained myself to play all my bass drum parts using the more aggressive 'stamping' style where only the toes and ball of the foot are in contact with the pedal, and the motion is driven from the hip rather than the ankle. This resolved the issue completely, and I had no further problems playing 'Passage'.

I managed to record the rest of my drum parts satisfactorily, and generally the basic recording of all the elements proceeded quickly and smoothly. I'm not one for sitting around doing nothing, and studio control rooms don't particularly excite me if I'm not at the desk myself, so once all my parts were down, I was quite happy making teas, coffees, and sandwiches for everyone. I guess these are the jobs which typically most people don't want to do, so

I became Mr Popular around the studio. Once the mixing and production phase began, things started to go wrong. Not immediately. At first, the mixes sounded great over the big monitors in the studio control room, and we were all really excited. But then John Fryer gave Brendan a cassette copy of a couple of mixes to take away and listen to. When we put this in a standard cassette player back at home, it sounded completely different – really muddy and muffled. It was a shock, and we hurried back to the studio the next day to find out what had gone wrong. But there was no obvious answer. The problem continued. Brendan would get a mix he was really happy with in the studio control room, but then we would take a cassette copy and play it on a standard domestic player and it sounded like mud.

We couldn't understand what was happening and didn't have the experience to deal with it. We were now into the second week and panic set in. The relationship between Brendan and John deteriorated rapidly, which only served to exacerbate the problem. By the end of the two-week session, everybody's nerves were in tatters. Brendan was looking pale, sick, and exhausted. He hadn't been able to sleep or eat for several days and was really broken. After a brief recuperation, Brendan went to see Ivo and it was agreed that some additional studio time would be allocated for remixing. These sessions took place in mid-September 1983. The final mixes that emerged from Blackwing were not as bad as the first efforts had been. Ivo listened to them and seemed reasonably satisfied, and we were told that they could be brightened up a bit in the final mastering before the records were pressed. This later proved correct, and some improvements were made, but the fact remains that our first album suffered greatly from an unfortunate mix of circumstance and our lack of experience.

There are some great songs on that album – when we played 'Ocean' live and Lisa's voice took off into the chorus, there was always a huge dimension that simply wasn't captured on the recording, and while 'Wild in the Woods' remains one of my favourite DCD songs both to play and to listen to, that original studio version is a shadow of its real self. Nevertheless, there was no going back. 4AD couldn't afford for us to rerecord any part of the album (and we couldn't even afford the bus fares to get back to Blackwing again without further subsidy). The album was recorded and that was that. And to underline the finality, Paul had quit the band following the initial Blackwing sessions and at the end of August returned to Australia. The recording process had taken more out of him than anyone had realised, and he was terribly homesick. I don't remember how he got his ticket – perhaps his family sent him some money, and I think maybe Jeff Earp helped him out – but it all happened very quickly, and he was gone.

We had to put the recording process to the back of our minds and focus on the next step. Although we had our reservations about it, we were now eager for the album to be released and to see what the response would be. Frustratingly there's always a gap of a few months between completion of recording and release as the record label needs to put it into the schedules and work up the prerelease promotions. On 17 October, Brendan, Lisa, and I went to 4AD's offices in Alma Road, Wandsworth – coincidentally adjacent to the location of my father's first childhood home in Melody Road – and formally signed the recording contract with Ivo. It was also confirmed that we were to embark on an eight-date tour of Holland supporting fellow 4AD artists the Cocteau Twins starting in two weeks' time. My old Mischief mucker Peter Hicks had filled in on bass for a couple of rehearsals after Paul's departure, but we now needed to seriously prepare ourselves for our first tour including the rapid initiation of the new bassist 4AD had found for us – actually via a recommendation of Cocteau guitarist Robin Guthrie – a seventeen-year-old Scottish lad called Scott Rodger.

FOUR

Cocteau Twins were now the duo of Liz Fraser and Robin Guthrie, original bassist Will Heggie having recently departed. They were a well-established act and had their own general manager/roadie/driver – Colin Wallace, a friend of Robin and Liz since schooldays in Grangemouth (Scotland), and whose favourite word was 'brelliant' – and tour manager/sound engineer – Ray Conroy, who we'd already encountered on the mixing desk at the Xmal gigs and whose brother, Mick, was bassist in another 4AD band, Modern English. We, on the other hand, were just us band members. Brendan didn't want a manager, so we'd agreed to have a crack at handling the management between us. As I was the only one with any formal administrative experience, I was nominated DCD tour manager, and we informed 4AD accordingly. My first task, then, was to organise the Carnet . . . The what?

This was pre-European Single Market days and it was explained to me that, to tour overseas, you had to temporarily 'export' all your equipment from your starting country, temporarily 'import' it into and 'export' it out of each country you pass through, and finally 'reimport' it into the country you started from. The Carnet is the controlling document and has to list everything in detail. You can't just say two guitars, a bass, three amps, and a drum kit – you have to list every individual drum, stand, pedal, effects machine, guitar, strap, amp, tool kit, plug box, and so on, and in every case give the serial number (where applicable), country of origin, value, and weight. A financial bond has to be lodged with your local Chamber of Commerce and, if you fail to account for every item of your equipment at every border (where you must stop and get your Carnet stamped), you can be charged duty as if you've sold, acquired, or changed anything which doesn't tally with the Carnet. What had I got myself into?

So, in the couple of weeks before we left for Holland, we had to sort out transport arrangements and this Carnet, in addition to inducting Scott into the DCD setup and rehearsing for the tour. Jim Pinker joined our tour party as sound engineer, and Brendan's dad Mike was enlisted to drive us and all our equipment in the Perry family's old VW camper van. By the time we were due to leave, I'd just managed to organise all the documentation in the nick of time, had been over to 4AD's offices to collect our cash float (money to eat and buy fuel until we started to pick up performance fees), and had organised myself a last minute British Visitor's Passport as I'd never owned a full passport and suddenly realised I'd need one to travel. I was knackered before we started. On 29 October 1983, we rolled off the Isle of Dogs with six of us wedged into the bright orange camper van along with amps, guitars, drum kit, etc. I really should've been wondering what on earth I was doing, but I was on a high. Here I was going on tour to a foreign country with a band – amazing!

Nevertheless, the trip rapidly became less glamorous still. Our ferry crossing was from Sheerness to Vlissingen – two of the gloomiest places imaginable in the murky grey cusp of autumn merging into winter. We met up with the Cocteaus at Sheerness and, although I immediately warmed to Robin, he does love a good moan, so he was complaining about everything, while Liz seemed to veer unpredictably between a resigned boredom and sudden outbursts of enthusiastic, quick-fire conversation. Liz was lovely, and had a vulnerability that made everyone feel protective of her, but I really struggled to understand her softly spoken, broad Scottish brogue. I quickly struck up a good rapport with Colin and Ray, and they gave me a crash course in tour management during the ferry crossing, stressing the essentiality of getting the Carnet stamped at every customs point, and of keeping strict control over the 'PD's (the 'per diems' – daily cash allowance handed out to each member of the tour party for basic subsistence).

Our pairing with the Cocteaus would inevitably generate comparisons between Liz's and Lisa's vocal styles. It was certainly a coincidence that two singers, both with such distinctive, untrained (in a formal sense), soaring voices, and who both preferred sounds to discernible words, should suddenly appear on the same label, at much the same moment. With the Cocteaus being better established, there would be murmurs that Lisa had set out to copy Liz, and/or that it was another premeditated component in establishing a '4AD sound', but it really was nothing more than pure coincidence, both Lisa and Liz having developed their styles before either knew the other existed and before either had any notion of being taken on by Ivo. While there are similarities in their motivations – both finding greater freedom of expression in not being constricted by the meanings and interpretations of words or phrases – Lisa's style came very much more from her Irish heritage. I already mentioned that her father's love of 'Sean-nós' was a big influence in her formative years, but many moons later Irish TV presenter and chat show host Graham Norton's answer to an interview question in the UK's *Observer* magazine as to whether the Irish have storytelling in their blood made me smile with recognition:

> Irish people talk in a different way. It's like birdsong. Often it doesn't have much meaning – we just enjoy making the sounds.

Fig. 8. Performing in Den Haag on DCD's first tour of The Netherlands supporting Cocteau Twins, November 1983: we would have been playing 'Ocean' – my chance during that set to come to the front of the stage, shoulder-to-shoulder with Lisa, to play yang ch'in. Photo by Tony Hill.

Once off the ferry, I headed to Dutch customs to get my prized Carnet stamp, and then we were on the road again, all carefully watching Mike to make sure he kept to the right side of the road, and yelling in unison whenever he looked about to take a roundabout in the wrong rotation. On arrival in Amsterdam the glamourometer took another plunge as we found our hotel was in the same building as a particularly seedy-looking 'massage parlour' (complete with gaudy red neon sign which lit up all the rooms at the front) and we could see fleas jumping about in the beds. I was worried Lisa would be freaked out, but she seemed the least concerned of any of us. I think she was so glad to be out of East London for a while, and that we were finally engaged in the activity she'd left home and crossed the globe to pursue, that she'd have accepted anything. I came to realise that she typically responded with admirable stoicism to situations like this – a very valuable asset.

Despite the hotel, we were in Amsterdam – and Amsterdam is beautiful. Once we'd lugged all our equipment into our hotel rooms (it wasn't safe to leave anything in the Perrymobile overnight), I spent several hours wandering the streets by the canals and soaking up the atmosphere. Exhaustion served me well and, despite the dampness and mustiness of the hotel and its resident wildlife, I slept soundly. The following day we received our venue passes and tour schedule from Dutch promotors Mojo Productions. My collection of notes, records, and keepsakes lets me down here because I can't find a definitive list of the order of shows and precise dates, but I've reconstructed the itinerary as best I can as follows:

Netherlands:
Sunday, 30 October, Amsterdam, Paradiso
Tuesday, 1 November, Nijmegen, De Vereeniging
Wednesday, 2 November, Rotterdam, Arena
Thursday, 3 November, Leiden, LVC
Saturday, 5 November, Appledoorn, De Giant
Monday, 7 November, Sittard, (Schouwburg?)
Saturday, 11 November, Den Haag, Paard Von Troje
Sunday, 12 November, Groningen, Vera

For just the opening show at the Paradiso in Amsterdam there was another band on the bill between us and the Cocteaus – The Europeans, whose singer and keyboard player Steve Hogarth would go on to replace Fish as lead singer in Marillion some years down the line. As first band on stage, we were last to soundcheck and were given little time, so as soon as our moment came, we rushed our gear onto the stage and a frenzy of activity ensued. Crisis! None of us had realised that continental Europe uses a different style of electric plug. All our electronic equipment was fitted with UK three-pin plugs, and all available sockets were European two-pin. The promoters arranged a 'gofer' to dash out to the nearest hardware store and buy a batch of plugs, and they all had to be changed. Fortunately, this was achieved with only slight disruption to our soundcheck, and we were ready.

We were soon back on stage. The venue wasn't yet full, but it was getting there, and our opening number was well received. I was settling in, trying not to be distracted by watching our performance, which was being filmed and projected onto screens at the back of the hall. We were about halfway through the third or fourth number – probably something like 'East of Eden', in which Brendan was in full flight, singing and pounding into his guitar – when there was a startling bang. Brendan was physically lifted off his feet by several inches and there was a vivid blue flash around him like a fleeting aura. He then started to shake violently. Scott and I shot each other alarmed glances, unsure in that split second whether we should carry on playing (but I'd now been hardwired never to stop). Lisa reacted instantly and rushed to help Brendan. Fortunately the onstage sound engineer immediately realised that Brendan's guitar had gone live and he now had full mains voltage earthing through his body into the floor. He ran onstage, screamed at Lisa to get back, and aimed an incredibly well-judged kung fu–style kick at Brendan's guitar that not only prised it from his grasp, but lifted it high enough that the strap flew over Brendan's head allowing him to throw down the guitar, breaking the circuit. Brendan staggered to the side of the stage, the power was shut down and we rushed to his aid. The audience, who initially thought they were witnessing some groovy new stage pyrotechnics, now also realised there was a problem, and a concerned hush descended.

Thankfully Brendan, though somewhat dazed, was otherwise unharmed, but he was in no state to continue. While we packed up our gear, safety checks by the crew revealed that in the rush to get all the replacement plugs fitted, the plug to Brendan's guitar amp had been live-neutral wired in reverse. Then Mike blurted out that it was he who had rewired the plug and became traumatised by the realisation that he'd come perilously close to being the cause of his own son's demise. All because of a stupid oversight over the different plug types.

After this unpromising start, things improved rapidly. It was a lowkey tour for the Cocteaus, and beyond Amsterdam they'd been booked into relatively small venues by their standards – clubs with capacities of around three hundred to four hundred. The result was they were all packed to bursting point, and people arrived early to stake their positions, so we got to play to pretty much capacity audiences everywhere. Furthermore, the audience responses were amazing. We got great receptions, lots of encores, and people crowding round to congratulate us after the shows. At some point around this time – I'm not sure if it was directly related to any damage Brendan's guitar had sustained from the Paradiso incident – Robin Guthrie took pity on him having to perform with the cheap Tokai 'Les Paul'-copy that was all Brendan could afford, and gave him his Kawai (with Di Marzio pick-ups to boot). Taken aback, but hugely grateful, Brendan used the Kawai as his main guitar for several years, but only found out much later it was the very guitar Robin had used to record the Cocteau's wonderful *Garlands* album – Brendan was gobsmacked!

Scott had fitted into the DCD setup incredibly well. He'd struggled to get to grips with some of Brendan's bass parts, but had practised until his fingers were raw and was coping well with being thrust onstage with far less time than it had taken me to acclimatise. At twenty-five, I was the oldest member of the group and eight years older than Scott, so I felt a particular responsibility for him. I think he appreciated my concern, but he wasn't in any need of my support. He was a bright lad, confident, outgoing, and cheerful, and was as thrilled as me about the opportunity that had come his way. Jim was also good to have in the tour party, his experience particularly helpful to me as a drummer.

Fig. 9. DCD promo shot from a session in early 1984 in the run-up to the release of our debut album. Possibly taken in the Photographers' Gallery just off Leicester Square, London. Left to right: Scott Rodger, Jim Pinker, Lisa, Brendan and me. Courtesy of 4AD Records.

Playing eight concerts in thirteen days was another completely new experience for me, and I was surprised how much it sharpened us up and how much tighter the playing became. I was happy that Brendan had rearranged 'Ocean', so I now played yang ch'in rather than the tuned metal pipes used for earlier shows and the album. Not only was it more enjoyable to play and suited the song better, it also gave me the chance to go to the front of the stage beside Lisa. The yang ch'in was mounted on a special wooden stand built for us by Mike and which also held our percussion. Lisa's vocal mic had to be located right next to the yang ch'in for the songs in which she played and sang simultaneously, so when we played 'Ocean' I would stand shoulder-to-shoulder with her. It was incredible to be right next to her as she sang and the emotion poured out. Her whole body would tremble with the power of her singing, and often she would grab the stand for physical support, leaving me chasing the yang ch'in around as it shook with her effort.

Not only were our performances going well, but after our show each night we got to see the Cocteaus play for free. I loved their performances and became a big fan but, sadly, Robin and Liz weren't enjoying it. With his customary cynicism, Robin had predicted that critics would be damning of the fact that, following Will's departure, so much of the music was on backing tape, with only Liz singing live and Robin performing what he could of his multilayered guitar parts. His response was to set his reel-to-reel tape machine centre-stage on a table and spotlight it, while he and Liz stood either side to perform. The message was clear – 'That's what you've come to see and hear, and if you don't like it, you can fuck off.'

To me it was a bold and amusing statement, and I still felt there was more than sufficient presence in their live performance from Liz's singing and Robin's guitarwork on stage. But they felt exposed and uncomfortable with just the two of them, and unfortunately the problem was exacerbated by touring with us. At that time we were playing everything live (not a sample or backing track in sight, other than me 'playing' the Tensai Rhythm Box on a couple of songs), using a variety of instruments which meant we swapped around the stage a bit, and so our performances were comparatively dynamic. To make matters worse, the Cocteau's spotlit tape machine jammed in midsong on at least one occasion, leaving Liz stranded while Robin undertook onstage maintenance before they could restart. Nevertheless, their shows were going down great – and I was out in the audience for everyone except the Paradiso – but Robin and Liz's moroseness seemed to grow in inverse proportion to our excitement during the course of the tour. We were sad for that, and told them their performances were fine, but it didn't help.

With some time to kill during the afternoon before the show in Nijmegen, the DCD party was installed in a local cafe where we were joined by some people who introduced themselves as another band. While we chatted, they handed us a few copies of an EP they'd recorded – *Subsequent Pleasures* by Xymox. We swapped contacts and promised to keep in touch. We liked the EP, which included a standout song called 'Muscoviet Mosquito', and when we returned to London, Brendan passed on a copy to Ivo, who would later sign them to 4AD as Clan of Xymox.

I always preferred to eat after a performance rather than before, but sometimes this wasn't possible and the choice was eat before or miss out. This was a no-brainer for me, and I have no self-control when food is on the table. After the soundcheck in Leiden, it was such an occasion when the meal provided by the promoter had to be taken at a local restaurant before the show, so we trooped down there. I'd just finished demolishing everything in sight, when someone came running into the restaurant and called out, 'Dead Can Dance on stage in five minutes.' We'd lost track of time and now found ourselves running back to the venue, me groaning and cradling my bloated belly. It was straight in the side door, onto the stage and into the first number. I had violent indigestion, and well recall 'Passage in Time' getting progressively slower as Brendan shot me angry glares and flicked his head at me to pick up the tempo. Another lesson learned. This same Leiden show was also notable for the presence in the audience of a battalion of skinheads. The dressing rooms were under the stage and there were small peepholes looking out into the auditorium at its floor level. Through these holes, all we could see was a forest of Doc Marten boots. Fortunately, we seemed to go down well enough to avoid experiencing the massed ranks of DMs flexed in anger.

I struck up a friendship with Brendan's dad, Mike. There was a midtour interlude for us while the Cocteaus went off to play shows in Paris and Brussels for which we weren't booked, so we had a couple of free days to explore Amsterdam. One night Mike and I somehow decided we must have a game of darts. Back home, dart boards were common in pubs, but not so in Amsterdam. We must have walked for a couple of hours, poking our heads into every bar we passed, and it turned out to be a great way to see the backstreets and less obvious parts of the city. At one point we found ourselves passing through the red-light district when Mike tugged my arm excitedly and told me a woman had smiled and winked at him from a shop window. I didn't have the heart to disillusion him and told him he clearly still had 'it'. We eventually found an 'English pub' with the requisite dartboard – I've no recollection of who won.

The contrast between ours and the Cocteaus' experiences of the tour came to a head in Den Haag. Our performance was greeted with exceptional rapture by the audience, Ray Conroy had nodded us the approval to play an extra encore, and we came off the stage to crowd noise threatening to bring the house down. But then Robin and Liz overheard through the thin walls backstage someone in our dressing room say something along the lines of 'Let's see them follow that.' Brendan later told me it was Jim, and they'd had an argument over it, but it hadn't been intended to reach the ears next door, and we didn't realise at the time. As a result, Robin went on stage in a foul temper and Liz's confidence was at an extra low ebb. On the night it could least afford to happen, the guy operating the smoke machine (which was used to create a brief cloud from behind which Robin and Liz would appear) overcranked it to such a degree that the pair were engulfed in a choking smog for their entire first number. It finally cleared to reveal Robin crouched over his FX pedals trying to make out the settings for the next number, and Liz coughing, spluttering and wiping tears from her eyes, altogether entirely killing the atmosphere. The next song was visibly unsettled and the audience responded with some agitation. It was too much for poor Liz who ran off-stage, locked herself in the dressing room and refused to come out.

On Sunday, 13 November we were on the ferry back to England, Robin and Liz hugely relieved to be going home, while we were feeling exuberant after completing our first overseas tour, and ready for more. I got our final stamp on the Carnet from UK customs and Mike was able to get the Perrymobile back on the normal side of the road. We later heard that, to compound their misery, the Cocteaus were detained at customs where their van was stripped out (including removing all the interior panels and floor) and searched with sniffer dogs. They were there for hours and I can only imagine what Robin was muttering about officialdom.

The awaiting news was that 4AD had arranged for us to record a session for the legendary *John Peel Show* on BBC Radio One the following Saturday. Brendan decided the four songs would be two from our forthcoming debut album – 'Ocean' and 'Threshold' – plus two from our live set which were otherwise unrecorded – 'Labour of Love' and the as-yet-untitled piece which was simply referred to as 'Instrumental'. Brendan was concerned about the amount of time available – four songs to be completely recorded and mixed in a single session of around eight to ten hours – so chose three songs which didn't feature the drum kit as it always took a long time to set up all the individual drum and cymbal sounds. This gave us two songs in which I 'played' the preset rhythms on the Tensai, 'Ocean' in which I played yang ch'in, and 'Threshold' in which I only used bass drum, snare, and two toms.

Having been an avid listener to John Peel's show pre-DCD, I now found myself in the famous Maida Vale Studios where so many bands I loved had recorded before – many I've already mentioned plus the likes of Echo & The Bunnymen, Television, The Skids, Vic Goddard and Subway Sect, Human League – the list goes on and on. It was another 'pinch myself to be sure this is happening' moment. The song plan worked well and still being fresh from the tour, we got everything recorded quickly and efficiently, giving Brendan the maximum time for mixing with producer Dale Griffin, the former Mott The Hoople drummer. The session went smoothly and Brendan emerged relatively unscathed.

Unlike our album, which as yet had no official release date (and wouldn't be released until well into the new year), the result of the Peel session was almost immediate. We only had to wait a couple of weeks for its first airing on Monday, 28 November. Peel introduced us as 'the enigmatic Dead Can Dance' and lots of people were contacting us afterwards to say they'd heard it. Brendan and Lisa even heard from friends who were in a cafe in Morocco and suddenly heard Peel introduce 'Dead Can Dance' as the show went out on the BBC's World Service. It was the norm for Peel sessions to be played four times, with any further repeats at John's personal discretion. Our session was broadcast again on Thursday, 15 December, and repeated at intervals up to the release of our album which made for a great prerelease build-up. All four songs recorded for this Peel session were released on CD many years later by 4AD as part of the white box retrospective – *Dead Can Dance 1981–98* – with the instrumental track given the title 'Orion'. Personally I think they sound great, and these versions of 'Ocean' and 'Threshold' are more dynamic than the versions that appeared on our first album.

We were now officially a five-piece group with Scott and James as permanent members, and I was organising to get everyone signed up with the Performing Rights Society for future royalties. Some confusion arose over Scott being still under eighteen and James being a New Zealand national, but I managed to resolve it, and we were all enrolled. For the design of the album cover, we were introduced to Vaughan Oliver who ran an independent art and graphics studio from within 4AD's offices in Wandsworth. Under the banner of '23 Envelope' (later 'V23'), Vaughan was creating a signature style which would become iconic and widely imitated. He created the '4AD' logo and classic album covers for many 4AD artists, including Cocteau Twins, Pixies, Throwing Muses, and Ivo's This Mortal Coil project, for which he regularly worked with images provided by photographer Nigel Grierson. His wide-ranging portfolio also included a set of instantly recognisable covers for a series of Ian McEwan books, and the cover for David Sylvian's *Secrets of the Beehive* album. Brendan had very specific ideas about the cover design – providing the main image and selecting all the other elements – so Vaughan was tasked with compiling rather than creating the artwork. We were all very happy with the final design, featuring a mask from Papua New Guinea which Brendan wanted to symbolise 'Dead Can Dance'.

It took us by surprise that the 'Dead Can Dance' name came to give the band its early association with the gothic community, though with hindsight, it's perhaps not so strange the assumption was made that it derived from the medieval Dance of Death concept. We had no particular problem with the misapprehension, and always much appreciated our goth following, but this wasn't the intention. Brendan describes the meaning behind the name as being an allegory for the way in which art forms create life out of essentially lifeless – 'dead' – raw materials. When an artist paints a picture, the materials are the canvas, the brushes, paints, pigments, oils, but once the picture is created, it takes on its own life force. Similarly, musicians take instruments made of wood, wires, skins, nuts, and bolts from which songs are borne and life is created. 'Dead Can Dance' is a description of the process of making music, with 'Dance' symbolising the life in music. The mask on the album cover was another manifestation of the same concept – carved from a lifeless lump of wood, but once fully formed and placed over the wearer's face, becoming imbued with a life force.

Brendan and I went to Tape One studios in Tottenham Court Road for the album mastering. We now heard the final version – as good as it was going to get – and Brendan had resigned himself to it, though he was at least relieved that it was possible to brighten up the sound to a certain extent at this last stage. The release was scheduled for the following month, February, and 4AD were preparing to dispatch prerelease copies to the press. While the promos clicked into gear, Brendan and I had some preliminary meetings with publishing companies – EMI, Carlin, and Chappells. The meeting at Chappells was with Jeff Chegwin. It was an unusual surname and, at the time, a UK television entertainer called Keith Chegwin – known as 'Cheggers' – was at the height of his popularity. When we stepped into Jeff's office, he was the spitting image of Keith, and spoke just like him too. Sure enough we found out afterwards they were twins. Although Keith was in the public limelight, Jeff was building his own notoriety. A few months earlier, he and agent Alan Melina had heard John Peel mention he was hungry during one of his live radio broadcasts. Being in their offices only a few streets away, they swiftly delivered a mushroom biryani to Broadcasting House for Peel, together with a recording by a singer/songwriter called Billy Bragg, for who they'd agreed the publishing rights, but who was as yet unsigned by a record company. Legend has it that Peel gratefully downed the biryani, played the tape while he ate, and in so doing, launched Bragg's career. Jeff seemed to genuinely like our demos and gave us the most positive response we'd had up to this point, but in the end no deal came about.

Ivo advised us to wait and see how the album launch went as it might put us in a stronger bargaining position if initial sales were good, so publishing went on the backburner. The album release was now imminent. John Peel had been sent an advance copy and moved from playing the session to playing tracks from the album. We had professional photos taken in a studio session at the Photographers Gallery in Leicester Square for 4AD's promotional work, and Debbie was in overdrive organising reviews.

On 26 February, DCD supported the Cocteaus at the Victoria Palace Theatre. Major London theatres are often hired out for one-off gigs on Sunday evenings when, traditionally, the resident theatrical show is not performed. The running show at the Victoria Palace at the time was *Hi-De-Hi*, a musical comedy version of a daft TV show based in a holiday camp. When we were called for our soundcheck, we found all the props for *Hi-De-Hi* tucked behind the curtains at the back of the stage. I dragged out a human-sized HP sauce bottle and managed to get Brendan inside it briefly, but nobody had a camera handy to secure the evidence, so he got away with that one. When it came to our time to perform, the theatre was already almost full. It was clear that many in the audience were really aware of us now and were well up for seeing DCD and the Cocteaus on the same bill.

The following day, the eponymous *Dead Can Dance* album was released on 12" vinyl – still the principal album format in this pre-CD era. I went into London's West End to visit the big record stores, wanting to see our albums in their racks, but I couldn't find any. Nevertheless, it *was* filtering out through the distribution chain, and it *was* starting to sell. In their 24 March 1984 issues, *Sounds* listed the album at number four and *NME* at number five in their respective 'Indie Charts', nestling in amongst albums by the likes of The Smiths, Cocteau Twins, and Fad Gadget. We were there . . . indisputable evidence that people were buying our album.

Unreserved reviews helped sooth our concerns about the album's sound – the intent, emotion, and craft of our songs clearly still cutting through. John Wilde in *Jamming* wrote: '[DCD] have achieved a dramatic wash of feeling that is not too far from impeccable'; Marina Merosi in *Melody Maker*: 'The emotional strains harnessed by Dead Can Dance are of a spiritual beauty above and beyond the realms of the imagination'; Robin Gibson in *ZigZag*: 'No doubting . . . that this debut is a complete and beautifully realised entity, that it is certainly one of the few truly important albums of the year, and that it reaches further than most are able, or willing to reach.'

While I don't remember any bad reviews, there are always some quirky ones. London listings magazine *Time Out* ran its review under the misnomer 'Dead Can Bounce' which I seriously doubt was an accidental typo. And a review appeared in our local newspaper, the *East London Advertiser*, with the unexpected result that Brendan received a letter from a local council inspector instigating a review of his unemployment benefit. Excitedly imagining he'd exposed the fraudulent activities of a wealthy popstar, the overzealous official was mightily peeved to discover that we still hadn't earned a penny at this point, still lacked the proverbial pot to piss in, and he could find no grounds to withdraw any of the fortnightly pittance that was just about keeping Brendan and Lisa alive.

We were scheduled to appear at the London School of Economics on Friday, 2 March for our first London headliner. We turned up midafternoon with all our gear, but there had been some organisational cock-up, and after hanging around for hours of 'It's off . . . no, it's on again . . . no it's definitely off . . . etc,' it was cancelled. At some point during the wait, I was wandering amongst the audience that was gathering when I heard someone whistling a melody I recognised. It was very familiar but I couldn't place it. Then it dawned on me that it was Brendan's guitar refrain in our own 'Instrumental' from our Peel Session. It hadn't immediately registered with me simply because it hadn't occurred to me that we were now accumulating our own audience who knew our songs – I was quite startled.

The disappointment of the cancelled LSE gig was soon forgotten when I got a phone call on the Sunday morning asking if we could play that evening at another prestigious London venue, The Lyceum Ballroom just off the Strand, supporting Fad Gadget and Pink Industry. I legged it over to Bowsprit to alert Brendan and Lisa, as they still had no phone, then after a few quick calls and arrangements, we were on our way. Fad Gadget (aka Frank Tovey) had an elaborate stage show with costumes, props, theatrics, and a bit of crowd diving/surfing. His over-the-top stage presence was in marked contrast to the demure figure we encountered backstage in a tracksuit manoeuvring his young child around in a pushchair. It was another good opportunity to play to a sizeable audience and spread our recognition.

A one-off gig in Paris on 5 April had been set up for us through an organisation called La Sébale which ran Goth Club Nights at a venue called The Opera Night. La Sébale had agreed to pay the full cost of us travelling over for the single performance, so it made it feasible. There were still arrangements to be made – including another bloody Carnet – but we were excited about going to play in Paris. The show was supposedly recorded for broadcast on French national radio, though I don't recall ever hearing any more about that. The trip was spread over three days, in order to include some interviews and promotions, so we managed a bit of sightseeing as well, and I fell in love with the Sacré Coeur and Montmartre.

Before we left, Lisa, Jim, and I went in search of some special French cheese to take home. Confronted by a vast selection in the *supermarché*, we asked what was their strongest *fromage* and were advised 'Rouy'. We each bought a pack and stashed it in our luggage which was then locked in Mike's van for the Channel crossing. As the ferry pulled in to Dover docks, we reopened the van to an overwhelming stench. Instantly hatching a cunning plan, I ushered everyone in, got all the doors shut and told them not to open any windows. Despite protests, they went along with me and once we'd driven into the customs enclosure, I instructed them to keep the van sealed while I went to get the Carnet stamped. If I returned with a customs officer, they should wait until my signal and then throw the side doors open. Sure enough, the customs officer wanted to take a look. I warned him we'd bought some cheese in France and there was a bit of a strange smell in the van, to which he smirked a warning that he wouldn't be so easily deterred. As we neared the van, I gave my signal, doors were thrown open, and the compressed aroma of Rouy exploded out of the van like an atomic cloud. The officer visibly staggered backwards, gulping back a wretch, signed off our Carnet, thrust it back at me, and ran for cover. So there you have it – the DCD quick customs method (patent applied for).

Whilst in Paris, we had what turned out to be a fateful meeting with La Sébale's prime mover – a highly ambitious guy around our age called Philippe Jauer who was juggling the beginnings of a successful banking career by day with being a promotor of clandestine indie music clubs at night. He was a powerhouse of energy, enthusiasm, and charm, as well as being very obviously besotted with Lisa, and set about convincing us he could organise a national tour of France for us. Back in London we discussed his proposal with Ivo and Debbie and, despite some reservations on their part, it was agreed that we go ahead with lining up a six-date tour in June. Meanwhile, we had our first London show as headliners coming up at the October Club in Brixton on 14 April, followed by a studio session to record some new songs, followed by a small UK tour for which we were inviting Xymox over from Holland to support us.

The October Club was resident in The Loughborough Hotel, just off the main drag through Brixton. On the first floor was a large function room with a dramatic domed ceiling, but no permanent stage. The temporary stage was constructed of builders' duckboards laid across a series of upturned plastic beer crates – classy! The support band was Living in Texas, who we knew of but hadn't met before. It was a new experience being first to soundcheck, and then having to shift our gear to the sides to make way for another band. It was a strange pairing as Living in Texas proved to be a pretty wild thrash punk outfit – they were lovely guys, but I couldn't help thinking that the promoters had thrown us together without much thought.

I was getting a beer while the audience filtered in when Ivo caught my attention.

'Does the name Mark Cox mean anything to you?' he asked, walking over.

'Erm, there's a tennis player called Mark Cox, and it's also the name of someone I was at school with,' I replied, wondering what was coming next.

'Well,' said Ivo, 'The one you were at school with is over there and he's in another of my bands.'

Turned out Mark was a member of The Wolfgang Press, one of 4AD's established bands, which I'd heard of but knew nothing about at this point. He'd been in the same year as me at John Lyon – though not in the same class (he was A-stream, me B-stream). We'd got on OK without being close friends, and I hadn't seen him for about eight years, but now we greeted each other warmly, both amazed at the coincidence. It was particularly surprising because neither of us had been aware of the other having any musical abilities or inclinations at school, but now we discovered a lot in common and a good friendship was rekindled.

Living in Texas came on and I enjoyed their set, particularly because I was transfixed watching their drummer Mat Fraser. Mat has thalidomide-induced phocomelia, resulting in much reduced length of both arms, but is one of those amazing people who, rather than being hampered by a 'disability', is inspired to greater achievement by it. He appeared to be on a mission to prove that he could drum harder, faster, and more frenetically than any other drummer. With his rack drums and cymbals all specially mounted within a reachable radius, he tore into the kit like a whirlwind from the outset in a compelling performance. The next time I would see Mat was on TV in the Closing Ceremony of the 2012 Paralympic Games guest drumming with Coldplay and the Paraorchestra conducted by Charles Hazlewood to a global audience of millions – some progress!

Eventually my attention was drawn away from Mat when the Texan's singer, Daniel Glee, climbed the PA stack at one side and leapt dramatically into the middle of the insubstantial stage. The boards collapsed and he disappeared into the hole, before emerging slightly shaken but apparently unharmed. During the interval, the stage was repaired before we could set up, but it was a bodge job and when we went on, we found the boards bouncing up and down alarmingly. There was nothing we could do about it once our performance had started. It wasn't quite so bad for Brendan and Scott who were more towards the sides of the stage, but poor Lisa in centre stage looked like she was trampolining in sync with my bass drum beats. She clung on to the percussion and yang ch'in stand to steady herself as best she could while she was singing and, as ever, she coped admirably, even turning round to me to let out a fit of giggles at one point. Worst of all was trying to play the yang ch'in with the stage bouncing. The yang was difficult to play at the best of times because the stage lights would reflect up in your face from the polished soundboard and blur the strings (all fifty-eight of them, or thereabouts), but with it leaping around as well . . . ! Maybe, after all, that subeditor at *Time Out* had a premonition when he labelled us 'Dead Can Bounce?' It's amazing how every venue seems to present its own individual peculiarities which have to be dealt with, but that's a big part of touring and, of course, an important factor in preventing monotony. You also come to realise that audiences are largely oblivious to these kind of technical quirks going on.

Entirely without Ivo's blessing – in fact, much to his consternation – 4AD had an occasional football (soccer) team which played ad hoc games against other record labels and music biz entities. Colin Wallace was the clandestine organiser, self-appointed captain, and star striker, and had lined up a fixture with the *Sounds* paper. Brendan and I joined a team which along with Colin included Mark Cox and Mick Allen (Wolfgang Press), Vaughan Oliver, and artist/musician Russell Mills who worked on various 4AD-related projects down the years and who had reputedly trialled at England Schoolboy level in football. At a time when fashion dictated that footie shorts were styled like hotpants, Brendan raised a few eyebrows by turning up in a pair of 1950s long baggies, earning him the 'Stanley Matthews' soubriquet and position of right wing, while I formed a defensive line with Mark and Vaughan. Twenty minutes or so into the game, Vaughan called to deal with a long ball, so Mark and I had already started moving up when we were stopped in our tracks by a sickening crack and yelp of pain behind us. Vaughan had caught his foot in the AstroTurf surface, snapping his Achilles tendon, and was in agony. The match was abandoned and another game against ZigZag was overshadowed by the incident, after which I don't think either Vaughan or 'Athletico 4AD' played again.

From Monday, 21 May 1984, 4AD booked a week for us in Vineyard Recording Studios in South London to record some new songs. Brendan and Lisa had told Ivo they didn't want to put out a standard single. They were uncomfortable with sacrificing one of their songs to the 'hit-or-miss', 'here today, gone tomorrow' commercial circus of the singles market, but Ivo advised it would be beneficial to building DCD's profile to try for a presence in the indie singles charts as well as the albums charts. The compromise was that we'd release a four-track 12" vinyl EP, but without specifying any of the tracks as the dominant 'single'. The format would qualify for the 'singles' chart, but radio stations and DJs would be left to decide which, if any, particular song they wanted to focus on.

Vineyard was chosen because, within our budget range, it was about as different from the Blackwing environment as could be found, and this was necessary for Brendan psychologically. Vineyard had a huge, bright and airy main studio, with a smaller 'live' room off to one side. The 'live' room was all polished wood floors and walls, giving a great natural reverb, and proved ideal for some of our drum sounds, and especially for the yang ch'in. It was a whole new experience to have these different sound environments to experiment with, and we had to be careful not to get carried away and lose track of time. With the lessons learnt from Blackwing and the experience of the John Peel session under his belt, Brendan was itching to take control as producer in his quest for the 'DCD sound' that he envisioned in his head and which he now felt more capable of reaching out for. He struck up a good working relationship with the studio engineers, Joe Gillingham and Kenny Jones (not to be confused with drummer Kenney Jones), and the atmosphere was upbeat. We recorded four quite different songs, two each for Brendan and Lisa to sing. Lisa's two songs both featured yang ch'in as lead instrument, with no guitar, and both had a joyous, celebratory feel to them. 'Carnival of Light' featured bass, kit drums, and additional pang cymbal, while 'Flowers of the Sea' dispensed with all elements of the standard rock format, utilising yang ch'in, congas, and tambourine. It was the first time I'd played congas as I'd always used bongos prior to the studio session, but Brendan wanted to hire congas for extra depth in the recording.

Brendan's songs reverted to the more standard guitar, bass, and drum kit instrumentation. 'The Arcane' was a dark, brooding song with dramatic rises and falls, and with a spacious drum pattern which I had to lock into and play with metronomic accuracy. Under Brendan's direction, it featured a single use of the crash cymbal midway through the song. This typified Brendan's attention to detail, and the way he was already approaching DCD composition like a classical composer might score a symphony. In contrast to much rock drumming in which the crash cymbal is typically hit every time the song goes into a change, that single crash in 'The Arcane' would be the only time I ever used that cymbal in a DCD recording, and would often be the only time it was used during an entire DCD live set, thus ensuring maximum impact.

Although the EP was to have no track selected as 'the single', Brendan's other vocal track was the obvious contender with its richly melodic guitar and bass lines and relatively accessible lyrics. Sensing that this song was dangerously close to commercial crossover territory, Brendan very purposely (I believe) gave it the decidedly uncommercial title 'In Power We Entrust The Love Advocated' – imagine your average radio DJ trying to spin that one off the tongue. He also gave it a typically nonconformist drum pattern in that the song starts with a single snare beat after which it is entirely played with just bass/kick drum, ride cymbal, and hi-hat (pedal cymbal). Nevertheless, with different marketing that song could well have been a mainstream commercial success. But that wasn't the route of Brendan's vision, and fortunately Ivo provided a safe haven for such an attitude at 4AD which would've been hard to find elsewhere.

The recording and mixing process generally went well. There were still some problems in relating the sound achieved in the studio control room to the reproduction on a home audio system, but these mixes represented major strides in the right direction and, although our album had been out less than three months, we were all eager for people to hear the much-improved sound quality of these songs. However, it would again be a while before the EP would hit the streets, and in the meantime we had a pressing schedule. The following Saturday – 2 June – we were back at the BBC's Maida Vale Studios to record our second Peel session. Brendan and Lisa decided to go for three of the songs we'd just recorded for the EP – 'Panacea' (which was then the working title for what became 'In Power We Entrust The Love Advocated'), 'Flowers Of The Sea', and 'Carnival Of Light' – plus one new song – 'Penumbra'.

I was particularly excited about recording 'Penumbra'. This song had developed from a drum pattern which I contributed. I'd taken what is essentially a standard drum fill – that is a busy interchange of hi-hat, snare, and tom-tom which would normally be used only at the end of a four or eight bar sequence, or where there is a change in a song – and constantly repeated it. The effect was to create a busy, driving rhythm over which Brendan set bass and guitar parts with an Arabic North African flavour. This provided a backdrop which Lisa's voice suited perfectly and when all the elements first came together in the rehearsal studio, I was stunned by what we'd created. As we worked on it further, Brendan developed the guitar part such that it built up to a frenzied finale. I loved playing the song live – even though it was physically demanding maintaining this repetitive drum fill for over five minutes – and it would be great to have a good recording of it.

But bad omens were looming. While recording the EP, we'd discovered that Kenny Jones did regular production for Peel sessions. So, as three of the four songs planned for our Peel session were from the Vineyard recordings that Kenny had just worked on, logic surely dictated it would be ideal for Kenny to engineer it. Brendan duly phoned the BBC and spoke to Peel's producer John Walters to ask if this were possible, but Walters merely looked at the schedule, told Brendan that Dale Griffin was booked and put the phone down. Brendan called back and tried to explain the logic of letting Kenny do the session – it would only require for Kenny and Dale to make a simple swap of sessions – but Walters wasn't having anyone phoning up and interfering with his organisation, and the answer was a firm 'No.' Whether or not Walters then made deliberate mischief by telling Dale Griffin that Brendan had requested his removal from the session, we don't know, but certainly there seemed to be 'an atmosphere' from the outset. Recording the parts went relatively smoothly, and we had all the tracks laid down in good time, again giving Brendan as much of the allocated time as possible for mixing. But from there the situation rapidly deteriorated. While Brendan struggled to get things sounding as he wanted, Griffin maintained an air of indifference and further exacerbated the problem by disappearing periodically to keep track of a cricket match on TV somewhere else in the complex. This, of course, had the proverbial 'red rag to a bull' effect on Brendan and his exasperation led to a heated argument. The session was completed in a tense standoff.

Word of the blowup was reported back to Walters who then presumably poisoned our reputation with John Peel. Our second session was played the minimum number of contracted times and, as far as we know, Peel never played anything by Dead Can Dance again. There is another entirely different (or additional) theory as to why DCD might have dropped out of the Peel playlists which I only discovered years later through the pages of Peel's posthumous autobiography *Margrave of the Marshes*. I knew, as any Peel listener would, that the man was a passionate supporter of Liverpool Football Club, but a quote from his book reveals his only prejudice to be that:

> Musicians I suspect of supporting Everton or Arsenal have a bugger of a time getting their ponderous tripe on to the programme.

Furthermore, I learned that Peel and his wife Sheila became season ticket holders at Ipswich Town FC during the years they lived in rural Suffolk. The point here is that Brendan is an Arsenal supporter, while I'm a member of Norwich City FC (traditional bitter rivals of Ipswich Town), so if Brendan and I had unwittingly revealed either, or worse still both, our allegiances in the wrong earshot . . . who knows?

Whatever the reason(s), it saddens me that we fell out with John Peel without ever even meeting him. Personally, I've never held any grievance over this, and continued to enjoy his programmes and maverick dealings with the established order. While Peel's autobiography pointedly omits any mention of DCD, Michael Heatley's biography – 'John Peel, A Life In Music' – includes Dead Can Dance in a list of 4AD bands which featured prominently on Peel's playlists in the 1980s, along with Cocteau Twins, Bauhaus, This Mortal Coil, the Birthday Party, Colourbox, Xmal Deutschland, Xymox, Throwing Muses, and the Pixies. There's no doubt his early patronage gave us a big start, so now we were up and running, we just had to move on without him.

Our album held its place in the indie charts over the coming weeks, but our proposed UK tour with Xymox hit problems. The booking agents originally had a schedule of eight dates, but one by one they fell through, apparently for entirely disparate and unconnected reasons. My heart sank as we lost the opportunity to play renowned venues on the indie circuit like the Leadmill in Sheffield and the Warehouse in Leeds, and by the time Xymox arrived in London, just two gigs were still standing. It was bad enough for us, but a huge disappointment for Xymox, and also threatened to be a financial disaster for them as they'd calculated their costs based on receiving eight performance fees. Nicki and I offered to put them up in our flat so at least they could cut out hotel bills, and our living room floor became a makeshift dormitory to Ronny, Anke, Pieter, Frank, and Willem.

The first of the two surviving gigs was on 8 June at a club called JB's in Dudley, just north of Birmingham. JB's turned out to be a brick shed in the middle of a municipal car park in a less than salubrious part of town. As we unloaded the equipment, Scott was approached by a local punk with huge Mohican hair and the full chain, stud, and razor outfit who demanded to know if we were anything like hardcore punk band The Exploited. Not wanting to disappoint, Scott assured him we were very similar, at which news he grunted his approval and went off to fetch all his mates. As onstage time for Xymox approached, the brick shed was already uncomfortably full and the atmosphere quite heavy, with no apparent security in sight. Ronny rose to the occasion admirably and put in a storming performance, while most of the male members of the audience seemed content gawping at Anke on bass, who at over six feet tall and strikingly attractive had little trouble holding their attention. When our turn came, Lisa made no compromise and glided on stage in her customary white makeup, deep red lipstick and flowing gown. The audience was either entranced or bewildered by her audacity – maybe both. When we started to play, we seemed to naturally respond to the atmosphere and played harder and more aggressively than I'd known before. We pumped Scott's bass up, I was beating the crap out of my little kit, Brendan scythed into his guitar to such a level that the brick shed threatened to crumble, and Lisa's manic percussion interludes were the icing on the cake. I've no idea if we won any new fans that night, but I reckon it must have been the wildest DCD performance of all time, certainly post-Oz.

The following night we were back at the October Club in Brixton for the second and final show of our 'UK Tour'. This time the stage held firm and the show ran smoothly. This was possibly the night that Ivo decided to sign Xymox – I'm not sure how that worked out – but our visitors seemed happy enough as they left the following day to return to Holland.

That next day – Monday, 11 June 1984 – we set off for our first tour of France. Once more we shoehorned ourselves and all the gear into the Perrymobile and headed for the cross-channel ferry, me with my tour manager kit. My accounts records let me down again here as, although they show where we played (by listing our performance fees), I didn't record the dates, and subsequent research hasn't turned up a definitive list. It turned out to be such a crazy and chaotic tour that recollections of individual incidents remain vivid, but we have varying recollections of the order of proceedings. With Brendan's help I've pieced together the evidence, and we think it went like this:

France:
Tuesday, 12 June Lyon
Friday, 15 June St Brandan, St Brieuc, La Mèche Bleue
Tuesday, 19 June Paris, Petit Forum

Thursday, 21 June Paris, Place de la Concorde
Friday, 22 June Perpignan
Saturday, 23 June Nice
Sunday, 24 June Marseille, Eldorado

The first disaster struck en route between Paris and Lyon, when Mike's trusty old VW Transporter shuddered to an ominous halt somewhere near a town called Nemours. I know VWs have a reputation for being reliable workhorses, but looking back on it now, the amount of people and gear we were trying to shunt around Europe in it was just a trifle excessive. A local breakdown service was summoned to haul the stricken vehicle to a local garage, where the Perrymobile was pronounced well and truly 'mort'. Hours of rearrangements followed. We emptied the VW and saw Mike depart sadly for home, we cancelled that night's show in Lyon – which meant we not only lost our performance fee but actually incurred a 'breach of contract' fee of two thousand francs (pre-euro days), and we waited while Philippe Jauer organised for some friends to drive out, collect us and the gear and take us all back to Paris where we were dispatched to different people's homes to hole up for a couple of days while frantic rearrangements were made.

Philippe had an extraordinary capacity to remain cheerful and utterly convinced this was merely a minor blip which he would soon have resolved. In the meantime, we should enjoy the delights of Paris, and specifically visit one of Paris's lesser-known tourist 'attractions'. Apparently, during the time of the French Revolution, so many people were guillotined that the cemeteries became full, and the Authorities dug up thousands of old graves, removing the skeletons of the long dead to create space to bury the newly dead. In some kind of conscience-appeasing gesture, it was ordered that all skulls and femur bones exhumed should be kept and stored in specially built catacombs under the city. Miles of tunnels were constructed under the streets of Paris, a section of which is open to the public to walk through. You file along a narrow passage with low ceiling, musty air, and an eerie yellow artificial light (to preserve the bones), and all along on both sides is a stack of femurs on top of which are piled a few layers of human skulls. A very odd experience, and not exactly what we were in the frame of mind for at that moment.

Meanwhile, Philippe hired a Renault commercial van, enlisted a friend called Walter to share the driving, and a couple of days later we were back on the road, heading for deepest Brittany. We were booked to play a venue in St Brieuc, which didn't appear where it was supposed to according to our map (pre-SatNav days), and after driving around for an hour or so hunting down ever-more remote country lanes, the van's fuel gauge touched empty. The engine spluttered, gasped, and cut out, and with the last of our momentum we cruised silently and serenely onto the forecourt of what seemed to be a small country hotel which had magically appeared. To our amazement, it turned out to be both our venue and our accommodation – a real change in our fortunes! It was certainly a curious location for a gig, seemingly in the middle of nowhere, but people turned up from all around, and it was a really good night.

Fig. 10. A change over between songs during our performance at La Mèche Bleue in St Brieuc during DCD's first tour of France, June 1984: Lisa, me, and Brendan. Photo by Frédéric Abgrall-Detrézien.

We'd finally managed a show, but now had another break – albeit a scheduled one – of a couple of days before our next gig back in Paris. Philippe secured us the use of a large house in southern Brittany (I think in the vicinity of Lorient, possibly down towards Quiberon) which belonged to the family of the girlfriend of Patrick Rognant, a journalist friend of Philippe's who arranged some of DCD's earliest press coverage in France. The house was idyllic, set in a forested valley on a narrow road leading down to a picturesque fishing village, where we bought a magnificent freshly caught fish, some great local bread and salad, and copious quantities of wine and beer. Back at the house, I cooked the fish, we feasted, got utterly drunk, smoked some hash, and fell asleep in the garden under one of the most beautiful star-filled skies I've ever seen. The following day, Philippe talked Lisa into taking her yang ch'in into an old stone church nearby which was open but deserted. The huge natural reverb of the interior made the sound of the yang ch'in and Lisa's voice completely envelope us – a special moment amongst my treasured memories of Lisa's intimate, spontaneous performances.

Finally we were back in Paris, first to play our scheduled gig in a small but central venue called The Petit Forum, and secondly for an additional show where Philippe had managed to get us added to the bill for a big street event in which we'd play on a temporary open-air stage at the Place de la Concorde facing down one of Paris's famous long, wide, tree-lined boulevards. We'd be last on – scheduled for 11:00 p.m. – which wasn't 'headlining' as the optimum crowd size would be reached earlier in the evening, but the streets should still be teeming with people. Headliners on the bill were East German actress/singer Eva-Maria Hagen (mother of Nina) and the band Eskimo, whose rehearsal earlier in the day Brendan got to sneak in on for a while. The show inevitably ran late, and the organisers hurried us on with warnings that the police might enforce a midnight deadline on amplified music. We started around quarter to twelve and had only played three songs when it became clear that urgent discussions were taking place behind the stage between the police and organisers. On Brendan's cue, we quickly launched into another number, but at the end of the song, the plugs were pulled. Nevertheless, it had been an experience in that setting, and somebody estimated we'd been playing to about five thousand people. I think that included people way off in the distance who couldn't really be considered to be active audience members, but it must still have been the largest crowd we'd played to by some distance. And on top of that, we received our full performance fee which helped reduce our losses.

The downside of the additional Paris show was that we now had to drive through the night to get to Perpignan on the Spanish border in time to sound-check and play the following night. The hired van, being a commercial rather than passenger vehicle, had seats only in the front for the driver plus two passengers, so the rest of us had to travel, not entirely legally, in the rear compartment with the equipment. This was one thing during the night, but as we headed into the south of France in the mid-June heat the next day, we had no option but to open the sliding side door to avoid a roasting suffocation, and thankfully escaped the attention of the Gendarmerie. It's probably much-changed since, but at that time Perpignan was a barren and desolate-looking place littered with construction sites. It felt a bit like arriving at a frontier outpost in the 'Wild West' of nineteenth-century America. Our venue turned out to be a small seafront bar with a tiny triangular stage across one corner which could barely accommodate my drum kit – it was certainly the first place I'd played with DCD that was smaller than the East London bars I used to play with Mischief.

Despite its size, they still crammed a PA system into the place – admittedly a relatively small one, but even so, it was going to sound mega in these confines. The PA was a homemade affair with old valves and was struggling with the heat, and we were sure it was hissing out steam in the late afternoon. Come the evening, the heat hadn't abated, the bar was packed, and many more people milled around outside. The sound system was intended to ensure that those outside were still at the gig (with a constant stream of people forcing their way in and out to get to and from the bar). Inside it was deafening, airless, and oppressively hot. Brendan, Lisa, and Jim had experienced playing in heat like this in Australia, but Scott and I were new initiates and were struggling. We got through the set and spent several hours afterwards rehydrating.

Next stop was Nice. My vague recollection is that the venue, although unremarkable, was a pleasant-enough small club close to the sea front, and that the gig went well and was politely received. We moved on to Marseille where an entirely different experience lay in wait. Arriving at the venue in the early afternoon, we were ushered into an unremarkable building down a side street bearing the overambitious name 'Eldorado' in which a disco was already in full operation. It was very strange to step out of the heat and brightness of the middle of a Mediterranean day into a darkness punctuated by flashing lights and thumping dance music. The club wasn't full, but the afternoon session was specifically for young teenagers and there were a fair few in. We had to dodge between them on the dance floor as we carried our equipment through to the stage – undoubtedly the most surreal prelude to a soundcheck I ever experienced.

The disco continued while we set up and was finally wound up around 6:00 p.m. before the venue was cleared and we were given a chance to soundcheck. A group of guys in the rock uniform of long hair, shades, black Ts, leather, and denim had wandered in with an entourage and set up camp on one side of the room. We'd seen them earlier in a nearby restaurant where lunch had been provided, and now one of them sauntered over to the stage with a girl hanging from each arm, took a look at Brendan's guitar and amp, and, without so much as acknowledging any of us, turned to someone behind and pronounced 'Yeah, they'll do.' He turned out to be guitarist Brian James, formerly of The Damned and now of Lords of the New Church (fronted by Stiv Bators), who were a big-name act in France at the time. The local promoter was wetting himself with excitement over their presence and had a special request that, after our set, we'd introduce them and let them come up and play a few songs as a special surprise for the audience. While we had no problem with anyone playing after we'd finished our set, we weren't letting them loose on our equipment. Lords of the New Church had a reputation for smashing up gear on stage – which was fine for them as they could afford to replace it, but our tour was already in financial peril. We couldn't afford any further disasters, so we refused the request.

The promoter wasn't at all happy that this bunch of unknowns who were getting the opportunity to play his club weren't cooperating, and to appease his honoured guests – already clearly stoned – he started plying them with champagne. To heighten tensions further, Brendan and Jim told him of their serious concerns about the quality of the PA system. The same homemade one we'd used in Perpignan had turned up and was both seriously underpowered for this size of club and wasn't fitted with the usual protective limiters. Although there was no outright argument, the atmosphere turned very obviously hostile. By the time we went on stage, the club was packed, and the first couple of numbers went down well. But then we started getting heckled from the Lords of the New Church's mob – marvellously inventive jibes like 'Where's your barbie, mate?' in mock Australian accents. Then one of them grabbed a champagne bottle and, as he aimed it at the stage, Walter (the guy Philippe had enlisted to help with driving and roadie-ing for us during the tour, and who we'd only known up to this point as a really sweet, placid character) suddenly came flying across the tables and laid the bottle-thrower out with a perfectly executed punch. Within seconds, the place erupted into a wild, John Wayne western-style barroom brawl, with everyone apparently hitting anyone in sight, and glasses, tables, and chairs flying through the air.

At first, we carried on playing – partly hoping we might regain the audience's attention so the fight would fizzle out, and partly because we really weren't sure what else to do. But then the PA system blew and the sound went. This seemed to turn a section of the audience against us, thinking we'd stopped playing deliberately and we were to blame for the entertainment they'd paid for being curtailed. Things were now being hurled onto the stage and we decided we had to get out . . . but in one of those decisions that's made in the midst of chaos when you act on instinct rather than logic, we thought we couldn't leave without our gear. So having carried it all into the venue dodging prepubescent afternoon boppers, we were now carrying it out trying to evade flying fists and furniture!

We'd managed to get most of our equipment out, and Brendan had gone off looking for the promoter to try to extract our performance fee, when suddenly, without warning, the club bouncers, notable by their absence during the dancefloor brawl, turned on us. We were attacked by a dozen or so trained karate fighters in full fight clothing, in what now seemed to have transformed into a scene from a Bruce Lee film. I can remember Lisa screaming at them from behind me as they came at us. I'm no fighter and had no idea how to react. Before I could take any evasive action, I was caught in the groin by a flying kick which temporarily poleaxed me. As I staggered to my feet I saw my snare drum come flying through the air and ducked just in time to avoid it smashing into my head. Instead I groaned with dismay as I heard it hit the wall behind me. I grabbed the snare and another drum that was in reach and stumbled outside to the van.

Lisa, Jim, Philippe, and I had managed to get out, but there was no sign of the others. Then police arrived, the club bouncers vanished into thin air and the situation started to calm down. Brendan reappeared unscathed, having been locked in a heated argument with the promoter in an upstairs room. The promoter was apparently blaming us for blowing the PA, and had ordered the bouncers to prevent us removing our equipment while he demanded compensation, but the bouncers had gone well beyond their remit. We found Scott and Walter who had both been trapped further inside and given a sound beating. They had to be taken to hospital, but were later discharged having sustained cuts and bruises but fortunately nothing more serious. Amazingly we also escaped with all our equipment, and nothing had been badly damaged. All we wanted to do, once Scott and Walter returned, was to get out of Marseille, so we piled into the van and hit the road.

Brendan had managed to extract one thousand francs of what should have been a fee of 2,500 francs from the promoter, and we later received a further one thousand francs from Lords of the New Church's management so at least, I assume, they must have felt some regret for the trouble, unless Philippe had threatened them with legal action. We dropped Philippe in Paris, and Walter drove us back to London. My accounts from this brief but eventful tour show that we paid out 3,200 francs for promotional posters, and recouped 220 francs from selling some of these at gigs. I suppose these must have been the first dedicated Dead Can Dance tour posters, and maybe there are still some in existence somewhere. I certainly don't have one, and can't remember what they looked like, but perhaps there's a die-hard DCD fan somewhere with one still clinging to a chambre wall?

Only after our return did I discover that, amidst all the chaos of our French adventure, romance had blossomed between our Scotty and Philippe's sister Elizabeth. The reputation of Paris had been upheld.

FIVE

The week after we returned from France, we were back in Vineyard Studios for a couple of days to finish recording our EP, and the following day Brendan and I went for a meeting at the Islington offices of Station – a professional booking agency. I presume this was set up by 4AD in response to the alarm caused by our chaotic experience in France, and it was felt that future tours should be organised via the established network. I subsequently sent a letter to Station boss Andy Woolliscroft setting out a guide to DCD's financial requirements for overseas touring, including £200 for return ferry tickets to cross to 'the continent', £35 per day van hire (following the demise of the Perrymobile), £12.50 per hundred miles for petrol, average of £7.50 per hundred miles for road tolls, minimum of £5 'per diem' per person for food and drink, and £50 for the carnet (admin, not bond). It was assumed that accommodation would be provided by the local promoters. These still felt like great sums of money for us to be asking at the time and, without cutting us short, I'd erred on the conservative side with my estimations.

Meanwhile, what seemed a curious gig had been arranged for our next headliner – the 'Bedford Boys Club' on Saturday, 7 July 1984. Bedford is a provincial town some sixty miles north of London and at the time was not, to my knowledge, serving a large enough populace for us to draw on. However, some canny Bedfordian had spotted a lack of decent venues in a substantial radius, and managed to establish the Boys Club on the indie circuit, with New Order having played there a couple of years earlier, and Cabaret Voltaire scheduled to play a few weeks after us. It was an unusual venue, featuring a sunken dance floor, originally built to house a boxing ring, surrounded by higher standing areas, so the audience were on different levels.

The show attracted a decent crowd – a testament to the effect the John Peel exposure was having (despite its premature end) – and, for the first time, I became aware that we'd started to accumulate fans who were following the band around. One of these in particular, Tony Hill, became a good friend of the band over the years, and another, Lee Kimber, maintained contact with me for some years. 4AD arranged for a minibus to come up from London for the show and invited artists, staff, and associates along. Both Ivo and Debbie came, as did Cocteaus, Robin, and Liz. Robin surprised me by telling me how calm and assured I always appeared on stage. I told him I was actually a bundle of nerves, at least when we first went on stage, and that to me, he was the epitome of onstage cool. He retorted that he could only get up on stage if he was off his head. There may have been a degree of truth in that, but I never believed Robin would allow himself to be entirely out of control of the situation. The Cocteaus must have been sufficiently impressed with the Boys Club as they played it themselves a few months later together with Dif Juz. Some footage later appeared on YouTube of various bands at Bedford Boys Club – including us – though these sequences tend to be mostly taken during soundchecks as presumably the person with the movie camera preferred to watch the actual shows with the naked eye rather than through the lens. The quality is poor, but for Dead Can Dance these snippets of video are amongst the few in existence of us around that time.

More meetings with publishers took place – Chappells again and Intersong – but still no concrete offer appeared and the matter remained in limbo as our new EP was released on 17 August entitled *Garden of the Arcane Delights*. This featured a cover illustration painstakingly hand-drawn by Brendan which I'm not sure was warmly welcomed around 4AD HQ, but I loved it, and still do. The concept is best explained in Brendan's own words:

> The naked blindfolded figure, representing primal man deprived of perception, stands, within the confines of a garden (the world) containing a fountain and trees laden with fruit. His right arm stretches out – the grasping for knowledge – towards a fruit bearing tree, its trunk encircled by a snake. In the garden wall – the wall between freedom and confinement – are two gateways: the dualistic notion of choice. It is a Blakean universe in which mankind can only redeem itself, can only rid itself of blindness, through the correct interpretation of signs and events that permeate the fabric of nature's laws.

It seems unlikely these kind of images and reference points were circulating widely in indie 'rock' circles, and this passage hints strongly at the future direction both Brendan and Lisa were already envisioning. Meanwhile, that same August day found us at 4AD discussing a prospective tour of Scandinavia. 'Tour' was perhaps overstating the case as the proposal was to play just four shows, though the distances to be travelled would certainly qualify. And while our trips to the Netherlands and France had been exciting, they were a quick hop over the Channel. Scandinavia was quite another world, and the idea of going there seemed positively exotic.

The meeting at 4AD also touched on how royalties were to be dealt with – sales were being made and the prospect of future payments now appeared on the horizon. Small amounts of money were already dribbling in from performance fees and subsidies from 4AD, which were immediately invested in gathering more equipment. I now had protective travel cases for my drums which made me feel like a real pro, and Brendan and I took a trip to Croydon to buy an original Vox AC30 valve amp he'd seen advertised in the 'Exchange & Mart' paper. Between us, we lugged it back to the Isle of Dogs via a series of buses, thus fulfilling a long-time ambition for Brendan and giving a new dimension to his guitar soundscapes. We were also improving our rehearsal facilities – having initially graduated from the Barkantine Hall to a local studio called 'Hotbox' (undeniably sweaty and claustrophobic, so no contravention of the Trades Descriptions Act there), we now went up a further notch to a more spacious and better-appointed studios in Wapping rather appropriately called 'Ocean'.

On 18 August, the first full-page interview feature on DCD appeared in the *NME*. Written by Adrian Thrills, the headline immediately badged DCD an 'enigma', and the intro to the piece emphasises the group's uniqueness and refusal to be defined, pigeonholed. Even at that early stage, Adrian wrote 'the range of the group is staggering' (little did he know what was to come!), while simultaneously noting the 'disciplined economy' of the compositions. In response to answers Brendan and Lisa supplied to his questioning, he went on to observe:

> For all the power in the awesome crescendos and haunting lulls of a Dead Can Dance song, the group talk about their music as if it were an electric blanket or a mug of Ovaltine. They see their music as a panacea to the pressures of an urban existence . . .

September brought another trip to Paris for a one-off performance at a festival called 'Les Nuits de la Saint Vitus' held at a venue called L'Eldorado (thankfully no relation to the like-named scene of our debacle in Marseille). We were billed to be appearing with Sisters of Mercy, but arrived to find they'd cancelled and we were now on a bill with Play Dead and Flesh for Lulu. All went to plan until we arrived back at Dover the following day and had our gear checked by UK customs, revealing Scott's bass guitar to be missing. As well as being a personal blow for Scott and the collapse of our finely balanced budget for the trip, we were now unable to get our Carnet signed-off and could face further penalty. As the Carnet was issued to 4AD, who always stumped up the bond, I had to ask Ivo to sign a form for the London Chamber of Commerce accepting liability should the French authorities come after us in pursuit of a perceived heinous act of international tax evasion. It certainly felt like our forays into France were jinxed, and yet the audience responses we were getting there were probably the most positive, so we couldn't afford to get 'les pieds froid'.

Back in London the buzz was around the imminent release (on 1 October) of This Mortal Coil's debut album *It'll End in Tears*. The album release came just over a year after the release of lead single 'Song to the Siren', which, as well as receiving almost universal critical acclaim, had been something of a commercial success by 4AD standards. This Mortal Coil was very much Ivo's personal project. The general principle was that he would invite artists he admired – both from 4AD and beyond the label – to record cover versions of songs he loved, all recorded at Blackwing Studios with John Fryer engineering and coproducing, and himself as lead producer and sometime arranger and contributor. 'Song to the Siren', written by one of Ivo's all-time favourites Tim Buckley, was arranged and performed by the Cocteaus – Liz's voice soaring with an incredible combination of strength and fragility over Robin's minimal, shimmering guitar chords.

Lisa and Brendan were invited to participate and managed to buck the trend by getting Ivo to let them record two self-penned tracks – 'Waves Become Wings' and 'Dreams Made Flesh' – the latter built around Lisa's yang ch'in as lead instrument. Other artists featured included my rediscovered schoolmate Mark Cox, Martyn and Steve Young of Colourbox, Cindytalk singer Gordon Sharp, Howard Devoto (Magazine/Buzzcocks), Robbie Grey of Modern English, Manuela Rickers of Xmal Deutschland, and string players Gini Ball and Martin McCarrick who worked regularly with some big names including Siouxsie & the Banshees and Marc Almond. 'Dreams Made Flesh' subsequently became a regular feature in DCD live performances, and I variously got to play either the bass drum or yang ch'in part.

On Friday, 5 October 1984 we played Fulham Town Hall in West London, and the following night supported The Fall at The Woughton Centre in Milton Keynes. They could hardly have been more different environments – the former a grand, historic Victorian building, the latter a bland, utilitarian leisure centre – and they were correspondingly very different gigs. Fulham was a showcase for our now established London following, while at Milton Keynes we played to what one reviewer described as 'a small handful of bemused Fall fans'. Encountering The Fall backstage was interesting. This was the era with Mark E Smith's American wife, Brix, a relatively recent recruit on guitar, and towards the end of the first of two periods in which they performed with two drummers – at this time Karl Burns and Paul Hanley. Karl was very friendly and invited me to join them in their dressing room. Passing the open door of their dressing room on my way to the stage, I noted a large table laid out with a cornucopia of pills and powders. Coming back past their dressing room after we'd played, the table was empty. Those guys then went on stage and gave a barnstorming performance which I went out front and watched, marvelling at them being able to hold it together when I'd gone weak at the knees just looking at what they'd imbibed. Needless to say, I never made it into their dressing room, which probably saved me from never making it out again.

My records show that we were paid the grand fee of fifty pounds for our support slot in Milton Keynes. Less than a week later, we departed on our trip to Scandinavia for which we were being paid the princely sum of two thousand pounds for three gigs (a fourth in Gothenburg, Sweden, had fallen through at the last minute) and we ended up turning a small profit. On the morning of Thursday, 11 October I had to scurry into London's West End to pick up our work permits, and a few hours later we bundled six of us – five band members plus Colin Wallace as borrowed tour manager/driver – plus all our equipment into a modest hire van and set off. We drove from London to the east coast port of Harwich, before taking a seventeen-hour ferry crossing from Harwich to Esbjerg on the west coast of Denmark. Then a three-and-a-half-hour drive across Denmark to the northeast coast port of Frederikshavn to pick up the onward ferry to Gothenburg. It seemed a great shame to be in Denmark for the first time, but not stopping and playing there, and only seeing 250-odd miles of motorway – particularly for me as my 'Ulrich' clan has been traced to Copenhagen origins.

While Scott demonstrated a remarkable capacity to sleep through everything – even contorted between amplifiers in the back of the van – the rest of us were already knackered and desperate to reach the hotel that waited in Gothenburg, but as we sat in the ferry queue at Frederikshavn, news filtered through that the car exit ramp on our ferry had jammed and the boat was unable to dock. Through the evening we sat on the quayside, tired and hungry, watching a large, taunting, LED temperature display gradually creep down the centigrade scale from six degrees, to five, four, three . . . It hit zero and we audibly shivered in unison. The hours crawled by and it was around eleven in the evening when a ferry finally docked that we could board. Once on the boat, we headed for the cafeteria in search of hot food and drinks. As we waited in the queue for the counter to open, a couple of other passengers came past and carelessly bumped into us. We exchanged perplexed glances and, in our frazzled state, came close to reacting. We then noticed that a few people were visibly staggering about, and a little way down a nearby corridor, someone threw up. It dawned on us that virtually all the other passengers on the boat were raging drunk. One of our few compos mentis fellow travellers explained that alcohol prices were so high in Sweden that it was common practice among young Swedes to book a return ferry crossing, hit the on-board duty-free shop as soon as the boat left port, and spend the entire trip drinking without ever leaving the boat. So we now had a three and a half hour crossing to look forward to, surrounded by people getting ever more smashed and with the vomit count increasing by the nautical mile.

Fig. 11. Brendan's hand-drawn cover design for DCD's second vinyl offering, the *Garden of the Arcane Delights* EP, 1984. The original was a pen and black ink drawing, then reversed white-out-of-black for the finished artwork. Art by Brendan Perry.

The only benefit of the ferry being a floating drinking den was that the car deck was far from full and, once docked, we were able to make a quick exit, never more relieved to get off a boat. We finally made it to our hotel in Gothenborg at around three in the morning – but what a hotel! It was a magnificent, brooding, gothic pile with enormous rooms that each had its own marbled hallway leading into a vast twin bedroom, and with two separate bathrooms. We briefly marvelled at our accommodation before collapsing into comatose sleep. By sod's law, we had to be up again at eight to depart by nine and head to our first venue. But at least we were warm again, had managed some deep sleep, and were now able to gorge on an enormous breakfast. This was back in the day when many hotels, particularly for their basic rate, served a 'continental breakfast' comprising a small, dry croissant, a smear of jam, and a single cup of tea or coffee. This hotel had a spread of food the like of which we'd never seen before, with every type of cereal, bread, meat, cheese, and condiment imaginable alongside a Scandinavian smörgåsbord of various fish, seafoods, and salads. I was eventually dragged screaming from the buffet and out to the van, stomach the size of a football.

Outside we discovered that The Cult had been staying in the same hotel that night. They were just exiting Sweden having finished this leg of their tour. They looked much like we'd felt before our few hours kip, probably having spent the night partying. A handful of young goth girls with mascara-smeared ashen faces were gathered, shivering on the pavement in the misty gloom after a night with their heroes, and were now tearfully waving them off. It struck me as particularly tragic, and made me glad to clamber back into our van and get out of there.

A few hours later, after seemingly endless long, straight roads cutting through forests of pine trees, we arrived at Hultsfred where we were booked to play that night, 13 October. The venue was a soulless gymnasium – all wood floors and bare brick walls with a makeshift stage. The acoustics were probably the worst we ever had to contend with. The soundcheck was virtually impossible as the sounds ricocheted off every surface and bounded back into a maelstrom in the middle of the empty hall. We spent so long trying to achieve a half-decent sound that we went way over scheduled door-opening time and the venue manager was getting frantic. Finally the doors gave way to a rush of seemingly drunken teenagers whose excited squealing failed to abate as we started playing. It gave Jim a frantic first five minutes or so at the sound desk once the show was underway, essentially redoing the soundcheck on the hop during the performance and trying to get the overall levels above the audience noise without distorting. It wasn't a disastrous gig, but we finished with very much a sense of 'we came all this way for this?'

Fortunately, our other two Scandinavian shows were to be in recognised venues in capital cities, so on we headed to Stockholm. Word had reached us via the promoters that we were booked into what would now be described as a 'boutique' hotel in Stockholm, but that The Cult had stayed there a couple of nights earlier and had trashed the place (tellies out the window and all that super-cool rock'n'roll stuff), as a consequence of which the hotel had banned all further stays by bands. Under pressure from the promoters, the hotel had been forced to honour its booking for us, but after us, no more. So now a terrified hotel was awaiting the coming of a band called 'Dead Can Dance', and we were headed for the frostiest of greetings. On our arrival, Lisa rose to the occasion magnificently. Leaving the rest of us in her wake, she glided across the hotel's entrance foyer with her hair piled high and her long coat billowing around her and, speaking very softly to the cowering maître d' and a couple of staff, said with her most eloquent enunciation something along the lines of 'We heard what those horrid boys did, and I promise you we'll look after your beautiful hotel.' The staff visibly almost fainted with relief, and the maître d' looked for all the world like she was going to vault the reception desk and embrace Lisa. It was indeed a beautiful hotel, full of quaint antique furniture, and we really did treat the place with kid gloves to restore their faith in humanity.

We had very little time in Stockholm and saw next to nothing of the city. My brief impression was that it was very clean, but at the same time quite stark and impersonal, though I'm sure this isn't true once you get under the skin of the place. We went straight on to the venue – the Kolingsborg, a curious circular, concrete bunker, but centrally located and a well-established club. The gig went smoothly and was met with a kind of reserved enthusiasm. Next morning we were out and on the road to Oslo to play that evening – so another city we would see nothing of other than venue, hotel, and roads in and out. The Oslo venue was the Ratz Club – essentially a large bar with a stage where they packed the locals in. It was well-established on the indie circuit and many of our contemporaries also played there, but it apparently didn't have the greatest of reputations. I believe the venue still exists under the name Studio 26, but probably much changed. Coming off stage I thought our performance had been fine, and the audience response had been very good, but Brendan was slinging things around the dressing room and shouting that we'd been shit. Lisa, Jim, and Scott seemed as surprised as me, and it was unusual that we should have such a different perspective, but it shows how the sound can distort in these small clubs. It emerged later that there was an unofficial video made of the gig. A supposed copy was sent to me, but it turned out to be a blank tape – either that or I accidentally erased it. Next morning we were back in the van for the forty-eight-hour journey home, and, exhausted, we arrived back in London just a week after setting out.

Two days later – Friday, 19 October – we played King's College in London with 4AD labelmates Dif Juz, and with Nyam Nyam supporting. Nyam Nyam had formed a link between the Factory label and 4AD in that their second single was produced by Joy Division/New Order bassist Peter Hook and released on Factory's Benelux imprint, following which the band had recently signed to one of the Beggars Banquet group labels, Situation Two. We also managed to get a friend of Jim and Brendan from New Zealand onto the bill – a wonderful Maori didgeridoo player called Tony Waerea who would go on to tour with us. It was good to hook up with Dif Juz, and to see them play – I loved watching their drummer Richard Thomas who had an unusual kit setup and a very individual style, fluid and distinctly reggae-influenced. At some point a minor altercation occurred backstage involving their bassist Gary Bromley – not sure what happened, but it seemed to sour the atmosphere a bit. A gig supporting The Fall again, together with The Membranes, at the Lyceum Ballroom scheduled for the end of October was cancelled, and the live work eased off for a while, giving us a chance to take stock, and Brendan and Lisa the space to start writing again.

A few weeks later I had a meeting just off Holloway Road at the offices of Anglo-Scandinavian Trading run by Harry Magee. Harry had arranged our recent Scandinavian mini-tour, but now wanted to talk to me about playing some timpani (orchestral 'kettle' drums) on a project called *Ten Portraits* – an album of musical portraits of ten renowned artists – with a musician he was promoting called Michael Dee. It sounded interesting, and we had a second meeting a week or so later, but in the end nothing came of it, or at least, not of my involvement. I lost touch with Harry after that, but heard he went on to become a manager of mainstream artists ranging from Katherine Jenkins and Alison Moyet to One Direction and Olly Murs.

The hunt for a publishing deal for DCD finally went full circle, and we ended up back at 4AD's parent company, Beggars Banquet, signing our first publishing contract at their Wandsworth offices on 22 November 1984. Next day I was banking an advance cheque for three thousand pounds from which our first investment was a Yamaha CX5 music computer which would come to play a significant role in shaping the direction of DCD's music. The programming capabilities were very basic (and it had to be laboriously programmed – there was no real-time play and record function), and the synthesised sounds were of somewhat dubious quality, but it gave Brendan the capacity to write and arrange music with strings and brass parts. He started learning a bit of music theory and could now print out scores, enabling him to hire the services of classical musicians and hand them the sheet music – all very pro! For guidance he turned to a renowned eighteenth-century study of counterpoint, *Gradus ad Parnassum* by Johann Joseph Fux, referenced in the groundings of both Bach and Mozart. And for inspiration, he could now start to properly embrace some of his cherished influences including John Barry, Nino Rota (whose soundtrack to Federico Fellini's *Satyricon* is an amazing work that Brendan introduced me to) and the soundtracks German band Popol Vuh created for Werner Herzog's movies. Both Lisa and Brendan were also influenced around this time by the beautiful choral arrangements in Arvo Pärt's *Tabula Rasa*. Before long the first strains of what would become the *Spleen and Ideal* album started to emanate from the thirteenth floor of Bowsprit Point.

DEAD · CAN · DANCE

Fig. 12. Promo picture for the release of the *Spleen and Ideal* album, 1985: the session was done on the balcony of Lisa and Brendan's flat on the 13th floor of Bowsprit Point, with the view out over the River Thames in the background. Courtesy of 4AD Records.

DCD didn't hit the road again until the end of March 1985 for a brief sortie across the Channel with the Cocteaus, initially to Ghent in Belgium. The

Cocteaus were now restored to a trio, with the arrival of Simon Raymonde on bass the previous year. Liz was much more comfortable on stage with the increased activity around her, and Robin seemed to enjoy having the new input into writing material, though you could never be quite sure what Robin was thinking. On 1 April, we set off for the venue and thought we'd unwittingly wandered into an elaborate April Fool's jape. We found ourselves delayed in a traffic jam in a narrow side street while officials tried to lift an illegally parked car onto a recovery truck, only to hoist it into the air and drop it! The extraordinary reaction of the uniforms was to jump into their truck and drive off, leaving the stricken and now damaged car straddling the pavement and road, surrounded by a crowd of bemused onlookers, to await the return of its unsuspecting owner. We managed to negotiate our exit, and reached the Vooruit Arts Centre, which turned out to be a beautiful, listed monument building dating from around 1914 – albeit dilapidated and in the early stages of a restoration project.

We headed on to Bourges, France to play the Grand Theatre on 3 April as part of 'Le Printemps de Bourges', an annual, week-long festival across ten venues. We arrived the evening prior and wandered the lively streets of Bourges, which were full of busking musical and theatrical performers, and heard the strains of the late 'French Elvis' Johnny Hallyday drifting across from the night's main event in the stadium. Next day backstage at the Grand Theatre, the footballer Pat Nevin showed up, having managed to 'negotiate' a day off training with Chelsea. His fellow players at Chelsea reputedly nicknamed Pat 'weirdo', partly due to his self-imposed isolation on away game travel to lose himself in the writings of Camus and Chekhov, partly because of indie music reviews he wrote for the club newspaper in a column called 'Hooknotes', and partly in frustration that he was so skillful, nobody could get the ball off him in training! A huge Cocteaus fan, he'd principally come over to see them, but had also heard some of our stuff on John Peel and was keen to see us as well. We had a good chat with Pat, who clearly knew his music and greatly enjoyed both sets, but we didn't give him any footballing tips in return.

A phone call came out of the blue from Ivo asking if I could sit in and drum for a few rehearsals with 4AD labelmates Modern English. By now, Richard Thomas of Dif Juz and I were the only two drummers on 4AD (XmalD having moved on to Red Rhino) so if anyone needed a drummer from within the stable, one of us was going to get the call. Modern English were not only well established on the UK indie scene, but had also worked themselves a foothold in the notoriously hard-to-crack American market, with their 1982 single 'I Melt with You' reaching No. 78 in the main US charts, and their album of the same year *After the Snow* selling half a million. We heard they even had screaming teenage girls in their audiences lobbing cuddly toys at them! They'd recently been recording and playing live with a drum machine, but wanted to try getting back to the human alternative. I did four consecutive days of rehearsals with them at Sleazy's Studios in Wapping. However, whatever beat/drum pattern I tried to either give them to work with, or put behind something they were playing, they would stop after a while and have me go back to a straight 4/4 with pumping kick drum, snare on every third beat of the bar, and running two-handed hi-hat. So, four days of that and I had a great physical workout, but at the end of it they decided to stick with their drum machine (lower maintenance costs and never answered back). They ended up parting company with 4AD before their next album and moving to the Sire label.

July of 1985 witnessed 'Live Aid'. Whatever your take on the coordinated concerts, their purpose and legacy, it was undeniably a momentous event. The stats say it was watched – one way or another – by an estimated 1.9 billion people in 150 countries, representing 40 percent of the world's population. I was never particularly a fan of Queen, though they certainly made some interesting recordings, but while I felt most of the 'Live Aid' performers – even 'big' names – seemed dwarfed by the occasion, the manner in which Freddie Mercury came on and dominated the stage genuinely merits that much-overused tag 'awesome.' I think anyone who has ever stood on a stage in front of an audience, no matter how large or small and under what circumstances – and, in truth, probably most people who have not – can fully appreciate just how amazing a performance that was.

Over the following months I was involved peripherally in developing material for the new DCD album – principally working with Lisa on percussion accompaniments to yang ch'in themes – but there were only a very few band rehearsals as Brendan was now focused on writing, programming, and multitracking everything with the CX5 music computer plus a Roland drum machine and Tascam eight-track tape recorder that had been acquired with our publishing advance. This gave Brendan complete control over all the parts, and an ease of recording compared to the setup time and experimentation needed to record acoustic instruments. A new collaborator had also been brought into the fold. Robert Lee, despite being only around eighteen or nineteen when we met him, was a multi-instrumentalist with technical/engineering abilities, as well as his own Tascam eight-track. He'd recently moved to the Isle of Dogs and met us through the local musos network, and had been able to help Brendan in the early stages of getting to grips with the multitrack recorder. Of Korean/Canadian descent, Rob also extended the multinational flavour of DCD.

A more substantial recording budget was on offer from Ivo for the new album, and the opportunity arose to use the Woodbine Street Studios of John A Rivers in Leamington Spa. John had come to the attention of 4AD through working with Love and Rockets – the band of former Bauhaus members Daniel Ash, Kevin Haskins, and David J. He had a state-of-the-art setup and a clean, bright, airy studio located in the basement of his house in the historic Midlands spa town, and getting out of central London was also good for the creative juices and the soul. We had our first week in Woodbine from 15–22 September 1985. We were booked into the local Grand Union Hotel, nestling beside a bridge over the Grand Union Canal and run by the flamboyant Julian. Julian's forté was making scrambled egg for our breakfast each morning, in which he insisted that each person's portion must comprise at least six eggs and half a pint of double cream. Admittedly it was delicious, but we were lucky to make it through our stay without any coronary failures. We'd then head to the studio to be greeted each day by John's two cats – Rosemary and Basil – in their sentinel positions, one atop each brick gate pillar at the head of the entrance path. It was all very relaxed and in stark contrast to our previous studio experiences.

Although we'd shipped all my drums and percussion up to Woodbine, Brendan was quickly seduced by the range and quality of the library of samples and electronic sounds which John had available. He broke the news to me that he was going to record the drums and percussion with these as it would save an enormous amount of time, and would give him much greater flexibility. I was disappointed, but not distraught or even that surprised. I certainly didn't want to see him go through the torment he'd endured in Blackwing making our first album, and in any case, they were mostly parts he'd written himself and programmed electronically during the writing process. I discovered that upstairs from the studio, John had a similarly state-of-the-art kitchen, so I appointed myself head chef and got to work.

After that first week, I didn't attend the further studio sessions while the new album took shape. The bulk of it was recorded by Brendan and Lisa, with classical musicians brought in for parts where Brendan wasn't happy with the rigidity of the programmed options, including cellist Martin McCarrick, who'd been involved in This Mortal Coil. Also on cello was Gus Ferguson, another of the Scottish contingent with 4AD connections who would become an integral part of DCD over the coming years. Jim was on hand to play timpani, which started his transition to the performance side of DCD rather than engineering, some trombone parts were contributed by Richard Avison, who would also join DCD's touring band, and a close friend of Lisa's from Australia who happened to be visiting the UK – Andrew Hutton – found himself singing a soprano vocal part on 'De Profundis'.

Lisa and Brendan also struck up a good rapport with a young studio engineer working alongside John at Woodbine, Jonathan Dee. Though he'd taken the job in a studio catering principally for rock recordings, Jonathan's first love was classical music. Not only was he delighted to be involved in recording the new DCD arrangements, he also had very useful knowledge and ideas to impart which were a great help to the nascent orchestral DCD. It was evident that Jonathan was something of a fish out of water at Woodbine and he didn't stay long. He would come to London and get himself a job at a studio called the Chocolate Factory (where Brendan and Lisa later made an early demo of 'Persephone') before gravitating to the famed Abbey Road Studios. But for now, he'd played a significant role in helping Brendan and Lisa embark on the realisation of their new musical vision.

When I finally got to hear all the studio mixes I was amazed – the transition from where we'd been musically only a few months earlier was truly incredible. The only song I felt a little disappointed over was 'Avatar', a reworking of the one song we'd written together in band rehearsals and previously recorded for the second John Peel Session with the working title of 'Penumbra'. The new album version, recorded with programmed drums and a zither taking the guitar part, had a totally different feel, and at first seemed overly homogeneous compared to our live rendition, which built to a crashing climax. On further listening, though, I got it completely. The album version is beautiful in its own way – a reimagining of the song – and for live performance we continued to revert to the original arrangement for contrast.

The recording, mixing, and mastering processes all went incredibly quickly, and the *Spleen and Ideal* album was ready and released by 4AD on 25 November 1985, a little over two months after recording had begun. That seems such an impossibly short period that I've had to go back and check the dates several times over while writing this and have still failed to dispel all trace of doubt from my mind. Photographer Colin Gray's striking cover image of the red-cloaked figure holding aloft a ghoulish white star features in its background a historic grain elevator at Salford Quays in the Manchester Docks which partially collapsed but refused to yield during its attempted demolition, leaving it in this eerie, crumbling lean. This location provided an unforeseen connection many years later when I came across an article by Mancunian poet John Cooper Clarke on the inspiration he's derived from the works of nineteenth-century French poet Charles Baudelaire. 'Spleen et Idéal' is the title of the opening section of Baudelaire's collection *Les Fleurs du mal*, a source used by Brendan and Lisa for the album. Clarke notes that the French poet took unexpected inspiration from his drab surroundings:

> The Paris of Baudelaire, like the New York of Lou Reed, and the Salford of yours truly, had been considered barren ground poetry-wise. Too cacophonous for such a reflective medium, and ugly, ugly, ugly. (*The Daily Telegraph*, 3 April 2021)

The parts of the cities referenced here by Cooper Clarke are, of course, the aesthetically grim underbellies rather than the attractions on the tourist trail, and it takes no great leap of the imagination to draw the parallel with the thirteenth floor council flat on the Isle of Dogs where the new DCD album had been created.

In the meantime, feeling the need to express myself in recorded form, and suddenly having the possibility to make home recordings on eight-track at our disposal, I formed the idea of a multitracked percussion piece. I visualised a scenario in two distinct parts – the first with animals relaxed and leisurely, gathered at a watering hole, then a sudden attack startling them into panic and a stampede. So while the DCD recording was taking place in Leamington, I took a case of hand drums and percussion round to Robert's flat on the Isle of Dogs and set about constructing my composition. It was quite spontaneous, and came into being very quickly and easily, with each track inspiring the next. Soon we had six tracks of overlaid percussion, and the overall shape was there. It was only a short piece – less than a minute and a half – and had plenty going on, but it needed a couple of additional flourishes. I used the seventh track to introduce two short melodic phrases using an ocarina (clay flute) which pre-empted first the change between the two distinct rhythmic elements, and then the end of the piece.

On the final available recording track I wanted to create a very dramatic crash at the start of the faster rhythm section. I could've simply used a crash cymbal, but I wanted something more explosive and less obviously a musical instrument. We decided to try smashing a glass bottle with a club hammer in the plughole end of Rob's bath. The natural reverb created by the tin bath and tiled walls would add to the effect. It would be a one-off attempt, so I'd have to get the timing spot-on first go, and be careful not to follow through with the hammer and crack the enamel surface of the bath. Rob set the mic up and we tested sound levels as best we could. I geared up with gloves, eye mask, headphones, and hammer, and we went for it. It worked a treat and achieved exactly the effect I'd hoped for.

Rob made a mix for me and transferred copies onto a couple of standard audio cassettes, one of which I packaged up, labelled with my title 'At First, and Then', and sent off to Ivo with some kind of 'see what you think of this' message. Ivo's response took me completely by surprise as he replied saying he'd like to incorporate it into the second This Mortal Coil album which was just taking shape. I later took the original eight-track tape over to Blackwing Studios for John Fryer to transfer it onto the main studio twenty-four-track so that Ivo could work on it, adding some effects and ambient guitar to create what would become track nine on the *Filigree and Shadow* album.

By this time DCD's *Spleen and Ideal* had been gathering strong reviews and critical acclaim, albeit tempered by some minor concerns that the new direction might be viewed as over-grandiose or pretentious. David Burton, writing in the UK's mainstream weekly pop magazine *Record Mirror*, and presumably unused to having such an offering to assess, opened with . . .

> Named after decadent poet Baudelaire's *Les Fleurs du Mal*, this hints at a healthy disregard for authority. DCD's Brendan Perry admires the poet so much that he even looks like him . . .

. . . referencing the fact that Brendan had now grown his hair longer and acquired a moustache and goatee beard – albeit a rather more Shakespearean look than pictures I've seen of the French poet. Robin Gibson in *Sounds* wrote:

> It's tremendously serious and ambitious and could easily, these days, be written off misguidedly as po-faced pseudo-grandeur. But to do that would be a bit silly. It's very, very good.

John Best, reviewing for the UK's trade magazine *Music Week*, opined:

> Lisa Gerrard and Brendan Perry . . . create the ultimate 4AD record – sumptuous, desolate, pompous and unique.

Jon Homer, in *What's On and Where to Go*, weighed in with:

> It's the spectral beauty of Lisa Gerrard's voice that hits the heart hardest, that haunts. This is not to be dismissed as gothic, too original for rock. *Spleen and Ideal* is like nothing I've ever heard, and something that you have just got to hear.

Spleen and Ideal reached number two in the UK Indie album chart, held off the top spot by the Dead Kennedys' *Frankenchrist*. The album was DCD's first to be released on the relatively new format of 'compact disc' (CD) as well as the original vinyl, and a tour of Holland, Belgium, and Germany was being planned to promote the album. We were using Jim's home – a squat in a beautiful period house in Bonnington Square, Vauxhall on the south side of the River Thames – for smaller scale acoustic rehearsals, both for Dead Can Dance and for an ensemble formed by Jim, Scott, Gus, and Rob under the name 'Heavenly Bodies'. The plan was that the Bodies would provide the support act for the DCD tour, so we could use a lot of shared instruments and onstage amps to streamline soundchecking and minimise the need to alter the stage setup between acts. Lisa would make a guest appearance on a couple of the Bodies' songs, I was invited to play some additional percussion, and Brendan would be house engineer!

At the beginning of May we moved to a professional rehearsal studio in Greenwich for the final tour preparations, and with a much-expanded lineup. The nucleus of Brendan, Lisa, Scott, Jim, and I was now augmented by the addition of Jim's wife Yvette on cello and keyboards, Gus and Nick Payne both on cello, Richard Avison and John Singleton on trombones, and Andrew Claxton on French horn, with Rob as house desk engineer. Yvie was pursuing an acting career, but nevertheless happy for the opportunity to give her musical abilities an airing, and it was good for the balance of the band to double its female quota. Nick, John, and Andrew were classically trained musicians, though while Nick had generally stuck to classical circles, John had a broader range and was playing regularly with a Blues Brothers-style band called The Fabulistics!, and Andrew was involved in scoring all manner of works. Richard had come to us via the Isle of Dogs music scene, playing in one or two soul/reggae/R&B groups with our drummer friend Tony Wright from Knighthead Point, and also featured in big band The Happy End (with singer Sarah Jane Morris, latterly of The Communards).

The DCD set list expanded as we now had two albums plus one EP's worth of material to choose from. Jim and I were performing acoustically various of the percussion and drum parts which were programmed on the studio recordings for *Spleen and Ideal*, with 'Advent', 'The Cardinal Sin', and 'Indoctrination (A Design for Living)' all included. It took me many hours of practice to master a couple of the rhythms which Brendan had written with the drum machine and which contained syncopation of limbs that didn't come naturally, but it was good discipline and further developed my technical ability, though it did cost the lives of a few smashed drumsticks. From a purely personal point of view, I was also very happy when Brendan and Lisa decided to include 'Dreams Made Flesh' in the set, with me to come front of stage to play the yang ch'in part (amazing, as ever, to be right next to Lisa when she was in full flow), and then completely bowled over when Brendan asked me if we could try developing an extended live version of 'At First, and Then' for inclusion.

Another change was that our new travelling orchestra could no longer be compressed into a van – something grander was required. 4AD's go-to company for this at the time was Griersons Coaches, the family firm of Vaughan Oliver's photographer colleague at 23 Envelope, Nigel Grierson. The firm was located about as far from London as you can get within England, being based in Sedgefield, County Durham, so we got not only a particularly brightly coloured, full-sized coach, but also a driver with a wonderfully broad Northumbrian accent. We were heading out in style. Our Carnet from that trip shows that, in addition to the various brass and string instruments, our stage setup now included a Commodore 64 computer as well as the Yamaha CX5, and an Ensoniq Mirage sampling keyboard – so our previous basic band lineup had expanded in both traditional/orchestral and tech directions. Setting up, soundchecking, and breaking down became a major operation, and venues with sufficient stage size and power capacity had to be carefully selected by our booking agents.

On 8 May 1986 we loaded up and hit the road with the following schedule ahead of us:

Netherlands:
Friday, 9 May, Zoettermeer, Boerderij
Saturday, 10 May, Zaandam, Drieluik
Sunday, 11 May, Amsterdam, Melkweg
Thursday, 15 May, Maastricht, Combi
Friday, 16 May, Leeuwarden, Schaaf
Saturday, 17 May, Haarlem, Patronaat
Sunday, 18 May, Groningen, Vera
Tuesday, 20 May, Nijmegen, Doornroosje

Belgium:
Wednesday, 21 May, Brussels, Halles de Schaerbeek

Netherlands:
Friday, 23 May, Wageningen, Unitas

Germany:
Monday, 26 May, Bochum, Zeche
Wednesday, 28 May, Bremen, Römer
Thursday, 29 May, Hamburg, Kir
Sunday, 1 June, Cologne, Luxor
Monday, 2 June, Frankfurt, Batschkapp
Tuesday, 3 June, Berlin, Loft
Thursday, 5 June, Hannover, Soxs

The schedule seems obviously somewhat 'light' on Belgium. This certainly wasn't deliberate on our part as we didn't really have any say in the matter. Our booking agents had a circuit of venues that were deemed to be of the right size and demographic for the level of sales and recognition we had reached, and schedules were generated accordingly. I can only assume that, outside the Belgian capital, we were not yet big enough to command the size/type of venues we could in provincial Holland and Germany.

On the Dutch leg of the tour, the Milky Way (Melkweg) was a venue I was particularly keen to add to my 'done it' list as it's a legendary club on the Amsterdam scene, established in the early 1970s in an old converted milk factory, initially patronised by hippies and subsequently following the trends through punk and post-punk. The Schaaf in Leeuwarden turned out to be a beautiful old theatre dating back to the late eighteenth century, and provided a setting perhaps better suited to orchestral DCD than the general club circuit – a taste of things to come.

Didgeridoo maestro Tony Waerea had travelled with us and was providing an additional solo support slot to Heavenly Bodies. We had a day off in Groningen and in the evening I went out drinking with Tony, Rob, and John from which we arrived back at the hotel in the early hours in high spirits. Tony decided it was the ideal moment to provide our neighbours with some impromptu entertainment. He positioned the bottom end of his didge in the plughole of the bath (seems to be a theme of musical bath plugholes developing), and began his circular breathing. The wondrous organic rumblings of the didgeridoo began to build and build, but by the positioning of the instrument, the sound now entered the hotel's plumbing system and travelled wherever the pipework went. Within a few minutes the entire building was alive with the shimmering growl of the didge, and was physically vibrating. Alarms started sounding, pyjama-ed guests were running up and down corridors shouting in confusion, and we heard later that the hotel's switchboard jammed.

I was in uncontrollable hysterics, rolling around the floor of our room, laughing so much I was struggling to catch my breath, while Tony just kept going without a hint of distraction for what seemed like hours, but was probably only about ten minutes. For my money, it beats all the better-known rock'n'roll hotel stories – Keith Moon aficionados may beg to differ.

Pretty much every show we did on this tour had its fair share of technical problems – computer disk loading failures (all the data was stored on floppy diskettes back then, which had limited data capacity and had to be swapped over during stage blackouts between songs), sound balance issues between the acoustic and electronic instruments, onstage feedback because of the complexity of the monitoring, etc. Despite this, we were soon in the groove and the performances were generally going well. Audiences seemed to respond very warmly to the ambition of the set, both Lisa and Brendan were singing beautifully, and 'At First, and Then' had become a regular finale number, with all of us playing percussion, and was going down a storm.

I was still tour manager, keeping the books, dealing with the Carnet, dishing out the 'PD's, checking us in at hotels and venues, etc. It was also my task to make sure everyone was ready and on the coach for all the departures, which had become quite a job with our expanded entourage. My nemesis in this role was cellist Nick, who was forever trying to resolve some personal crisis or other, always needed another three cups of radioactive-grade coffee and a dozen cigarettes to make it through the next half hour, and was constantly losing some essential part of his kit. While I ground my teeth and cursed him, Lisa found him endlessly fascinating and hilarious, which only served to encourage him to greater heights of barminess. Meanwhile, I struck up a particular friendship with trombonist John, largely through somewhat similar backgrounds and much the same sense of humour – DCD performances were always taken very seriously, so it was important for that to be counter-balanced with some light relief behind the scenes. Richard, our other trombonist, also had a good temperament for handling life on the road and, amongst various pranks, altered all the setlists (except Brendan's) so we now had a song called 'The Cardinal's In'. And when Brendan was otherwise distracted, John and Richard would periodically slip in a little horn section dance routine.

After the performance in Bochum, John and I were chatting while I was packing up the drum kit when we were approached by a member of the audience who told us how much she'd enjoyed the show before informing us that her two favourite bands were Dead Can Dance and Bucks Fizz. For the uninitiated, Bucks Fizz was a pop group with two male and two female singers who were largely about image and commercial success, and represented the UK in the notorious Eurovision Song Contest with a jaunty number called 'Making Your Mind Up'. Back home, it was extremely unlikely you'd find anyone with this combination of tastes, and even if they did exist, they'd never dare air such an opinion in public for fear of instant ridicule and social exclusion. John and I both laughed, but assured the startled girl that we were very touched by her kind accolade. And actually, I must sneakily admit that the video for Bucks Fizz's song 'New Beginning' is worth a look.

The following night we were at the Römer in Bremen, where someone in the audience with a handheld camcorder recorded several songs and years later uploaded them on YouTube. The quality isn't great, but as with the previously mentioned fan footage from Bedford a couple of years earlier, these clips are the only audio-visual records of DCD from that time as we weren't getting offered any TV appearances, and weren't in the market of making videos to support singles. Then it was on to the Kir Club in Hamburg, which Brendan assures me occupied (at that time) a converted former WWII air-raid shelter, and where the local promoter turned up in a white suit with matching white briefcase – must confess I've no recollection of this, but Mr Perry seems sure of his powers of recall so who am I to argue? Brendan further recollects that we really struggled to fit on the stage at the Kir – he had to keep ducking whenever the trombones started extending behind him – and it was like a sauna when we played.

May segued into June and we rolled on through Cologne and Frankfurt until next up was Berlin. Back in 1986 this involved a transit through the German Democratic Republic, more commonly referred to as East Germany, which had been established from the Soviet-controlled zone after the Second World War. East Germany was governed by a strict, old-school 'socialist' regime, and had retained its very austere image. It entirely surrounded the enclave of West Berlin, a quirk of the Potsdam treaty signed at the end of the War, creating a marooned outpost of West Germany. In response to being surrounded by the perceived repressive East German society, and in the shadow of the Berlin Wall which was built in 1961 to ensure the separation of the two sides of the city, West Berlin had become overtly decadent, loud, and colourful.

Arriving at the border crossing, the East German guards couldn't conceal their disdain. Our coach, decorated in bright primary colours, contained a motley crew, the debris of a few weeks on the road, a hoard of curious musical instruments . . . and Robert! The East German guards were highly intrigued by this strange alien with South East Asian features and long black hair trailing over his shoulders, and a pair of them boarded the bus and stood observing him while their colleagues outside pored over his passport and visa for what seemed an eternity, even threatening at one point to confiscate his documents. Finally we were given permission to pass through and the coach trundled onto the East German motorway, on which we had a set time limit to make it to West Berlin. The coach soon became like a mighty ocean liner, with a flotilla of small boats around it – in this instance the collected Trabants and Wartburgs of the local populous, their drivers and passengers all gaping up at us slack-jawed. At every junction we passed, one division of Trabants and Wartburgs (in regulation grey, slightly darker grey or sort of beige-grey) would grudgingly leave us at the exit, only to be replaced by the next batch of gawpers who surged down the entry slip and immediately surrounded us.

We reached the border, reentered Western civilisation and headed for The Loft, a legendary venue even by Berlin standards. It was run by the equally legendary Monika Döring, who was one of the great characters to meet on the alternative arts circuit. She had taken over the spacious former headquarters of 'The Jesus People' above the Berlin Metropol a few years earlier and created a venue where she could put on bands she liked and party with them. Her taste included pioneers of the New German Wave – such as local industrialists Einstürzende Neubauten and Mania D – and generally the contemporary UK indie scene. We had a great night there with some exuberant post-show indulgence, particularly as it was our penultimate show in Europe.

The following day we managed a quick sighting of the Brandenburg Gate and Checkpoint Charlie, before returning to board the coach. As we walked back towards the hotel, a curious rumbling sound started to build, and the ground beneath us was shaking. I was wondering if there was an earthquake, or if Tony had managed to hook his didge into the city drainage system to upstage his trick at the Groningen hotel. While we were looking around for the cause of the now considerable commotion, all the locals continued about their business without batting an eyelid. Finally the source became apparent as a division of American military tanks came into view, rolling down the middle of Berlin's old stone streets – a stark reminder of the Allied Forces' occupation which still continued over forty years after the end of the war.

And so we left Berlin's crazy island of decadent excess, wartime hangover, and forbidding wall, made our way back along the river of Trabants and Wartburgs, crossed once more onto West German soil, and headed for Hannover and its goth outpost the Soxs club. Final show, all good, and next day we were headed for the ferry back to Old Blighty. By this time the 1986 World Cup Football

Tournament had begun in Mexico and England's second game – against Morocco – was due to be played while we were on the high seas. England had lost their first game to Portugal 1–0 so the Morocco game had become critical to our progress, and Brendan and I in particular were anxious to see it. We couldn't find a TV in any of the public areas of the boat, so we asked a member of the crew who kindly managed to get us into a private TV lounge of the Captain's and find the live match coverage just getting underway.

Several of us snuck in and settled down to watch, but as the ferry headed out into open waters, we found ourselves on a seriously rough crossing. This was also pre-satellite TV transmissions, so the further we went from land, the worse the TV reception became. Watching a deteriorating picture whilst being tossed about on some ferocious waves is an open invitation to sea sickness, and before long only two of us were left. I made it through the dull and goalless first half, but that was my lot and I left 'Iron Guts' Perry as last man sitting. Fortunately, as it was a night crossing, we had cabins, so I had somewhere to go and lie down. I passed by the washrooms en route where a bunch of teenage lads were providing running commentaries on the unfortunates succumbing to the ocean's upsetting of stomachs, bellowing observations like 'Waaaah – trap one's gone again!' It had the effect of nearly tipping me over the edge, and I virtually fled the final yards to my cabin, laid down immediately, and promptly fell into an exhausted sleep. I woke the following morning as the ferry glided serenely into port on now calm seas. I hunted Brendan down to find that he'd only seen part of the second half before the picture was finally lost, but the game had ended 0–0 which left us in a precarious position. Luckily, England saved their best performances for our return to home turf and we were able to see (on dry-land TV) our next two games, in which we beat first Poland and then Paraguay both by 3–0, the former courtesy of a Gary Lineker hat trick. This set us up for the notorious quarter final against Argentina, won apparently by the 'hand of God' with a little assistance from some bloke called Maradona.

Before all this, our current tour wasn't quite finished as two days after we arrived home, we had our biggest London show to date at what was then called the Town and Country Club (later to become The Forum) in Kentish Town on Sunday, 8 June. With an audience capacity of around two thousand, this was a step up. It was to be a 4AD Festival of sorts – even awarded a DCD-generated title 'The Carnival of Light . . . and Other Tall Stories' – with both Dif Juz and Wolfgang Press playing between the Heavenly Bodies' opening set, and DCD, plus the midpoint showing of a film *Maelstrom* by 23 Envelope's Nigel Grierson and a performance by dance company The Cholmondeleys, choreographed by Lea Anderson. The T&C was packed and the overall show tipped six hours.

I've heard Cocteaus bassist Simon Raymonde in an interview dismiss the idea that a '4AD family' ever existed, but on that night at the T&C I'd have disagreed. I got to perform with Heavenly Bodies, then to watch Dif Juz and the Wolfies plus Nigel's film, and then perform with DCD, which had an extra edge that night, an extra magic. The show really had the 'WOW' factor for me, and the backstage atmosphere was great, with Ivo, Debbie, and Vaughan also in the throng – I'd say there was a special bond created by 4AD. I was buzzing afterwards like never before and suddenly the scale of what we were doing felt so much bigger. In the following days reviews appeared in the national music press:

> DCD KNOW. . . that they have mastered pop's possibilities and that they will be one of the very few groups from this decade to be part of the next. A moment worth seeing.
> —Jim Shelley in *Melody Maker*

and:

> Dead Can Dance are precious and delicate and special; they're reaching out for a piece of heaven and they've almost made it. You have to admire their nerve.
> —Mr Spencer in *Sounds*

And the Town & Country/Forum would forever be my favourite venue.

SIX

Backtracking a little, while we'd been touring, 4AD put out a highly unusual release – one that was only feasible because of Ivo's very personal and uncommercial approach to label management. The story goes that Ivo had been producing Peter Murphy's post-Bauhaus solo album at Blackwing, and regularly at the end of sessions, Murphy would play an old cassette tape of the Bulgarian State Radio & Television Female Choir. Although the quality wasn't great, Ivo was smitten by the extraordinary sound created by the open-throat vocal technique of the singers. The recordings had been made by Swiss ethnomusicologist Marcel Cellier and released on his own label in 1975 under the French language title *Le Mystère des Voix Bulgares* but the release had gained little exposure. Ivo was sure he could – indeed *should* – bring this amazing, spine-tingling music to a wider audience. He contacted Cellier and licensed a rerelease on 4AD, which successfully introduced the Bulgarian Choir to an entirely new audience – and, incidentally, featured probably my favourite of Vaughan's cover designs. Ivo was delighted to have played such a significant role in bringing them the attention they richly deserved, and in the years to follow, Cellier was able to produce a series of albums with major label releases, and the Choir began to tour the world.

Closer to home, the Bulgarian Voices had a dramatic effect on Lisa, who adored the sound and set about teaching herself the technique, which in turn had a major influence on her future writing and performing. Nicki and I went to see the Bulgarian Choir live at the Royal Festival Hall in London. The singing was wonderful, but it was also amusing to discover from the programme notes that these incredible voices, in their complex arrangements, were actually singing about subjects like taking the family goat down to the local market (I don't guarantee that was an *actual* subject of one of the songs, but you get the idea – simple, everyday life in rural Bulgaria).

Around this time, Lisa was also starting to indulge herself in another of her passions – grand opera. I knew her to be a big fan of Maria Callas, but with a small trickle of income newly at her disposal, she would now squirrel away funds to periodically purchase a ticket for the Royal Opera House in Covent Garden. She discovered that, if she dressed in her finest stage gown and employed her stage makeup and hair, she could buy the cheapest seat in 'the gods', scour the lower tiers during the first act for an unoccupied seat, then at first interval descend to the appropriate level, glide swiftly and serenely past the ushers – daring them to challenge her for her ticket – take up the spare seat she'd identified, and stay put for the remainder of the performance.

The enclave in Bonnington Square where Jim lived was a magnet for musicians and artists, and a collective formed to put on a concert at St Peter's Church on Vauxhall Cross under the banner 'Echoes from the Cross'. The concert was on 6 September 1986 which meant I couldn't attend as it was the wedding day of Nicki's sister Debbie. Nicki was briefly back for the occasion from Spain. She'd taken a year out from her career at home to teach English at a language school in Reus, a provincial town in Catalonia. It was something she had a burning passion to do, and she had my full support, but at the same time I'd been missing her badly. I'd been out to visit her once, around Easter time, but I needed to be available back home for DCD commitments and didn't have the money to keep going back and forth. I wanted to spend as much time as possible with her while she was over. So I didn't attend the 'Echoes' event, but Brendan and Lisa performed a piece – possibly an early version of what would become 'Persephone' on the next DCD album. The Heavenly Bodies also performed, and the success of the event gave rise to a likelihood of more to follow.

On 20 September 1986, the second This Mortal Coil album, *Filigree & Shadow*, was released, with my track 'At First, and Then' included. With vinyl still the primary format, *Filigree & Shadow* was a 'double album' (i.e. two 12" discs) and to much of the media was overlong and ponderous, with no standout single to come close to TMC's first album's 'Song to the Siren'. Although *Sounds* made the track 'Come Here My Love' a Single of the Week, both *Melody Maker* and the *NME* gave the album negative reviews, and generally the reception was mixed. However, many fans speak very fondly of the entire This Mortal Coil output, and it undeniably represents a very important element of the classic 4AD period in the 1980s. More to the point, Ivo was happy with it and believed in it, even though he was stung by some of the criticism. But this exemplified the ethos he created at 4AD, where artists were able to create their music unhampered by commercial and promotional considerations. In a review of DCD's *Spleen and Ideal* for *Melody Maker*, writer Steve Sutherland had observed that: 'Dead Can Dance care nothing for the fluctuations of fashion.' Which was absolutely true, and emphasised our good fortune to have settled in the rare and fertile environment which Ivo created.

Brendan and Lisa were back at the writing 'coal face', working on material for the next album, interrupted briefly by preparations for a brace of gigs to see out 1986. On Friday, 21 November we played the University of London Union (ULU). 'Persephone' and 'Xavier' were both included in the set to give the audience a taster of the new material being written, which was still much in the same orchestral vein as *Spleen and Ideal*, with Brendan in particular looking more towards Stravinsky as a source of inspiration than anything in the indie circuit which we effectively still inhabited. Next day we headed down to Bristol for a gig organised by music journalist, local promoter, and self-confessed DCD fan Dave Massey. Dave had interviewed Brendan and Lisa for *Jamming* magazine shortly after the release of *Spleen*, concluding:

> Dead Can Dance, for me, offer a deeply personal sense of hope, solace and respite, bringing light to darkness of mood and outlook. Saying this to Lisa brought a smile to her face. 'If that's the effect we have, what more can we ask for?'

Dave had booked us into the beautiful St George's Church, which I think was in its relative infancy at the time as a venue, but which has since become a landmark on the alternative/folk/world music circuit. It was a lovely environment for the semi-orchestral Dead Can Dance show, and great to work with a local promoter who had real empathy for what we were about.

I received another call from Ivo, this time on behalf of The Wolfgang Press, who were looking for some additional percussion on a track for their next EP. A cassette tape came through the post to give me an idea of what they were working on and in early December I headed down to Blackwing again, this time with my original pair of bongo drums tucked under my arm. When I arrived, Mark had also brought in a goblet drum, which we subsequently decided against using, though looking back on this I think perhaps I simply didn't know how to play it. The Arabic goblet drum, which I have subsequently come to love and use extensively, has an entirely different sound in the middle of the drumhead or skin than near the rim, and the two different areas are played in different ways to obtain the effective sounds. With hindsight, I think I was trying to play it as if it were a single bongo drum, with flat hands, which would have sounded terrible!

Fig. 13. On holiday in Brittany, August 1987: Brendan striding out in fine style. Photo by Peter Ulrich.

So we reverted to my trusty old bongos. These, however, by the nature of their construction cannot be tuned and are notoriously susceptible to changes in temperature and humidity. I picked them up to play along to the track, only to discover that the skins had gone slack and the drums had lost all their tone. Fortunately, not being too large, the bongos could fit on a shelf in the fridge in Blackwing's kitchen, and after ten minutes or so, the skins had tightened sufficiently. I prepared for a take, but while John Fryer (engineering the session) was getting the mic in position and setting the record levels, the skins went slack again, so it was back to the fridge. The bongos weren't happy at all in Blackwing that day, and wouldn't hold their tension for more than a few minutes, so I spent the session running back and forth between recording booth and kitchen. We got there in the end, and I made my guest appearance on the track 'The

Wedding' on the Wolfies' *Big Sex* EP. My fellow DCD-er Richard Avison was also drafted in, playing unrefrigerated trombone on 'That Heat' on the same EP.

The beginning of 1987 was a decidedly happy new year for me, with Nicki back from Spain. Brendan continued writing with his ever-developing tech setup, so band rehearsals continued to be thin on the ground. Amongst other diversions for me was Max! Maxwell Bailey was a fifty-something Trinidadian who lived a couple of floors below Brendan and Lisa in Bowsprit Point, believed he had attained some kind of Jesus-like status, and would often disturb Brendan, Lisa, and their neighbours during the night with his bellowed conversations with God from his balcony. He also suffered a moderate amount of hassle from the police during his preaching stints on the streets of London's West End, and would periodically write letters to Her Majesty the Queen to complain about his treatment. He had a big stature, accentuated by baggy clothes and a thick beard, but was actually quite softly spoken, had a very gentle nature and a wonderful deep, chuckly laugh. He'd befriended Brendan and Lisa, and in turn, me and Nicki. If we called on Max, he'd proudly show us black and white photos of himself when he was an eighteen-year-old boxing champion back in the Caribbean, before the manager of one of his main opponents allegedly used black magic against him to render him virtually crippled. He fled to Europe, married a Portuguese lady after praying to God for a wife, discovered and embraced the Oahspe Bible and Kosmon Church, and had re-invented himself as a, or the, son of God (later renaming himself 'Alric').

Max (I'll stick with this) was very sincere, but not overbearing with the religious tack, and had a past full of curious stories. He'd regularly call at our flats for a cup of tea and a chat, and we all grew very fond of him. He'd enrolled on a lino cutting course at the local arts centre and in no time was producing striking pictures of flying horses inspired by visions from his dreams. One day I was waiting for a bus across the road from Knighthead when he came along on his bicycle (which, despite being full adult size, looked like a child's toy with Max balanced precariously on it). 'Peter, where can I see cows?' he asked as he glided to a halt beside me. Unsure if they yet had a bovine division at the local Mudchute urban farm, I could only think that he would need to head out towards Epping, on the outskirts of London, where the first farmlands would appear. He tipped his hat to me and off he went. A few days later, he knocked at our door and presented me with the most remarkable model of a cow, fashioned out of wire coat hangers. He made a number of these wire frames, took them to the Arts Centre and covered them with papier maché. They varied from plump, healthy creatures, to others which had cavities between their ribs and the hollow eyes of famine victims – again all images drawn from his dreams.

I wasn't the only one impressed with Max's output, as a month-long exhibition of his work was scheduled at Bethnal Green Library, and I volunteered to be publicist. In addition to ensuring that details were in the London listings magazines – *Time Out*, *City Limits*, and *Event* in those days, as well as various local papers – I had Max make me a dozen or so A3-size prints of one of my favourite of his horse images, and sent them to art critics at the main newspapers. A few days later my home phone rang and, to my surprise, it was the art critic of the *London Evening Standard* – Brian Sewell. Brian had a formidable reputation as one of the toughest critics, and didn't pull any punches when reviewing works which he considered unfit for public admiration. He told me he'd try to come to Max's exhibition and review it, though he couldn't promise. He then gave me his private phone number and told me to call if he hadn't appeared in the first few days. He didn't appear, and I did try to call, but only reached his elderly mother who got very confused trying to take down my message. But although Brian never did make the show (as far as we know), it was a tribute to Max that the print sufficiently grabbed this leading critic's attention, and a tribute to Brian that he took the trouble to show an active interest in an entirely unknown artist.

DCD were booked into Woodbine again for sessions for the next album. I assumed I wouldn't be required until Brendan told me he had one track on which he wanted me to play a snare drum roll. However, my kit snare drum didn't have the right sound and he wanted the depth of a military marching band snare – Brendan fanatical as always about ensuring that every small detail in his recordings is the best he can make it. This was a specialised item, not readily available, and I had to order the marching snare drum, with its polished mirror-effect stainless steel shell, through Central London dealers Chas Foote, travel first to their shop (at that time near Piccadilly Circus) to make the payment, then take a train from King's Cross to Leicester to go to the Premier drum factory to collect the drum, and then take another train across to Leamington Spa to get to Woodbine. I spent three days at Woodbine around the end of April, beginning of May, during which time I performed the snare part as well as a timpani part, reacquainted myself with Rosemary and Basil (oh, and John), and then headed back to London to await the fruits of Brendan and Lisa's labours.

On arrival back in London, Nicki greeted me with the life-changing news that our first child was on the way. I was thrilled. I always wanted children, but had left it to Nicki to decide when the time was right – that's a mighty undertaking to grow another human inside your body! We hadn't been trying long, and hadn't expected it to happen so soon, but I was massively excited and immediately on the phone to all my family and friends. After the initial morning sickness, Nicki blossomed during her pregnancy and looked radiant, even though she was still working full time in a demanding job, having moved to her first senior teaching post at a school in the neighbouring London Borough of Newham. I wanted to be fully involved – I attended the scans, we did the ante-natal classes together, and we amused ourselves for hours lobbing potential names at one another.

Fig. 14: Brittany holiday, August 1987: Brendan, Lisa and Nicki looking curiously furtive over their lunch order. Photo by Peter Ulrich.

In June 1987 4AD released a compilation album called *Lonely is an Eyesore* – a collection of nine tracks from various 4AD bands/artists, including two from DCD. The first was a reworking of 'Frontier', the second – and the album closer – was a long slow-burner of a piece called 'The Protagonist', which Brendan had composed and recorded very much as a soundtrack for a short film. One of the main driving forces behind the release was a collaboration with art studio 23 Envelope, with videos made for each track by Nigel and the package artwork created by Vaughan. Nigel's film for 'The Protagonist' was to some degree an extension of ideas and techniques employed in his film *Maelstrom* which had been shown at DCD's Town & Country Club gig the previous year and – I think I'm correct in saying – Brendan's piece was the only track on the album specifically written for this purpose (the others being Nigel's visual interpretations of preexisting songs, albeit bespoke remixes).

The *Lonely is an Eyesore* title was taken from a line in the song 'Fish' contributed by recent 4AD arrivals Throwing Muses – the first American band Ivo signed. Vaughan went to town on the packaging, one of the incarnations being a special and very limited edition set of beechwood boxes containing the album in all audio formats, a video of Nigel's short films, and various etchings. Just one hundred of these wooden box sets were produced and, as a fine example of the extremes of fate, one is now a prized artefact in the collections of London's Victoria and Albert Museum, while another was allegedly last seen (by undercover agent R Guthrie Esquire) in use as a cat litter tray in the kitchen of Colourbox's Martyn Young.

While the new Dead Can Dance album was taking shape, I received the offer of another session from Ivo, this time with former Xymox member Pieter Nooten who was in Blackwing making an album with guitarist/producer Michael Brook. Michael's work – particularly his distinctive guitar textures – had come to Ivo's attention via his recent 'Hybrid' project with Brian Eno and Daniel Lanois. Ivo felt a similar treatment would work well with Pieter's music, and Michael had accepted Ivo's invitation to get involved. I was looking forward to seeing Pieter again as I think it was the first time since Xymox had stayed at our flat and done their first two UK shows with DCD. I arrived at Blackwing to be presented by Michael with a number of oriental paper fans – not the 'concertina' type, but rather flat, taut, thin paper stretched on simple wood frames. He wanted me to try some rhythms, played lightly with the fingertips on the paper, held close to the microphone. Pieter was keeping out of it, but looking rather bemused. I was always up for something unusual, but despite trying various techniques, the sound from the fans was consistently dull and lifeless, so in the end we resorted to standard percussion and out came my trusty old bongos again.

Fortunately, the Blackwing climate was kinder on this occasion and the fridge wasn't needed. The track I was to play on – 'Time' – was quite different to the rest of Pieter's album, with a jaunty feel in contrast to the generally more contemplative moods. Pieter was clearly in need of a little light relief, and while I tried to concentrate on playing, he was on the other side of the glass screen in the control room miming a rider on a horse, bouncing along from one side of the room to the other while descending into a mock valley (by bending his knees and disappearing from view) and then gradually reascending (straightening up again, and coming back into my view through the glass). We both got the giggles, which was made worse by Michael trying to ignore Pieter's antics and studiously continue with the task at hand. Finally we were done and I had my feature spot on Pieter's lovely *Sleeps with the Fishes* album which would be released the following October.

Before that came the release of the new Dead Can Dance album *Within the Realm of a Dying Sun* on 27 July 1987. The album was very much a natural progression from *Spleen and Ideal*, with similar styles and arrangements, but even more orchestrated and ambitious. Although Brendan was extensively using some of the classic electronic equipment and sampled sounds of the era, these two DCD albums don't have a 'mideighties' sound. Brendan actively steered away from the sounds which a lot of the popular, mainstream synth bands were obsessed with, picking only the most natural sounds and, where the digital samples didn't come close enough, bringing in musicians to play the acoustic instruments for the parts he'd sequenced – hence the contributor lists that appear on those albums. The cover image shows a detail of the family grave of nineteenth-century naturalist François-Vincent Raspail in Paris's Père-Lachaise cemetery. Ivo has gone on record as saying of *Realm*: 'It's probably my favourite record of theirs.'

DCD album releases were accompanied by the statutory round of reviews and interviews. Almost without exception, these would begin with the setting of the scene in Brendan and Lisa's flat in Bowsprit Point which writers found so compellingly at odds with DCD's musical world of ethereal beauty. This obsession was exemplified in the opening lines of a feature by Mr Spencer in the *Sounds* issue of 25 July 1987:

> SIMPLY EVERYBODY begins by telling us that Dead Can Dance live in a council flat on the 13th floor of a tower block in Millwall. The location invariably comes as a surprise, because most people who've heard their music expect Dead Can Dance to reside in a grand old castle or a palace or on top of a big white fluffy cloud.

Once into the meat of the interview, these features would regularly be characterised by Brendan and Lisa gently, and often amusingly, contradicting each other. In the same *Sounds* feature, Mr Spencer asks Brendan about the origins of his inspirations and whether, as a kid, he dreamed of being in an orchestra rather than a pop group, to which he receives the responses:

I was put off at a very early age. I can still recall my first music lesson vividly. You had the classic situation where the music teacher would come around handing everybody recorders and we'd all have to play the basic melody to 'Three Blind Mice' in unison. That's a terrible way of going about things.

Lisa: 'I remember being very moved by "Three Blind Mice". Awe-inspired. I love it.'

The release of *Realm* found us midway through rehearsals for an exciting festival in the south of France under the banner 'Veni, Vidi, Vici'. We were booked to play on 1 August in an historic Roman amphitheatre dating back to the first century at Fréjus, nestling just inland from the resort of St Raphael. The venue had a large stage and Brendan determined to make full use of it, assembling DCD's largest 'orchestra' to date – ten of us, including Lisa's younger brother Mark, who was over on a visit from Australia, on trumpet – and asking me to hire a couple of tunable orchestral timpani drums. The now-regulation Griersons coach was booked, and we were to be joined on the adventure by Ivo's latest signing to 4AD – A R Kane, comprising Alex Ayuli and Rudy Tambala, who were gathering some excited critical acclaim and would provide one of the support acts. Also on the bill with us would be Xymox, who would meet us there.

A change to DCD's core had taken place, with the departures of Scott and Jim. What had seemed a mutually beneficial arrangement of Heavenly Bodies touring with DCD the previous year had generated some friction and the rift remained unresolved. The Bodies continued long enough to release an album in 1988 on the Third Mind label. Scott played bass briefly with Dif Juz, covering for Gary Bromley, who was having some health problems, before carving himself a career in artist management, firstly for Björk, and later with Sir Paul McCartney and Arcade Fire. Jim toured on drums with the Jesus and Mary Chain (later to be followed onto the JaMC drumstool by Dif Juz's Richard Thomas), and contributed to a recording collaboration between Michael Brook and Nusrat Fateh Ali Khan on the Real World label amongst other projects.

Either Gus and/or the 4AD tartan division moved swiftly into gear to dish up another replacement Scottish bassist for DCD – Colin Cairns. I gelled well with Colin between bass and drums, and he also had a wicked sense of humour. Our set for Fréjus would be the longest to date, comprising eighteen songs/pieces plucked from all four albums, the *Arcane Delights* EP and This Mortal Coil contributions, and supplemented by Lisa's solo 'Swans' (which would surface some years later as a track on her first solo album *The Mirror Pool*) and a first outing for 'Severance', which Brendan had already written for the next DCD album and which was destined to become a live staple.

Griersons provided two drivers so we could do London to St Raphael in a straight run with no overnight stop, but we hit a major problem at the French border when Lisa's and Mark's visas were rejected. After some urgent phone calls with 4AD, it was arranged that Lisa and Mark would return to London for an emergency appointment at the Australian Embassy, and then fly down to the South of France the following day, while the rest of us continued as planned. It would be touch and go whether they'd make it, and we might have to contemplate performing without Lisa!

On the morning of the show, we went to the amphitheatre early to start setting up and found that, because the area was never bothered by rain in August, the stage had no covering. This also meant there was no shade and by midday the sun was beating down on us mercilessly. I suddenly became aware that the large plastic heads on the timpanies were physically 'bubbling' in the intense heat – I panicked and screamed for help, and we rushed the timps off stage and into a patch of shade. With hindsight it was a stupid error on my part, but having no previous experience of either using such large, flat drums or setting up in the glare of such an intense Mediterranean sun, I simply never thought about it. We had no replacement heads with us, and I was convinced I'd ruined the possibility of using the timps in the show, which were really essential for some of its dramatic moments. However, to my amazement and overwhelming relief, the plastic heads as they cooled went back into shape and I was able to retune them.

Panic over, lesson learned, and better still, Lisa and Mark arrived with a couple of hours to spare. AR Kane provided a very different opening set to usual DCD shows, with their heady mix of dub-styled pop tunes morphing into everything from psychedelia through free jazz to Hendrix-style guitar licks and screaming feedback. Xymox we were familiar with and it was good to see them perform again. Our set had a few technical and onstage sound balance issues, which were almost inevitable given its ambition, but overall it worked and got a great reception from the audience. And, of course, the setting and ambience of the show were fabulous. Promoter Jean-Luc Martin was very happy and had laid on a wonderful aftershow party at a local villa with food and wine flowing which, I guess, probably went on through much of the night.

Back in London a couple of days later it was straight into rehearsals to keep us sharp for two UK shows, the first at the Tower Ballroom in Birmingham on Thursday, 6 August, and the second back at the Town and Country Club in London's Kentish Town on Sunday, 9 August, for which a support set would be provided by Rob Lee's latest project, Peran Orphis, which would involve more multitasking DCDers, me included. Also on the T&C bill was to be one Enrique Juncosa. With DCD now a bit of a 'name' amongst the London hip squad, Brendan and Lisa were attending a few trendy arts events and mixing with the in-crowd. They'd befriended Enrique and his partner Farid. Farid was reputed to be of Afghan nobility – royalty even – and rumoured to have fled his homeland from the Soviet invasion. He didn't speak of it, but had the air of someone who carried the weight of something momentous but unresolved. He'd been educated in the UK, spoke perfect English, and blended seamlessly into London society.

Enrique was Spanish, a near descendant of the artist Joan Miró, and a fledgling writer whose first book of poetry, *Amanacer Zulú*, had been published a year earlier. He went on to become not only an established poet and writer of art history and critiques, but also a curator of exhibitions at major galleries across Europe (including Tate Britain and the Whitechapel in London) and Director of the Irish Museum of Modern Art in Dublin. Some years later, Brendan was visiting Enrique at the family home in Palma de Mallorca where he witnessed a private ceremony arising from a legacy of Miró that, on the occasion of their twenty-first birthday, each direct descendant receives an original artwork of the painter from the family vault, on this occasion bestowed on one of Enrique's cousins. When we first knew Enrique in London he was also a budding composer who jumped at the opportunity to 'perform' a new work to a London audience at our upcoming T&C show – I put 'perform' in quotes because Brendan later told me that Enrique actually just ran a preprogrammed sequencer and mimed his performance – with some considerable gusto – while Brendan played a live bass accompaniment!

First though, it was off to Birmingham. Our trip got off to a bad start when, after collecting the timpanis from the hire company, our driver, in trying to negotiate the narrow back streets in Kings Cross, caught the side of the coach on a concrete bollard and punched in a section of the metal panelling. The poor guy was mortified and we felt really sorry for him, but there was nothing to be done other than press on. The Tower Ballroom turned out to be a strange venue – an apparent misnomer as it had no discernible tower, and had the appearance of a cross between a Mecca Bingo Hall (for Anglophiles of a certain age) and a lock-up garage, marooned at the end of a large car park next to an expansive reservoir. It was also famed for its plastic palm trees, but it was well established on 'the circuit' and had hosted the likes of New Order, The Smiths, and The Damned prior to us.

Years – decades, in fact – later I came across an online recollection by a member of the audience from that night called Keith Bate from which I hope he will excuse me for quoting the following extract:

> After the encores she [Lisa] stepped off stage and walked through the audience. As she walked past me she was stopped by a USA/goth girl who told her she could make her look 'more beautiful'. I said I think Miss Gerrard is already beautiful. The girl agreed but said to LG 'yes but I can make you even more beautiful with my makeup.' LG's reply and expression will stay with me until I die. She looked blankly at the USA goth girl and without an expression on her face said very slowly 'thank you very much' then she wheeled away and walked off!

Playing the T&C again was a joy, as always. Despite being an out-and-out 'rock venue', we were hugely grateful for the reverence and support we received from the audience. A subsequent review in *Music Week* noted that: 'A packed Town & Country Club paid its respect in the pin-drop silence that fell during some of the spiralling vocal sequences in Gerrard's songs' and went on to observe of Brendan and Lisa: 'each the other's perfect foil – Perry in his workaday, Fair Isle pully, the wraithlike Gerrard mesmeric in spectral white robe.'

Meanwhile, I was quietly chuffed that the review finished with a reference to our live rendition of 'At First, and Then', describing our finale as: 'An electrifying volley of percussion for the encore, strikingly concluding Dead Can Dance's apocalyptic musical visions.'

A break in the schedules after the Town & Country gave us the opportunity to take a holiday. Brendan, Lisa, and I had fallen for Brittany when we'd recuperated there during our ill-fated debut French tour, and Nicki was eager to go as she'd never been. It would also be my and Nicki's last child-free break for a couple of decades! Nicki hired a traditional 'gîte' for a fortnight in the second half of August – apparently some kind of old converted water mill – and as the only driver amongst us, was also designated chauffeur. We set off appropriately in her old Peugeot 304 estate car which she'd bought on return from Spain from an 'honest John' second-hand car dealer on the Romford Road near Ilford.

The gîte was lovely – a remote spot in the middle of beautiful countryside, set beside a fast-flowing stream, and with a substantial colony of bats nesting under its roof beams which would come jetting out each dusk, shooting past us in all directions. A bigger contrast to our concrete towers on the Isle of Dogs was hard to imagine. Nicki discovered a less welcome member of the local wildlife when, on one of her middle-of-the-night trips to the loo (a consequence of pregnancy), she was stealthily stepping across the living room in the dark trying her best to be silent when a mouse ran across her bare foot causing her to let out a blood-curdling scream. Lights shot on and Brendan, Lisa, and I appeared from respective rooms to find Nicki quaking and wanting to go home! She got over it, and was permitted to put lights on for future nocturnal wanderings.

Time was split between chilling out at the gîte and exploring the hinterland, which included chancing upon some traditional folk music in the town square in Guingamp, where Brendan was smitten by the sound of the bombardes (like bagpipe chanters played without the windbags), and discovering the amazing menhir stones of Carnac which Lisa found particularly captivating and spiritual, I think in a similar manner she had experienced before at Aboriginal sacred sites back in Australia. Lisa also possibly invented the 'selfie' at Carnac, taking what turned out to be a somewhat distorted image of herself in front of one of the stones.

Towards the end of the holiday, we were involved in a minor road accident when a local driver ran into the back of Nicki's car. I jumped out to remonstrate with the culprit. Casting around wildly in my schoolboy French, I blurted out 'Vous etes mal aux yeux?' – which literally translates as 'you are sick of the eyes?' The poor recipient, who was already trying to apologise in broken English (having seen our registration plate), looked bewildered. Fortunately, Nicki joined me at this point and, being both more sensible than me and able to speak French, shoved me aside and took over while Brendan and Lisa laid low in the back. A quick check of the car revealed no discernible damage, particularly as it was far from pristine anyway, and the 'shunt' had been at low speed and flat-on, so it was agreed no further action was needed. However, the expression 'mal aux yeux' entered our vocabulary and, to this day, if either Nicki or I can't find something or fail to spot something, the other will casually enquire . . . 'Vous etes mal aux yeux?'

Next assignment on return to London was to prepare for the second 'Echoes from the Cross' concert to be held again at St Peter's Church in Vauxhall on Saturday, 12 September 1987 at which Brendan and Lisa would appear under the banner of their own names, but this time it would be more of a mini-DCD performance. It wasn't, however, a performance of music taken from the DCD live set, but rather two pieces specially for the occasion – 'Synaesthesia (A song cycle)' and 'The Poison Tree (From Songs of Experience by William Blake)'. This was actually the second concert of what had expanded into a two-night festival. The previous evening's roster had included The Heavenly Bodies and John Foxx (formerly of Ultravox), while the Saturday night also featured performances by Roger Eno and Michael Brook, with the audience including Roger's brother Brian and David Sylvian.

Alongside such gentle, cultural happenings, the hitherto relatively calm waters of 4AD were about to hit some wild rapids. Earlier in the year, the idea of a collaboration had been mooted between Colourbox and A R Kane to create a dance track. The officially touted version is that Rudy, Alex, and sometime ARK collaborator Russell Smith were keen to work with dance producer Adrian Sherwood, but Ivo suggested that working with Martyn and Steve Young might produce something more 'unusual'. But I also heard a story circulating at the time that, in an evening of lubrication at 4AD's local hostelry, one, other or both Youngs had bet Ivo they could make a hit single and Ivo, in an unguarded moment, accepted the challenge. Whatever truly lit the touch paper, the upshot was a few sessions at Blackwing with John Fryer at the controls, the emergence of a specially created entity called M|A|R|R|S (an acronym of first name initials of the participants) and a single called 'Pump Up the Volume'. The track, constructed largely of samples of other recordings, took its inspiration from the emerging house music scene in the US, and was given a ground-breaking edge by the addition of sampling and scratch mix effects by DJs Chris 'CJ' Macintosh and Dave Dorrell. The track's title came from the vocal phrase sampled from 'I know you got Soul' by Eric B and Rakim.

4AD pressed up a batch of anonymous white label 12" vinyls and sent them out to UK clubs. It was widely played and clubbers were clamouring to know what it was and where they could get hold of it. In August 1987, 4AD revealed its hand and officially released a 12" single, though without any of the usual media promos. It hit the official charts at No. 35 pretty much entirely with the patronage of the club scene as it wasn't yet receiving radio airplay. A 7" remix was made and sent out to radio stations and then it really took off. The peace at 4AD's little office was shattered. The phones turned red hot. Shops were selling out stock as soon as it came through the door, distributors were frantic for fresh supplies, the pressing factory had to put on extra shifts and was running 24/7, legal actions were threatened by artists/labels whose material had been sampled and used on PUTV without permission, Stock Aitken and Waterman obtained an injunction to prevent further use of an unauthorised sample from their single 'Roadblock', and further remixes were needed to amend and edit the now outlawed samples. Alongside this, the relationship between the creators, which had been volatile from the outset, descended into acrimony, with disputes between Colourbox and A R Kane, and both sides taking against Ivo.

'Pump Up The Volume' hit No. 1 in the main UK charts and the BBC were on the phone to 4AD pleading for either M|A|R|R|S to appear, or at least for a video, for their weekly chart show 'Top of the Pops' – they'd never before encountered a No. 1 single with no artist available, no supporting video and apparently no interest in having made No. 1! Ivo phoned Martyn in desperation, who reputedly said bluntly: 'Tell them to fuck off!' and put the phone down. The BBC, I think, ended up having to put together a makeshift dance group to perform to the single for the couple of weeks it held the top spot. Meanwhile, PUTV was going global, making No. 1 in Canada, Italy, Netherlands, New Zealand, Zimbabwe, and the US Dance chart, with top ten placements in a raft of other international territories. 4AD's offices remained under siege from both trade and media. The single sold a couple of million, and 4AD also now had to contend with money pouring in – this might not seem like such a 'problem', but when you're trying to run the planned and carefully controlled cashflow of a small-to-medium-sized business, suddenly being swamped with cash can be as difficult to manage as suddenly being starved of it.

We were aware of the chaos going on, but removed from any direct involvement or fallout, and we had to stay focused on our own progression. DCD was now on the books of London agency Fair Warning run by Jeff Craft which would become an enduring relationship, and Jeff a good friend of the band. He'd set up our next European tour and, following a week of intensive rehearsals in the now well-established Greenwich studios, we departed on 28 October with a slimmer lineup. We were seven performers, including, for the first time, Brendan's younger brother Robert. Robbie was only about fourteen when I'd first joined DCD and was wide-eyed, watching everything and questioning how everything worked. Now, still a teenager (just), he was already competent on a range of instruments, and was almost certainly technically a better drummer than me. He seemingly had the ability to pick up any instrument, shut himself in a room with it for a few hours, and emerge playing it to a reasonable standard. He also had a great sense of humour and got on famously with everyone except Brendan, with whom he had a classic fraternal love-hate relationship. So Robbie came on the tour principally as a percussionist, Nick Payne shifted from cello to keyboards leaving Gus as lone cellist, and Colin Cairns continued on bass.

While the onstage group had contracted, the overall tour party now expanded to include a dedicated onstage monitor engineer – a brilliant Dutch guy called Renee de Zoute who effortlessly sorted out problems and kept things calm – front of house sound engineer Tom Pollock, and lighting engineer Dave Sherry. This would ensure more continuity from show to show and help enormously with setup and breakdown each night. We also had a new driver from Griersons Coaches – Malcolm West – who I struck up a good friendship with. Despite this upping of our game in the tour entourage stakes, I continued moonlighting as makeshift tour manager, with Robbie renaming me 'PD-Pete'. In my defence, it was now a bit more than getting the Carnet stamped at borders and handing out the daily allowances. I was liaising with local promoters, collecting more substantial performance fees, and had also been given a contact list of 4AD's licensees in the various territories we were scheduled to play so I could coordinate press interest and arrange interviews with Brendan and Lisa – so I was kind of full circle and back into my old press and PR role.

The 'lighting engineer' – Dave Sherry – was not (as far as I'm aware) really a lighting engineer at all, but rather a mate of Gus and Colin who went under the moniker of 'Looby', the dictionary definition of which is an awkward, clumsy fellow, but this didn't ring true. He was a larger-than-life character, as well as being physically quite large, who always wore a suit (though I think it was the same suit throughout the tour, and was dishevelled even before we left) and trilby hat, had the affable gait of Yogi Bear, was extremely funny, and had the broadest Scottish accent of the three. Reputedly a semi-pro golfer (amongst other talents), he would, when required, assume the role of lighting technician and push a few sliders around if a particular venue didn't have an in-house tech, and on occasion he'd even pop up on stage during 'At First, and Then' brandishing a tambourine and doing a turn reminiscent of Bez from Happy Mondays.

The bulk of the tour would take us through places where we'd been building our audience in Belgium, Netherlands, France, and Germany, but also through northern Italy for the first time, as well as playing a one-off in Switzerland. Our full schedule was:

Belgium:
Wednesday, 28 October Brussels, La Gaite

Netherlands:
Friday, 30 October Amsterdam, Paradiso
Saturday, 31 October Utrecht, Tivoli
Sunday, 1 November Rotterdam, De Lantaren

France:
Tuesday, 3 November Rouen, Exo 7
Wednesday, 4 November Paris, Rex Club
Thursday, 5 November Rennes, Ubu
Saturday, 7 November Lyon, Salle Moliere

Italy:

Monday, 9 November Genoa, Teatro Verdi
Tuesday, 10 November Turin, Studio 2
Wednesday, 11 November Milan, Prego
Friday, 13 November Treviso, Palasport Montebelluna
Saturday, 14 November Novellara (Reggio Emilia), Ritz

Switzerland:
Tuesday, 17 November Zurich, Theatersaal Rote Fabrik

Germany:
Wednesday, 18 November Frankfurt, Batschkapp
Thursday, 19 November Bochum, Zeche
Saturday, 21 November Berlin, Loft
Sunday, 22 November Hamburg, Markthalle
Monday, 23 November Muenster, Odeon

Playing the Paradiso in Amsterdam meant returning to the scene of our first ever European mainland show, which had been aborted when Brendan narrowly survived electrocution by his own guitar. Thankfully, that incident had been a complete one-off, and long-since put behind us, so the venue didn't hold any bad karma for us.

My unofficial managerial duties still included rounding up the entourage and making sure everyone was on the tour bus each time we moved on. It seems I'd become a bit over-relaxed on this front as the morning after the show in Utrecht, we'd just set off en route to Rotterdam when Malcolm noticed in his rear view mirror someone running down the middle of the street behind us waving frantically. When it turned out to be young master Perry, Brendan was all for driving off (at least as far as out of sight around the next bend) to teach his brother a lesson, but he was out-voted and Malcolm pulled over to allow the panting Robbie to catch up and jump in.

After Rotterdam, we headed to France with the prospect of a day off before the first show in Rouen, but disaster struck. Lisa contracted a severe throat infection and lost her voice. I had a series of frantic phone calls with French promoter Salomon Hazot, who arranged for a doctor to attend the hotel, then medical prescriptions to be collected. Things worsened as Brendan went down with the same, or similar throat condition, and their hotel room was soon piled high with medications, throat pastilles, herbal teas, honey pots, etc. Our show in Rouen had to be cancelled and while the rest of the entourage moved on to Paris to prepare for the show at the Rex Club, Brendan and Lisa remained confined to bed and would be brought to Paris by hire car if they recovered in time.

They were seen by a doctor who suggested they'd be able to sing that night if he injected them with cortisone. Fortunately, they were aware that, while cortisone can provide a remarkable 'quick fix' for the voice, the longer term effects can be disastrous and turned him away. There are horror stories aplenty of the damage cortisone can inflict on singers – that of Diamanda Galás, for example – and it was alarming that the doctor should propose this treatment without warning of any potential risks, presumably in pursuit of a quick buck. So, Paris was cancelled, the show planned for the Rennes Ubu on the Thursday night was cancelled, and an attempt to reschedule the Rouen show for the Friday was abandoned. We finally got on stage again – even then with Brendan and Lisa some way short of fully recovered – at the Salle Moliere in Lyon on Saturday, 7 November. We'd lost three performance fees and shelled out £123.80 on doctors' fees and medications, plus nearly £80 on hotel phone bills with all the calls to promoters, doctors, and back home to 4AD. Despite our progress, these were still significant costs to us – losses that would be covered for the time being by 4AD, but ultimately it all gets deducted from artist royalties (and that's not a shot at 4AD, that's just how the business works).

Brendan and Lisa had clearly become run down and, looking back, it seems likely that the pressure had taken its toll without anyone realising. They both always seemed very natural on stage, very comfortable performing, and I'm sure they never doubted either the quality of their music or their ability to perform it. But perhaps there's a period which many performers experience during the transition from being a small act in its infancy to a 'name' headline act where things become unsettled. In the early days, everything is very new and fresh, you do the support gigs and then start headlining in small clubs, and it's all an exciting whirl. Then you reach a point where you're headlining to a thousand-plus people per show, and they're now paying serious ticket prices, and you're aware of becoming an 'established artist'. For a while it creates a pressure; once you pass through this phase, you can go on to scale greater heights and an entirely new level of confidence instills itself. But you have to make it through this transition, which I think is where a lot of bands struggle, maybe reliance on drink/drugs kicks in to get people through, and often breakups take place, seemingly inexplicably, just at the point when it appears the 'big time' beckons, because the tension becomes too much to bear.

With Lisa and Brendan recuperating, the rest of us divided our time between sightseeing and bar-crawling. Returning to our hotel on one occasion, I entered the lift (elevator) to find it occupied by a guy hovering over the buttons. He spoke, presumably asking what number I wanted. I confidently requested what

I thought to be the fourth floor in my finest French (yup, I keep trying) in response to which, although he did press the '4' button, he gave me a strangely quizzical look. I was due to phone home to Nicki on return to my room, so I recounted the incident. She asked me to repeat what I'd said in French, and when I told her, fell about laughing on the other end of the line. When she finally recovered her powers of speech, she told me I'd asked my lift companion for the fourth century.

Fig. 15. Day trip to Carnac during our Brittany trip, August 1987: Lisa invents (?) the 'selfie' to get a pic of herself in front of one of the menhirs. Photo by Lisa Gerrard (having snatched my camera!).

We were staying in a small, centrally located hotel on Boulevard de Clichy in the Montmartre district, which didn't have a restaurant and only served breakfast by room service. Hating to be defeated, the morning before we left I determined to attempt the local lingo once more. After a couple of practice runs, I called reception and asked '*Ah bonjour, puis j'ai petit déjeuner à chambre quarante-deux?*' to which I received the tired reply 'Yes, and whadyou want for breakfast?' I invisibly stuck two fingers up and flippantly ordered a 'full English'. *Naturellement*, I ended up with the regulation dry croissant.

Leaving France, I presented our Carnet at Italian customs and was told to go back to the coach and wait. An hour passed so I walked over, only to be sent back. Another half hour passed, then Malcolm twigged and told me they were waiting for us to offer an 'incentive'. I hadn't yet changed any money, so had no lira to offer. The only thing we could come up with were a couple of DCD albums which we had on board for promo purposes. I went and presented our offering, which wasn't rapturously received, but it was enough to get the stamp and we were on our way. After a brief currency exchange stop, Malcolm tried to catch up on a bit of lost time but promptly fell into the Italians' next trap. The foot of a long descent shortly after crossing the border was clearly a favourite entrapment point of the local Polizia and had me delving into my new fund to pay an on-the-spot speeding fine of twenty-five thousand lira, which sounds alarming but was actually about twelve quid. Our first destination was Genoa, with the benefit of another show-free evening to give Brendan and Lisa a little more recovery time. It was also a chance to hook up with old friends Jeff Earp and Stella Robertis.

During his Bowsprit residency, Jeff had become romantically entwined with Stella who was also studying in London, and the arrival of consignments of her mother's homemade pesto had become a source of considerable anticipation and excitement in our concrete towers. When time came for Stella to return home to Genoa, Jeff had gone too and they'd settled there, so we now had ready-made tour guides and interpreters as they joined us for the rest of the Italian dates. The show the following night in the Teatro Verdi was pretty much sold out to fans already familiar with DCD's recorded output and now eager to hear the live renditions, and the receptions proved continuously strong as we played our way west to east across the alpine region of northern Italy, seeing the pristine fashion malls of Turin and the beautiful Milan Cathedral along the way, and ending in Reggio Emilia – home of gastronomic favourite Balsamic vinegar – the following Saturday.

With two free days in the schedule, and none of us having visited before, we clubbed together to give Malcolm a bonus in return for taking us on a daytrip to Venice. After doing the tourist trail and buying the obligatory carnival mask miniatures to take home to Nicki, I bumped into Brendan and Lisa towards the end of the afternoon and we decided to get a meal in before we were due back at the bus. All the restaurants in the central area looked very formulaic, very expensive and very full – we wanted an authentic trattoria frequented by locals. Jeff and Stella had to leave earlier in the day, so we were now unchaperoned. Brendan stopped a small, older woman weighed down by bulging shopping bags almost as big as her. She spoke no English and Brendan was trying the classic 'Brit abroad' approach of speaking in English very slowly and over-enunciating the words – we believe this makes us understandable anywhere on the planet. Eventually, and apparently based on recognition of the single word 'Ristorante' combined with Brendan's best eating mime, the woman signalled with a flick of her head that we should follow her, and set off into the backstreets at a pace we could just about keep up with.

On and on we followed her, twisting and turning through ever narrowing streets and alleys, wondering how we'd ever find our way back. Finally she paused, turned and indicated a small restaurant on the opposite corner of the street with another slight flick of her head, and was gone. We found ourselves a table, but the menu was useless to us as it had never anticipated being consulted by foreigners. With more sign language and the odd mutually recognisable word, we managed to place our orders. It turned out that the regional speciality of the Venice area is squid/calamari in ink with polenta. It was the first time I'd eaten it – I've had it many times since and it's become a firm favourite, but I'm not sure ever as good as that first time. Lisa recalls this adventure a little differently to me. . .

> I remember that night in Venice, it was freezing cold. We did walk, you, Brendan, and I, and we met with two young Italians, a man and a woman. I remember her black hair and red lipstick, all dressed in black; she was beautiful. I can't remember his face, but they were rich-looking punks. They had been to our concert, so they recognised us.
>
> The restaurant was tiny and we went down stairs into a candlelit room. I can still see you with a white wall behind you. I remember being horrified and fascinated by your dish; it was a pasta with a rectangular block of bright yellow polenta and black sauce. You said it was squid ink. I couldn't understand why you would eat such a terrible thing – I was silently horrified. I remember we walked back through the damp little streets with the sound of dripping water.

. . . take your pick!

On Tuesday, 17 November, we played the only gig of my times with DCD in Switzerland – at the Rote Fabrik Theatre in Zurich – before heading on for the German leg of the tour with three of the five shows taking us back to venues we'd played the previous year, including another traversal of East Germany to reach West Berlin and play The Loft. We had a little more time than the previous year and went to visit the Wall where there were wooden viewing platforms to climb onto and peer over. It was a very strange experience to look into East Berlin, across the barbed-wire delineated 'no-man's-land' between the streets and the wall, guarded by armed soldiers on foot and in watchtowers, and see this other Germany of bowed people trudging through their colourless environment only a matter of yards away. It felt wrong to be treating them as a 'tourist attraction', and we didn't linger.

Fig. 16. Poster for DCD's show at La Gaité, Brussels on 28 October 1987.

Arriving back in London, we had our final show of the year to prepare for – and one of particular resonance for me. One of the first prime central London venues I was taken to as a child by my parents was Sadlers Wells Theatre in Islington, then home to the D'Oyly Carte Opera Company, famed for its productions of Gilbert and Sullivan light operas. Back then I would've chuckled at the antics of Nanki Poo in 'The Mikado', and sung along with 'I am the very model of a modern Major-General' in *The Pirates of Penzance*. I'd long since grown away from all that, but it was a surprise to learn that we'd been booked to play the theatre which remained principally a home of opera and increasingly ballet/dance, and I was excited about it.

On starting the soundcheck, I found that as soon as I started playing the bass/kick drum, it set off down the stage in a manner I hadn't experienced before. I repositioned it and started again – same thing. It transpired that the stage at Sadlers Wells is purposely sloped. It's a gentle slope, such that I hadn't been aware of it while setting up, but once you become aware of it you realise it's actually quite pronounced. It's apparently not uncommon for stages primarily used for dance to slope forwards (i.e. downward from back to front), and is also used in some theatres to create an extra illusion of perspective. All very interesting, but now a problem to stop my drums running off, and we had to obtain permission for me to nail wood blocks to the stage floor in front of some of my drums and stands.

A R Kane were with us again for this show, and Rudi and Alex seemed remarkably unaffected by all the fallout from 'Pump Up The Volume'. It was a little strange to have them supporting us in the midst of their global chart success, but of course, their A R Kane set bore no relation to M|A|R|R|S and perhaps many of the audience were unaware even of the connection.

Nicki came to the show, heavily pregnant with less than nine weeks until she was due. Our unborn responded actively to the sonic frequencies of Colin's bass and was kicking away vigorously in the stalls – perfectly in time, of course. Those final weeks after Sadlers Wells flew by, and on 6 February 1988, in the less than glamorous location of a bathroom floor in the London Hospital at Mile End, Nicki gave birth to our first daughter. We called her Louise, and when I left mother and daughter resting an hour or two later, I was walking on air through the streets of East London.

Fig. 17. Slipping a day's sight-seeing in Venice into our European tour schedule, November 1987. Left to right: Stella Robertis, DCD fan/friend, me, Lisa and Brendan strolling across Piazza San Marco. Photo by Jeffrey Earp.

SEVEN

I was filled with wonderment at the tiny being who'd taken over our lives. I was sleeves up, changing nappies, sterilising bottles, rocking her to sleep, proudly taking her out in the buggy – totally smitten. It was also time to take my share of responsibility and learn to drive. I was never interested in cars for cars' sake, having always preferred to spend my money on instruments and records. But now I needed to share duties with Nicki, and a few weeks after Louise arrived I passed my driving test and bought my first car, which immediately also proved so useful for moving band gear around, I wondered how I'd ever managed without it.

Just before Louise was born, I was invited back for another percussion session with Wolfgang Press, this time at Smokehouse Studio in Wapping, to guest on the appropriately titled track 'Swing Like a Baby', which would feature on their album *Bird Wood Cage* released later in the year. As Brendan and Lisa worked on new material for the next DCD album in their ever-expanding home studio in Bowsprit Point, across the way in Knighthead I had the beginnings of my own studio coming together. Brendan was handing down bits of equipment to me as he upgraded his setup – I now had the Yamaha CX-5 which enabled me to start composing, and I'd also invested in a four-track cassette recorder. Lisa lent me her yang ch'in, on which I wrote a song called 'Smiling She Rose', and Brendan helped me arrange a trumpet-led song called 'Marriage of Minds'. Peter Hicks called by regularly and helped with some of the recording, but dubbed me 'the swinging vicar' on account of what he considered my choir-boy vocal delivery.

The CX-5 had some good built-in tuned percussion sounds – xylophone and marimba – which I used as the basis for a song called 'Rainforest', and I was moved by some contemporary news footage to write a song about the plight of a child soldier – an early version of a song called 'Taqaharu's Leaving'. I compiled a demo-cassette, added my own simple cover design and sent it to Ivo, but my voice didn't appeal to him. The demos were very rough and ready such that I didn't feel sufficiently confident to go 'cold-calling' around other labels with the tape, so there the adventure ended for the time being.

Brendan and Lisa were back in Woodbine Studios in May, working again with producer John Rivers on the next album. I helped with transporting gear up there before leaving them to it. But then I heard things weren't going to plan. It was almost a reprise of the old issues from our early Blackwing sessions – Brendan was getting mixes he was happy with in the studio, but when taking them away to check on other systems, they sounded all out of balance, totally lifeless. When Brendan confronted John over the problem, he confessed that he'd turned the studio monitors upside down – apparently some kind of funky techie experiment (?) – so all the while in the control room, the treble frequencies had been coming to them at ear level, while all the bass was going straight over their heads! Brendan was apoplectic over the time and energy wasted and walked out.

Urgent discussions were convened with Ivo, in which it was agreed that 4AD would advance DCD the funds to build a fully-fledged home studio as a preferable alternative to continuing to shell out for studio hire fees. The following day found Brendan in the Argent's Music Store in Denmark Street – London's 'Tin Pan Alley' – with a twenty grand budget burning a hole in his pocket. He splashed the cash and within days the now legendary thirteenth-floor flat in Bowsprit Point was fully kitted out. And that's where the new album was recorded, with the exception of 'The Host of Seraphim' which was already at an advanced stage at Woodbine, and needed the facilities there for its completion. So Lisa returned to Woodbine and worked again with John to obtain a workable final mix.

'The Host of Seraphim' was destined to become one of DCD's signature tracks, a glorious showcase of the development of both Lisa's vocal technique and Brendan's orchestral arranging. In a reflective interview many years later with Glen Johnson (more of Glen further down the line), Brendan provided the following insight, in response to being asked about the emotional response which DCD is capable of inducing in so many listeners:

> We kind of strive to do that, especially in songs where there's less cognitive stuff to work on, like lyrics. So, it tends to happen more so in Lisa's songs where it's not so much about the words, where it's more emotive voice and instruments. It's a very special place, a very special emotion to tap into but you can't predict when it's going to happen. It's when all the elements come together. There's a specific moment. With 'Host', when I was putting the string arrangement down, I was working from the bass upwards – that's the way a lot of baroque composers work

too – the basso continuo, when the organ pedals were played by foot. I put that down and thought that sounds nice, the drone but once it started moving, I had a chord above the bass and then the basic counterpoint and then you just overlay it and with every pass, it's something new. You just go with the flow – it's like a river, music when it's working and you're on this raft, floating downstream and you feel great, everything around you looks wonderful and you completely forget about your surroundings. And then the cello and the strings and you haven't planned it and this is when you get these amazing meshes of harmony and dynamics.

In the same interview, Brendan goes on to recount an unexpected issue which arose during the mastering session:

We had real problems cutting 'The Host of Seraphim' onto vinyl. We like a lot of stereo panning and the bass was really heavy but the dynamics were so rapid that every time the needle got to that point, it would jump out of the groove. We had to sacrifice quite a lot of audio quality to make it work on vinyl so – and I don't normally say this – it's best heard on CD, that one.

With recording completed, we did some preliminary work on which of the new pieces would be included in the set for a tour being scheduled by Jeff Craft for later in the year before an entirely new project came on the scene which levered Lisa in particular, and Brendan to a lesser extent, away to Barcelona over the next few months. Lisa had accepted a lead acting role in a film being made by Spanish director Agustí Villaronga called *El Niño de la Luna* (*Child of the Moon*), for which Brendan and Lisa would also compose the soundtrack. The film would be released the following year and was accepted as an entry to the prestigious Cannes Film Festival in 1989, but despite that, it didn't break through onto the mainstream cinema circuit and remains something of an underground cult production.

As so often happens, the filming overran its schedule and it started to become touch-and-go for Brendan and Lisa to return in time for rehearsals for our November tour. Back in London, I was plunged into a family panic over Nicki's mum Jean – a wonderful woman who we all adored – who was seemingly in a positive recovery from treatment for cancer when she relapsed alarmingly and was rushed back into hospital. Nicki, her dad, and sisters were distraught and, with Louise to look after if Nicki was suddenly called away, it was clear there was no way I could contemplate disappearing on tour. I had to call Brendan and break the news to him. He was totally understanding and supportive, but being away from the situation, had to ask me to take charge of the process of finding a replacement drummer.

I placed a small ad in the NME for a drummer immediately available for a tour with a 'name band' and was a bit surprised to receive only three replies. I booked a rehearsal room at 20th Century Studios in Bethnal Green for Monday, 7 November and invited the three along at half hour intervals. In between making the booking and the day of the audition, we lost Jean. She was just forty-nine years old and Louise was the only one of her grandchildren she would ever see and hold. The sense of anger and utter bewilderment that such a lovely person with so much to live for can be taken by this sinister and pervasive disease is overwhelming.

I was still reeling when the day of the audition came, and thankfully had both Gus and Rob Lee, who had recently returned to the fold, come with me to help me through. The three respondents to my advertisement couldn't have been more different, and recounting this feels a bit like telling the story of Goldilocks and the three bears. The first guy was simply a beginner who couldn't yet hold a basic beat in time. It was hard to imagine what made him think he was ready for the level he'd applied for – he didn't even have the air of someone whose supreme self-confidence enables them to believe they have ability way beyond the reality. We gave him a polite five minutes and said we'd let him know. Number two was the opposite end of the spectrum – an experienced session drummer who copied the drum parts I'd laboured to learn with a nonchalant ease – but to the extent that he gave the impression of being bored to the verge of nodding off. Gus, Rob, and I exchanged glances, clearly all thinking exactly the same – that Brendan would have his hands round this guy's throat within two minutes. He seemed as glad to leave as we were to see the back of him. Number three had some experience playing with a band that had released a couple of indie singles and was much more in our zone. He struggled a little to get to grips with the drum parts – but in much the same way I had initially, and I could see he'd get there as I had done. The job was his.

A few days later I was driving gear down to Quay Sounds rehearsal studios in Greenwich. Brendan had just made it back from Barcelona by road trip, sharing the driving with Javier Navarrete, an aspiring composer he and Lisa had met in Spain and who was being initiated into the DCD lineup for the tour; Lisa was due back a day or two later. The band now also included keyboardist John Bonnar – recruited from the Bonnington Square brigade – together with Colin Cairns on bass, Robbie Perry on whatever he was needed to play, and Rob Lee handling the out-front sound engineer duties.

I'd given our replacement drummer the dates, times, and locations, and we waited for him to show up . . . but he didn't, and our efforts to reach him by phone failed. We started rehearsals with me drumming, and hoped he'd appear the following day, but again no sign of him and no contact. The 4AD office was now involved, trying to track him down via his regular band's label. By day three it was clear he'd blown out and gone to ground. Brendan had a decision to make, and in true Perry family style, turned to his brother and simply said 'You'll have to do it,' to which Robbie replied equally simply 'OK' and jumped onto the drum stool. Robbie was amazing – he picked up all the parts in no time and, although his drumming style was a little too fluid for some of the more rigid beats, it provided Brendan with ammunition for periodic bouts of brotherly castigation, and the DCD roadshow took shape. It gave me some comfort that my replacement had come from within our ranks, but it was still with a heavy heart that I waved them off on the tour without me.

DCD's fourth album *The Serpent's Egg* had been released a few weeks earlier – 24 October 1988 – the name taken from the title of a 1977 Ingmar Bergman film which, in turn, is taken from a line in William Shakespeare's *Julius Caesar*, the cover an aerial image of a serpentine tributary of the River Amazon. The schedule for the tour to support the release was:

Belgium:
Sunday, 27 November Brussels, Ancienne Belgique

Netherlands:
Monday, 28 November, Utrecht, Muziekcentrum Vredenburg

France:
Thursday, 1 December, Bordeaux, Salle du Grand Parc
Friday, 2 December, Toulouse, Theatre des Mazades
Saturday, 3 December, Lyon, Le Truc
Monday, 5 December, Paris, Elysee Montmartre

Germany:
Wednesday, 7 December, Munich, Fabrik
Thursday, 8 December, Wiesbaden, Kurhaus
Saturday, 10 December, Hamburg, Audimax
Sunday, 11 December, Berlin, Quartier Latin

Austria:
Tuesday, 13 December, Vienna, Arena

Italy:
Wednesday, 14 December, Udine, Auditorium Zanon

Thursday, 15 December, Bologne, Sala Europa
Friday, 16 December, Firenze, Casa del Popolo di Grassina
Sunday, 18 December, Milan, Teatro Ciak

France:
Monday, 19 December Marseille, Espace Julien
Tuesday, 20 December, Paris, Elysee Montmartre

Of a couple of incidents recounted to me after the tour, the first was at the Kurhaus in Wiesbaden, Germany, which turned out to be a grand and imposing building, fronted by six great Corinthian columns and a frieze featuring carved gryphons, and set in grounds with a tiered fountain and 'bowling green' lawns. Seemingly inspired by this lavish display of classicism, much of the audience had turned out in elaborate Victorian evening dress, replete with top hats and canes.

In marked contrast, across the border in the Austrian capital, the Arena reputedly started life in the early twentieth century as an 'urban slaughterhouse for pigs'. In the 1970s it became a theatre/arts space and by the 1980s had become an established music venue with a reputation for attracting anarchists and Satanists. The local chapter of Hell's Angels had been given the role of stewarding, possibly as a means of discouraging them from disrupting events (I seem to recall there was a notorious Rolling Stones show where a similar tactic didn't go to plan). When the audience filed in, a strange group of five or six figures shrouded in voluminous monk's habits with tall pointed hoods positioned themselves centre-front by the stage and went into a choreographed swaying routine once DCD's performance started. The effect was distracting to both band and audience, and after a while Lisa decided to take matters into her own hands and threw a potful of lukewarm tea over them from the stage. Cue the Hell's Angels to spring into action and Brendan recalls the bizarre scene of these heavies, wearing polished chrome-plated German military helmets, dragging out the fake friars by their be-sandaled feet. After the show, the local promoter told the band that the expelled group had formed themselves into a cult with Lisa nominated as their high-priestess – the ex-church lectern which Lisa had by now taken to using as a stand for her yang ch'in had proved irresistible for their private ceremony.

Otherwise it seemed all had gone smoothly enough; gigs had been as well-attended as ever, *The Serpent's Egg* was selling strongly, the general upward momentum was maintained, and I put behind me the disappointment of missing the tour. I also had a new project to occupy my thoughts, having placed an order with a supplier in Hong Kong for a consignment of musical instruments manufactured in China. The idea had been in my head ever since Lisa first told me that one of her yang ch'ins had come from Hong Kong and cost the equivalent of about thirty pounds. I thought to start up my own independent instrument wholesale and retail business under the name 'Full Circle Music'. These were pre-internet days, but somehow I'd identified and established 'fax' contact with a supplier. The prices were very low, though admittedly the quality was 'variable'. I included a few items for my own use – a yang ch'in (of course), a yuet ch'in (moon guitar), an erhu (two string fiddle), and a guzheng (a long, multistringed zither, similar to the Japanese koto). The consignment also included a range of Wu-Han brand classic 'China-type' cymbals and a few gongs – the largest of which was 36" in diameter and could create an earth-shattering crescendo – a selection of marching bass and side drums, and some beginner level classical guitars and violins. After sorting the UK customs clearance, I took a delivery a couple of days before Christmas and had to pacify Nicki who suddenly found our flat transformed into a warehouse.

As a commercial enterprise Full Circle Music didn't make the cut, but it got me some additional instruments I'd long wanted and also brought me into contact with a guy called Keith Lowe who was based in Greenwich, traded under the name Salamander Music, and was an established importer and distributor of Egyptian percussion. He'd commissioned and was retailing an educational video showing how to play a range of Arabic percussion featuring Tim Garside, a well-known musician on the UK's North African and Middle Eastern music scene, which gave me some useful guidelines. I ended up trading a few instruments with Keith, via which I acquired my first darabuka (Arabic goblet drum) – a really nice, heavy, metal-shelled drum from Alexandria.

In late March 1989 we began preparations in earnest for the next DCD tour with a significant upgrade to our rehearsal space, transferring to No-mis Studios across London, located in a maze of streets tucked behind the Olympia event halls in Kensington. Nomis had been set up in the late 1970s by Simon Napier-Bell who variously managed a string of big names from the Yardbirds and Marc Bolan to Japan and Wham! He converted the studio complex at considerable expense from a former Victorian dairy which had the natural sound proofing provided by two-feet-thick walls and ceilings. The cost reportedly overstretched Napier-Bell and his partners who were forced to sell out to Sanctuary Group, but nevertheless he achieved his aim to create a state-of-the-art rehearsal hub which was used by an array of global superstars – the Rolling Stones, Tina Turner, Dire Straits et al – and now DCD.

I'd upgraded to a larger car and was chauffeuring back and forth from the Isle of Dogs. One morning, as we turned off North End Road onto Hammersmith Road just in front of Olympia, another car changed lanes without warning and cut me up, causing me to brake hard and swerve to avoid a collision. In a fit of road rage, I chased after the other driver, got alongside him, shot the window down beside Lisa who was in the front passenger seat beside me, leant across her and screamed 'Fucking dickhead!' at the offender who returned in kind before the traffic moved on. I calmed down again, but then became aware that Lisa was staring at me, frozen statue-like, with her bottom jaw dropped as far as it could go. I was supposed to be the calm one who sailed serenely through all situations, and in the seven years she'd known me, she'd never seen such an outburst. Although clearly shocked, I think she was also quietly impressed. I think it must have also been around this time – though I don't recall what prompted it – that Lisa told me I'm the 'most English' person she'd ever met. I think it was an impartial observation, but I took it as a compliment.

The lineup for the tour was Brendan, Lisa, me, Colin Cairns on bass, John Bonnar and Javier Navarrete on keyboards, and Rob Lee on the sound desk again. Our 'go-to' stage monitor supremo, Rene de Zoute, was in the party to provide continuity to the onstage sound balance, which was a big comfort for Brendan and Lisa in particular. On 4 April we left for a tour which sandwiched just two dates in Italy between a string of shows in France:

France:
Wednesday, 5 April, Rennes, Salle Jean Vilar
Friday, 7 April, Bourges, Pavillon D'Auron

Italy:
Wednesday, 12 April, Turin, Teatro Colosseo
Thursday, 13 April, Milan, Teatro Orfeo

France:
Saturday, 15 April, Nice, Theatre de Verdure
Monday, 17 April, Marseille, Espace Julien
Tuesday, 18 April, Montpellier, Mas des Grilles
Thursday, 20 April, Clermont-Ferrand, Maison du Peuple
Friday, 21 April, Grenoble, Le Summum
Sunday, 23 April, Mulhouse, Le Phoenix
Monday, 24 April, Strasbourg, Palais des Fetes
Wednesday, 26 April, Reims, Theatre du Chemin Vert
Thursday, 27 April, Rouen, Espace Duchamp Villon

Our French road crew were a good-time bunch, comprising sound guys Gilles Gautrois and Jean Jacques Terrones, and superb lighting designer Jean Luc 'Rosko' Jacquinot. They rose admirably to the challenges posed by DCD's array of instruments which, alongside guitars, drums and percussion, keyboards, and Lisa's two yang ch'ins now included a lap mandolin, two piano accordions, a saz (Turkish guitar), a concert whistle, flageolet and shawm, and a hurdy-gurdy. Amongst the percussion added for this tour was one of my Chinese gongs. During rehearsals back at Nomis, I had the idea to construct a stand from plumbing fittings and had bought lengths of copper pipe plus various brass elbows and straight connectors from the local builders' merchants. Although a bit cumbersome (and heavy!), it did the job, and my assembly and dismantling of the gong stand became a feature of setups and breakdowns before and after shows, much to the amusement of the stage crew, who took to calling me 'le plombier'.

The tour started at the Salle Jean Vilar, the principal space in the National Theatre of Bretagne, in the beautiful city of Rennes. Next up was a return to the 'Printemps de Bourges' Festival which we'd previously played with the Cocteaus in 1985. Back then we played the nine-hundred-capacity Grand Theatre; this time we were in the festival's second-largest venue – the three-thousand-capacity Pavillon – so some measure of our progress. We were excited to be sharing the bill with Uilleann piper (Irish bagpipes) Davy Spillane but ultimately disappointed that he chose to perform a middle-of-the-road rock set rather than the more ethereal Celtic folk side of his repertoire. The Pavillon had hosted Dr John a couple of nights before us, and had Womack and Womack due a couple of nights after, while the lineup for the biggest venue – the Bourges Stadium – included over the course of the festival Kool & The Gang, Stevie Wonder, Nina Simone, and, in a somewhat different vein, a night of Nick Cave & the Bad Seeds plus The Pogues.

En route between Rennes and Bourges, we'd detoured via Paris for a personal appearance and signing session at the flagship FNAC record store, organised by Virgin Records, who were 4AD's French distributor at the time. Brendan was in no mood for it, but Lisa was up for it, provided she didn't have to go alone, so asked me to accompany her. I was happy to, even though we both knew she would have to deal with being the focus of all attention. A taxi was summoned to take us across town, which turned out to be one of the most terrifying experiences of both our lives. The driver had been given a deadline and was already running late even before we dived into the grindingly slow Paris traffic. He proceeded to accelerate wildly into every minute gap that appeared, immediately then having to slam on his brakes, shouting and horn-honking all the while, mounting kerbs, and at one point even drove along a section of the pavement/sidewalk. Lisa and I sat in dumbfounded silence, rolling our eyes at one another and gradually sinking down behind the seats. When we eventually arrived at our destination – the car somehow unscathed – we crawled out feeling like a pair of boxers who'd just shared a points decision after twelve rounds.

We were ushered clandestinely into FNAC via a back entrance and upstairs to a reception area. Over a calming cup of tea, we were informed that there were 'hundreds' of fans downstairs waiting and that DCD's current album – *The Serpent's Egg* – had been their biggest-selling album ever on its first day of release in the store, overtaking a record previously set by Michael Jackson's *Thriller*. Lisa and I were once again struck dumb, looking at each other wide-eyed. To this day, I'm not sure if we misheard or misunderstood something, but before we could question it, we were whisked downstairs to the signing desk, set in front of a backdrop of *Serpent's Egg* cover artworks, and the flow of fans began. Even without us playing a show in Paris, the queue was out of the doors and 'round the block – several hundred people, many in goth uniform, and a fair few decked out to mirror Lisa's typical stage appearance, some managing to look almost more 'Lisa' than their heroine herself. Lisa handled it brilliantly, smiling, chatting, and dispensing pearls of wisdom, while I pretty much stood by providing moral support (or so I like to think).

Following the Bourges Festival, we had an unusually long four-day break for which we were booked to stay a couple of nights in St Raphael on the south coast, close to where we'd played the Fréjus festival a couple of years back. We arrived to find a lovely, slightly ramshackle old hotel in classic French style with wooden shutters on the windows, and situated almost on the beach. That evening, to placate a rumbling stomach, I unusually opted not to head for the local bars with 'the lads', but instead went with Lisa in search of food. We found ourselves a quiet restaurant, chatted over a leisurely meal, then returned to the hotel relatively early. Not knowing where my roommates had gone (not yet carrying personal phones), I decided to turn in. I was woken abruptly sometime later by a commotion as the rest of the entourage came in, all dripping wet. After a bar crawl, they'd hit the beach, demolished a bottle of Jack D, then spotted a stack of unsecured pedalos. Unable to resist the temptation, they 'borrowed' one, launched themselves onto the Med, and, spotting an American battleship moored in the bay, decided the obvious thing was to storm it. Having pedalled some distance out, they suddenly capsized. Rapidly sobering up, fully clothed, in the water, in the dark, and a good stretch from shore, Brendan vividly recalls the panic, particularly for a couple of the lads who couldn't swim. One had actually gone under and only quick reactions by Rob – diving under and hauling him up – prevented tragedy. Eventually they managed to haul themselves back to the beach and up to the hotel where an astonished (and decidedly unamused) concierge watched them file in. When we went down to breakfast the following morning, there was a distinct salt trail along the hotel's corridor and stair carpets, and I was quietly thankful I'd given that one a miss.

The tour resumed and we headed east into Italy. Javier was providing the support act, and some scribbling in Italian on the back of an old schedule I kept seems to be notes that one of the promoters had used to introduce his act – a single piece called 'La Litania del Fuoco' receiving its first public performance in Italia. In stark contrast to Javier's Litany of Fire, it poured with rain nonstop for over twenty-four hours, and as we departed Italy we looked out from the tour bus over vast tracts of flooded farmlands. Back across the border into France and along the coast to Nice where we played in a large tent, or marquee, on the seafront. A group at the back of the audience started heckling during the performance, shouting out 'Acieeed' – presumably in homage to an underground club track doing the rounds at the time, 'We call it Acieeed' by D Mob feat. Gary Heisman, but absurdly irrelevant to a DCD performance and a killer for some of the quieter and more fragile parts of our set. Brendan was highly agitated by the disruption and, when the local promoters failed to stamp it out, he walked off stage in protest. By a twist of fate, UK music paper *Melody Maker* had sent reviewer Ian Gittins and a photographer out to cover just the show in Nice, but fortunately Ian was supportive and made the best of it for us.

Our next leg of the tour took us through Clermont Ferrand – dramatically set amidst the Chaîne des Puys volcanic mountains – and on into the eastern regions of France towards its borders with Switzerland and Germany, an area of France we hadn't previously covered. There's a markedly different feel to these eastern borderlands, with their Germanic influences, taking us through to the Palais des Fetes in Strasbourg, an unusual venue, built in 1903 to provide a home for the city's male choral society. Onwards north to Reims – known as the capital of the Champagne region – and then west to Rouen in Normandy, both these final destinations featuring magnificent gothic cathedrals. Everything was running remarkably smoothly. Three days later – on Sunday, 30 April – we were back at the Town & Country Club in London in what now felt like an established tour-ender. On this occasion, Javier was performing a composition called 'Whale Songs' and there was a guest appearance by Shelleyan Orphan – essentially, the duo of singer Caroline Crawley and guitarist Jemaur Tayle. Shelleyan Orphan were signed to Rough Trade at the time, but Ivo would subsequently invite Caroline to sing on four tracks on This Mortal Coil's third and final album *Blood*, so the seeds of a 4AD connection were being sown.

The tour established John Bonnar as a regular member of the DCD entourage for some time to come. By contrast, it would be Javier Navarrete's second and last tour with the band, following which he pursued his solo work and has gone on to achieve international acclaim as the composer of some notable film soundtracks, including *Pan's Labyrinth*, *Byzantium*, and *Wrath of the Titans*.

After the tour we returned to our largely separate routines. Although there'd been no point at which I was aware of an official 'split', I think it's fair to say that Brendan and Lisa's personal relationship was over by this stage (and possibly had been for some while). There was still a connection between them, a bond that in some ways was probably as strong as ever – but at the same time a realisation that that they could no longer cohabit under the same roof. They worked on their music almost entirely separately, and I occasionally got together with one or other of them to develop a few ideas, but the need for them to be in geographical proximity was gone. Lisa decided to return to Barcelona where she'd been based while making the film the previous year and had loved the city. It seemed strange that she was no longer just across The Quarterdeck in Bowsprit Point, but I don't recall feeling that the future of Dead Can Dance was under threat.

The effect on Brendan was that he withdrew even further into the hermitic refuge of his home studio. I sensed he didn't want to discuss Lisa's leaving, so I let it ride. Musically, as ever, he was exploring new territories. We were listening to a lot of 'early' music by this stage – European medieval and Renaissance period – and discovering its astonishing range of everything from mesmeric, floating, polyphonic choral pieces to wild, cavorting songs featuring exotic instruments like serpents, sackbuts, and the aforementioned hurdy-gurdy along with a range of percussion, much of which is from Turkish and wider Arabic descent as a result of such instruments being brought back to Europe by knights returning from the crusades. But although we continued to share our discoveries with each other and discuss sources, Brendan more than ever wanted to write his music in isolation, so he and I tended to connect more over football.

Both our teams had been doing well in the old First Division, but while Norwich's season had faded near the end, Arsenal's finished on a knife edge. (*Note: if your eyes glaze over when football reminiscences kick in, please skip this paragraph.*) Liverpool were top, Arsenal second, and in their final game, the two were due to play each other at Liverpool's fortress stadium of Anfield where Arsenal would have to win by two clear goals to take the League title. The odds were stacked against the London club and the sympathies of most neutrals were with Liverpool as both Club and City struggled to deal with the aftermath of the terrible Hillsborough tragedy, which had happened only some six weeks earlier. On the evening of Friday, 26 May 1989, Brendan came over to watch his club's fate on TV, we got the requisite beers in, and I grudgingly agreed to be an Arsenal 'sympathiser' for the match duration. After a goalless first half, Arsenal scored and briefly their dream was alive, but as the ninety-minute mark passed, Liverpool fans were already in full celebration and Brendan was slumped dejectedly on our sofa. With seconds remaining, the ball fell into the path of Arsenal's Michael Thomas who found himself one-on-one with Liverpool keeper Bruce Grobbelaar. Momentarily the world stopped before Thomas flicked the ball over Grobbelaar into the Liverpool net. Arsenal fans everywhere exploded with unbridled joy and I found myself rolling around the floor of my living room in Brendan's full embrace. It was the moment Nick Hornby labels 'The Greatest Ever' in his book *Fever Pitch*, and you'd be hard pushed to find an Arsenal fan born pre-1980 who'd disagree. Naturally, I have a bulging kitbag full of preferred Norwich moments, but nevertheless, sharing that experience with Brendan is a fond memory (with apologies to John Peel (in memoriam) and my various Spurs-supporting mates).

As Brendan and Lisa settled to independently writing material for what would become the fifth DCD album, *Aion*, I was becoming musically restless having written the few songs of my own that were sitting on the proverbial shelf. I called John Rivers at Woodbine and sounded him out about costs and feasibility of recording a couple of my songs with a view to releasing a self-funded 12" single. Although DCD's relationship with John had cooled, I still felt I'd be comfortable recording at Woodbine. I didn't have the money, but I was formulating a proposal to my bank for a loan. It'd be a long shot, and I didn't really hold out much hope of the bank agreeing – funding arts projects rarely strikes bankers as a smart investment – but I'd been with the 'NatWest' since I was eighteen, had a well-managed account history, and I had my connections with DCD and 4AD to give me credibility. So in late November 1989 I submitted my application, which included a business plan and cash-flow forecast based on predicted sales of ten thousand singles. The bank responded not with the anticipated instant rejection, but with a request for some further details, then followed this up with an invitation to attend what turned out to be a cordial meeting. Although the amount of my application was a big sum to me, to the bank it would be modest, so there were grounds for optimism. After another exchange of correspondence, a letter arrived granting an overdraft facility of nine thousand pounds at an eye-watering 'minimum' interest rate of 14 percent. Today, that would frighten the life out of me, but back then I had no doubt I could conquer the world and I was off and running.

Meetings were rapidly arranged – I went up to Woodbine to discuss my recording plans with John, I went to Mayking Records in Battersea (the vinyl pressing plant used by 4AD) to line up the manufacture, I met up with John Singleton (who I'd kept in touch with after the 1986 DCD tour) to discuss him playing trombone and putting me in contact with oboist Ruth Watson who recorded with DCD on *Within The Realm*, I lined up the mastering and cut of the record with Tape One in Soho, and I went to St Albans to visit old friends Chuck and Ange Silverman – two wonderful folk musicians I'd known since college days who I wanted to sing with me on the recordings. Everyone was enthusiastic and the pieces of my jigsaw slotted neatly into place.

I decided the two songs to be recorded would be 'Taqaharu's Leaving' and 'Evocation', the latter a new piece using a similar formula to 'At First, and Then', but extended into a longer composition with vocals and other instrumentation. My record label would be called 'Corner Stone Records' because it was the first block laid in the empire I was going to build. I had grand visions of following in Ivo's footsteps, not only releasing my own music but also that of other emerging artists I would discover and provide an outlet for. I was buzzing with excitement and Christmas and New Year passed in something of a blur. My session was confirmed for the week of Monday, 22 January, and I was counting the days.

The week before, Brendan came over to dinner with me and Nicki and told us he too had decided to leave the Isle of Dogs. A few years back his parents had settled in his mother's hometown of Cavan in Ireland and he'd decided to follow on and grab himself a slice of the beautiful and inspiring Irish countryside. County Cavan forms part of Ireland's 'Lake District' and the scenery is spectacular so, with no longer any need to be based in a high-rise council flat in London, it was really a no-brainer. It would certainly be strange not to have either Brendan or Lisa just across the way from us anymore, but work was to continue on the new album and plans were starting to be made for the next tour, so still I felt no threat to the continuation of DCD.

I arrived at Woodbine the following Monday, car crammed with various drums, percussion, a selection of bamboo flutes, and an 'angklung' – a curious Indonesian instrument like a miniature set of tubular bells made of bamboo –

which I'd recently found in an Oxfam charity shop. The session started with just me, John 'in the chair', and a young engineering trainee called Adam. It suddenly struck me as strange that I'd been to Woodbine numerous times with DCD, I knew John and his studio set up well, and yet all I'd ever recorded here was one roll on the military snare and a small timpani part. Yet now here I was, the epicentre of the entire week's sessions. 'Taqaharu's Leaving' made a good starting point – it has a simple structure which enabled us to progress quickly and efficiently. We programmed the drums as it suits the song to have a very rigid rhythm and the sampled drum/percussion sounds we selected were a better fit than the acoustic options I had (yup, influence of a certain Mr Perry right from the off). Layered on top of that, the whole song works off a repeated three chord progression, for which I wanted a rich orchestral sound to create a solemn, processional feel. John sequenced the part with a big strings sample, but then we looked for something to further enrich the sound. John came up with a saxophone sample, but set some way below the instrument's natural register. He blended it with the strings and it sounded mighty over the studio monitors (thankfully, by now, the right way up again!). Then we were ready for my debut on vocals, for which John produced a prized new microphone which had apparently cost him ten thousand pounds – a lot now, but back in 1990 . . . ! If he could make my relatively thin and one-dimensional voice sound good, he'd be my hero.

I'd expected to be more nervous, but because I was in control – it was my session – and I had so many things to occupy my mind, I didn't really notice any jitters. I asked John to be a harsh judge of what he was hearing – not to go easy on me but to keep making me do retakes until he was happy with each phrase. Even so, we progressed at a good rate once I'd warmed into the process, and when I went through to the control room and listened back to what we had, I was amazed to hear what he'd achieved with his super-mic and a dollop of 'reverb' effect. I added the gong crash in the middle of the song, and its shape was coming together nicely.

We set 'Taqaharu' aside for the moment and I started laying down drum tracks for 'Evocation'. Here the approach was totally different – this was going to be an organic piece with pretty much everything performed acoustically. I wanted it to be a mix of elements – partly inspired by Olatunji, partly a progression of ideas in 'At First, and Then' (including the way Brendan had developed it for DCD's live performances), and partly harking back to the discovery that had fascinated my teenage self of drum rituals that can induce trance. Lyrically, the slower first part was to be an invocation of the spirits, while the pounding second part would feature a constantly repeated phrase to be evocative of the trancelike state. In between the two, instrumentally, there would be a moment of frenzy in which the spirit possesses the body. So, I laid down a bunch of drum/percussion tracks to give us the outline shape of the piece to build on.

Fig. 18. My cover illustration for the 'Taqaharu's Leaving/Evocation' single, done with pen, ink, and watercolour, all in mono/greyscale, 1990. Art by Peter Ulrich.

The following day we were back to 'Taqaharu' as my additional participants began to arrive. Although I'd spoken to her by phone when making the arrangements, I'd never actually met Ruth Watson before – and now I had this professional oboist performing a part I'd written under my direction. Hearing the human expression added to the performance of what had only previously been a part sketched with a sampled sound was a joy – wow, these were big moments happening in my life, and maybe I was now experiencing the same kind of thrill Brendan had when he first heard his programmed orchestral parts being played by the musicians he brought in. Chuck and Ange arrived – and would be staying for a couple of days – and we started adding vocal parts in the end section of the song. Chuck and I sang the lower parts, for which his richer, deeper voice was much better suited, but the two voices together created a nice overall breadth. Then I gave Ange free range to experiment, and she added some wonderful, soaring parts – even though she was later disappointed that some of the crescendo she built up to was lost in the fade-out which John and I subsequently programmed.

Back to 'Evocation', my old compatriot John Singleton pitched up and, as he readied his trombone, I asked him to give me marauding elephants – a task (I was tempted to say 'tusk') he rose to with aplomb. Then Chuck, Ange, and I started building the choral arrangement in the second part. I didn't have this preplanned – we were improvising parts as we went, but with Chuck's lower register, my mid-range, and Ange up high, the voices blended well. Before we knew it, we'd multilayered no less than seventeen vocal tracks. Each time we added a layer and John played back the developing effect to us over the monitors in the recording room, we were more excited, and inspired to add the next part. I was exhilarated and couldn't believe how it was coming together, like it had assumed its own life force. When we finally decided we'd laid down enough, we went through to the control room to hear the working mix on the main monitors and I was completely blown away – I must've slept the whole night with a beaming smile on my face.

'Evocation' needed a few finishing touches, mainly in the contemplative outro after the vocals finish. I added a marimba part on one of John's keyboards (one of only two sampled sounds we used), then a bamboo flute, and then the angklung, gently shaken, to create an effect like trickling water. The recording was done, and we moved on to mixing. John had been doing a lot of mix preparation as we'd been going along and it was all sounding amazing to me already. John gave me a few different effects and level balances to choose from in different parts, but we knew we were pretty much there, and by the end of the day on the Thursday we had both tracks 'in the can' as them good ol' studio boys like to say. On Friday morning we listened again with fresh ears, made a few minor adjustments, and then John set about making the two-track master for me to take to the cutting studio.

The following day I drove back to London with a handful of treasured cassette copies of my final mixes, stopping off in St Albans on the way to drop one off to Chuck and Ange. I then had to finish the cover artwork which I was doing myself in a naïve style to give the whole thing a handmade feel. 'Taqaharu' – a name I made up which, as far as I know, doesn't mean anything and is not specific to any race or culture – is a ten-year-old boy excitedly enlisting as a child soldier to the horror and fear of his mother who has already lost her husband and another son to futile conflict. I wanted the artwork to reflect the innocence of the child and the despair of his mother, both set against the beauty of their homeland and culture. And, although I made the name nonspecific, there is an intentional Arabic element to the design because the song was inspired by heart-rending accounts of the deployment of child soldiers in the Iran-Iraq war which was in the final throes of its eight year duration when I wrote the song, and that contrasts poignantly with my love of so much Arabic art, design, and music – the same contrast I tried to represent in the song itself.

The next few weeks were a flurry of activity – going to Tape One to have the record mastered and get the final cut, delivering the 'lacquers' and cover art to Mayking, studying contract offers from distributors Pinnacle and APT, applying for a barcode which had to be incorporated into the design of the back cover of the sleeve, checking the test pressings that came back from Mayking – the excitement of holding a 12" vinyl disc of my own songs in my hands for the first time and putting it onto the turntable! – designing the central labels for the discs, doing a photo-session in Victoria Park with my old mate Bob Bridges on camera duty so I had new artist pics to send out to the press, collecting purpose-designed record mailers ready for sending out my press copies, drafting my press release, compiling press lists, paying the up-front mechanical royalties to the MCPS (Mechanical Copyright Protection Society), adding my songs to the publishing deal I was already signed into as a member of DCD with Beggars Banquet's publishing arm, Momentum Music, notifying the songs to PRS (the Performing Rights Society), and on and on.

Amidst all this activity, Brendan dropped by our flat to say goodbye as he departed for Ireland. So, just as I was about to launch my first solo record, my musical mentor was making his getaway. Although he hadn't been directly involved in the process since helping me make the early demo of 'Taqaharu' a while back, it had always somehow been a comfort that he was close by. He left the keys with me to the flat in Bowsprit to deliver back to the Council's housing office for him. Before doing so, I couldn't resist one last visit. Rooms that had witnessed the creation of music held dear by more people in more places than we could ever have imagined now stood empty, and my footsteps echoed hollowly over the background hum of the city outside. It was hard to grasp that both Brendan and Lisa were gone from here for good, but they were, and life moved on.

On 16 March, I collected 800 records from Mayking along with 650 posters. The other 1,700 records (total pressing of 2,500) were collected by APT Distribution, who I'd decided to go with. I delivered 625 of the posters to a guy I knew from my old Riverside Studios days who did fly-posting around the streets of West London – not strictly legal, but he knew the less sensitive sites where it was tolerated. The records – mostly for my promo campaign – went back to the flat in Knighthead Point, so that Nicki and Louise once more found themselves living in a warehouse. Debbie at 4AD gave me an invaluable list of press contacts and my packages of records, press releases, and publicity photos started going out in daily batches from the local post office.

Weekly music paper *Sounds* gave a brief mention to my release in its 7 April issue, noting in tabloid 'double-entendre'-style, that it was produced by 'renowned indie knob-man John A Rivers along with Ulrich', and UK music trade mag *Music Week* listed the release in its New Singles column on 21 April alongside *Staring at the Sun* by 4AD stablemate Ultra Vivid Scene and Neil Young's 'Rockin' in the Free World', but frustratingly, neither publication deemed it worthy of review. And so it was that, with a marked absence of fanfare and anticipation, my debut single was released. Finally, the 5 May 1990 issue of *Melody Maker* ran a brief review in its new singles column by Jon Wilde which read:

> Somnambulistic epic, that might have starred Peter Ustinov and David Niven, in which ex-Dead Can Dance drummer tells of ten-year-old boy drawn into religious war with bold arrangements of oboe, trombone and flute. Strangely beguiling.

I was left guessing whether (a) Jon actually liked the record or not, and (b) if he knew something I didn't about my tenure of the DCD drumstool. The same day I did a phone interview with Ian Gittins which gave rise to a mini-feature in *Melody Maker* a few weeks later in which 'Taqaharu' was described as: 'a stately, haunting litany recited at funereal pace over bells and drums'.

In recent weeks I'd compiled various mailing lists of hundreds of targets – music press, national press, national radio stations, local radio, hospital radio stations, consumer magazines, record shops, record labels, music venues, and so on – and sent out heaps of promo singles, leaflets, posters, stickers, press releases, photos and letters, but seemingly all to no avail. The UK national newspapers and monthly music magazines all completely ignored the release, and radio airplay was nonexistent. After the huge effort – and expense – of my promo campaign, that was it. Nothing. No second chance. My release had passed virtually unnoticed. I was deflated and exhausted.

While I'd been bound up with my single release, Lisa had visited Ireland to work with Brendan on the new DCD album. Brendan had rented a large house in Bailieborough in County Cavan which now housed his studio. The bulk of the album was recorded here, with a brief trip to Woodbine for tracks 'The Arrival and the Reunion' and 'The End of Words'. On 11 June 1990, *Aion* was released. I got my copy from 4AD and found myself listening like an excited fan to songs that for the most part I'd never heard even the slightest element of before. This enabled me to be completely objective about my opinion – and I loved it. The cover, showing part of the wonderful Hieronymus Bosch painting 'The Garden of Earthly Delights', set the scene for the very specific influences of medieval and Renaissance musics that now appeared, including 'Saltarello' – a fourteenth-century Italian dance, 'The Song of The Sybil' – a sixteenth-century ballad from Catalonia, and 'Fortune Presents Gifts Not According to the Book' – setting to music the words of Spanish Baroque poet Luis de Góngora, while the album's instrumentation featured tenor and bass viols, bagpipes, and hurdy-gurdy.

It seemed to be finally becoming more broadly recognised in the media that Dead Can Dance was very much *not* an indie rock band, even though it still released albums on 4AD, featured in 'indie' charts, and hadn't entirely freed itself of playing venues on the rock circuit. It was becoming a sport in its own right to see the media trying to categorise the new release, one I spotted having come up with 'Neo-Classical Darkwave Neo-Medieval Folk', which trips sweetly off the tongue. It would become apparent that DCD was now not only inspiring other bands and artists who inhabited classifications including goth, 'ethereal', and 'darkwave', but also bands ploughing the very specific furrow of 'early' music while feeling newly enabled to combine authentic acoustic instruments with electronics and sampled sounds. The likes of Corvus Corax, QNTAL, and Faun (notably, all German bands) have been said to have followed in DCD's footsteps in this respect, though I don't know if those bands accept the influence.

I was in touch with Brendan as the next DCD tour was being planned for later in the year, and there was the exciting prospect of us heading across the Atlantic for the first time. Meanwhile, at the end of July I received a sales update from APT for *Taqaharu* – to date 574 'units', and even those were not definite sales. That was how many had been supplied to fulfill orders, but some were on sale-or-return so could yet come back into distributor stock. So much for my business plan and cashflow forecast, but I'd used only around half the overdraft facility up to this point, so it wasn't yet a cause for outright panic. If we were going to do a European and American DCD tour later in the year, that would hopefully give me some promo opportunities and maybe another chance to kickstart sales. I would at least be able to leaflet the venues we played.

Nicki discovered she was pregnant again – a brother or sister for Louise on the way. I was up in the clouds about that, but frustrated and despondent that *Taqaharu* was still failing to gain any traction. I felt I should try to grab the attention of someone with the clout to get me into the public eye. Amongst various avenues I tried, I sent a record to Peter Gabriel (care of the Real World Records address). A few weeks later I received a courteous reply letter from 'Anne Parsons on behalf of Peter Gabriel' thanking me for my submission and explaining that PG was currently up to his eyes in writing and recording his next album which should take until the beginning of the following year. 'After that,' the letter concluded noncommittally, 'he should have some time to catch up.' It seems to be taking longer than anticipated.

Around the end of September, *Taqaharu/Evocation* received what I like to think of as its first 'rave' review. It came in well-respected indie fanzine of the time 'Peace & Freedom', written (if I remember rightly) by editor Paul Rance:

> Incredible stuff. Very innovative, uplifting tracks, with oboes, trombones and flutes. 'Evocation' is a percussion jamboree, with emphasis on melody, while 'Taqaharu' is a sort of antiwar hymn, with a beautiful arrangement. Music made in heaven.

Well, there at last was the quote I'd been waiting for. However, it came at just a moment when I didn't have time to use it for a new round of promotions. I'd just purchased tickets for a ferry crossing in early October to Ireland where our rehearsals for the next DCD tour were due to begin. Shortly before I was due to depart, I received a distressed phone call from my mother. My father had suffered a massive stroke during the night which she'd been unaware of until she woke. He was now in Brighton General Hospital, but almost completely paralysed. I jumped in the car and drove down. I was heartbroken to see my dear father in a semi-comatose state with my poor mother sitting helpless at his bedside. Stroke is such a terrifying thing, the manner in which it strikes without warning and can leave the victim conscious but unable to move or communicate. And amidst the grief and shock of what had happened, the alarm bells of déjà vu were ringing in my head about the impending DCD tour.

I stayed a couple of days with my mother, and we spent the time at my father's bedside getting over-excited at any flicker of an eyelid or twitch of a finger. But the nursing staff were preparing us for a long-haul and gently counselled against getting our hopes up. As she recovered from the initial shock, my mother's stoic strength returned and she insisted that I should go with DCD – she understood how much it meant to me. It was hard walking away, and despite her insistence I should go, I felt a heavy guilt of selfishness. I'd call her each day, but there was no change in my father's condition, and she gradually took on the role of nursing him, washing him, and generally assisting the hospital staff wherever she could. I thought about her going back to their flat on her own each evening, and felt I should've been there supporting her. We both secretly cried – we kept it from each other, but we both knew.

On 8 October, I picked up John Bonnar and we set off for Anglessey in north Wales to get the ferry to Dublin. We drove up the M1, turned onto the M6, and straight into the embrace of a monumental traffic jam. After crawling for a couple of hours, we eventually got free of it, but now were really struggling to make the ferry departure. I hit the accelerator and we made good time while we were on the motorways, but once we got into Wales and had to tack across country on narrow, winding roads, our progress slowed considerably, even taking the Welsh lanes like we were rallying. We reached Anglessey port just in time to see the ferry's ramp being raised and the barriers come down to prevent any more vehicles approaching. We jumped out of the car and waved frantically, but to no avail, and we watched our boat sail away.

We had hours to wait – there were only a couple of sailings a day – and instead of arriving the evening before rehearsals started and having time to settle in, we now reached Cavan next morning, having had no sleep, and had to go straight into rehearsal. Still – good acclimatisation for the tour. Our rehearsal space, which Brendan had hired for the week, was the function hall of a bar in Bailieborough, close to his house. And this was quite a new-look Dead Can Dance, with guitar, bass and drum kit exorcised and two entirely new band members plucked from Brendan's new circles. The tour programme would list the band thus:

Lisa Gerrard: voice/yang-ch'in/percussion
Brendan Perry: voice/hurdy-gurdy/saz/flute/recorder/harp/percussion
Robert Perry: Uillean pipes/bagpipes/flute/mandora/percussion/voice

Peter Ulrich: percussion/voice
John Bonnar: keyboards/voice
Joseph Burns: trumpet/percussion/voice
James Lee: violin/percussion/voice

It was also to be an ambitious set, comprising in excess of twenty songs/pieces and touching a couple of hours including encores. It featured fragile choral arrangements, pipe and percussion reels, a medieval dance, Arabic rhythms, an Irish folk ballad and – I'm happy to say that our extended live version of 'At First, and Then' retained its place. For the first time I was also to use electronic percussion in addition to our acoustic batterie. Brendan had acquired a Roland Octopad – as the name suggests, a board of eight electronic 'pads' to which different sampled sounds could be assigned. Amongst songs I would play on this was one from the new *Aion* album – 'As the Bell Rings, the Maypole Spins'. Although perhaps not one of DCD's more well-known songs, I grew to particularly love playing it – the rhythm meshing with the bagpipes played by Robbie – and it became a highlight in the set for me.

The set would also feature three songs in which we formed a vocal chorus, hence all of us being listed as 'voice'. These were 'Song of the Sybil', 'Orbis de Ignis', and one that features in my rehearsal notes as 'Twilight's Curtain', an early version of what would become 'Towards the Within'. Another song entirely new to the set – 'Oman' – would feature an outburst of group hand-clapping. So, plenty of movement around the stage and different configurations to keep us on our toes. On the downside, we had to drop new song 'Black Sun' because of me. Brendan showed me the core drum part he'd written and programmed for the recording of the album version, and it seemed fairly straightforward. But there was some inflection in the pattern which for Brendan was absolutely essential to the feel of the song, and I wasn't getting it. No matter how many times he showed me and explained, I just couldn't grasp what I wasn't doing correctly. We went back to it periodically and tried again, and apparently sometimes I'd get it, but other times not, and I still couldn't hear the difference. Brendan decided to drop the song from the set – I knew he was very reluctant to do this as it was a powerful song and one he craved to perform live, and I was gutted to be letting him down.

Despite this spanner I'd stuck in the works, the set came together. It was good to be together with Brendan and Lisa again, and didn't feel like we'd grown apart since they left the Isle of Dogs. Robbie was always great to have around, full of energy and enthusiasm, while John was a very calming influence, reliably creating the required symphonic bedrock from the keyboards. Newcomers Joey and James slotted in well, albeit they were very different. Joey was a stocky guy with a big laugh and presence; James was waiflike, fidgety, with a lovely fluency on violin in the Irish fiddling tradition. And I was free of tour manager duties. For the first time we had professional on-the-road management provided by Barry Bartlett (tour manager/sound engineer) and Ian Stewart (assistant tour manager/accountant). Monsieur Rosko was in the party as our regular lighting maestro, but Rene wasn't available for onstage monitoring duties so new man Sean O'Malley stepped admirably into the breach.

On 16 October, we all headed for London. The following day we had a final rehearsal, then I shot down to Brighton to see my parents. There was no change of any substance to my father's condition, and my mother was looking pale and tired. Pangs of guilt returned as I had to swiftly depart again, and these only increased when I got home to finish packing. Nicki was once again blossoming, but was now having to cope with her pregnancy in addition to her demanding teaching work and the two-and-three-quarter-year-old-Louise while I disappeared on tour. Next day, I was with the DCD entourage on a flight to Athens.

We were scheduled for two nights – 19 and 20 October 1990 – at the Pallas Theatre, a beautiful early 1930s venue built in French style and naturally featuring a grand marble entrance. We'd been warned prior to the trip that bands touring in Greece regularly encountered all manner of technical issues, mainly resulting from unreliable power supplies, but I think this applied to the smaller rock club circuit. Although it was our first time playing in Greece, we arrived with an advanced status. There was a hardcore legion of Greek fans who knew DCD from early days – the *Within the Realm* . . . album had made No. 2 in the mainstream Greek charts (held off the top spot by Metallica, who were a virtual permanent fixture), and *Aion* had now reached No. 3. As a result, we were bypassing the tour circuit used to establish a following, and heading straight into a higher tier concert venue.

We were greeted by a group of around twenty to thirty excited fans as we came through 'Arrivals' at Athens airport, and on our first night in the city we were taken out by the promoters for a veritable feast in a fine restaurant, which had been taken over by the great and good of the Greek music industry. To my personal astonishment, two or three people came over to me at various points in the evening, having actually recognised me, and complimented me on my recent single release. One was Nick Sarikostas, who at the time was running a record shop in Athens through which he told me he'd sold around seventy copies of

Taqaharu/Evocation – which at that moment must have constituted at least 10 percent of my total sales worldwide! Nick subsequently became a good friend and we've remained in touch.

The two shows were sold out and went down a storm. Such was the magnitude of DCD's arrival in the city that the mayor of Athens attended the first night. After a whirlwind three days we were back on the plane to London, still buzzing and fully hyped up for the rest of the tour. We squeezed in another rehearsal, I made another flying visit to my father's hospital bedside, said my farewells again to Nicki and Louise (who was slightly bewildered by her father's comings and goings), and it was onto the Griersons tour bus for the next leg, which would take us briefly through each of Germany, France, Belgium, and The Netherlands, before returning to 'Blighty' for an actual mini-tour of England. The scheduled dates were:

Germany:
Thursday, 25 October, Cologne, Gurzenich
Friday, 26 October, Hamburg, Musikhalle

France:
Sunday, 28 October, Besançon, Le Mont Joye
Monday, 29 October, Lyon, Transbordeur
Wednesday, 31 October, Rennes, Salle Jean Vilar
Thursday, 1 November, Paris, Olympia

Belgium:
Friday, 2 November, Brussels, Cirque Royal

Netherlands:
Sunday, 4 November, Amsterdam, Carré Theatre

England:
Tuesday, 6 November, Middlesbrough, Little Theatre
Wednesday, 7 November, Manchester, University (Student Union Hall)
Thursday, 8 November, Nottingham, Royal Albert Hall
Saturday, 10 November, Brighton, Gardner Centre
Sunday, 11 November, London, Town & Country Club

When we were in Athens, I'd sent a postcard to my father in hospital back in the UK. I'd beaten the postcard back on my most recent brief visit, so it had yet to make any impression, but nevertheless I resolved to send postcards to him from as many of our tour stops as I could. Although the cards were sent to my father, it was my mother who derived the greater benefit. They gave her something to look forward to on her visits, gave her something to read out to my father and make a one-sided conversation of, and the growing collection of cards at his bedside from their son's glamorous occupation acquired her a mini-celebrity status with the nursing staff. My mother kept all the cards, and many years later they found their way back to me, so they make an unusual record of the tour. The card I sent from Cologne on 25 October notes: 'Tasty hotel – had my first ever sauna this morning!' and generally all was going well until my card of 29 October from Besançon reports:

> Unfortunately we have problems. Virtually everybody (except me) has flu and we have been forced to cancel two shows. We hope to resume the schedule in Rennes on Wednesday.

The same card goes on to note that I'd heard (presumably via phone calls home to Nicki) that my father was sitting out of bed and eating again, which was great news. A card sent two days later gives the update:

> We're now in Rennes and Lisa is fit to sing again so we are due to perform tonight – the first time for 5 days!

After the soundcheck in Paris, we were taken for a pre-show meal at an Armenian restaurant where a hammered dulcimer player was providing background music. His playing was lovely and Lisa invited him to our show. When he came backstage afterwards, despite us having just received a wildly enthusiastic reception from a capacity audience of around two thousand, he was clearly underwhelmed by what he'd seen and heard. He was perfectly polite, not at all derogatory, but rather than comment on our performance, he set about demonstrating some elements of his classical Arabic musicianship, particularly some rhythms which he played on a hardback book. I was intrigued, but completely lost when I tried to follow what he was doing. He scribbled down four words on a scrap of paper and handed it to me: 'dumbak, zarb, family Chemirani', telling me that the first two were different names used for the goblet drum in the central Middle Eastern region, and the Chemiranis expert exponents. I kept the scrap of paper until one day, years later, I saw a poster for a free lunchtime concert as part of a City of London music festival featuring the Chemirani family playing in a church (possibly St Olave's?). I went along brimming with anticipation. The audience only numbered about thirty so it was very intimate.

The performers were a father and two sons playing dumbaks, and a daughter playing a large frame drum with bells and singing. I emerged an hour or so later having experienced something extraordinary and glorious, yet which had passed virtually unnoticed in the UK capital.

My postcards from Brussels and Amsterdam confirmed things continued to run smoothly. In Brussels, we stayed in possibly our grandest hotel to date – the Pullman Astoria, with its magnificent foyer and broad, palm-lined staircases down which I half expected a Busby Berkeley dance troupe to appear at any moment. In Amsterdam, we played the Carré Theatre, a beautiful building on the banks of the River Amstel which I'd often passed when previously wandering the city streets and craved it being booked for one of our shows. Originally designed in the 1880s to house a circus, I think the Carré has in more recent times been home to both the Dutch National Opera and Ballet companies, and has at some point also acquired 'royal' status. So it was a treat to get to play there.

The following day we were on a ferry from Rotterdam to Hull, and then driving to Middlesbrough in the northeast of England to play our first gig in my home country outside London for three and a half years. The UK 'market' is a mystery where DCD is concerned. Over the course of the next five days we'd play the Little Theatre in Middlesbrough, where we attracted an audience of 248 in a theatre with a capacity of 486, Manchester University's Student Union Hall, where apparently there were an estimated six hundred people crammed into a venue whose official capacity was 450, the 'Royal Albert Hall' in Nottingham, where we only half-filled an auditorium with a capacity of 650, and finally the Town & Country Club in London, which had sold out its 2,000-odd capacity in no time and where we were told tickets were selling via touts outside for up to five hundred pounds each. And in the UK ever since, DCD has sold out performances in major London venues in a flash, while outside London, promoters apparently find a DCD booking too uncertain to take a punt.

For reasons nobody seems to recall, the show scheduled for the Gardner Centre in Brighton on 10 November was cancelled. On this occasion, I don't think it was down to any health or other issues with the band – rather some problem with the venue itself – but it removed the one opportunity I might have had to get my mother to ever see me perform live. Instead, I took the opportunity to go down to Brighton anyway with Nicki and Louise to visit my father and mother at the hospital. Although he was still unable to talk or move unaided, my dad was now at least able to sit propped in a chair beside the bed and could chew and swallow a little solid food. He was clearly full of anger and frustration at his condition, but Louise's visit brought a hint of a smile onto his face for the first time since he had the stroke, and we were all in bits. Louise, in fact, found the hospital so fascinating that we were obliged to buy her a replica doctor's outfit complete with toy stethoscope which she insisted on donning for future visits.

Back in London, all our tour party passports were back from the American Embassy with our US visas stamped in them, our equipment was collected from the Town and Country and shipped off to air freight, and on Tuesday, 13 November, we flew from London Heathrow to Paris Charles De Gaulle where we transferred to an Air France 'Jumbo' to Toronto to begin our first tour of Canada and the States. I'd never been on such an aircraft before and it seemed enormous, but I was so conditioned to short haul flying that I remained in my seat for the entire flight and just read or dozed, musing over the prospect of a tour that lined up as follows:

Canada:
Thursday, 15 November, Toronto, Music Hall
Friday, 16 November, Montreal, Le Spectrum

North America:
Saturday, 17 November, Boston, Berklee Performance Art Center
Tuesday, 20 November, New York, Symphony Space
Wednesday, 21 November, New York, Symphony Space
Friday, 23 November, Washington DC, Gaston Hall
Sunday, 25 November, Chicago, Vic Theater
Tuesday, 27 November, San Francisco, Palace of Fine Arts Theater
Thursday, 29 November, Los Angeles, Wadsworth Theater
Friday, 30 November, Los Angeles, Wadsworth Theater

Arriving in Toronto, we had a day off to acclimatise before the first show. It immediately seemed a really friendly city, very relaxed, and we were surprised at the low cost (relative to London) of food and clothes. The latter was particularly fortunate as Air France had lost Lisa's luggage, so I went with her to trawl around vintage clothing stores to find some replacement stage dresses and gowns. Lisa has a sharp eye and knows instantly whether or not something is right for her, so no time was wasted with deliberations and she quickly compiled a replacement wardrobe. This afforded time for a bit of sightseeing and we went to the CN Radio Tower, the viewing platform of which at that time was the world's highest. You could step onto a sloped glass panel at the edge and look straight down. It was all enclosed so there was no danger to it, but you had to be solidly nonvertiginous all the same. As we took the elevator back down, Lisa and I were the only passengers and the operator offered us one of four speeds of descent. He told us that in the case of the fastest, the elevator was released from its cables and went into freefall, before being caught again near the bottom. Thinking about it afterwards, I take it that was a joke (?) – but in any event we opted for speed No. 2 and lived.

The venue for our show the following night was then called The Music Hall (now the Danforth Music Hall), originally a 1920s movie theatre and boasting a fine, ornate ceiling. Our equipment had arrived safely, Lisa seemed pleased with her new outfit and, although we hadn't completely sold out the fifteen-hundred-seat auditorium, it was near full with an appreciative audience and our expansion into the new world was underway. After the show, it was another new experience – we'd travel the eight-hour drive to Montreal overnight by bus fitted with bunk beds. Not only that, it had a front lounge fitted with TV monitors, fridge and mini-kitchen area, a loo-cum-small-washroom, and a private rear lounge which Lisa made her own. As ever, Lisa coped admirably with being the only female in the party, and – as far as I recall – never (or very rarely) complained about being suffocated by blokey behaviour.

As happens all too often on tour, we saw nothing of Montreal apart from the inside of the venue – Le Spectrum. Another former cinema, this one dating from the 1950s, it was apparently demolished in 2008 so we were part of a relatively brief history. An added twist arrived in the form of Julee Cruise. She'd been booked as the support act to DCD for this one show, but in between the time the booking was made and this day of the show, her single 'Falling' – the theme song for director David Lynch's *Twin Peaks* – had become a major global hit (selling over half a million in the US alone) and she had been transformed from underground artist to international star. Inevitably, we were approached by the promoters asking if we would swap roles and be support act to Cruise, but Brendan was having none of it. Not that we were overly bothered about the hierarchical structure – the key point for us was that, as main act, we would get by some distance the longer and more focused soundcheck, and with our complex stage set, we were reliant on this. The promoters and management were powerless to do anything as we were only sticking to our contractual terms, and so it was that on the night of 16 November 1990, in downtown Montreal, international chart-topper Julee Cruise opened for new kids on the block Dead Can Dance.

An added irony to this encounter was that David Lynch had reputedly originally wanted to use This Mortal Coil's version of 'Song to the Siren' as lead song in the soundtrack to his classic film *Blue Velvet*. He'd called Ivo directly about it, and even asked about having Liz and Robin mime to it in a scene in the film. But the idea came to grief when lawyers who controlled the late Tim Buckley's copyrights reputedly demanded a usage fee of $20,000 which was way beyond Lynch's budget. Instead, composer Angelo Badalamenti was commissioned to write a song in a similar style and came up with 'Mysteries of Love' which was sung by Julee Cruise. This had garnered her some attention, but it was the subsequent success of Lynch's prime time television series *Twin Peaks* which had catapulted her into the musical big league.

I don't recall any hostility from Cruise and her entourage, but there was no love lost either, and I think they just performed their contracted set, packed up and left us to it. However, it seemed the show was destined to be jinxed after all. Our electronic equipment was all rated at the UK standard 240v whereas the standard in Canada is 110–120v. It's standard practice for this to be overcome using a step-up power converter, but inexplicably the converter at Le Spectrum had a fixed upper limit of 106v which, in turn, didn't provide the full conversion we needed. It could just about handle the guitars/amps, but the computer equipment kept crashing. As a result, we had to do a semi-acoustic performance, dropping out around 50 percent of our setlist, with Lisa busking a couple of additional solo a capella songs to give the audience their money's worth. To top things off, the venue itself was set out like a cabaret club, with the audience seated around numerous small, circular tables with continuous waiter service through the show – altogether a bit of a weird one.

After the Montreal experience, it was back in the mobile hotel for a seven-hour overnight drive across the border onto American soil and down to Boston for a show the following night at the Berklee Performance Arts Center on the campus of the renowned Music College. DCD was very much an unknown quantity in Canada and the States. We had no official distribution in the territories at this point and could only have been heard on the international grapevine, so the promoters had no idea what to expect and had taken some level of risk by booking us into some 1,000+ capacity venues. But so far the audiences were turning out, recognition of our music was apparently strong, and it seemed we were creating the much lauded 'buzz'.

With no show the following day, we were afforded the luxury of an overnight hotel stay in the palatial Hyatt Regency in Cambridge Massachusetts, and happened to arrive on the day of the annual Harvard vs. Yale Football Match (in this case that hands, oval ball, crash helmets 'football'). My two recollections of the Hyatt are the place being full of middle-aged men around seven feet tall and the same width (being the proud fathers, uncles, etc. of the current

University squads), and the most enormous breakfast buffet which stretched the full circle of a gallery around a vast central atrium in which I spent a good couple of hours gorging myself. Overall, a truly American baptism.

In my peculiarly English way, I hadn't expected to like America. Not to say that I went with an intention of not liking it, but my limited experiences of American tourists in London had been that they were too loud (both vocally and in appearance), too brash, and over-confident. With hindsight, mentally tarring the entire populace of the US with this bigoted brush was of course ridiculous stereotyping on my part. And now I was immediately won over. In their own back yard, Americans seemed comfortably 'right', incredibly friendly, helpful, and enthusiastic, and I completely got why their culture fills them with confidence and openness. I was loving it, and our next stop was New York City where we were going to have a bit of time to explore. We had a couple of free days, and then were booked to play two consecutive nights at a venue called Symphony Space which was actually *ON* Broadway . . . OK, upper Broadway, but Broadway all the same. Not everyone can say they played Broadway on their first visit to NYC. First up, we headed off to do the tourist thing and bizarrely found ourselves travelling up the Empire State Building with a visiting basketball team. After the mountainous footballers in Boston, we were now dwarfed by these towering stick figures who were having to fold their heads down to fit in the elevator. From the viewing zone in the Empire State we marvelled at the architectural wonder that is the Chrysler Building, then back at ground level we were fascinated by the steam geysers emanating from venting points in the streets, we took a rollercoaster Yellow Taxi ride downtown, lingered in Times Square, and got cricks in our necks from staring up as we walked the blocks of Manhattan.

The shows were sold out and DCD was making an impression in the Big Apple – the promoters weren't saying too much, but we knew they were more than impressed by both the ticket sales and the rapturous receptions our shows were receiving. The 22 November issue of the *New York Times* ran a review by Jon Pareles, who was clearly wrong-footed by having turned up for a rock concert only to be confronted with a 'seven-piece group' more 'like a classical early-music broken consort' and a performance in which 'There were no guitars; many songs didn't even have a drum beat.' Ultimately it seems he was won over, albeit reluctant to surrender his rock critic status, concluding: 'It's easy to be fond of a rock band whose idea of a dance number is a fourteenth-century Italian *saltarello*.'

Playing two nights in a row at the same venue is always a joy, because you don't have the break down after the first show, and particularly you don't have the set up and full soundcheck the following day – just a quick refresher to make sure everything is still set. Some shopping was on the agenda as we continued to marvel at the buying power of our English pounds. Back in 1990, in rather different economic times, the exchange rate was hovering around two US dollars to one pound sterling. I went to the 'Cockpit' clothing store and splashed out $395 on an Avirex flying jacket – so this was the equivalent of around £200 and the same jacket in London at the time cost over £550. It's an amazing garment, but so bulky and heavy that it almost doubled the volume of my tour luggage, and I've only ever worn it a few times since because it's so hot!

An odd incident occurred in New York when Ian Stewart, the assistant tour manager, sheepishly claimed to have been the victim of a mugging, somewhat oddly alleging that he was travelling in a taxi with an envelope on the seat beside him containing a not inconsiderable cash sum comprising our performance fees and tour float, when someone suddenly opened the taxi passenger door, snatched the envelope and ran off. It was an incident that generated more questions than answers, particularly as Stewart seemed resistant to having it reported to the police. Not wanting to become embroiled in a matter which might cast a shadow over the amazing experience we were having, we (as a band) decided to report what we knew back to 4AD and leave them to sort it out. It was soon forgotten and to this day I've no idea what the upshot of it was. It made us reflect, however, that we'd made a good decision in managing ourselves for as long as we did.

All too soon, our New York experience was over. The day we left was Thanksgiving Day, and we managed to catch a little of the annual street parade before we clambered back on the tour bus to head for the capital and Presidential seat, Washington DC. We stayed in a suburb of the city and were warned it wasn't safe to go wandering the locality, so off I wandered. I didn't encounter any trouble, but the area had a strange coldness and blandness, in stark contrast to my other impressions of America up to that point, and that would follow. I was still sending postcards back to my dad in hospital whenever possible, and one I sent from DC notes: 'Haven't managed to see the White House but then George Bush hasn't been to see my flat!'

In contrast to the drab surrounds of our DC suburb, the venue turned out to be both elaborate and historic. Gaston Hall is the ceremonial hall of Georgetown University and its ornate ceiling bears the coats of arms of the sixty Jesuit universities which existed in the world at the time of its construction in 1901, while behind us at the back of the stage was a decorative structure housing the

Georgetown University seal. Although we were unaware of it at the time of our show – it may well have been covered by the backdrop for our lighting rig – this seal apparently incorporates a 'Christogram' (Christian religious symbol) which years later would be the subject of controversy when it was covered at the request of the White House during a speech by President Barack Obama. There's a gallery at the back of the hall on which, to my bemusement during our performance, a group of half a dozen or so audience members enacted a phenomenon I'd never seen before (nor since) – 'air' yang ch'in players, miming along to Lisa's dulcimer hammering!

Back in the bus for a fifteen-hour drive to Chicago. It was possibly on this leg of the journey that we watched either the first (or certainly a very early) episode of a new American cartoon which was causing a stir – something called *The Simpsons*. I couldn't watch TV and play games for hours on end, so periodically I'd go and chat to Lisa and sup tea for a while in the rear lounge while she regaled me with tales of Melbourne suburban life. These ranged from contending with the midsummer heat when, despite the thermometer topping forty degrees, her Irish father would still insist on having the full Northern Hemisphere traditional dinner on Christmas Day before lying out on his back in the middle of the lawn and visibly turning blue (to the horror of the family), to the hilarious adventures of Joan and Ron Ferguson, friends of her mother. Eventually I ached from laughter so much I had to go back up the bus to recover. At some point during the journey we stopped for a meal at a diner. We were gawped and scowled at by the locals like we were a freak show, so didn't linger over our deep-fried delights and it gave us a taste of how removed the 'outback' in the States can be from its cities.

Sadly, the 'Windy' city was another we saw nothing of. We arrived fairly zombified after the journey and barely strayed from the venue, The Vic Theater. The following morning we were on a plane to the west coast, contemplating putting flowers in our hair. San Francisco is a truly extraordinary city, an architectural anomaly that defies the rules. The hills are so steep that a local taxi driver told us he goes through a set of brake pads every three months. The iconic image of San Francisco is its cable cars. Although often referred to as 'trams', they're not. They're actually hauled up and down the hills by a phenomenal 'wire rope' cable housed in channels through the streets, and you can visit the engine room in which a labyrinth of great cogs and pullies run the system. I discovered it was invented in the 1870s by Scottish immigrant Andrew Smith Hallidie who'd been appalled by the regular sight of cart-pulling horses becoming exhausted before reaching the hill summits, losing their footing and being dragged all the way back down, such that they would break their legs and have to be shot on the spot.

San Francisco also boasts reputedly the largest 'Chinatown' outside China and Hong Kong, and part-surrounding the Bay is the Fisherman's Wharf complex, with its piers converted into various restaurants, bars, and clubs to cater for just about every lifestyle taste imaginable. Then, of course, there's the Golden Gate Bridge and the spectre of Alcatraz sitting out in the bay. Luckily, we had a couple of days to explore. Our show at the Palace of Fine Arts Theater was put on by legendary 'Frisco' promoter Bill Graham, who was synonymous with the famous Fillmore Auditorium and had been involved with many of the biggest names on the tour circuit since the 1960s. The city made a huge impression on me, right up to our flight out where the plane had to climb steeply on full thrust immediately after take-off to clear the local mountains and we were pinned in our seats by the G-Force.

The band flew on to our final tour location of Los Angeles, while the truck with all our gear took the Pacific Coast Highway. I'd like to have experienced the drive down State Route 1, but taking the plane meant we had more time to explore the city. Having been warned that LA is pedestrian-unfriendly to the extent that they didn't even bother to make pavements/sidewalks to many of the roads, I hired a car. I was a little nervous about the left-hand drive thing, and the multiple-lane freeways, but I soon got into the groove, and actually found the local drivers surprisingly friendly and unaggressive. Robbie, John, and Joe jumped in and we started with an American staple and went to a 'drive-thru' diner, then proceeded to check-out all those famous LA place-names that feature in so many songs, books, and movies. We drove through Beverly Hills and saw little more than endless rows of high security walls and gates, then took a ride out to Venice beach which was sparsely populated by people but heavily by signs warning of a pollution threat – this wasn't the glamour we'd anticipated. We went to visit the Forecourt of Stars where all the famous handprints are made in the pavement outside the Chinese Theater, but even this was a bit underwhelming on a day when no ceremony was taking place.

Then, as we took a wander along Hollywood Boulevard, a huge commotion broke out, with police cars screaming in from all directions. At first we thought we'd walked onto a movie set, but it soon became clear this was for real. The police surrounded a car and officers were crouched behind open car doors with guns cocked and pointed. A police helicopter whirred overhead and instructions were barked through a loudhailer. Slowly the door of the suspect car opened, its driver clambered out and dropped to the ground, hands behind head and legs spread as instructed. While we cowered in a shop doorway a good hundred yards down the street lest we should get caught in a sudden hail of bullets, a group of locals gathered within feet of the incident and casually watched the armed arrest with a tired indifference that suggested this wasn't an abnormal occurrence.

Our final show – the second of two nights at LA's Wadsworth Theater – brought down the curtain on a first US tour which had been a resounding success. Venues had been mostly sold out, audience responses had been great, promoters wanted us back, and music biz notables were raising an eyebrow here and there. The aftershow party was underway and a local journalist was asking me about our live version of 'At First, and Then'. I told him over-candidly that I'd been a little disappointed that on TMC's *Filigree & Shadow* the track had been blended into the tracks immediately before and after and, being such a short piece, felt a bit like it had become a bridge between these other tracks rather than being allowed its own space. There was a tap on my shoulder and I turned to find Ivo behind me had heard the conversation. I wilted with embarrassment and cursed myself for being so loose-tongued. There is some truth to what I'd said, but it needs more explanation to the extent that I remain very happy about my inclusion in TMC, and had I known how Ivo wanted to incorporate 'At First, and Then', I would have liked the opportunity to make the recorded version a little longer and further developed.

I shouldn't have been so ready to be critical out of context to a journalist I'd never met before, and I certainly shouldn't have been disrespectful enough to do so within Ivo's earshot after he'd given me so many opportunities. I regret that I've never had the opportunity to properly apologise to Ivo for that. To add insult to Ivo's injury, I discovered years later a footnote in Martin Aston's 4AD biography *Facing the Other Way* that reads:

> When 4AD trailed the This Mortal Coil box set via a brief video posted on You-Tube, Ivo was frustrated to discover that the soundtrack chosen was the instrumental 'At First, and Then' written by the former Dead Can Dance collaborator Peter Ulrich. 'It was given to me by Peter, and so it was the only piece on *Filigree & Shadow* that I didn't commission, write or play on! I was told it was the only piece that fit the trailer!'

Two days later I was back in London. The sustained adrenalin high had dissipated and the jet lag of the long-haul flight back from LA, with its eight-hour gain, kicked in. I was so tired I didn't know what to do with myself, but couldn't sleep more than a couple of hours at a stretch, and made it through the next few days on autopilot. It had been an extraordinary year.

EIGHT

Everything changed.

I found out shortly after returning from America that, entirely unknown to me, Lisa had a whirlwind romance with a guy she'd met in LA, Jacek Tuschewski. Lisa now headed back to resettle in Australia and he upped sticks and moved to be with her. They would subsequently marry and have two daughters – Teresa and Lashna. Of course, I was very happy for Lisa, but we weren't in general contact once she was back in Oz, so news would trickle through some time later and the opportunity to even send a message or card passed, which seemed weird after we'd been living in and out of each other's flats for so long.

Brendan had returned to Ireland and was devoting his time to expanding and upgrading his studio setup. As happened with many musicians around this time, he became submerged in exploring the rapidly expanding boundaries of computer/recording technology and was sucked into an ever more hermitic existence.

The 4AD camaraderie seemed to me to have evaporated, though it may have simply moved on. But Ivo and Debbie had separated in recent months, having been romantically together all the time we'd known them. Debbie left 4AD and Ivo was spending increasing amounts of time in the States. The Cocteau Twins had flown the nest amidst some acrimony, This Mortal Coil was drawing to a close (final album *Blood* was being finished and would be released in April 1991), and Xymox, Modern English, Colourbox, and Dif Juz had all departed or disbanded. Simon Harper, who had joined 4AD a couple of years earlier to work up the label's international expansion was valiantly trying to hold things together, but Alma Road in Wandsworth was not at all the same place – not necessarily in a negative way, but it was now strictly an office whereas it had previously been more like popping round to Ivo and Debbie's place. Aside of DCD, 4AD's focus had shifted across the Atlantic and the primary acts on the label now were the Pixies and Throwing Muses, but I never saw or met any of them.

On New Year's Day 1991, I was in Brighton with Nicki and Louise, accompanying my mother on her daily visit to my father's bedside. This day was different as he'd just been moved to a nursing home. The upside was a change of environment for Mum after three months of daily visits to Ward E2 in Brighton General Hospital; the downside was the unspoken understanding that there was nothing more the medical staff at the hospital could do and Dad's condition wasn't going to improve. Dad knew there was no hope, and suddenly convulsed. I ran into the corridor screaming for help and staff came running. Mum, Nicki, Louise, and I were ushered out, and Dad was gone. I stayed on a few days in Brighton to be with Mum. There were things to be done which had never previously crossed my mind – a funeral to organise, my father's 'estate' to be identified and calculated, the probate to be completed and registered, accounts to be closed or transferred to my mother, government offices to be informed, and so on.

All the while Nicki was getting closer to the end of her pregnancy, the opposite end of life, newness, hope, and joy. On 9 April 1991, in the London Hospital at Whitechapel, Nicki gave birth to another daughter who we called Eleanor (which she subsequently shortened, and is now universally known as Ellie). The memory of the now three-year-old Louise as a baby already seemed distant, and it was a source of amazement all over again to have this tiny newborn to hold and care for. Though thrilled at our new family addition, I knew I'd toured with DCD for the last time. With two young children and Nicki's commitments to her teaching career (which provided our financial stability as a family), I could no longer periodically disappear on tour for two to three months at a time. It was my choice, I'd made it knowingly and had no reservations about it, but I had to tell Brendan and Lisa. It was a personal wrench, but no threat to DCD.

The Isle of Dogs was changing . . . massively! The derelict acres were being regenerated and the old West India Docks were being developed into a new commercial centre for London – 'Canary Wharf'. The Isle of Dogs had previously been like a village community in the heart of London, but now it was a vast building site, with trucks rumbling past 24/7 and dust and dirt everywhere. It wasn't an environment we wanted for our young children so Nicki and I decided it was time for us to move on too. We agreed that Nicki would apply for jobs which would be the next step up the teaching ladder for her, and wherever she was successful, that's where we'd go. Committing such a big life decision to the hand of fate can so often bring an unexpected twist. And so it was, that out of the three or four jobs Nicki applied for – spread from Brighton to Dunstable – the one she was offered was at my own first school in west Harrow – Vaughan. I'd never had any desire to return to Harrow, nor in fact to any part of the London suburbs – I much prefer being either in the heart of a city, or right out of it. But our decision was made and in January 1992 we bought our first house, an Edwardian end-of-terrace with some beautiful traditional stained glass windows, a bedroom each for the girls, and a little patch of suburban garden.

DCD slipped into hibernation – although there was 'behind the scenes' activity, there were no live performances throughout 1991 and 1992, so for a while it seemed like I hadn't left. I guess Brendan and Lisa must have been periodically in touch with 4AD, but I'd now lost all contact. I heard from Brendan that our 1990 North American tour had resulted initially in 4AD licensing DCD's recordings through the Rykodisc label for US distribution, and then as a result of a strong showing, DCD being fully taken on by Ryko parent Warner Music Group. This meant some serious muscle was being put into promotions, and sales were growing strongly. But Brendan was absorbed with creating the right studio environment for his writing and wasn't going to be hurried to complete a new album or to get back on the road, major label deal or not.

A compilation album was released in the US in 1991 under the title *A Passage in Time* to introduce DCD to a wider audience. Conversely, it didn't include the song 'A Passage in Time', but comprised a selection from *Spleen and Ideal* onwards plus two previously unreleased tracks – 'Bird' and 'Spirit' – which had been written and recorded after completing material for *The Serpent's Egg* but had thus far not been used. The album was later remastered and given a worldwide release in 1998.

I continued to promote *Taqaharu/Evocation* and in April 1991 forked out 300 quid on hiring a radio promotions agency called 'Push & Plug' to do exactly that to regional stations across the UK. A couple of months later I received their 'Radio Reaction Report' which included:

> Radio Forth, Edinburgh odd plays – one to watch
> Radio Trent, Nottingham quite a few plays
> Radio Hereward, Peterborough not likely to play
> Westsound, Ayr 'interesting' – couple of plays
> BBC Leeds one play
> BBC Oxford don't like it

So, while I interested the good folk of Ayr and was under observation in Edinburgh, there was brief hope I could be big in Nottingham, but sales failed to materialise. In June, I placed a small ad in the NME offering sales direct from me to Joe Public by mail order. The ad cost £80; I sold ten records at £3.75 a pop, and each cost me about a pound in post and packing – not good business, and I was running out of steam.

By contrast, our old 4AD compatriots Wolfgang Press suddenly found themselves with an international hit single on their hands – *A Girl Like You (Born to be Kissed)* reaching the dizzy heights of No. 2 on the *Billboard* Modern Rock chart in August 1992. The song was subsequently covered by no less a megastar than Welsh maestro Tom Jones, who further commissioned the Wolfies to write another song for him – 'Show Me (Some Devotion)' – and would even appear live on stage with them for a 4AD anniversary show in Los Angeles a couple of years later.

Brendan bought an old, decommissioned church amidst the spectacular scenery of the Irish lake district – Quivvy Church in Belturbet – and set about converting it into a recording and rehearsal studio. He was also once more romantically entwined, now with Françoise (Fran), who he'd known in London, but they'd recently discovered that each had been harbouring a secret desire for the other. He was happy and bubbling with enthusiasm again, which was great to see. Fran, originally from Bretagne (Brittany) in northern France, had given up a modelling career to devote her time to her true passion of looking after animals, and it was healthy for Brendan to be with someone not directly involved in his music.

While DCD slumbered, its musical influence continued to grow. A segment of Lisa's singing from 'Dawn of the Iconoclast' was sampled into Future Sound of London's 'Papua New Guinea' (1991) which hit No. 22 in the UK mainstream charts and became a rave anthem on the club scene. 'The Host of Seraphim' was featured to great effect in the beautiful documentary film *Baraka* (1992). Also in 1992, a duo called the Dust Brothers released on single their interpretation of 'Song to the Siren' which, in turn, sampled This Mortal Coil's version of the same, along with a reversed sample of Lisa's vocal on 'Song of Sophia' – the song would be included on the duo's debut album *Exit Planet Dust* in 1995, just around the time they changed name to the Chemical Brothers.

I hooked up with Brendan when he visited London in March 1993 and took him to a couple of specialist instrument retailers I'd discovered through my dalliance in the trade with Full Circle. He was also visiting 4AD as preparations were underway for an event to mark the label's thirteenth anniversary and he'd been invited to do a solo performance. He was back in London to headline 'The 13 Year Itch' at the Institute of Contemporary Arts in The Mall on 24 July, and, so out of touch was I with 4AD by this point, I turned up on the Saturday for his gig not realising it was the culmination of a week-long mini-festival, the first five nights of which had been and gone. I'd missed performances by The Breeders, Red House Painters, Kristin Hersch, Pale Saints, Lush, His Name is Alive – even the Wolfies – and by all accounts it had all been a riot.

Anyway, there I was on the final night, acknowledging the occasional familiar face here and there, exchanging a brief hello with Ivo, though his attention was naturally in high demand, and enjoying Heidi Berry's performance in the slot before Brendan. Heidi had signed to 4AD a year or so earlier and I love her songs. At the time of this show, she'd just released her debut album, and she went on to release a second album – *Miracle* – on 4AD a few years later. They're both beautiful and I never understood why she didn't achieve a much higher level of recognition. The probable explanation is that her compositions were too close to folk music to appeal to the indie scene, and at that time the UK folk scene was in the doldrums. It's since blossomed into fine health and if Heidi had been on this scene twenty years later, I'm convinced she'd have been one of its stars. Stuffy English magazine *Folk Roots* had apparently returned the review copy of Heidi's album sent by 4AD with a note saying 'this isn't "Folk" music' (or words to that effect). *Folk Roots* did something similar to me a couple of years earlier – they ran a small review of *Taqaharu/Evocation*, but essentially said they didn't know why I'd sent it to them and described it as 'an object lesson in how to flummox a critic'. *Folk Roots* magazine has since expired, but I'm not gloating – we can't afford to lose any media which provide a public platform for specialised music sectors, and I was sorry to see it go.

Back to the ICA and the headliner . . . Brendan gave a storming performance and there was a genuine 'WOW!' buzz in the audience afterwards. Hard-bitten music biz pros could be seen indulging in a bit of thoughtful chin-stroking as they supped their end-of-evening chasers. I think Brendan only played about eight songs, including a couple of DCD's, a couple of Tim Buckley's (specially for Ivo's benefit), and a couple of pieces he'd been working on for a slow-burning solo album which was still in the pipeline. There were whispers of a great solo career in the offing, and anyone other than Brendan would have scooted back to the studio, polished off his album and released it while the iron was still hot. But not him. He would toil over the project for several more years before deeming it ready for the world, and that particular moment passed.

What did get completed was a new DCD album. *Into the Labyrinth* – released on 13 September 1993 – was the first album to emerge from the new Quivvy Studio, the first DCD album to be recorded entirely by Brendan and Lisa (with no other performers), the first DCD record (I think) to be principally a 'CD' format release, with the vinyl version in support, and the first to be launched in the US through Warners. The effect of the last of these firsts was dramatic – with the album shifting in excess of half a million copies.

Labyrinth opens with two songs which would come to feature prominently in the DCD canon. 'Yulunga (Spirit Dance)' has its roots in native Australian Aboriginal traditions and is perhaps the track that, in a more measured way, comes closest to recapturing what Brendan and Lisa had spontaneously created with the original version of 'Frontier' a dozen years earlier. 'The Ubiquitous Mr Lovegrove' is arguably as close as DCD will get to a pop song with an actual sing-along chorus – though, of course, being DCD there's Middle Eastern percussion, a snake charmer popping up here and there, and the title wasn't exactly aimed at chart DJs. The title is taken from an episode of 1960s UK TV series *Danger Man* (shown in the US as *Secret Agent*) and forerunner to weirdly wonderful cult series *The Prisoner*. Warners put 'Lovegrove' out as a single and it was playlisted by influential LA station KROQ ('*Kay-rock*') bringing DCD a whole new level of exposure. The song would also later provide the soundtrack to the strip club scene in Sean Penn's 1995 movie *The Crossing Guard*. Both songs are real 'hip-swayers', if you'll pardon the expression – they have a real groove to them – and at any DCD live show to this day, as soon as the intro to either song starts, a distinct shiver of expectation ripples through the audience.

Shortly after the release, DCD embarked on the first tour since my departure and it finally hit home that I was no longer involved. Brendan had hooked up with the wonderful Irish band Kíla from whose ranks he recruited percussionist Rónán Ó Snodaigh and guitarist/bassist Lance Hogan. Brother Robert retained his place, as did John Bonnar on keyboards, and the tour lineup was completed by the return of Andrew Claxton, who'd been working on some material with Lisa, including the song 'Sanvean' which they wrote together during rehearsals for the tour. The European leg lined up as follows:

Ireland:
Wednesday, 29 September, Sligo, Factory Theatre

Netherlands:
Thursday, 30 September, Amsterdam, Muziektheater

Belgium:
Friday, 1 October, Brussels, Cirque Royale

France:
Saturday, 2 October, Rouen, Theatre de la Ville
Tuesday, 5 October, Paris, Le Grand Rex
Wednesday, 6 October, Lyon, Le Transbordeur

Germany:
Friday, 8 October, Stuttgart, Ludwigsberg Forum im Schlosspark
Saturday, 9 October, Cologne, Philharmonie
Sunday, 10 October, Berlin, Hocheschule der Kunste
Tuesday, 12 October, Hamburg, Musichalle

England:
Thursday, 14 October, London, The Forum

I couldn't wait for the tour to hit London and went and spent the day with the gang catching up. The atmosphere at The Forum (the renamed former Town & Country Club in Kentish Town) was great as always, and I found it both a joy and a disappointment to experience my first DCD show as a member of the audience. And then they were gone again, headed across the Atlantic:

North America:
Wednesday, 20 October, Atlanta, Roxy Theater
Friday, 22 October, Washington, Lisner Auditorium
Saturday, 23 October, Washington, Lisner Auditorium

Canada:
Sunday, 24 October, Montreal, Salle Pierre-Mercure
Monday, 25 October, Toronto, Music Hall

North America:
Wednesday, 27 October, New York, Town Hall
Thursday, 28 October, New York, Town Hall
Friday, 29 October, Boston, Berklee Performance Center
Saturday, 30 October, Philadelphia, Theater of Living Arts
Tuesday, 2 November, Chicago, Victoria Theater
Thursday, 4 November, Denver, Ogden Theater
Sunday, 7 November, Berkeley, Zellerback Auditorium
Monday, 8 November, Los Angeles, Royce Hall, UCLA
Thursday, 11 November, Seattle, Moore Theater

Canada:
Friday, 12 November, Vancouver, Vogue Theater

North America:
Monday, 15 November, Los Angeles, Wiltern Theater
Tuesday, 16 November, Los Angeles, Mayfair Theater, Santa Monica
Wednesday, 17 November, Los Angeles, Mayfair Theater, Santa Monica

The last two shows were filmed for a commercial video release which came out in 1994 under the title *Toward the Within* which for me gave rise again to mixed feelings. While it was great to see a professionally made concert recording of DCD, I was sad not to be in it. Throughout my involvement, we never officially had a show filmed or did a TV performance, so I've only ever seen myself in bootleg video clips, mostly of dubious quality. *Toward the Within* was filmed by Mark Magidson who produced *Baraka* and subsequently made a music video for 'Yulunga (Spirit Dance)' composed of *Baraka* clips. There was also a live CD/vinyl of *Toward the Within* released on which eleven of the fifteen songs were previously unreleased, so it was effectively like a new DCD album.

After the tour, Brendan and Lisa once again retreated to opposite sides of the planet and DCD went back into storage. Meanwhile, 4AD caused a fair few eyebrows to be raised in 1994 when American singer/songwriter Lisa Germano signed up, having previously been on Capitol, a pretty much unprecedented switch from a US major label to UK indie. In fairness, it was apparently an exec at Capitol who suggested what was, initially, effectively, a label collaboration. Germano had no knowledge of 4AD at the time, so Ivo wooed her with a selection of releases – including some DCD and This Mortal Coil – which instantly won her over (so the story goes). Seemingly revelling in her new artistic freedom, Germano went on to release five albums with Ivo between 1994 and 1998, including a reworking of her previous Capitol-released album *Happiness*. Though I never met Germano, I'd guess she also appreciated being on a label which made no demands on her gender. Unusual in the music industry, 4AD provided a home for many strong female singers/songwriters on the basis of their music alone – to the best of my knowledge, image/style/look were never raised. Artwork was, of course, given great importance, and the styling of a personal image may have been discussed in this context, but I'm not aware that Ivo ever tried to manipulate the stage or media image of any of his artists.

Entirely out of the blue, Brendan called me one day in April 1995 inviting me over to Quivvy for a week or so in late May to join a percussion ensemble to record rhythm tracks as the basis for new DCD material. Lisa would be over for the sessions, and Robbie, Rónán, and Lance would also be there. I was overjoyed at the prospect and it brought home to me that I'd been in a deep denial about how much I'd been missing my involvement. After checking with Nicki that she could manage for a few days, I confirmed with Brendan and booked my return flight to Dublin. The sessions took place at Quivvy between 27 May and 3 June. Brendan had been listening to a lot of Brazilian samba-style rhythms and the sessions were to work around and develop his own take on some of the basic patterns. Samba rhythms are typically underpinned by a deep root drum called a 'surdo', and my role was to play these equivalent parts on an orchestral bass drum laid on its side. The others would play various hand drums, shakers, cymbals, and bells, and the sessions were engineered by a new collaborator, German electronic composer Klaus Vormehr who also had a grounding in Afro-Brazilian percussion. As ever, Brendan had everything impeccably organised and our daytime sessions were regimented and productive.

Aside of the sessions, I had time to take in the church and its spectacular setting, to catch up with Lisa who'd been working on solo material and was to have her first album released by 4AD later in the year, to clown around with Robbie and to get to know Lance, Rónán, and Klaus a little. The five of us lads were being accommodated in holiday log cabins on a nearby farm owned by a wacky German expat – Fred Müller. Fred lived off the land as far as possible and the kitchen door always stood open while we ate at the communal table so he could grab his shotgun from the wall at any opportune moment and take out a passing pheasant or rabbit – alarming at first, but entirely commonplace after a few days. On one night during our stay we had an impromptu Irish percussion jam in one of the cabins – a regular happening for the others, but an unforgettable 'craic' for me.

On another evening towards the end of the week, I was supping a few beers with Brendan in a bar in the local town of Belturbet and discussing a shared love of Massive Attack. As usual Brendan was one step ahead of me and had a solo album by Shara Nelson, the voice of Massive Attack classic *Unfinished Sympathy*. He asked the barman to play it so I could hear it, and I was just getting nicely chilled out to 'What Silence Knows' (highly recommended) when our conversation took a strikingly unexpected turn. Brendan asked me if I was still writing my own songs, which I vaguely had been, but without any great focus or direction. I replied in the affirmative, to which he offered that if I could get a set of songs together for an album, I could come to Quivvy and he'd record them for me. I was stunned. I thought my commercially doomed 12" had been the beginning and end of my solo career. It was a big commitment and I must have asked him several times if he was really sure, but even in the sobriety of the following day, he was adamant that he meant it. So I returned home at the end of the week, not only having had a ball being part of DCD again, but also brimming with the very real possibility of making my first full album.

I started developing a few ideas but was conscious of the limitations of the equipment I had available. I trawled around some music stores in London's West End trying to get my head around the current crop of music computers and what my non-tech brain might get to grips with. I settled on the idea of a 'workstation' – a keyboard with an in-built sequencer and bank of sampled sounds – and plumped for a Korg X3 as it appeared to be among the simplest to operate. Even then the poor, defenceless X3 came within a hair's breadth of being jettisoned out the window on a few occasions, but eventually I had a 'road to Damascus' moment and found myself capable of multitrack composition.

In August Lisa's album *The Mirror Pool* was released. A few of the songs I knew as she'd performed them in earlier DCD concerts, but much of it was new and it was fascinating to hear what she'd been working on. And, at a weighty 68+ minutes, it was evident this had been a long time brewing. The tracks 'La Bas' and 'Gloradin' were featured in the soundtrack of Michael Mann movie *Heat* released that December. With a cast including Al Pacino, Robert De Niro, Val Kilmer, Natalie Portman, and Jon Voight, and a soundtrack setting her songs alongside those of Brian Eno and Moby, Lisa was in impressive company. It would also be the start of an ongoing working relationship with Michael Mann who, a few years earlier, had included Brendan's DCD song 'Severance' in an episode of US TV series *Miami Vice* on which he was executive producer.

In my less elevated world, *Melody Maker*'s 16 September issue included publication of a reader's letter from 'Claire Moody, Harrow' which read:

> Is it true that Peter Ulrich from Dead Can Dance has released a solo album? I've looked for it everywhere, but with no joy at all. Most record shops haven't even heard of him. Can you help?

Suspicious, you might think, that it should be submitted by a reader claiming to be from Harrow, and with the name 'Moody' to boot, but I swear I wasn't behind it, and I never did find out who this is/was. Nevertheless, I'm grateful for the interest, and to *MM* for providing a brief but informative response about my *Taqaharu* single, though without knowing of the album now in the pipeline. Sadly no spike in sales resulted from this unexpected blaze of publicity.

DCD's *Spiritchaser* was released in June 1996, shortly after Lisa's brother Mark had died suddenly and tragically, and the album is dedicated to his memory. This naturally had a profound effect on Lisa, as well as resulting in her and her mother taking on the upbringing of Mark's young son Jack. But with a major DCD tour lined up to support the album release and kicking off in Dublin on 2 June, Lisa had to throw herself into preparations to depart for three months.

Release of *Spiritchaser* threw up an unexpected consequence when it was alleged that a melodic theme in the track 'Indus' was overly similar to that of Beatles' song 'Within You Without You' on their *Sgt Pepper's* album, penned by George Harrison. No imitation had been intended, but Brendan had to contact Harrison for permission to continue using the piece. Harrison agreed, but his record company insisted that he be given a partial songwriting credit from that time on. I guess that kind of makes 'Indus' a DCD-Beatles collaboration?

The album's eight tracks included two which used rhythm sections from the previous year's Quivvy sessions – 'Nierika' and 'Dedicacé Outò'. Less well known is that a special programme was produced for the American leg of the 1996 DCD tour which included a single-track CD of an instrumental called 'Sambatiki', also based on one of our rhythm sections from the Quivvy sessions. This track was subsequently included on the retrospective DCD Box Set (2001), but the original CD single in the tour presentation box is, I think, quite rare now. For me personally, it felt nice to have this connection with the tour, which was the most extensive yet for DCD. And Brendan's programme notes revealed a pasttime hitherto unknown to me – dragon hunting! The European leg lined up as follows:

Ireland:
Sunday, 2 June, Dublin, Olympia Theatre

Belgium:
Thursday, 6 June, Antwerp, Queen Elisabeth Hall

Germany:
Friday, 7 June, Cologne, Philharmonie

Hungary:
Sunday, 9 June, Budapest, Budai Parkszínpad

Czech Republic:
Tuesday, 11 June, Prague, Palace of Culture

Germany:
Wednesday, 12 June, Munich, Circus Krone
Friday, 14 June, Frankfurt, Alper Oper

France:
Saturday, 15 June, Paris, Salle Pleyel
Sunday, 16 June, Paris, Salle Pleyel

Greece:
Tuesday, 18 June, Athens, Lycabettus Theatre
Wednesday, 19 June, Thessaloniki, Sileon Theatre

Spain:
Friday, 21 June, Barcelona, Palau de la Música Catalana
Saturday, 22 June, Madrid, Teatro de Monumental

Germany:
Monday, 24 June, Berlin, Tempodrom
Tuesday, 25 June, Hamburg, Musikhalle

Netherlands:
Thursday, 27 June, Amsterdam, Carré Theatre
Friday, 28 June, Amsterdam, Carré Theatre

England:
Sunday, 30 June, London, The Forum

Turkey:
Thursday, 4 July, Istanbul, International Jazz Festival

DCD's lineup comprised Brendan, Lisa, Robbie, John, Lance, Rónán, and additional percussionist Nigel Flegg. The schedule included some grand venues, not least the Palau de la Música Catalana in Barcelona – a designated UNESCO World Heritage Site. Chief Talking Head David Byrne turned up in Thessaloniki and met the gang backstage, and all had been running smoothly when the dreaded tour lurgy struck between Hamburg and Amsterdam. The first night at the Carré had to be cancelled, and then, to my great dismay, the only UK show at The Forum was also struck off – so that was my only chance to catch the tour gone.

With the band holed up in London before going to the unusual scheduling of an appearance at a major Jazz Festival in Istanbul, I met up with Brendan one evening to discuss, amongst other things, progress with songs for my album. He anticipated being able to give me some studio time later in the year, so it was straight back to the X3 for me. After Istanbul, DCD headed for the Americas:

North America:
Wednesday, 10 July, Philadelphia, Keswick Theater
Thursday, 11 July, Washington DC, Warner Theater

Canada:
Saturday, 13 July, Montreal, Maison Nueve
Sunday, 14 July, Montreal, Maison Nueve
Monday, 15 July, Toronto, Massey Hall

North America:
Wednesday, 17 July, New York, New York City Center
Friday, 19 July, Boston, Harbor Lights Pavilion
Sunday, 21 July, Ann Arbor, Michigan Theater
Monday, 22 July, Cleveland, Lakewood Civic Theater
Wednesday, 24 July, Chicago, Riviera Theater
Friday, 26 July, Minneapolis, Orpheum Theater
Tuesday, 30 July, Santa Fe, Paolo Soleri Amphitheater
Thursday, 1 August, Boulder, Fox Theater
Friday, 2 August, Salt Lake City, Kingsbury Hall
Monday, 5 August, Seattle, Paramount Theatre
Tuesday, 6 August, Portland, Arlene Schnitzer Concert Hall

Canada:
Wednesday, 7 August, Vancouver, Orpheum Theatre

North America:
Friday, 9 August, Berkeley, Greek Theatre
Saturday, 10 August, Los Angeles, Universal Amphitheatre
Sunday, 11 August, San Diego, Humphreys Concerts by the Bay
Wednesday, 14 August, Dallas, Majestic Theater
Thursday, 15 August, Houston, Cullen Performance Hall
Saturday, 17 August, Atlanta, Symphony Hall
Monday, 19 August, Miami, Gusman Center

Brazil:
Wednesday, 21 August, Sao Paulo, Olympia Hall
Thursday, 22 August, Rio de Janeiro, Morro da Urca

Argentina:
Sunday, 25 August, Buenos Aires, Dr Jekyll

Mexico:
Wednesday, 28 August, Mexico City, Teatro Metropólitan

Thursday, 29 August, Mexico City, Teatro Metropólitan
Saturday, 31 August, Guadalajara, Teatro Degollado
Sunday, 1 September, León, Teatro Manuel Doblado

At the LA show held within Universal Studios' own 'city', Brendan later told me it was like a typical Hollywood social event, the backstage area teeming with freeloaders and networkers who had no interest in the music. The band had to walk through this party to get to the stage, which set him on edge before their performance got underway, and then as they were playing, the hum of conversation, punctuated by yells and shrieks of laughter, was clearly audible on stage. Although they made it through most of the set, Brendan – sensing that interest levels front of stage were not that much greater than in the backstage soirée – finally lost it during 'Cantara', kicked a cymbal into the audience in frustration and stormed off. Some years later, the venue would be demolished to make way for The Wizarding World of Harry Potter attraction, so Brendan's curse on the luvvie muggles eventually did the trick.

There were a few other hiccups – the Boston show had to be abandoned after Lisa fainted, Salt Lake City was cancelled due to sickness in the ranks, and Guadalajara was ruled out as a result of a bizarre scheduling clash with the city's annual Mariachi Festival! But otherwise the tour had generally played to packed houses in a string of impressive venues and DCD continued to go from strength to strength.

A couple of months after the tour, Brendan told me we could start on my recordings and I booked return flights to Dublin for the weekend of 6–9 December. The World Wide Web was destined to have an unimaginably huge impact on every aspect of the creation, production, and circulation of music, but back in 1996 we were only seeing early glimmers of this. Although personal computers were becoming a regular feature of the domestic environment and people were getting hooked up to the internet, these were still on 'dial-up' connections and download speeds were excruciatingly slow. There was certainly no possibility for the remote file sharing that is now ubiquitous, and I couldn't send Brendan my X3 programming on the 'floppy disks' that were then used for data storage as the data would be incompatible with the systems he was using. So, the main purpose of this trip to Quivvy was simply to take the X3 itself so that Brendan could transfer my programming to his recording setup. At least most electronic keyboards and recording systems by now featured a system called MIDI (Musical Instrument Digital Interface) which allowed them to talk to one another.

As it was just me visiting this time, I stayed at Brendan and Fran's home in Killyvally on the outskirts of Cavan town, a beautiful old farmhouse at the end of a track with rolling fields leading down to a lake – the kind of place I dreamed about living in! And under Fran's influence, there were animals everywhere – I woke the first morning with a strange weight on my head and reached up to find a sizeable long-haired cat using my crown as a mattress, while downstairs in the living room, humans were frequently relegated to sitting on the floor as the two sofas were occupied by a pair of Irish Wolfhounds, each the size of a small horse.

Over at Quivvy we transferred my sequencing, the elementary standard of which left a lot to be desired, and poor Brendan was alarmed by the volume of repair work facing him to pull it into a usable shape. We decided 'Taqaharu's Leaving' and 'Evocation' would be included on the album in their original formats from my sessions with John Rivers – the 12" had received relatively little exposure and I still believed in those songs, so it was an opportunity to give them a new lease of life. I then wanted to include a new recording of 'Smiling She Rose' (the yang ch'in-led song which Brendan had helped me demo back on the Isle of Dogs) and a new version of the song from my teenage years, 'Time and a Word'. To these would be added five entirely new songs written since Brendan had offered me the recording opportunity. We discussed the styles and instrumentation, and I had some very rough cassettes which I'd made at home with the four-track to indicate how the vocal melodies would sit. And that was it – I was off back to London leaving it all in Brendan's hands.

While Brendan worked his magic and developed the instrumentation, I wrote and rewrote lyrics. A song that had started out as 'The Maze' morphed into an entirely different song called 'Nocturne' to which Brendan added gorgeous Spanish guitars and soaring strings. The subject of a piece I'd written in the style of a medieval dance with swirling bagpipes unexpectedly became a reflection on how quickly childhood passes and the parental need to cherish every moment – 'Life Amongst the Black Sheep' was my response to Louise and Ellie turning nine and six respectively. 'Time and a Word' retained the words I'd written as a fifteen- or sixteen-year-old largely intact, but needed a few additions. Brendan intuitively picked up on this song having been written in an entirely different era and gave the arrangement a hefty twist of psychedelia plus a good lick of 'prog'. While I was generally amazed and thrilled with the directions my songs were being taken in, my one sadness was that Brendan was unable to make 'Smiling She Rose' work. He tried a number of different angles, but couldn't find his way into the song and we had to drop it. The early demo I'd made some ten years earlier had been popular with most people who heard it, and was Nicki's, and had been my dad's, favourite of my songs.

I made two further trips to Ireland for sessions at Quivvy. The first was in March 1997 during which we recorded the bulk of my vocals. The second started with an overnight stop in Dublin on Saturday, 25 April, where Brendan was doing a one-off solo gig at the Red Box as support on a bill headed by Nick Kelly, former front man of Irish band The Fat Lady Sings. Over the following week we added the remaining parts to my songs and settled on final arrangements for the six Quivvy tracks, and I left Brendan to do some additional mixing and polishing. On my homebound trip to London on Sunday, 4 May, I found myself on the same flight as Katrina and the Waves, still on a bender following their victory the previous night in Dublin at the annual Eurovision Song Contest with their song 'Love Shine a Light'. It was a strange contrast to be contemplating the gravitas of finalising my first album which the waiting world as yet knew nothing of, while they celebrated having the most popular song in Europe.

By mid-June I'd received the final mixes from Brendan, pressed a batch of demo CDs, and started approaching labels in pursuit of a release deal (having long since decided that Corner Stone Records was not, after all, going to be the foundation block of my own label empire). 4AD were quick to tell me it wasn't for them, and it also didn't find a home with any other labels within the Beggars Banquet stable, so I was out on my own, cold-calling at labels who would know of DCD, but nothing of Peter Ulrich. My obvious targets initially were the leading indie labels of the day including Mute, Rough Trade, Factory, Cherry Red, Creation, Cooking Vinyl, Dedicated, and so on, but I also circulated the majors – EMI, Universal, Polydor, Epic, Virgin, Warner/WEA, RCA, Mercury, Sony, Chrysalis, etc. on the off-chance. No response whatsoever – no interest, and no feedback so I had no idea whether my samplers were even getting listened to, let alone what the reaction was if they were given an airing.

I started sending sampler packs to labels in the US, by now well established as DCD's largest market (by album sales), a more costly and protracted process. The odd package would be returned to me with a 'thanks, but no thanks' letter, sometimes with an encouraging note. Charles Powne, head of the label Soleilmoon, liked the album but didn't feel it was right for his niche market.

Catherine McLaren at Nettwerk, Canada wrote: 'I listened to your sampler, which I really enjoyed, but . . .'

Daniel Savage at Beloved Records in the States wrote: 'The vocals are great, and the string arrangements. Have you tried Projekt?'

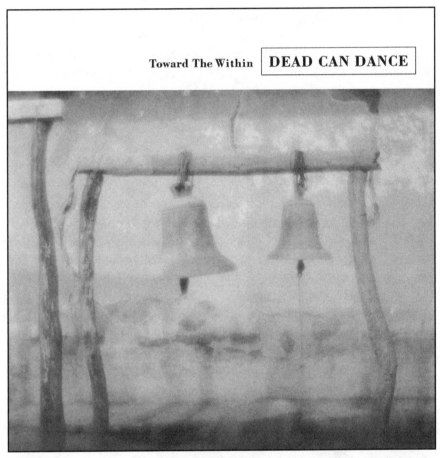

Fig. 19. Cover artwork for DCD's *Toward the Within* CD album recorded and released alongside the official video of the shows at the Mayfair Theater Santa Monica, LA, November 1993. Courtesy of 4AD Records.

Yes, I had tried Projekt, but received no response. The label was one of my first ports of call in the States as it had a reputation for being modelled to some extent on 4AD and laid claim to being the leading indie label for goth and ethereal music. I had high hopes of a response, but nothing had come through. Every now and then I'd have to listen to my mixes again, just to remind myself that I was really happy with my songs and that Brendan had made a wonderful job of the arrangements and production. The lack of response was disappointing, but it didn't shake my belief that I had something worthy to offer.

In early March, Brendan was in London briefly and we met up and visited JAS Musical store in Southall which specialises in classical Indian instruments. He was still working on his solo album, but punctuated with work on some other projects. He'd done the soundtrack for an Irish movie called *Sunset Heights* and had been collaborating with French composer Hector Zazou on an album due for release later in the year called *Lights in the Dark* which would also feature contributions from Peter Gabriel and Egyptian percussionist Hossam Ramzy. (Both Brendan and Lisa had previously contributed to Zazou's 1992 album *Sahara Blue*, and Brendan to 1994's *Chansons des Mers Froids*.)

'Nierika' had won the annual award for most played song on US College Radio in the year following the release of *Spiritchaser* and, against his better judgement, Brendan went with Fran and Momentum Music publisher Andy Heath to an American music awards ceremony at the Dorchester in London where he found himself brushing shoulders with various pop luminaries and sat at the same table as Spice Girls manager and 'Pop Idol' creator-in-waiting Simon Fuller. Brendan had never felt more like a fish out of water and vowed never again.

April saw the release of Massive Attack's *Teardrop*, featuring Liz Fraser's vocal – a strong contender for my all-time favourite single. It was only later I heard the backstory, that in the midst of writing the lyrics and recording the track, Liz received news of the tragic and unexplained drowning of Jeff Buckley. As the Cocteaus had limped towards their final album *Milk and Kisses* (1996), and following her personal split from Robin, Liz reportedly had a brief but intense relationship with Jeff after he'd contacted her having heard her sing his father's 'Song to the Siren', and they'd become obsessed with each other's voices. At the time of working on *Teardrop* – for which she was allegedly chosen over Madonna by a two-to-one vote within the Massive ranks – Liz had been looking through old letters and thinking about Jeff when the news of his death came through, and has said that the song became about him. It's extraordinary how Ivo's passion for 'Song to the Siren' inadvertently created a spine through so much of the 4AD story, with epic highs and lows, extremes of joy and pain.

Another curious home for a piece of DCD music cropped up when 'Nierika' appeared behind the opening titles of Mexico's TV Azteca soap opera *La Chacala* which would run from 1997–98. The action was based in Chacala, a Pacific beach town whose name apparently translates as 'where there are shrimp'. In April 1998, Lisa's second album *Duality* hit the streets – a collaboration with Australian composer/engineer/producer Pieter Bourke who had been a guest musician on her *Mirror Pool* album and a subsequent member of her live band. The album includes the riveting vocal delivery of 'Sacrifice', a fine example of the extraordinary power and fragility that Lisa can combine to such a mind-blowing effect. Many years later, I spotted beneath a YouTube post of a live rendition of 'Sacrifice', a comment by Elvin Haceliyev:

> Doctor: You have only five minutes to live.
> Me: Play this music.
> Doctor: But it's eight minutes.
> God: It's OK.

My search for a release deal continued to find a dead end down every street and I was struggling to resist a loss of heart. Nicki, Louise, Ellie, and I went to stay with my mother in August to mark my fortieth birthday, but on the morning of my big day, Nicki and I were woken by the girls telling us that granny had fallen on the floor. I ran through to find my mother having what I recognised instantly as a stroke. The memories of everything we'd been through with my father came flooding back, and the ambulance came to take us to the same hospital where Dad had seen out his final months. Mum was seventy-seven and until the previous night had been fit, healthy, and active – now she was struck down, unable to move or speak. I sat by her bedside all day and evening, with little change. When I returned next morning, she looked brighter and . . . spoke to me! I was stunned – I'd thought she would never speak again like my father. Fortunately, the rapid attention she'd received enabled the medical staff to minimise the effects and get her blood circulating efficiently again. I stayed on for a couple of days, and then went back and forwards over the next week or so, until she was discharged from hospital, declared able to largely resume her normal life, albeit with a daily aspirin prescribed by the hospital, and a daily glass of red wine by her doctor (off the record).

Despite Mum's recovery, the experience knocked me out of my stride and I lost impetus with my search for a release deal. As the year came to a close, Brendan and Lisa announced to the world that Dead Can Dance was over. They'd started work on material for a new album, but found that directional disagreements ran too deep and the spark simply wasn't there. Lisa was bouyed by her solo work and had further projects in the pipeline, while Brendan wanted to concentrate on finally bringing his solo debut to the world. I was bitterly disappointed as a fan that there would be no more DCD offerings, but this also now rendered me the ex-drummer of an ex-band with a solo album that nobody wanted – the light at the end of the tunnel was getting dimmer.

Early in 1999, I met up in London with Nick Sarikostas, who was over from Athens on behalf of Greek importer/distributor Penguin Records, and his friend Gary Levermore who'd previously released the Heavenly Bodies' album on his Third Mind label, worked with The Legendary Pink Dots among others, and was now running the UK arm of Nettwerk Records. The evening found us in The Castle pub on Pentonville Road, and the conversation wove round to my homeless album, which Gary had heard and been moderately complimentary about. He immediately instructed that I must send it to Sam Rosenthal at Projekt in Chicago as the obvious label for me. I gave him the old 'been there, done that', to which he replied simply 'Well send it again!' as if it were the most obvious thing in the world, with Nick nodding vigorously in agreement. It had never occurred to me to send again to a label I'd already sent to, but worth a punt I supposed? So the following day I made up another package, this time addressed personally to Sam Rosenthal, and with a covering letter which opened: 'I am writing to you at the suggestion of Gary Levermore. . .'

Another month had drifted past when my fax machine sprang into action and churned out a letter from Sam. It was noncommittal, but said that he was listening to my demo and I would hear from him again shortly. I only had to wait a couple of days and another fax came through. He enjoyed the way my demo 'falls somewhere between the work of Dead Can Dance and the vocal stylings of Brian Eno or John Cale', and then, following a bit of background info about his label, he wrote: 'I would be very interested in releasing your disc on Projekt.'

So, there it was . . . my offer . . . subject to terms to be agreed. Within a week we had a contract signed and sealed and, although the album release was not scheduled until September, I was suddenly immersed in activity to get everything prepared.

First I had to get final mixes to Sam for the album to be mastered under his control in Chicago. Next up was the cover artwork. My notion – a mix of primitive tribal designs and geometric compass which had been compiled under my direction by digital artist friend Tony Pinfold – was sent to Sam and immediately rejected as being entirely inappropriate. He wanted something that would fit with Projekt and have likely appeal to his established fanbase. I was put in contact with Timothy O'Donnell, a designer I didn't previously know, but who'd worked with Vaughan at 4AD/V23 and was now with London design agency Stylorouge who were doing some of the most high-profile album covers of the era for major labels. I had a couple of good meetings with Tim, and both Sam and I were very happy with what he came up with.

I did a photo session in Finsbury Park with my old mate Bob Bridges behind the lens to get a new stock of publicity mugshots. I got my first email account as it was clear that I couldn't continue with a combination of fax and Nicki's work email to communicate with Sam and the team at Projekt. Sam, meanwhile, had started circulating a promotional 3-track Projekt sampler EP featuring 'Taqaharu's Leaving' alongside songs from two of my new labelmates, Tara Vanflower and Mira. It was getting some good feedback, including a DJ called Michael on WRAS (Atlanta, GA) radio who emailed: 'The cut by Peter Ulrich is amazing!'

I was also in touch with Brendan to check he was OK with me being referred to in publicity as the 'former drummer of Dead Can Dance' and for him to be referenced as the arranger and producer of the relevant six tracks. Brendan was fine with it all, happy for me that I finally had my release organised, and told me his own solo debut was due for release in September. Funny that after all that led up to this point, we were going to release our first solo albums at virtually the same moment. As things turned out, my album release was brought forward by Projekt to 10 August 1999, while Brendan's was delayed slightly by 4AD to 4 October, so we didn't quite walk down the debutant steps side by side, but finally my album saw the light of day, with the title *Pathways and Dawns* and the track listing:

Taqaharu's Leaving
Always Dancing
Life Amongst the Black Sheep
Journey of Discovery
Nocturne
Evocation
The Springs of Hope
Time and a Word

These were still the days of people buying music in a physical format – mostly CD. The shift from brick and mortar stores to online vendors was underway, but the digital download revolution was yet to kick in. When *Pathways and Dawns* was released, it was theoretically worldwide, but in reality it was probably 95 percent in the US, so it was odd for me that all the activity on my album was happening across the Atlantic and I was detached from it. One of the big outlets at the time for Projekt releases was the Borders store group which was widespread and influential in the US market, and Sam had bought prime in-store display and listening post positions for *P&D*. I craved walking into a Borders in downtown NYC or LA and seeing a rack of Peter Ulrich albums sitting up front and in the collective face of the great record-buying public, but I had to leave that to my imagination.

What I ***could*** experience firsthand were the reviews landing in my new inbox. And they got off to a promising start. Dave Aftandilian writing in US magazine *Ink 19* noted tracks progressively as 'majestic' and 'joyous' to 'exquisite', throwing in complimentary references to Pink Floyd and Syd Barrett-like vocals, until he arrived at closing track 'Time and a Word' which he dismissed as 'Tangerine-Dream-on-a-very-bad-day'. But his overall summation was: 'This is a fine album by an artist I'd love to hear more from soon.'

And thankfully, an online review on *StarVox* by Blu came swiftly to the rescue of my teenage bedroom song: 'And like the hopeful but bittersweet ending to a movie, "Time and a Word" rounds off this CD sweetly and softly,' before summing up the entire album as: 'Simply beautiful.'

Lexicon magazine's September issue ran an interview with me in addition to a separate review which concluded: '*Pathways and Dawns* is a wonderful collection of songs that, while in the 4AD school, shimmers with an inner lightness that makes it very different from any other 4AD album.'

Then, in October came the review Projekt had primed me would be particularly significant for its reach into their established audience – *Alternative Press* magazine. Thankfully, writer Mark Burbey did us proud, first with the general comment: 'It's Ulrich's gifts as a composer, percussionist and vocalist that win over the listener,' and then with a completely unexpected and gobsmackingly favourable comparison to arguably the biggest band of all time:

> The excellent 'Nocturne' is Beatlesque, with Spanish guitar and rich orchestral bridges, and 'The Springs of Hope' sounds swiped from the same album the Fab Four might have made had they signed with 4AD instead of Capitol.

Wow – I didn't see that coming! Just as my head was swelling to the point of having to negotiate doorways side-on, Kira Mickle's review in the November issue of *Punchline* brought me crashing back to Earth:

> If *Pathways and Dawns* was more like Dead Can Dance, I might be able to listen without wanting to stick pencils in my eyes . . . Ulrich creates bland goth that I have no desire ever to hear again . . . He carries a tune like Nigel from Spinal Tap.

I've always held the opinion that, if you're going to put your work into the public domain, you have to be prepared to take whatever is thrown at you. At least the damnation was done with humour (I like to think!) and, having the cushion of my collected positive reviews for comfort, I could afford a wry smile.

The December issue of *Music Review* magazine ran its *P&D* review alongside the soundtrack album for new Michael Mann movie *The Insider* by a certain Lisa Gerrard and Pieter Bourke, referencing the post-DCD era that both offerings now represented. Although not a huge box office hit, the movie was critically acclaimed and notched up seven Oscar nominations, including Best Actor for Russell Crowe who would come to cross paths rather prominently with Lisa in the near future. Lisa and Pieter's soundtrack received a Golden Globe nomination, while the film also featured musical contributions from Graeme Revell, formerly the driving force behind 1980s industrial group SPK.

Meanwhile, Brendan's beautiful album *Eye of the Hunter* was being well received. I'd been surprised when I heard it as Brendan had played me some of the material he was working on a couple of years earlier at Quivvy which had been totally different, in a groove not dissimilar to Massive Attack or Portishead. In one respect it felt a shame that everything from that period seemed to have gone as it had been sounding amazing, but Brendan had gravitated back to the spheres in which he truly thrives, inhabited by Tim Buckley, and Scott Walker, and the resultant beautifully crafted, epic soundscapes embracing Brendan's ever-richening voice are something very special. A substantial interview feature with Brendan appeared in UK national newspaper *The Independent* on 8 October, and the following week he played a solo London show to support his album release at The Scala in Kings Cross. Nicki and I went along, and it was a lovely show, but we were surprised to find the audience only numbered a couple of hundred – a DCD show would have been rammed and I'd expected a solo Brendan show to have the same pulling power, but it doesn't work that way.

While Projekt's promotion of *P&D* was very much geared to its home market in the States, a few copies were reaching Europe 'on import', mainly via an Italian-based distributor called Audioglobe which handled a lot of Projekt's titles, and were also finding their way into the hands of reviewers. More positive coverage appeared in *Side-Line* (Belgium), *Sorted* (Ireland), *Elegy* (France), *Black Magazine* and *Ironflame* (Germany), and *Alter Ego* (Ukraine). The January 2000 issue of Italian magazine *Il Mucchio* included a free covermount CD for which Sam had granted permission for 'Life Amongst the Black Sheep' to be included and which also featured a live track by former 4AD stalwarts Bauhaus.

Alongside this, I'd been investigating the possibilities of getting a licensing deal set up from Projekt to a UK distributor so *P&D* could officially get into the retail chain in my homeland. The favourable reviews I'd been collecting did the trick and I secured a deal with Pinnacle – at this time the leading independent distributor by some distance. Their double page advertisement in the February issue of *MOJO* magazine included a feature panel on *P&D* and listed one hundred record stores covering the length and breadth of the country which now either stocked *P&D* or would supply to order. Pinnacle took a total of three hundred CDs, so clearly none of the stores had gone overboard with their stock, but at least it was out there. *MOJO* was by this point established as one of the leading influential monthly music magazines in the UK, and in their March issue they ran a brief *P&D* review:

> Ex-Dead Can Dance man Peter Ulrich walks with the ghosts of Japan, Tones on Tail and Depeche Mode while singing with an undeniable *Another Green World–* period Eno lilt in his voice.

Not exactly a 'rave', but some big-name comparisons which should help. *P&D* was also picking up radio airplay with some interesting variations. KUSP in Santa Cruz, CA reported playing 'Nocturne' and 'The Springs of Hope', 'Evocation' hit No. 13 in the Top 40 chart on CFBU in Ontario, Canada, and *P&D* struck the No. 1 spot in the New Age Voice Top 20 album chart on WSYC in Shippensburg, PA. In the UK, DJ Ashley Franklin featured several tracks on his *Soundscapes* show on BBC Radio Derby and included *P&D* in his 'Best of 99' review, while Meridian Radio ran a live interview with me, interspersed with four tracks from the album, on 'Dave Wright's Saturday Sizzler'! The April 2000 issue of *Losing Today* – an Italian-based English language magazine principally aimed at the US market – included the biggest interview feature I've ever had, extending over six entire full colour pages, and they even added a review of *P&D* elsewhere in the same issue, calling it a 'rich, well-made masterwork'.

The following month brought a phenomenon on a different scale entirely. Ridley Scott's epic movie *Gladiator* was released and became a global smash. The film propelled Russell Crowe into superstardom at the head of a cast which included Joaquin Phoenix, Connie Nielsen, Oliver Reed, Djimon Hounsou, Derek Jacobi, and Richard Harris. The soundtrack was written by Hans Zimmer and Lisa Gerrard, with Lisa performing the main theme and many other parts of the score.

I've heard a couple of versions of how this came about. Although perhaps slightly inaccurate in places, my favourite is this. Hans Zimmer, the go-to composer for so many leading Hollywood film-makers, was contracted for the soundtrack. He had in mind to feature a haunting female voice, with Israeli singer Ofra Haza in his original thinking. Tragically Haza died suddenly, aged only forty-two, before she was due to start work on the film, and Zimmer was at a loss to think of another voice which would work. During breaks in filming, one of the studio technicians was listening to Dead Can Dance on a portable music player such that Lisa's voice drifted across and found its way into Hans Zimmer's head, commanding his attention. He demanded to know who was this singer. His secretary was charged with contacting 4AD and ascertaining her immediate availability. Lisa was relaxing in Gippsland back in Oz when the phone rang and the caller asked if she could jump on a flight to LA and do three days' work with Hans Zimmer on a new movie soundtrack. She considered the proposition for a full three seconds and started packing. As soon as she and Hans met, they got on like a house on fire, and she ended up staying for three months and cowriting and performing much of the soundtrack, for which she subsequently won a Golden Globe award and an Oscar nomination jointly with Zimmer. And in such moments, the stuff of legend is created.

Lisa has worked with Zimmer on and off ever since, particularly touring live performances of the *Gladiator* songs internationally. He holds Lisa in the highest esteem, having been quoted as saying: 'There are lots of extraordinary singers in the world, but there's no one like Lisa. She can move mountains with her voice.'

He also tells a wonderful story of a moment during the making of *Gladiator* when, after a very long session, they'd reached a point where the development of a section of the soundtrack wasn't working and they'd seemingly run out of ideas:

> At about two o'clock in the morning, and at the last minute, Lisa said 'OK, what about this?' She got up in front of the microphone and from within her came this sound that you'd never heard before. I turned to Ridley, who was sitting on the couch, and neither of us could speak. His eyebrows were sky high, and with that voice, she pinned us to the wall.
> [quotes extracted from a feature in *The Australian*, 1 December 2018]

Working on *Gladiator* also brought Lisa back into contact with Russell Crowe and this time their friendship was firmly cemented. A singer and musician himself, Crowe also eulogises about Lisa's voice, while on a personal level describing her as 'some kind of ethereal angel and earth mother goddess, big sister combination in my life'!

Back in my world, Sam proposed including one of my P&D tracks on a compilation to be released on Projekt, which came out in August 2000. Titled *Orphée*, it was billed as 'an introspective descent into the male soul'. My song 'Life Amongst the Black Sheep' found itself sitting alongside tracks by original Ultravox singer John Foxx, Japan's David Sylvian, Steve Jansen, and Richard Barbieri, Bauhaus offshoot Tones on Tail and cult US band Christian Death. There was also a track licensed from Pieter Nooten and Michael Brook's 4AD album *Sleeps with the Fishes* and contributions from other Projekt artists, including Sam's own Black Tape for a Blue Girl. The key additional dimension to the release was an elegant twelve-page booklet, designed by Timothy O'Donnell and featuring an exclusive retelling of the Orphée myth by cult author Neil Gaiman. On the sly, I sent a 'reader' enquiry under a pseudonym to UK music monthly Q magazine asking if they knew anything about a mysterious release on an American label featuring John Foxx and former members of Japan. The letter was published in the December issue, together with a reply identifying the *Orphée* album and providing some information on it, but as an unwitting (I assume) punishment for my deception, they failed to mention the contribution of Peter Ulrich.

Despite all this activity and more positive reviews than I'd dared hope for, sales of P&D were disappointing. At the outset, Sam and I had impressed on each other that our expectations shouldn't be too high, but we'd both harboured hopes of more substantial figures. While never for one moment was I presumptuous enough to think that DCD fans would automatically like my music, I did believe that the connection would encourage the release to be widely listened to, and that it would then start to create its own audience. But, while a DCD album could now sell half a million plus, P&D was struggling to tip over 2,000 sales worldwide.

One obvious problem was that the release wasn't being supported by any live shows. P&D was entirely a studio project – there was no band and I didn't have the wherewithal to put any kind of live act together. This, of course, creates a classic Catch-22 – I needed sales to provide the funding for a live show, but I needed the live show to generate the sales. Over the course of the next eighteen months or so I continued to explore every avenue I could think of to kick-start some momentum, but only achieved the occasional isolated nice review. Sales ticked over at a slow trickle, and over time would creep up towards 5,000, but activity around the release faded and in the end I had to accept the need to move on. I was contracted to Projekt for a minimum of two albums and it was over four years since I'd written anything, so some new material was long overdue.

Lisa continued to be active with film soundtracks. For Michael Mann's *Ali* (2001), with Will Smith in the title role, she collaborated again with Pieter Bourke, and for New Zealand director Niki Caro's film *Whale Rider* (2002), whose soundtrack was released on 4AD the following year, she attributes a huge input to Simon Bowley who did the engineering and mixing and 'was a rock and brilliant'. Another Ridley Scott/Hans Zimmer collaboration on 2001's *Black Hawk Down* brought Lisa an invite to contribute an interpretation of the song 'Gortoz a ran' performed with Breton singer Denez Prigent. 2001 also saw the release of Canadian director Jesse Heffring's debut film *Coil* dealing with rape victim trauma, shot from the perspective of newsreels and video surveillance footage, and which played at several film festivals picking up awards for innovation. Lisa and Brendan both contributed to the soundtrack, which also featured 'Om Namaha Shiva' performed by English actress/singer Sheila Chandra who'd recently had a cover version of 'Song to the Siren' released on Real World compilation *Gifted*.

Brendan had gone off on a tangent, getting heavily involved in samba bands and organising workshops at Quivvy. He branched out from local groups to advertising online and ended up with DCD fans travelling from far and wide to attend. On one occasion, a group of them contacted me and came on to London to meet up. They'd had a great week at Quivvy drumming with Brendan, and were now regaled with my DCD recollections over dinner and drinks in London's Queensway. They included Wojtek Peczek from Poland, Deni from France who later unofficially uploaded some *P&D* tracks on YouTube with his own film sequences to help spread the word, and Saskia Dommisse from the Netherlands who kept me updated on her own music projects, including Poets to their Beloved, and would contribute to another of my albums some years down the line.

I dismissed the idea of approaching Brendan about working on new material of mine, partly because I felt he'd done enough for me and it would be an imposition, but more importantly I felt the need to prove to myself that I could write, arrange, and produce my material independently. I needed a new starting point. It doesn't come naturally to me to write lyrics from personal experiences. I have great admiration for songwriters like Jarvis Cocker and Guy Garvey who write wonderfully incisive, witty, and emotional takes on the loves and lives of the ordinary man – I can appreciate that, but I can't do it. Similarly, I love the strange and abstract world of Thom Yorke, but I'm too pragmatic to be inhabiting that kind of territory. I have to search out my subject matter.

In February 2001, Nicki and I saw an ensemble called Joglaresa at London's Queen Elizabeth Hall who specialise in early music of the Mediterranean lands. The concert programme introduced me to the concept of 'The True Cross', the surviving part of the wooden cross to which Jesus was nailed in the crucifixion, which became hugely symbolic during the period of the religious crusades, with both the Christian forces (holding Christ to be the Son of God) and the Muslim forces (not accepting Jesus as a deity, but rather a prophet second only in importance to Muhammad) seeking to possess the artefact which each believed would give them the edge in battle. I read up more on the phenomenon and a chorus started to form, questioning whether the blood spilled from the nailed hands was that of a mortal prophet or saviour god. I was underway and, having completed a basic arrangement and written more lyrics for 'The True Cross', I started the next song from the music rather than the subject matter. Long having loved the intro to Blondie's 'Fade Away and Radiate', I took the basic four-note hook, dropped out the second note to make it more ponderous, and transferred it to a grand, resonating cathedral organ sound, then built something entirely different. The result was brooding and suggested dark magic. I found an account by *Fortean Times* editor Paul Sieveking of a seventeenth-century tale of a spell being used to free a woman of an evil curse, from which emerged the song 'The Witchbottle of Suffolk', and into which I managed to slip an adapted quote from Shakespeare's *Hamlet*: 'He's hoisted by his own petard.'

I chanced on a book called *The Queen's Conjurer* by Benjamin Woolley telling the adventures of Dr John Dee, a controversial figure in the Court of Queen Elizabeth I who some considered a medical doctor, physician and scientist of high repute, while others – fearing his dabblings in alchemy, dark magic, and divination – plotted against him. Dee assembled a private library in his house at Mortlake consisting of rare books of religion, philosophy, astronomy, and astrology which he used in his lifelong quest to understand the mysteries of the universe. While I didn't want to create a 'concept' album – that much-derided ProgRock cliché – I liked the idea of a 'themed' album, a metaphor for entering a latter-day library like Dee's and dipping at random into books to discover different beliefs. I wrote 'At Mortlake' to open the album, following which each song would be an exploration of some belief or mystery.

For a song called 'Across the Bridge' which uses hammered dulcimer as lead instrument I wanted a sound closer to a Middle Eastern santoor. The sticks used for playing the santoor – known as mesrabs – are entirely different from the traditional Chinese bamboo hammers which Lisa and I had long used for playing the yang ch'ins. I'd recently bought a CD, *The Art of the Santoor from Iran*, by classical master Hossein Farjami, the booklet notes for which include that he is (or was at that time) based in London with his own workshop making and selling instruments. I contacted his record label – ARC Music – to ask for details of Farjami's workshop, and was surprised to be given his home phone number. I called him and he invited me to his flat which turned out to be in a tower block on a 1970s-built Council estate at World's End in Chelsea (the less 'glam' end of the King's Road) where the contrast between the brutalist architecture of the outside and the interior of his apartment strewn with Persian carpets and wonderful instruments couldn't fail to remind me of DCD's former world on the Isle of Dogs. After a fascinating chat with this renowned maestro of the santoor, I bought a pair of mesrabs for a measly few pounds and also came away with the gift of a cassette tape of music by classical Egyptian singer Oum Kalthoum as Hossein was horrified to learn that I claimed an interest in Arabic music but didn't have any of her works in my collection!

I needed to find a studio where I could bring my recordings up to release standard and properly record the vocals. I found a home-based professional studio in Watford – about four miles from home – operated by engineer and musician Hill Briggs who had done his time as a gigging and recording session musician, while his most recent brush with the limelight had been assisting in the writing, recording and production of former Rolling Stones guitarist Mick Taylor's album, *A Stone's Throw*. Hill was charging twenty-five pounds per hour, which was top end of my budget, but I could just about get that together to do a one- or two-day session (the time I needed per song) every month or so.

Although I was playing most of the parts, there were a few I needed help with. Hill added some lovely incidental piano to 'Another Day', his partner Debbie Marchant (who owned the grand house in which the studio was located) turned out to be a recorder player and was on hand to play a part in 'The Scryer and the Shewstone' which I was struggling to play as smoothly as I wanted, and the mother of one of Louise's school friends, Alison Bell, was drafted in to play an oboe part I'd written for 'The True Cross', actually performed with the more antiquated 'oboe d'amoré' as I'd unwittingly strayed fractionally out of the oboe's natural range.

About two-thirds of the way through recording the album, Hill's relationship with Debbie broke down (I think it had been brewing for a while), and he had to promptly move out lock, stock, and barrel. There was a brief hiatus while he reorganised his life, and when next I heard from him his studio had relocated to a ramshackle shed on the edge of a car park beside the Grand Union Canal in Hemel Hempstead, a little further for me, but we were into the home straight by this point.

My final song was in part inspired by the animistic religion of the Dogon tribe of Burkina Faso, as well as a reimagining of one of the elements of Brendan's naming of 'Dead Can Dance' – the belief in the wearer of a mask being inhabited by the spirit of the carved animal. As I worked on the demo at home, Louise and Ellie (by now fifteen and twelve) were showing an interest and I had the idea to make the chorus a 'call and response' with me and them singing alternate lines. I'd heard Louise singing in her bedroom when she thought nobody was listening, and she has a lovely voice, but was reticent about my proposal and I had to cajole her into giving it a try. As soon as I put her in front of a microphone, she became nervous and started trying to sing like a pop diva. I managed to get her to tone down the affectation, but couldn't get her to sing with the innocent purity I knew she possessed. Ellie's approach was much more matter-of-fact. She was always ready to perform and had recently taken the lead role of Maria in a school production of *The Sound of Music*, so their performances were very different and I couldn't be sure if this was going to work. I took the recordings to the studio where Hill managed to blend the girls' voices and, although he had to add quite a bit of 'FX' to get a balance, we reached something usable and it was a great thrill to me to have both daughters on the recording. Ellie was also learning to play violin and had joined our local youth orchestra – Harrow Young Musicians – so I wrote in a small violin part for her to play as well, and the song 'Through Those Eyes' came into being.

Recording and mixing were done. I knew it was far less polished than *Pathways And Dawns* in all respects – performance, arrangements, and production – but I was happy with my set of songs and that I'd controlled the process and done it all on my terms. So I was ready to put it out there and take whatever response I'd get. I sent the set of final studio mixes to Sam Rosenthal who had to break it to me that his response was only lukewarm. The new material didn't possess the qualities that had attracted him to *P&D*, which in itself had been a commercial disappointment. By this point online file sharing was having a significant effect – Apple's iTunes had launched in 2001 and Napster was also established – so sales were going to be considerably harder to come by. Sam couldn't take the risk on something his heart wasn't in, but he was very uncomfortable with giving me the bad news. Naturally I was disappointed, but I understood Sam's position, so we parted on good terms and he released me from my contractual obligations to Projekt. Now, though, I had to start trawling around labels all over again, and in this tougher new environment.

As before, I circulated dozens of labels in the UK, US, and Europe, and again there was patchy interest but nobody jumping to commit. Californian goth/industrial label Cleopatra seemed like they might go for it, but ended up just licensing the single track 'At Mortlake' for inclusion in their *Unquiet Grave Vol. 4* compilation released in November 2003. Ironically, Cleopatra chose my song to open Disc 2 of the double album, immediately followed by 'All My Lovers' from Sam Rosenthal's Black Tape for a Blue Girl. The contracted licence fee was US$100 which, at time of writing, I'm still waiting to receive . . .

Fig. 20. Projekt's press/promo photo of me issued for the release of my debut solo album *Pathways and Dawns*, August 1999. Photo by Bob Bridges. Logo by Projekt Records.

I was also in touch with a Dutch label called Music & Words. They'd caught my attention through promotion of Finnish band Värttinä who were receiving what I deemed an impressive level of recognition in the UK and Europe, and the label naturally had a strong presence in Benelux – a key DCD market – and had UK distribution via Proper, now established as the leading folk label and independent distributor in my native land. The folk scene was entering its blossoming renaissance and I felt comfortable positioning my latest offering in this area. M&W label owner Hans Peters immediately liked my demo, but was surprised I was looking at a Dutch rather than UK label – he was clearly tempted, but not sure enough he could provide the right exposure. We remained in contact, but he wouldn't commit.

Lisa was forging ahead with her third album, this time working with Irish classical composer Patrick Cassidy who she'd met in LA when working on the *Gladiator* soundtrack. They'd loosely planned to work together at some point, and finally a couple of months free from commitments coincided during which Cassidy could join Lisa in Australia. The resultant album *Immortal Memory* was released in January 2004, with Lisa taking a linguistic odyssey through Gaelic, Aramaic, and Latin alongside her more familiar 'idioglossia', and Cassidy writing a lament to his late father to close the album. Lisa and Cassidy also combined with Australian composer Christopher Gordon on the soundtrack for a two-part TV adaptation of the Stephen King novel *Salem's Lot* which, although an American production, was shot on location in southeast Australia, and was first networked in the States in June 2004. That same month witnessed release of *The Blue Album* by British rave duo Orbital to which Lisa contributed the vocals to closing track 'One Perfect Sunrise'. At the time this was intended to be Orbital's farewell song and, although they did reemerge a few years later, the song has a special resonance with many of their fans.

For me, life had taken another unexpected turn. My mother, now in her early eighties, had a couple of falls in the street, seeming to inexplicably lose her balance and become disorientated. The first time, she shrugged it off, but when it happened a second time, it spooked her. She lost all her confidence and entered a self-imposed exile in her flat in Hove. I found myself driving back and forth from London once or twice a week to take her shopping and give her some company, but the rest of the time she sat on her own in her flat and wouldn't venture out. The diagnosis was that some of the effects of the stroke a few years earlier had resurfaced, and it seemed likely she had experienced some further minor strokes which had passed unnoticed but were having composite after-effects. She wasn't going to improve and I had a big decision to make. After consulting with Nicki, I offered Mum the options of going into some form of care home or sheltered accommodation, or coming to live with us – I already knew the answer.

This became more involved. It entailed moving house to be able to accommodate my mother while, on the advice of a friend who was providing financial advice to Mum, Nicki and I grudgingly agreed to marry. I appreciate this doesn't sound wildly romantic, but it was purely a commercial decision to protect ourselves from UK laws which financially discriminate against happily cohabiting couples. We both fundamentally disagreed with the convention of marriage – not that we object to others marrying if that's their wish, but our view was, and still is, that we'll stay together if we're happy, and part if we're not. Anyway, one unremarkable Wednesday in February 2004, we 'took our vows' at the local Registry Office with Louise and Ellie as our witnesses, and the following day we moved a mile or so down the road, and within forty-eight hours I became a husband and a home-based carer for my elderly mother.

Around the same time I chanced to pick up an imported American music magazine at a Borders store on Charing Cross Road in London which contained an advertisement of a New York label I hadn't previously heard of called City Canyons. I duly sent a demo and swiftly received an enthusiastic response from CEO Trebor Lloyd. It was a fledgling label with only a couple of albums released – one by NYC singer-songwriter Jen Elliott and one by a Finnish rock band called Valerian – but there was plenty more bubbling under and it was clear that Trebor wanted to assemble a diverse catalogue free of genre restrictions. By late March we had a draft contract on the table, which was batted back and forth and eventually signed and sealed in September. In between I introduced Trebor to Hans at M&W and a licensing deal for Europe was provisionally agreed. Release of my new album was scheduled for spring 2005.

NINE

Brendan and Lisa announced the return of Dead Can Dance for tours of Europe and the Americas in 2005. This was great news to me on two fronts – first and foremost the excitement to see them play live again, but also, with my new album in the pipeline, a resurgence of DCD interest would surely help?

I gave my album the title *Enter the Mysterium*. Dr John Dee had written his own *Liber Mysteriorum*, so I was borrowing from that, while also suggesting an emporium of mysteries. I'd taken a couple of photos of old wood doors opening into unknown beyonds, and earmarked them for the cover artwork. Trebor asked me if I'd thought of using a symbol in the imagery. I hadn't, and liked the idea, but couldn't find an existing image that worked. I decided to create my own – my own 'logo' in effect – combining several traditional symbols so the composition included at least one that in some way represented each song on the album – the all-seeing eye, the sun, the Cardinal points, the serpent, rune signs for fire and water, the Islamic crescent moon, the Christian cross, and so on.

I sent my design to 'T', who loved it. I added a great photo of cave tombs in Turkey, strongly evocative of mysteries and beliefs, sent to me by online friends and supporters of my music Shane and May Beck, and all the material was passed to T's designer 'Knot' Watkins who brought the artwork to life. As an alternative to a bog-standard press picture, Louise made a couple of photoshopped promo images for us to use featuring my mugshot with a clay Medusa head she'd made for a school art project and the *ETM* logo.

Enter the Mysterium was released on 1 March 2005, with the track listing:

At Mortlake
The Scryer and the Shewstone
Across the Bridge
Nothing but the Way
The Witchbottle of Suffolk

The True Cross
Kakatak Tamai
Another Day
Through Those Eyes
Flesh to Flame

Nine days later, DCD kicked off the first leg of their tour in Dublin. Rather than the almost decade-long gap having diminished their pulling power, and despite the absence of a new album to promote, their return was greeted rapturously and demand for tickets seemed greater than ever. The tour would also see them venturing into new territories – Russia, Latvia, and Poland – where they would encounter huge popularity.

The DCD lineup behind Lisa and Brendan changed again, with only John Bonnar and Lance Hogan from the midnineties cast. Patrick Cassidy, fresh from his recent collaborations with Lisa, came in on keyboards, along with Australian composer Michael Edwards who'd worked with Lisa on the music for British crime film *Layer Cake* (2004). Skin-pounding duties were assigned to Simeon Smith and Niall Gregory, two Irish percussionists who both specialise in Latin American styles and who had come onto Brendan's radar via the samba scene. The set list comprised around twenty pieces garnered mainly from the last three albums and tour-only songs from the last two or three tours, previews of a couple of solo works – Brendan's 'Crescent' and Lisa's 'Hymn for the Fallen' (later re-badged 'Sleep') – old faithful This Mortal Coil song 'Dreams Made Flesh', and traditional Irish ballad 'The Wind that Shakes the Barley'. The tour lined up as follows:

Ireland:
Thursday, 10 March, Dublin, Olympia Theatre

Netherlands:
Saturday, 12 March, Den Haag, Prins Willem Alexander Zaal

France:
Monday, 14 March, Paris, Palais des congrès
Wednesday, 16 March, Lille, Salle Vauban (Grand Palais)

Belgium:
Thursday, 17 March, Brussels, Bozar

France:
Saturday, 19 March, Bordeaux, Théâtre Femina

Spain:
Monday, 21 March, Madrid, Teatro Lope de Vega
Tuesday, 22 March, Barcelona, L'Auditori

Italy:
Thursday, 24 March, Milan, Teatro dal Verme

Germany:
Saturday, 26 March, Cologne, Philharmonie
Sunday, 27 March, Munich, Gasteig Centre (Philharmonie)
Tuesday, 29 March, Berlin, Philharmonie

Poland:
Thursday, 31 March, Warsaw, Sala Kongresowa

Latvia:
Friday, 1 April, Riga, National Opera Theatre

Russia:
Sunday, 3 April, St Petersburg, Oktyabrskiy Big Concert Hall

England:
Wednesday, 6 April, London, The Barbican Centre
Thursday, 7 April, London, The Forum

That the German promotors had been able to secure the homes of their great orchestras as venues for this tour was a sure mark of the esteem in which DCD was now held, and generally the tour took in grand, historic concert halls. In London, The Barbican sold out so quickly that the promoters tried to add a second night, but the hall wasn't available so DCD found themselves the following night back in my old favourite haunt, The Forum. Technically it was a drag for the band and crew to have to shift the whole set a couple of miles across town and re-soundcheck everything, but Nicki and I went to both shows and the contrast was fascinating. The more orchestrated and ethereal pieces shimmered beautifully in The Barbican's seated, classical concert hall, while the more up-tempo, more obviously rhythmic songs rocked the largely standing audience in The Forum – both shows were great, and it was very unusual to have the opportunity to experience such markedly different settings on consecutive nights. Actor Adrian Dunbar popped backstage to say hello at The Forum – at the time he was probably best known for his movie appearances in *My Left Foot* and *The Crying Game*, but these days he's something of a superstar in the UK from his lead role in TV series *Line of Duty*, yet still (I believe) something of a closet wannabe lead vocalist.

Meanwhile, *ETM* was gathering reviews, generally positive, some enthused – and was getting picked up by the folk community, undoubtedly helped in Europe by the licensing to M&W and the active support of Hans and his partner Liesbeth Puts. In the UK, *Space-Rock* called it 'a dreamy, lush magic carpet ride which never fails to enthrall', *Kaleidoscope* 'hypnotic neo-folk', and *Tradition Magazine* 'Pure Magic'. *Side-Line* (Belgium) called it 'a pearl for you to discover', *Folkroddels* (Belgium) 'a small work of art', *Funprox* (Netherlands) 'a rich and varied album', *Heimdallr* (Switzerland) 'rich and varied . . . A Must!', *D-Side* (France) 'delicate, percussive and airy music . . . penetrated with intelligence', and *Elegy* (France) found it 'charms and intrigues from beginning to end'. T and his team were also pushing the release hard, with US reviews including 'a fascinating CD that is a pleasure to listen to' from *Green Man* and 'absolutely fantastic . . . strongly innovative. Totally recommended' from *Bliss Aquamarine*, while Cosmik Debris's September/October issue opined: '*Enter the Mysterium* might be the most eclectic, inventive record to date in 2005, a magnet for folk, world and dream pop fans.'

There were still numerous references to my associations with DCD, there were again favourable comparisons with Pink Floyd and Brian Eno, and this time with Alan Parsons Project and even Simon & Garfunkel! Trebor's efforts also achieved a healthy amount of airplay on the US college radio circuit, with around fifty stations picking *ETM* up. It made No. 4 in the charts on Seattle's Giant Radio, No. 10 in the World Chart on WMPG in Portland, OR, No. 20 on WGDR in Plainfield, VT, No. 23 on KSMF in Ashland, OR (where they loved 'Through Those Eyes'), and top 40 placings across a number of others. A playlist from Ethereal Goth Radio on KRCL in Salt Lake City pitched in sequence my song 'Flesh to Flame', Brendan's 'The Captive Heart', and Lisa's 'Glorafin', while DJ Thomas Schulte, on his Outsight Radio Hours show on 12 June, ran a phone interview with me and played five of the ten tracks from *ETM*. Edward Burke on WWPV in Colchester VT put *ETM* in rotation on his World Music show and was particularly plugging 'The True Cross'.

Bad reviews were relatively few. A couple of German magazines were severely unimpressed, with *Zillo* calling it '*grottenschlechten*' which – Saskia apologetically informed me – translates as something like 'massive crap'! A lengthy review appeared on a Canadian website called MyTown by Larry Sakin which, although quite damning, was very thorough in its analysis and raised some constructive criticisms. I wrote to the website, thanked them for Larry's considered appraisal and replied to some of his specific points. They were clearly more than a little surprised to receive my response, but to their credit, they welcomed it, published it in full, and even invited me to be a guest reviewer for them, which I took them up on and provided a couple of reviews including Saskia's *Poets to Their Beloved* album.

Later in the year, DCD headed out on the second leg of their tour – the Americas:

North America:
Saturday, 17 September, Seattle, Paramount Theater
Sunday, 18 September, Seattle, Paramount Theater
Wednesday, 21 September, Oakland, Paramount Theater
Thursday, 22 September, Oakland, Paramount Theater
Sunday, 25 September, Los Angeles, Hollywood Bowl
Tuesday, 27 September, San Diego, Humphreys Concerts by the Bay

Mexico:
Thursday, 29 September, Mexico City, Auditorio Nacional

Canada:
Saturday, 1 October, Toronto, Massey Hall
Sunday, 2 October, Montreal, Théâtre St-Denis
Tuesday, 4 October, Montreal, Théâtre St-Denis

North America:
Wednesday, 5 October, Boston, Orpheum Theater
Friday, 7 October, Philadephia, Tower Theater
Saturday, 8 October, New York, Radio City Music Hall
Monday, 10 October, Washington DC, Strathmore Symphony Hall
Wednesday, 12 October, Chicago, Auditorium Theater

While this itinerary also included many historic venues, the name that jumps out from the list has to be the Hollywood Bowl. Playing this legendary venue, which had previously hosted The Beatles, The Doors, Jimi Hendrix, Grateful Dead, Elton John, Prince, The Rolling Stones, The Who (the list goes on), was something on a different scale altogether for DCD. To an audience approaching eighteen thousand, they performed with the Hollywood Bowl Orchestra – a fluid association of professional musicians based in and around LA which provides an impromptu orchestral backing for events at the Bowl as and when required from whoever is available at the time. The orchestra has an independent sound system, with radio mics for the instruments and a dedicated mixing desk – a well-oiled machine. For the DCD show, the orchestra was guest-conducted by Jeff Rona who Lisa had met when working on the soundtrack of *Mission: Impossible 2* with Hans Zimmer shortly after *Gladiator*, and Rona also composed a short piece for the orchestra to play as DCD took to the stage. Percussionist Niall Gregory cites the show as the highlight of his career, and I have to admit to pangs of envy that I missed out on that one.

The show in Mexico City provided another sure indicator of DCD's progress during their absence – having played a 3,500-seat venue on the 1996 tour, they now found themselves packing out the 9,000-capacity Auditorio Nacional. And in New York, the show at the landmark Radio City Music Hall in the middle of Manhattan, with an audience of around 6,000, was the band's most prestigious yet in the Big Apple and, as with LA, was performed with a 'house' orchestra, conducted again by Jeff Rona. But while the tour statistics were impressive and shows would live long in the memory, Brendan and Lisa were once more finding it hard to work together as DCD, particularly after the long stretch of pursuing their solo ventures, and the tour ended with ominous declarations that neither could ever work with the other again.

Despite good exposure, *ETM* sales refused to kick in, and T and I were casting around for new initiatives. A while after the release of *Pathways and Dawns*, I'd been contacted by Greg Beron who runs high end audio business United Home Audio in the DC area. He told me he'd been using *P&D* to demonstrate his top-of-the-range rigs at major audiophile shows across the US, including the annual Consumer Electronics Show (CES) in Las Vegas and the Rocky Mountain Audio Fest in Colorado. The main driver behind this was the extraordinary width of soundstage which Brendan's production had created on *P&D*, but as a result of repeated listens, my songs had grown on Greg and his colleagues and they'd become fans! Greg seemed genuinely surprised when he got a personal and very grateful response from me, and we struck up an online friendship which encompassed not only music but also the marvel of fresh fenugreek (methi) as an essential ingredient of Asian cuisine (no idea how we got onto that).

Naturally I sent Greg a copy of *ETM* on its release, which he in turn gave a glowing review on the CD Baby website. We then had the idea to do an exclusive promo CD for Greg and his colleagues to give away from their demo room at CES in January 2006. A cooperation was arranged between T/City Canyons and Sam/Projekt so that both my solo albums would be represented, and Greg made a personal selection of the tracks to be featured:

The Springs of Hope
Through Those Eyes
Nothing But the Way
Another Day

'The Springs of Hope' from *P&D* was an unexpected choice for the opener, but apparently is the track on which Brendan's production had grabbed the attention of Greg and his colleagues for its remarkable sonic qualities. The closer – 'Another Day' – is Greg's personal favourite of my compositions. We had a thousand copies pressed and packaged in a slip-sleeve with the *ETM* cover photo on the front and *ETM* logo on the back. However, although show visitors appreciated the gift, and it created a talking point, the promotion didn't have any notable impact beyond the show. I'd hoped a copy might find its way into the hands of some influential Hollywood insider and lead to the licensing of a track or two to a forthcoming blockbuster – no such luck.

Physical music sales were collapsing. Cassette tapes were consigned to history, and only the audiophile community and a few DJs bothered with vinyl. CD was the sole surviving format for 'brick and mortar' stores, and sales were plummeting in the face of digital file sharing. The music industry seemed to accept the trend as inevitable and the epitaph of the high street record store was writ large. I refused to buy into this. Millions of home audio systems with turntables and CD players couldn't have evaporated into thin air, and there were surely still enough people whose ears could detect the difference between the heavily compressed sound of an 'mp3' (digital music file) and the greater width and depth of a disc, greater still on vinyl?

Record stores were closing and in early 2006 UK high street chain HMV was reportedly in trouble. It announced that chief executive Alan Giles, with twelve months left at the helm, intended to rethink the company's sales strategy. So, they'd waited until they were on their knees, and then a man preparing to leave decides to set about reviving their fortunes – the mind boggles, but at least it was a statement of intent. The tired old record store formula was way past its sell-by date – a few racks of new releases at the front of the stores selling mainstream pop on which they were being undercut in price by every supermarket and petrol (gas) station, the central bulk of the store dedicated to an A-Z of 'Rock and Pop' where the same albums sat for eternity generating only an occasional sale, and some 'specialist' racks in the dingy back corners where, for example, 'World Music' might be represented by Charles Aznavour, Julio Iglesias and a

Tango compilation by the Boston Pops Orchestra (no disrespect to any of those, but you take my point).

I wrote a six-page letter to Mr Giles setting out my blueprint for redesigning HMV's stores and turning them from passive hardware-type shops into buzzing boutiques where customers could discover a diverse range of regularly changing new titles. I secretly aspired to a consultancy role, and thus the opportunity to promote my own releases as well as a range of artists I love, but of course that was wishful thinking. HMV did write back, telling me they liked a lot of my ideas and that, in fact, some they were already incorporating and I would see the changes in their stores in the coming months. Fortunately I didn't hold my breath – nothing changed and many of their stores subsequently closed, including the two I used to frequent in Oxford Street in London, and my local store in Harrow.

January 2006 saw the US release of a Hungarian film *Sorstalanság* (*Fateless*) which had been made a year or so earlier, the soundtrack for which featured a piece on which Lisa collaborated with cinematic giant Ennio Morricone. The film received a string of nominations at international film festivals, and featured a cameo performance by British actor Daniel Craig shortly before he donned that most famous of all shoulder holsters for the first time. September brought the release of a film *about* Lisa – a documentary called *Sanctuary* directed and produced by Clive Collier and featuring interviews with Brendan, Hans Zimmer, Michael Mann, Russell Crowe, Niki Caro, and other of her notable collaborators. Lisa's year ended with the release of her fourth album (or second out-and-out solo album), *The Silver Tree*, which, perhaps more noticeably than before, had the feel of sitting plum on the ridge between her DCD and soundtrack personas, and featured a cool cover design by Collier. A note here to 'completists': the US CD version of *The Silver Tree* (released in 2007) features an additional hidden track at the end, conversely called 'Entry'.

For me, the year went on to be a mixed bag. On the plus side, Johnny Coppin gave 'Through Those Eyes' a spin on his folk show on BBC Radio Gloucester and likened it favourably to the Moody Blues. On the variable side, I was contacted by a musician called Steve Tyler (ha, no, not the one in Aerosmith who acts inappropriately in elevators) who'd been trying to buy *ETM* in the north of England without success. In following this up, I discovered that Proper – the UK distributor for Music & Words – had taken just twenty-five copies of *ETM* for the entire campaign and had never reordered. I'd been misled into believing that my album (in SACD format for Europe) had been made available throughout the UK via Proper's network of partner stores, but this was now obviously not the case. I told Steve he should at least be able to order the CD through Proper's official outlet in Durham called Concepts. He placed an order, waited, followed up several times only to be told it was still on back-order, and finally, after four months, gave up.

I was angry and frustrated that Proper would fail to support my album like this, but I had no direct association with them and could only complain via M&W, who were loathe to upset their relationship with Proper. Who knows how many other sales I'd lost as a result of Proper's complete disinterest? I ended up sending a CD directly to Steve, and in return received a CD of his latest project – *Passion, Pestilence and Polyphony* by Misericordia which is terrific. It turned out that Steve is one of the UK's leading hurdy-gurdy players, as well as being accomplished on a number of other instruments including hammered dulcimer, cittern, and harp, and we've kept in touch.

On the downright bad side was my most disappointing review to date. I've been a devotee of UK 'World Music' magazine *Songlines* since it started and have discovered many great albums through its pages, so I craved its endorsement. I'd pestered editor Simon Broughton since *ETM* was released, and he eventually confirmed he'd include it. But then I received an email from him warning that the review would be in the next issue, but was bad. He was apologetic, saying he'd sent it to a reviewer he thought would be sympathetic, but that he had a policy of not interfering with reviews once they were done. Fair enough – I get the policy, and he was decent enough to warn me in advance, but still it was a blow. The review appeared under the heading 'Emporium of Ponderosity' with a solitary rating star (I suppose it could have been none), and was surprisingly unintelligent and poorly written, seemingly dashed off in annoyance by someone given the task against his will. The only small comfort was that it appeared alongside a review (different reviewer) of *Comments of the Inner Chorus* by Tunng – one of my favourite bands – which only got a three-star review whereas it would get the full five stars in my book all day long. Ironically, elsewhere in the same issue, Proper had a full page advertisement promoting twelve of their current releases, one of which was *ETM* – why they were still promoting an album which they were actively preventing people from buying remains an enduring mystery.

Early in 2007, Steve Tyler tipped me off that Mark Coyle of alternative folk hub Woven Wheat Whispers was curating a compilation album exploring the darker side of British folk music – 'the mysteries of our ancient past and peoples, and the strangeness of their beliefs'. I emailed Mark asking if he'd be interested in including one of my songs and immediately received an affirmative response.

It was exactly the area where I wanted to pitch *ETM*, and his promotion was going out through – amongst others – *Fortean Times*, whose editor had provided the inspiration for 'The Witchbottle of Suffolk', and *Tradition Magazine*, which had given *ETM* one of its best reviews. Initially 'Witchbottle' was Mark's frontrunner for inclusion, but in the end he plumped for 'The Scryer and the Shewstone'. The album was released, naturally enough, on 'Lammas' (1 August – the Anglo-Saxon festival of the wheat harvest) on the Cold Spring label under the title *John Barleycorn Reborn: Dark Britannica*, and was later reissued as a four LP vinyl box set on Burning World Records in 2018.

Fig. 21. The 'Mysterium' symbol I designed following Trebor's suggestion that such an image would work well with the theme of my second solo album, released in March 2005: a simple pen and ink line drawing. Art by Peter Ulrich.

I met up with Steve at London's Shaftesbury Theatre on 29 April at a solo show by Lisa, where I also bumped into Gary Levermore amongst the audience, whose Nettwerk label had picked up the European release of Lisa's album *The Silver Tree*. The person I failed to see that night was Lisa herself, as she often heads off stage and straight back to the sanctuary of her hotel to preserve her voice. She was only in London fleetingly as she passed through on an international tour which had started a few weeks earlier with three shows in Australia – the Melbourne Forum Theatre, Sydney State Theatre, and Melbourne Playhouse – her first performances in her homeland since the earliest incarnation of Dead Can Dance back in 1981-82. To coincide with the tour, 4AD released a *Best of Lisa Gerrard* album comprising fifteen tracks including some DCD, some from her previous solo albums, and *Gladiator* anthem 'Now We Are Free' (which my daughter Louise nominates as one of her favourite tracks of all time). Although a shame not to meet, it was great to see her on stage again.

'The Host of Seraphim' made a Hollywood appearance in the 2007 movie adaptation of Stephen King's *The Mist*, with director Frank Darabont personally selecting 'Host' and describing it as 'a requiem mass for the human race'. More surprisingly, sampled segments from 'Host' seemed to be regularly popping up in various electronic/dance and hip-hop/R&B tracks, examples from around this time including 'Ye' by Nomagróf feat. Nova-Kane and Killer Falcon and 'Act of God (Thunderdome 08 Anthem)' by Endymion and Nosferatu. Altogether 'Host' has been sampled into a dozen or so tracks in these fields over the years – quite a rave staple.

Sam Rosenthal contacted me to say that Projekt's two hundredth album release was approaching. To mark this impressive milestone he was planning a three-CD compilation album spanning the label's back catalogue and would include 'Taqaharu's Leaving' from *P&D* amongst its thirty-two tracks alongside contributions from the Projekt roster including Black Tape for a Blue Girl, Voltaire, Lycia, Attrition, Lovesliescrushing, Human Drama, Lovespirals, Arcanta, Tearwave, Lowsunday, Audra, Fayman & Fripp, Vidna Obmana, Steve Roach, and many more. *Projekt 200* was released in August 2007 in a limited edition box set, and I was honoured that Sam would include me.

Lisa called me around Christmas time, apologising for having missed me in London and generally catching up, mostly family stuff. And then in the new year, Brendan contacted me to say he was parting company with 4AD and sounding me out as to labels he might approach, knowing I'd been doing the rounds for both my albums. He was at an 'advanced' stage with his next solo album, but his ever more extreme pursuit of sonic perfection dictated that it would still not see the light of day for another two years.

Not realising Krautrock had featured in Lisa's formative years as it had in mine, I was surprised to learn she'd become involved in a collaboration with Klaus Schulze, former member of both Tangerine Dream and Ash Ra Tempel. Originally a drummer before concentrating on synthesisers and electronics, Schulze is incredibly prolific, having churned out more than sixty albums since the early 1970s, several of which are live recordings. Lisa appeared as guest singer on his studio album *Farscape*, released in July 2008, after which she regularly joined him for concerts and features on live albums *Rheingold* (2008), *Dziekuje bardzo* (2009), and *Big in Europe* (2013/14).

In the months following the release of *John Barleycorn Reborn* (*JBR*), I worked on its promotion with Mark Coyle, and with Justin Mitchell of the Cold Spring label. With some trepidation I approached Simon Broughton at *Songlines* again. He readily agreed to run a review of *JBR* and promised me a different reviewer, this time passing it to Tim Cumming. The review appeared in the March 2008 issue, with the award of four out of five stars. Mark was delighted that (in his words) 'the review really does understand the intent and references', and it bore some useful quotes including:

> Like nothing else before it, *Dark Britannica* drills a deep musical borehole to explore the links between folk music and Britain's folklore . . . it's like opening a cellar door onto a truly strange underground culture . . . *Dark Britannica* will grab you the way a good ghost story – an MR James or Arthur Machen – will grab you over the course of a dark winter night.

While the *Songlines* review didn't specifically mention my contribution, Stuart Maconie featured *JBR* on his *Freakzone* show on BBC Radio 6 and 'Scryer' was one of the two tracks he chose to play.

Three years had elapsed since *ETM* hit the streets. I still believed in the songs, but the breakthrough continued to elude me. I was contracted to City Canyons for another two albums, but hadn't been writing anything new in the interim. It wasn't that ideas had dried up, simply that I'd been absorbed with trying to make *ETM* happen. As I started to think about new material, Trebor posed a question which would shape our next decade – would I be interested in working on a new song in collaboration with him and another artist who'd joined the label around the same time as me, New Yorker Sara Wendt (former singer with East Village cult band Homer Erotic)? I had no fixed ideas about where I was going next, and this sounded interesting, so I readily agreed.

T had the bare bones of a song which had been pinballing around his head for years. He'd made a rough sketch of the melody on his phone and sent it to Sara, who'd given him the basic guitar chords in return, so I now received that together with T's lyrics for 'Hanging Man' which had the feel of being set in an isolated nineteenth-century religious community, perhaps (I thought) located somewhere in the Appalachians. I had free rein to create the arrangement, and Sara would add the vocals. I set the song at a slow pace against a processional beat and menacing string arrangement, with pizzicato strings to add tension (somewhat in the way PJ Harvey has used them to great effect), then added a central bridge for Uilleann pipes. I now needed two external elements – a new pro-studio and an Irish piper. I found another local home-based studio run by an engineer called Marc Specter who could transfer my programmings to a professional audio format. For the pipes, a friend of Ellie's in Harrow Young Musicians, Catherine O'Grady, from a very musical local Irish family, was drafted in and played the part beautifully on both Uilleann pipes and Irish whistle, which we ended up blending in the final mix. There's something quite uniquely spine-chilling about those instruments!

The recordings were dispatched across the Atlantic to T, who added instrumentation to flesh out the arrangement and then recorded Sara's vocals. Having finished my input, I found it surprisingly tense waiting to hear how it would develop, having music I was involved in creating taken out of my control, but I loved the full version when I heard it. We were all delighted with it and I enlisted my artist friend Tony Pinfold to create a phased-slide video for the song to promote it online. YouTube had launched in 2005 and, while there were already a few unofficial postings by fans of my songs from *P&D* and *ETM*, we could now put up the first official and uniquely created video for a song by newly badged 'The Peter Ulrich Collaboration'.

For the past couple of years I'd been using MySpace for promotion – the first of the big international social networking sites, and which was in its heyday in the three or four years immediately following the release of *ETM*. I devoted a lot of time and effort to it, and built up a friend/fanbase of thousands, but this apparently sizeable following still didn't translate into sales. Nevertheless, I did make some great contacts through my time on MySpace. One was Adam Green, guitarist in highly underrated English band Fiel Garvie, who turned out to be a Norwich City season ticket holder and who I subsequently met up with at numerous matches. Another was Gesine Schreve of German medievalists

Media Noctis who has sent me some great music over the years. And one time, when we'd put my yang ch'in-led song 'Flesh to Flame' on my MySpace music player, I was seriously chuffed to receive a message from one of my favourite folk singer/songwriters, Lisa Knapp, saying simply, 'I do love a hammered dulcimer!'

Fig. 22. City Canyons's press photo of me issued for the release of *Enter The Mysterium*: a photoshopped image created by my then-teenage daughter Louise, sandwiching my mug between a clay Medusa head she'd made for a school project and a reversed out segment of the Mysterium symbol. Art and photo by Louise Ulrich. Courtesy of City Canyons LLC.

A very valuable contact made through MySpace was author/journalist Lisa Tenzin-Dolma, who became a staunch and highly valued supporter of my solo work and of the Collaboration. Lisa (T-D) was working on a psychology book – *Mind and Motivation* – a guide to increasing her readers' self-understanding and, in turn, maximising their potential. The book comprised nine chapters, each devoted to a particular aspect of the whole, and with each chapter split into an analytical section followed by an interview with someone Lisa considered exemplified that aspect. I was invited to represent a chapter on 'Evolution'. Other interviewees I found myself alongside include Glastonbury Festival founder Michael Eavis, extraordinary 'micro-artist' Willard Wigan MBE, *Chocolat* author Joanne Harris, and academics including Bryant McGill who has since become one of the world's most-followed online social influencers. An updated second edition of *Mind and Motivation* was later published in 2019.

Another MySpace contact was Nikola Uroševic, vocalist/guitarist of Serbian band Kinovia. He came to London and we met up for a chat over a few drinks, during which he asked if I could arrange for him to also visit Brendan. I explained that Quivvy wasn't the easiest place to reach, but he was determined on his mission. I called Brendan who said Nikola could visit if he wanted, but he was very busy working on his album and wouldn't be able to spare much time. Nikola wasn't to be dissuaded, so I gave him directions and off he went. Next time I heard from him, he reported finally making it to Quivvy following a gruelling journey only for Brendan to greet him by asking if he played table tennis. After confessing to having dabbled a few times, it transpired that Brendan had just taken delivery of an olympic grade table which had been installed in the crypt, and now he was on the hunt for opponents. So Nikola, having travelled all the way from Belgrade for an audience, found himself not trading guitar riffs or listening to Brendan's latest creation, but batting a ping-pong ball back and forth with an opponent determined on baptising his new table with a thumping victory. Diplomatically, he never revealed the result, and I wouldn't trust Brendan to tell me! Nikola did, however, subsequently send us both a copy of Kinovia's lovely album *Knjiga Pelinova*. Years later, I heard US chat show host Jimmy Fallon tell of a similarly unexpected table tennis encounter with Prince – a shame there's no opportunity to set up a paddle-off between the artists formerly known as 'Prince' and 'Ronnie'.

Also through MySpace came a connection with Canadian flautist Ron Korb. Originally inspired by the recorder (man after my own heart), Ron trained in classical flute, lived in Japan for a while to study traditional shinobue and ryute-ki bamboo flutes, travelled the world gathering a collection of over 250 flute variants, and amassed an enviable CV of collaborations, contributions, and solo recordings. We met when he was passing through London, he took me to the home of his latest collaborator, and I found myself supping tea and chatting with Jim McCarty, drummer and sole permanent member of The Yardbirds, whose alumni include three of *Rolling Stone* magazine's top five guitarists of all time – Eric Clapton, Jimmy Page, and Jeff Beck. Ron contributed extensively to, and coproduced, Jim's 2009 solo album *Sitting on the Top of Time*.

City Canyons released 'Hanging Man' as a standard single, and with a 'video-enhanced' version, while T, Sara, and I worked on another track and discussed the possibility of expanding the project to a three-track EP. This time Sara provided some initial ideas/words around a theme titled 'Pureland' which suggested something mystical, mantra-like. I created a cyclical male vocal chant set over a gentle rhythm on Indian tabla drums to which T added some sitar and great ambient sounds and effects. Sara put a stunning lead vocal onto it, with her own lyrics, and ultimately we created what I think is a really beautiful track. However, this one didn't come together as quickly as the first song due to various delays and technical issues, so in the interim, T headed off on a tangent and invited me to have an input to a new song in a totally different style which would be sung by another UK artist he'd signed to City Canyons, David Steele.

This time I received my starting point at a more advanced stage. T had written the lyrics, then the main melody and basic structure had been added by Anne Husick, a NY guitarist/bassist whose bottomless CV includes touring with Ronnie Spector and Wilson Pickett. The song therefore came to me to add percussion, but also to suggest any other additions to the arrangement. It was called 'Love's Skeleton', and tuned percussion instruments of the xylophone/marimba family make me think of a skeleton laid out, so I built the underlying rhythm section of the piece on these, adding some light hand percussion. T worked up the arrangement before sending it back across the pond to another recent addition to the City Canyons family, Kingsley Sage (founding member, keyboard player, and cowriter for Brighton-based band Anemo) who, because he had his own studio, could now provide a UK recording facility for our project. David Steele went and recorded his vocals with Kingsley, T made his final mix, and now The Peter Ulrich Collaboration had a new dimension – it was taking on a life of its own.

In early 2009 I was contacted by Glen Johnson, singer and driving force behind the band Piano Magic which had previously worked with John Rivers at Woodbine and been signed to 4AD between 2000 and 2002, releasing two albums on the label. Glen favoured a fluid, rather than rigid, band lineup and constantly approached other artists he admired to make contributions. These had included John Grant of the Czars and 1960s folk legend Vashti Bunyan who was lured out of a self-imposed thirty-year exile by Glen to sing on the track 'Crown of the Lost' on Piano Magic's second 4AD album *Writers Without Homes*. Bunyan went on to make her second solo album *Lookaftering*, released in 2005 a mere thirty-five years after her debut, and I saw her perform at the Barbican the following year in a 'Folk Britannia' concert which also featured Bert Jansch, Mike Heron (Incredible String Band), Adem, the rather wonderful King Creosote, and the eccentric Circulus.

Glen initially got in touch with me looking for a route to Brendan and I hooked them up. He then invited both of us to contribute to work in progress for Piano Magic's next album. He was thrilled when Brendan agreed to sing on two songs and, together with drummer Jerome Tcherneyan, went to Quivvy for the recording. Just before their trip, we did a session in a basement studio next to the Beggars Banquet/4AD HQ in Alma Road, Wandsworth – it was a blast-from-the-past going back there, even though I no longer knew anyone at 4AD. We had no real plan prior to the session and I took along a couple of bags of hand drums and percussion together with my yang ch'in. I'd been expecting mainly to be playing percussion, but after adding some darabuka and claves to 'A Fond Farewell', the yang ch'in came to the fore. I added parts to another largely pre-formed song – 'March of the Atheists' – and then we worked on adding a selection of different yang ch'in ideas to a drum track programmed by Jerome which he and Glen would take away to work with. When the album – *Ovations* – was released in October 2009, I was taken aback to discover they'd looped a couple of my parts over the drum track and worked the entire piece around the yang ch'in on an instrumental called 'La Cobardía de los Toreros'. Overall the album sounded great, and 'You Never Loved This City', sung by Brendan, is simply beautiful.

Fig.23. DCD live at Radio City Music Hall NYC in October 2005: Brendan and Lisa in front of the 'house' orchestra. Photo by Mary Kamphausen Shadbolt, Tiger-Fly.com.

In between making the recordings with Piano Magic, and the release of *Ovations*, Nicki and I took a trip to Venice where Ellie was on tour with Harrow Young Musicians, based in nearby Lido di Jesolo and playing a series of concerts around the area. Never known for his lack of ambition, the orchestra's conductor and director Mark Gooding had requested permission to perform in St Mark's Basilica itself. He didn't manage to negotiate access for the full orchestra, but HYM were invited to perform a choral piece during one of the services. So we got to see Ellie sing as a member of the impromptu choir in this magnificent historic setting – some experience.

It was a crazy-busy year for Lisa. She collaborated with California-based Italian composer Marcello de Francisci on two soundtracks, one for Vibeke Løkkeberg's anti-war documentary *Tears of Gaza* (which would be released the following year), and one for *Balibo*, directed by Robert Connolly and recounting the plight of five journalists captured and killed during the Indonesian invasion of East Timor in 1975, and which secured an Australian Music Industry Award for Best Score. The end of the year found her singing with the NHK Symphony Orchestra of Japan on the opening theme for *Ryōmaden*, the forty-ninth production in the nation's epic series of 'Taiga' dramas. Its forty-eight episodes subsequently screened weekly throughout 2010 on Japanese TV telling the story of Sakamoto Ryōma, a famous samurai of the Edo period.

In between, in October 2009 Lisa launched her own label, Gerrard Records, with a mission statement to create a catalyst for works that wouldn't otherwise be heard, 'like an Andy Warhol factory for artists'. The label swiftly released her third solo album *The Black Opal* which, as though a show of intent, includes an intriguing cover of Dylan's 'All Along the Watchtower' with Lisa making a radical departure from her usual singing style. She was understandably in great demand, and projects rolled out. Her label would provide an outlet over the next few years for collaborations with Klaus Schulze on *Come Quietly* (2009), with Marcello de Francisci on *Departum* (2010) and *Oranges and Sunshine* (soundtrack to the debut feature of English director Jim Loach, 2011), and with Cye Wood on *The Trial of Genghis Khan* (soundtrack to Australian adventurer Tim Cope's epic trek through Mongolia and the Eurasian Steppe, 2010). The label would run independently until the 2014 release of Lisa's fourth solo album *Twilight Kingdom*, before being taken under the wing of music services group Air-Edel to relieve Lisa of the administrative side.

Brendan, meanwhile, was still toiling over his second solo album, striving for ever-increasing heights of perfection, both in performance and production. Many years later, in an interview for guitarguitar.co.uk, interviewer Ray Mc-Clelland touches on the quandary thrown up by the boundless enormity of sampled soundbanks which draws a revealing response from Brendan:

> Yeah, I know, but it's like, I'm so OCD about them, that I have to go through every single one to find the one that's just right! Because, invariably, they're all different, and they all have little bits of expression and things, you know, that every library has. It's just, I try to exhaust all possibilities, and it's very time-consuming and

very over-the-top. I'm quite nerdy when it comes to that! I can be lost for hours, if not days, hunting for the right sound!

The Peter Ulrich Collaboration was gathering pace and breadth, and the previous EP idea had given way to murmurings of a full album. T was pressing me to get a proper home studio setup so I could share files and develop ideas more readily. His regular engineer, Mike Presta, sent me a guide to an intro-level Mac-based system with Pro Tools software – one of the music industry standards for multitrack recording. I duly trooped off to a local gear store and ordered my kit, the most exciting element of which to me was a Røde NT2 studio microphone which came in its own padded aluminium flight case complete with 'cradle' and 'pop shield' – I'd never owned anything like this before and handled it with kid gloves. T was embracing the notions of creating songs from very different starting points and using a different array of instruments each time. He was gradually involving not only more of the expanding City Canyons roster – Jen Elliott, and Mike Grosshandler of The Velmas – but also inviting musicians from his extensive contact book to participate. For my part, I got Saskia involved, contributing some vocals, didgeridoo, and bullroarer to a song called 'Children of the Rain'.

In June 2010, Brendan's second album – *Ark* – was finally released on Cooking Vinyl. The label deal had been brokered by former 4AD/Cocteaus stalwart Colin Wallace, who also became Brendan's manager for a period around this time, and saw Brendan tread the footsteps of Pixies's Black Francis who had also migrated to Cooking Vinyl post-4AD. Brendan sent me the heavy 12" vinyl format and, of course, he had again made a wonderful mix of exquisite songs, gorgeous arrangements, his ever-richening voice and stunning production with the kind of dynamic range that sends audiophiles into raptures – a real labour of love, a meshing of creative passion and intricate engineering that truly few others come close to. Brendan assembled a band and headed out on an extensive tour to promote the album taking in eighteen countries and including an appearance at goth staple the Wave-Gotik-Treffen Festival in Leipzig. Nicki and I caught the London show at Islington's Union Chapel where Piano Magic provided the support, and Brendan included a version of Glen's 'You Never Loved This City' in his set. Lovely show in a beautiful venue.

I was actually invited to guest with Piano Magic that night, but had to turn it down as I couldn't get to the venue early enough due to commitments with my mother. Her physical condition was deteriorating rapidly – a losing battle to keep her mobile – and she was showing early signs of dementia. I was having to move her even the shortest distances in the house by wheelchair and do pretty much everything for her – regularly taking four to five hours out of my day. I was determined to keep Nicki and the girls out of it and, as an only child, I had no siblings to share the load. With the benefit of hindsight, I'd been at breaking point for a while when, one morning, Mum lost her balance and I was unable to stop her fall. Paramedics came and pronounced her OK, but took her to our local hospital for a thorough check. When the medical staff, and then social services team became fully aware of her condition, they were incredulous that I'd been caring for her on my own. I was told in no uncertain terms that she was way beyond my home care. I could never have told this to myself – it would have been an admission of defeat and a betrayal of my mother – but to be told by healthcare professionals came as an overwhelming relief. I undertook an intensive period of research, settled on a good local care home, and my mother moved in. Although I continued to visit her typically three or four days a week, the freedom of life suddenly bestowed on me was revelatory.

To follow up on navigating his *Ark* around Europe, an American tour was in Brendan's offing but a planned pairing with former Bauhaus front man Peter Murphy twice fell through, even ending up in a bit of online mud-slinging. Having periodically remained in contact, Brendan turned to Robin Guthrie who, with new album *Emeralds* about to hit the streets, readily agreed. During a schedule of ten dates in the States, two in Canada, and one in Mexico City, Brendan invited Robin to join him on stage during his set to accompany his now customary rendition of 'Song to the Siren'. Word of this classic old-4ADians collaboration spread like wildfire and Seattle's Radio KEXP invited them in for a live-on-air performance which, according to a station insider, lived up to This Mortal Coil's original album title by ending in plenty of tears.

Curiously, over a decade after the release of *Gladiator*, lead soundtrack song 'Now We Are Free' peaked at No. 2 in the US *Billboard* chart in May 2011; overall the song clocked up a seriously impressive 460 weeks on the chart! Constantly in demand for soundtrack work, Lisa added to her catalogue the score for *Burning Man*, an Australian film written and directed by Jonathan Teplitzky and starring English actor Matthew Goode.

The June 2011 issue of *Record Collector* magazine (UK) carried a half-page interview with me, published in response to a reader enquiry about 'Taqaha-ru's Leaving', as a result of which *Record Collector* also listed the single in its Rare Record Price Guide with a value of ten pounds. Theoretically, my small residual stock had just soared in value, if I could only locate some customers.

The following month brought a performance by a steel pans band based at Vaughan School which I'd joined a few years earlier playing basses – a set of six full-height oil drums, each with three notes hammered into its horizontal surface, and played with homemade sticks fashioned from lengths of dowel with rubber dog-fetch balls on the ends! It was an entirely amateur group, comprising parents and teachers, and we did a handful of gigs each year – school fairs, summer garden parties, the occasional wedding or birthday – playing a set of Latin American, reggae, and rock/pop standards. But everything sounds great on the pans, and it was very useful to keep my hand in rhythmically and playing in an ensemble. The song arrangements had been created and taught to us by a brilliant panner and teacher – Dexter Joseph – who worked for the Harrow Schools Music Service and inspired many of our children to join pan bands and play locally, nationally, and even internationally. The particular performance on this occasion was to mark the retirement of Vaughan's long-serving head teacher Sheila Carnan, and also in attendance and performing that evening was saxophone maestro Courtney Pine who lived locally and whose children had been through the school. I'd hoped we might persuade him to jam with us on a version we did of jazz standard 'Watermelon Man' so we could all say we'd shared a stage with him. Sadly that didn't materialise, but we did get to see/hear him play a solo sax piece in a kind of impromptu and intimate 'in-the-round' which was a treat.

The Peter Ulrich Collaboration (by now initialised to a snappier 'TPUC') had been gradually amassing songs, and by early 2012 we had sufficient material at an advanced stage to start planning the debut album release. T wanted to have a licensed label or distributor based in Europe from the outset, so I was researching possibilities in the UK. I met with Gary Levermore, head of Ardent Music Ian Blackaby who'd been involved in the successful international marketing of Canadian world music star Loreena McKennitt, and Peter Muir of Market Square Music. Gary and Ian were both interested, but unsure they could offer TPUC anything viable in what remained a hostile commercial environment. With Peter I found a lot of common ground – he had many similar reference points in his past, and was involved in releasing music by artists including Kevin Ayers (from the Canterbury prog scene that had been a big part of my formative years), Alan Hull (of Lindisfarne), Michael Chapman, and Steve Tilston – father of Martha Tilston who is one of Nicki and my favourite artists (*Machines of Love and Grace* is a truly wondrous album).

While he was impressed with our music, Peter also had reservations about the commercial potential of TPUC, particularly without the immediate prospect of live performances (which we were looking at for the future, but not immediately, purely for logistics/costs reasons – same old Catch-22 I'd faced with my solo releases). My one negative about working with Peter was that Market Square's UK distributor was Proper. But he assured me he'd keep on top of them to make sure the distribution was, indeed, 'proper' this time around, so I introduced T to Peter (by email), a deal was thrashed out, and it was agreed that the debut TPUC album would be released jointly by City Canyons and Market Square. T set about finalising various mixes, while I provided one last song – a yang ch'in-led piece called 'Tempest' which would be the only track on the album for which I'd written the lyrics.

I'd met and befriended Spyros Giasafakis and Evi Stergiou who comprise the 'band' Daemonia Nymphe (in much the same way that Brendan and Lisa are DCD). Their work is a contemporary interpretation of ancient Greek traditions, both musical and dramatic. Their music incorporates traditional folk instruments such as lyre and pandoura, and their stage performances use costumes, masks, theatrical props, and dancers, as well as plentiful percussion. On 1 August 2012, they were booked to play a street festival on Exhibition Road in the Kensington museum quarter and invited me to join them as guest percussionist. They assembled a great band which included, among others, hammered dulcimer player Kate Arnold who turned out to be a close friend of a cousin of Lisa's, and singer Victoria Couper fresh from the cast of Damon Albarn's new opera *Dr Dee* (yup, same Dr Dee rearing his head again) at the London Coliseum. We played on a makeshift stage on a flatbed truck set between the Natural History and V&A Museums. Our initial audience of family and friends encouraged a healthy number of passing locals and tourists to join the throng and after the first couple of songs we'd gathered a sizeable crowd and the show went down really well.

On stage immediately after us was a solo performance by folk legend Dave Swarbrick. Extraordinarily, it seemed there'd been little or no publicity for this, such that the audience DaeNym had drawn knew nothing of what was coming, and when our dynamic set, involving several performers with masks, costumes and curious instruments, was replaced by this single guy on a violin (who sadly was not looking well at this point in his life), people drifted away en masse. Despite never having seen him live before – this man who had been a linchpin of Fairport Convention and their classic album *Liege and Lief* and had worked with luminaries of the folk hierarchy including Ewan MacColl, Peggy Seeger, Martin Carthy, Richard Thompson, and Bert Jansch – I felt extremely uncomfortable standing there with a couple of other people and a dog (truly) and I reluctantly slipped away and went to join the DaeNym aftershow in a nearby bar.

Brendan was back in touch with Lisa, initially with concerns for her safety after news reports of huge fires sweeping through the outback regions in Australia. The bush fires were truly terrifying and had come within touching distance of Lisa's home on the northern fringe of Moondarra State Park. She believes were it not for the sprinkler system fitted in the roof, she would have lost her house and studio. Thankfully, however, Lisa was OK and the conversation moved on to the possibilities of not only touring once again as DCD, but writing and recording a new album – potentially the first since 1996! I only got wind of this some time later when they called me from Quivvy to tell me Lisa was visiting to record her vocals. With DCD's 4AD recording deal long since expired, a new label deal was struck with PIAS. Formerly 'Play It Again Sam', PIAS is a Belgian company whose first ever release back in 1984 was an EP by the Legendary Pink Dots, and which provided distribution in the 'Benelux' territories to 4AD over many years, so had handled most of DCD's previous albums in that capacity. It gradually expanded to an international operation, and now released *Anastasis* on 13 August 2012 (14 August 2012 in the US).

'Anastasis' is the Greek concept of 'resurrection' or 'rebirth'. In an interview around the time of release with Jonny Mugwump for TheQuietus.com, Lisa was quick to quash a too obvious and literal interpretation:

> It wasn't about Dead Can Dance and some egocentric thing, oh you know 'Lisa and Brendan are coming back out of the ground, and being reborn' – it's not that at all – it's to do with impermanence and the repetition of life and when you see the dead sunflowers [reference to the cover artwork] they're still alive because the seeds are inside them and in the ground and they'll still carry on so it's the fragile context of renewal.

Personally, I was thrilled by the album and consider it right up with the best of DCD's works. As a number of reviewers commented, it was extraordinary how seamlessly it picked up from where DCD's recorded output had left off sixteen years earlier, and in her interview with Mugwump, Lisa pays a very warm and candid tribute to Brendan: 'His words on this album are the strongest they've ever been . . . I just think they're stunning.'

After securing the services of tour manager Richard Jones, whose same role for the Pixies had provided fair experience of handling 'combustible personalities', DCD hit the road for their most extensive tour yet, divided into three segments:

Part 1 – Canada & North America:

Canada:
Thursday, 9 August, Vancouver, Orpheum Theater

North America:
Friday, 10 August, Seattle, Marymoor Park
Sunday, 12 August, Berkeley, Greek Theater
Tuesday, 14 August, Los Angeles, Gibson Amphitheatre
Wednesday, 15 August, San Diego, Humphreys Concerts by the Bay
Friday, 17 August, Salt Lake City, Red Butte Garden
Sunday, 19 August, Denver, Temple Hoyne Buell Theater
Tuesday, 21 August, Chicago, Jay Pritzker Pavilion

Canada:
Thursday, 23 August, Toronto, Sony Centre
Friday, 24 August, Montreal, Centre Bell

North America:
Sunday, 26 August, Philadelphia, Kimmel Center, Verizon Hall
Monday, 27 August, Vienna, Wolf Trap, Filene Center
Wednesday, 29 August, New York, Beacon Theater
Thursday, 30 August, New York, Beacon Theater
Saturday, 1 September, Durham, Durham Performing Arts Center
Tuesday, 4 September, Nashville, Ryman Auditorium
Wednesday, 5 September, Atlanta, Cobb Energy Performing Arts Center
Friday, 7 September, Austin, Moody Theater

The personnel changed completely for this tour. Astrid Williamson (keyboards and vocals), Dan Gresson (drums), and Richard Yale (bass) had formed Brendan's band for the *Ark* tour and all now came into the DCD lineup, together with Jules Maxwell on keyboards and percussionist David Kuckhermann. This was now something of a 'Supergroup'!

Astrid is an established artist with already five solo albums under her belt at this point, and having worked with John Cale, The Stereophonics, Ivo's The Hope Blister and the Bernard Sumner/Johnny Marr project Electronic. Dan is a classically trained percussionist who plays across the musical spectrum, including being principal timpanist for the Birmingham Opera Company, touring internationally with the ensemble Icebreaker – with which he played the London Jazz Festival and the Brighton Festival with Brian Eno – and having played percussion for Bombay Bicycle Club in live sessions at Abbey Road Studios. Richard is both an accomplished bass player and a 'backline' and production technician who has worked with some of the biggest live acts around, from Metallica and Muse to Rihanna and CeeLo Green. In addition to touring as a pianist/keyboard player for several bands, Jules has composed for contemporary dance, for films including an Oscar-nominated short called *Dance Lexie Dance* (1996) and for theatre, including several works at Shakespeare's Globe in London. And David is simply one of the most astonishing percussionists I've ever encountered. He specialises in Arabic forms and has since provided the support act at numerous DCD shows in which he regularly performs a solo on the riq (an Arabic tambourine) during which, if you close your eyes, you'd imagine you were listening to an ensemble of at least half a dozen playing!

Nicki and I looked at the pre-tour schedule and decided that as (1) she'd never been to New York, (2) I'd only been the once on the DCD tour back in 1990, (3) DCD were playing two consecutive nights in the Big Apple, and (4) the first NYC date fell on my birthday, we had to go. We booked ourselves a four-day round trip, splashing out on three nights at the Beacon Hotel next to the Beacon Theater where DCD would grace the stage. Arriving the day before DCD hit town, we took the opportunity to meet up with Trebor and his partner Natasa at one of their local restaurants in downtown Manhattan, along the waterfront near Battery Park. I'd known T online for not far short of a decade, during which time we must have been in email contact on almost a daily basis, and we'd written and recorded an entire album together, but never met! T is a giant – I touch six feet myself, but he towers over me and is an imposing presence. It was great to meet and we had a lovely evening, kind of just getting to know each other.

The following morning, Nicki and I were delighted to discover a traditional 'Noo Yoik' diner on the corner of the next block for a hearty breakfast to set us up for a day of sightseeing before the show in the evening. Already well into the tour, the band was in fine form with a set that included the entire *Anastasis* album. After the show, Lisa quickly slipped away to the hotel, though we did get to meet her daughter Lashna – by now just turning twenty if I've got my maths correct – who'd come on the tour in a 'PA' capacity to her mother (sounds rather brave on both sides). Brendan was up for seeing my birthday out in style so once the crowd had dispersed, we headed round the corner to find a bar, happened upon the Amsterdam Ale House, and in the pleasant warmth of a late August evening settled on an outside table. There were still sufficient

DCD fans milling around for Brendan to be approached for a steady stream of photos and autographs, but he was in relaxed and charming mode and all was smoothly dealt with.

When we finally headed for our respective hotels, the sun was already starting to make itself known, and we decided meeting for lunch later was more realistic than planning anything for the morning. A little the worse for wear, we duly met up, had a stroll through Central Park, and grabbed a bite before Brendan needed to get back and prepare for the evening show. In between, I met up with Sam Rosenthal in a local Starbucks – he was on his way out of town and couldn't stay for the show, but could just manage half an hour before he had to run. Here again, it was the first time we'd actually met, in this case some thirteen-plus years after we signed the contract for Projekt to release *Pathways and Dawns*. Still, it was good to finally say a face-to-face hello.

The show on the night of 30 August 2012 at the Beacon Theatre in NYC turned out to be, I believe, the best DCD performance I have experienced. It's a little difficult to compare with those I played in because you're very much focused on your own performance within the overall, and you're also hearing the sound mix adjusted for your own needs through the onstage monitors rather than the auditorium sound. But of the shows I've experienced as an audience member, this was epic. Brendan was clearly very relaxed and it carried through to Lisa and the band. Both Brendan and Lisa sung exceptionally well, even by their standards, and Brendan's encore rendition of 'Song to the Siren' actually reduced me to tears, and that doesn't happen!

Backstage afterwards, Lisa and the others mobbed Nicki and I demanding to know what on Earth we'd done with Brendan between the shows, and asking if we could come back and do the same for every performance. But even before this, Lisa and Brendan were seemingly back in a good place with their working relationship. In a pre-concert interview which was published in New York's late lamented *Village Voice* newspaper on 29 August 2012, Lisa was quoted as saying:

> I've collaborated with lots of people and I get a really powerful, really lovely response working with other people, but there's something unique to working with Brendan that is like with nobody else.

A few days later, DCD played Nashville for the first time, one of the iconic music locations of the US. The venue – the Ryman Auditorium – is famed as home to the 'Grand Ole Opry', the great showcase of traditional country, bluegrass, and gospel music of the South. It's always a thrill and honour, and to some extent a humbling experience, to tread the boards of such stages. Then back across 'the pond':

Part 2 – Europe and surrounds:

Lebanon:
Sunday, 16 September, Beirut, Zouk Mikael Amphitheatre

Turkey:
Wednesday, 19 September, Istanbul, Harbiye Cemil Topuzlu Açichava Tiyatrosu

Greece:
Friday, 21 September, Thessaloniki, Earth Theatre
Sunday, 23 September, Athens, Lycabettus Hill Theatre

Netherlands:
Tuesday, 25 September, Utrecht, MCV

France:
Thursday, 27 September, Paris, Grand Rex

Belgium:
Saturday, 29 September, Brussels, Cirque Royale

Germany:
Monday, 1 October, Frankfurt, Alte Oper
Wednesday, 3 October, Berlin, Tempodrom
Friday, 5 October, Hamburg, Congress Center
Sunday, 7 October, Munich, Philharmonie
Monday, 8 October, Cologne, Philharmonie

Czech Rebublic:
Wednesday, 10 October, Prague, Congress Centre (KCP)

Russia:
Friday, 12 October, St Petersburg, Ice Palace
Saturday, 13 October, Moscow, Crocus City Hall

Poland:
Monday, 15 October, Warsaw, Sala Kongresowa

Hungary:
Wednesday, 17 October, Budapest, László Papp Arena

Italy:
Friday, 19 October, Milan, Teatro degli Arcimboldi

Switzerland:
Saturday, 20 October, Geneva, Batiment des Forces motrices

Spain:
Monday, 22 October, Barcelona, L'Auditori

Portugal:
Wednesday, 24 October, Porto, Casa da Música

England:
Friday, 26 October, London, Royal Albert Hall

Ireland:
Sunday, 28 October, Dublin, Grand Canal Theatre

The show at the Royal Albert Hall in London provided us with the opportunity for a family outing so Louise and Ellie finally got to see DCD live and really enjoyed it! The night also holds a special memory for DCD keyboard player Jules Maxwell who gave me this moving recollection:

> I'll never forget performing 'Rising of the Moon' with Lisa at the Royal Albert Hall. At the outset of the tour Lisa had asked me to accompany her with nothing more than an alternating pedal note. It started literally as two notes and a lot of listening. What began as a very simple exercise had evolved over the forty performances into a glorious last encore of the show. It was just Lisa and me on stage and we'd never really spoken about what we were doing, but I'd felt her faith in me grow as the months passed. By the time we got to London the piece had become an amazing four-minute improvisation with a huge dramatic arc. A full Royal Albert Hall felt like a sacred place to present it and I remember gazing up at the ceiling in the silence as the final note died away. Musical moments like that come rarely in life and it seemed to forge something profound between me and her which continues to resonate to this day.

The following day Nicki, Ellie, and I headed off to Dublin, met up with friends who had also travelled over for the last show of the European leg, and found ourselves amidst much excitement and interesting costumery as it was the closest weekend to Halloween which the good folk of Dublin like to go for . . . big time! We located a suitably touristic Irish music bar just off O'Connell Street for our Saturday night entertainment where copious amounts of Guinness were consumed and the dance floor was graced. On the Sunday we headed to Trinity College to see its magnificent library and the beautiful Book of Kells, before making our way to the Grand Canal Theatre in the evening. Brendan was by now sufficiently Irish to make it feel like a bit of a homecoming with family and friends in the audience, and at the aftershow I was reunited with Joey Burns from our 1990 tour in one of those 'is it? . . . it can't be . . . no, it is . . . how the hell are you?' moments.

Fig. 24. Time-out at Killyvally, Ireland after the European leg of DCD's 2012 tour. Left to right: me, Emma, Fran, Brendan, Nicki – with resident Irish Wolfhound keeping us in line. Photo by Ellie Ulrich.

The following morning I hired a car and with Nicki and Ellie headed for Killyvally – the first time I'd been back since staying with Brendan and Françoise during the recording of *Pathways And Dawns*. Fran had been pregnant then, but I'd never met their daughter Emma who was now just turning fifteen – it seemed crazy that so much time had passed. By now Fran had established a dog-minding business with an impressive purpose-built kennels alongside the house. While Brendan caught up on some sleep, we joined Fran to take the dogs for a walk. To our amazement, she let them all out at once, not bothering with leads, and set off across the fields with a dozen or more hounds of all shapes, sizes, fitness levels, and excitability. Some bounded off, some plodded, some barked ferociously, and some disappeared alarmingly from view. But Fran took no notice and strode down to the lake before looping round and up the far flank of the hill. Back at the house, the dogs were mostly already gathered around her, the stragglers were summoned and counted in, and all were safely returned to their pens.

I was hoping we'd have time to drive out to Quivvy for Nicki and Ellie to see the church and studio, but Brendan was exhausted post-tour so we just chilled, chatted, ate, and drank for a couple of days – a real pleasure in itself. For the final leg of our trip, Nicki, Ellie, and I headed off for a fleeting overnight visit to Sligo on the west coast, stopping off to visit the spectacular Glencar Waterfall on the way, and then back across to Dublin for our flight home. We left Brendan with a few weeks to recover before rejoining the DCD troupe for:

Part 3 – Central and South America:

Mexico:
Tuesday, 27 November, Mexico City, El Plaza Condesa
Thursday, 29 November, Mexico City, Nacional Auditorio
Friday, 30 November, Guadalajara, Teatro Diana

Chile:
Monday, 3 December, Santiago, Monticello Grand Casino
Tuesday, 4 December, Santiago, Espacio Riesco

Argentina:
Thursday, 6 December, Buenos Aires, Teatro Vorterix

It was a long way to travel with the entire entourage for six shows, but DCD played to over thirty thousand people on this leg of the tour, managing to avoid the Mariachi festivals of Mexico this time around, playing for the first time in a palatial casino in Chile, and passing up on slipping a cheeky tango into the set in Argentina. Nicki's dad Stan was in the audience at the Nacional Auditorio in Mexico City, having remarried and settled in the Mexican capital a few years earlier, together with his wife and her sons. Brendan and Lisa knew Stan from back in our Isle of Dogs days, so there was a bit of reminiscing to be done. Stan called us from backstage after the show and it sounded riotous – he does tend to have that effect.

Talking of reminiscing . . . around a year earlier I'd been contacted by original DCD bassist Paul Erikson who I hadn't heard from since he left London in 1983. We exchanged a few emails and I obtained some early DCD recordings from 4AD which he didn't have to send over to him, together with my solo albums which he hadn't heard, and a new issue of the UK's *MOJO* magazine which contained a major DCD interview feature by journalist Martin Aston. In November 2012, Paul sent me a lovely email thanking me and giving me some nice compliments about my music, including that '*Enter the Mysterium* has a really pure sound to it' while nominating 'Nocturne' from *P&D* as his favourite track. Responding to the *MOJO* feature, in which Brendan and Lisa were quite brutally frank about their fights and fallouts over the years, Paul also sent me the following recollection from formative DCD days in Australia:

> Been thinking about the early days of DCD, I put an ad in the local independent record shop for bands wanting a bass player. Brendan had Jim Pinker helping him out on drums. Jim sent me a letter, I went over to Nth Melb and I met Brendan. Then Jim left to join SPK and it was just me and Brendan. We had great fun mucking around with bass riffs and electronic syncussion drums with an old Teac reel-to-reel, and then Brendan announced the name of the band Dead Can Dance. I feel I met Brendan when he was going through a big transformation, from punk to gothic?, from Ronnie Recent to Brendan Perry. Lisa is an important part of his transformation musically and personally, and I still see it especially in the interview.

Paul attached to his email an mp3 file of a live DCD performance of a song I'd never heard before called 'Second Chance' recorded at the Seaview Ballroom, Melbourne in early 1982 before they'd departed for London.

Back to the future . . . planning for release of the first TPUC album was gearing up and T wanted to put professional support in place to try to gain some real impact. While he organised the release in the US, I had meetings with Prudence Trapani at Rocket PR in Brixton which would run our radio promo campaign, and Duncan Clark at 9PR in Islington who would run our press and online promo in the UK. Between them they wanted upward of 400 promo copies of the album to enable them to service the release properly. This was a big ask, and we scaled it down a bit, but essentially T and Peter Muir decided to bite the bullet and we agreed terms. (We also couldn't pass up on the opportunity to send regular emails starting: 'Dear Prudence . . .')

The prototype cover design and booklet texts were circulating for checks and approvals, a couple of final track mixes and edits were done, and before the end of the year we had the prerelease copies in our hands.

TEN

In early 2013, Dead Can Dance headed out on a second international tour built around the *Anastasis* album, starting with DCD's first shows in Australia since April 1982. On that last occasion they'd played their regular haunt of the time, the Seaview Ballroom on the corner of Fitzroy and Grey Streets in the bohemian St Kilda district of Melbourne. Now they played two consecutive nights at the iconic Sydney Opera House. Russell Crowe was in the audience for the first night at Lisa's invitation, an opportunity for Brendan to meet him at the aftershow. For old time's sake DCD then headed back to St Kilda – even though the artistic community of Lisa and Brendan's youth was long since displaced by the soaring rents and real estate prices of gentrification – to play the Palais Theatre, before concluding the Aussie leg with a Perth Festival appearance at the western capital's Concert Hall.

The full 2013 tour would sprawl over the following six months, falling into four distinct parts, the first of which lined up as follows:

Australia:
Sunday, 3 February, Sydney, Opera House
Monday, 4 February, Sydney, Opera House
Wednesday, 6 February, Melbourne, Palais Theatre
Saturday, 9 February, Perth, Concert Hall

Japan:
Wednesday, 13 February, Tokyo, Shibuya Club Quattro
Thursday, 14 February, Tokyo, Shibuya Club Quattro
Sunday, 17 February, Osaka, Umeda AKASO

The same day DCD kicked off their tour, I was recording with Daemonia Nymphe in London – darabuka and maracas for the title track of their *Psychostasia* album which would be released in May. In between (on 11 March in the UK,

19 March in the US) the debut album of The Peter Ulrich Collaboration was released – *The Painted Caravan* – with the track listing:

In This or Other Skin
Pureland
The Secret Gardener
Dark Lover
Starship (Golden Eye)
Children of the Rain
Drug of War
Hanging Man
Fanfare for the Lost Tribe
The Desert
Love's Skeleton
Tempest

It had been an extraordinary effort by Trebor to pull this album together, and at the final tally, it featured thirty-six performers and in excess of fifty different instruments. T will always underplay his role in the project – in a prerelease interview with Lisa Tenzin-Dolma he gave this typically modest appraisal of bringing one song into being:

The internet has really changed everything. It's quite easy to transport large and small musical files all over the world. For example, one of our recent songs, 'Children of the Rain', had didgeridoo, bullroarer and vocal tracks done by Saskia Dommisse at her studio in the Netherlands, vocals, percussions and various instruments done by Peter Ulrich in his home studio near London, vocals by David Steele tracked by Kingsley Sage at his Brighton (UK) studios and vocals added by Jen Elliott and Sara Wendt plus various instruments added at Engine Room Audio in Manhattan where it was also mixed and mastered. Not too many years ago this sort of trans-Atlantic caper would have been a huge and expensive undertaking, but now it's quite doable.

So now it was over to the promotions teams – press releases and promo discs flew out, and, gratifyingly, accolades rolled in.

HigherPlainMusic.com trumpeted: 'The Painted Caravan is utterly phenomenal from start to finish . . . Easily a contender for album of the year.'

ClosedWatchMusic.wordpress.com followed with: 'It is not very often that you come across a piece of work that completely blows your mind. For me, *The Painted Caravan* by The Peter Ulrich Collaboration is one such example . . . I honestly can't praise this album enough.'

In the UK, an unexpected source of interest came in the arts review section of the traditional London City gent's famous old pink broadsheet, the *Financial Times*: 'An insane throwback of a record, thrumming with bagpipes, mariachi brass, hammered dulcimer, Chinese guitar, a flutter of flutes and plainchant,' while aaamusic.co.uk also noted our delvings into the past: 'Captures the spirit of baroque, folk rock, global roots and psychedelia . . . Close your eyes, put some flowers in your hair and imagine you're happily amongst a hippy community in a park in San Francisco on a warm summers day in the sixties.'

My old school friend Rob Steen, now a journalist and prominent published author on sport as well as a sometime music critic, was smitten and put a review into UK trade magazine *Music Week* which included: 'A smörgåsbord of music past, present and future, and a bonafide contender. A collaboration to cherish,' while the mighty *Rolling Stone* weighed in with: 'A rich and song-filled showcase.'

Facebook had by now swiped the social media crown from MySpace and T was working the medium. Among the responders to his pushing of *TPC* was Richard Pearson who runs music promotions, events, and publications from his HQ in Scarborough, North Yorkshire in the UK. He'd been closely involved with the Albion Band/Fairport Convention scene back in the 1960s and 1970s and immediately warmed to the reference points he heard in *TPC*. He recommended we send a CD to legendary English folk singer Linda Thompson. When we enquired via Richard (Pearson, not Thompson – just to be clear!) as to her response, he reported that she was 'eulogising' about it. We asked if he could get an official quote from Linda that we could use in our promo – unfortunately that seemed to get lost along the way somewhere, but nevertheless, it was heartening to know we'd made our impression.

Radio airplay was once again pretty healthy across the US college radio network, but in the UK was limited to isolated one-off plays. Despite all the efforts of the pluggers, we couldn't break into the UK radio daytime playlists which was a big frustration. We felt we had a few songs on *TPC* strong enough and suitable, and we circulated a radio-edit of 'Children of the Rain' – chosen as the most immediately commercial-sounding track by a straw poll of fans, friends, and music industry folk – but the doors remained shut.

DCD 2013 tour part 2:

North America:
Sunday, 14 April, Indio, Coachella Festival

Monday, 15 April, San Francisco, Louise M Davies Symphony Hall
Wednesday, 17 April, Napa, Uptown Theater
Thursday, 18 April, Monterey, Golden State Theatre
Sunday, 21 April, Indio, Coachella Festival

Fig. 25. Promo picture of Brendan and Lisa for the release of the *Anastasis* album and tours in 2012 and 2013. Photo by Jay Brooks. Courtesy of Dead Can Dance.

The annual Coachella Festival is a big deal, attracting a crowd of quarter of a million. Its unusual feature is to repeat the same lineups on consecutive weekends – hence the double listing a week apart. DCD appeared in a billing headed by Red Hot Chili Peppers and also featuring Nick Cave and the Bad Seeds, Vampire Weekend, Wu-Tang Clan, Tame Impala, Rodriguez, and a relatively early career performance by Grimes, who'd signed to 4AD the previous year. The show on the first weekend took place in the midst of a fully-fledged Colorado Desert dust storm – footage of DCD's performance shows palm trees bending, lighting rigs swaying alarmingly, Astrid's hair dancing a wild jig in sync with Lisa's cape, and eyes squinting and blinking away the ingress, but doesn't fully convey the struggle against sand in the mouths, throats and equipment. Also appearing at Coachella were New Order, who Brendan finally got to meet through Astrid knowing Bernard Sumner from their previous collaboration. Before the next show a full spring clean of the gear was needed to remove all the sand.

After my experience of Proper's distribution failure with *Enter the Mysterium*, I wondered how *TPC* distribution was working out and if our CDs were in the record stores. I took a trip across London to Rough Trade East which I'd been told was sure to have *TPC* in stock. I checked the racks under the likely categories, but found nothing, so embarked on a systematic search of the entire store. Eventually I found a solitary copy of *TPC* in an avant-garde jazz section, misfiled because it had been over-stickered with a barcode label for a double album set called *Yasmina/Poem for Malcolm* by American saxophonist Archie Shepp. Without saying anything to staff, I took the CD to the cash tills and bought it and, sure enough, it came up on my receipt that I'd purchased the Archie Shepp offering. It's deeply galling to have devoted so much time, effort, and expense to bringing a creative project to this stage, only to be let down by careless incompetence in the final distribution/retail leg of the journey. Once again I was left wondering just how many sales we'd lost, or, in this case, sales we'd made but never known about as they'd registered to other artists. I tried to make a formal complaint to Proper through Market Square, only to get the message back that I should concentrate on making music and stop snooping around record stores like some kind of amateur private dick. Needless to say, I can suggest a few alternative names for 'Proper' Distribution on request.

Meanwhile . . . DCD 2013 tour part 3, Europe:

Spain:
Saturday, 25 May, Barcelona, Primavera Festival
Sunday, 26 May, Madrid, Teatro Circo Price

Portugal:
Tuesday, 28 May, Lisbon, Coliseu dos Recreios
Thursday, 30 May, Porto, Parque da Cidade

Italy:
Sunday, 2 June, Florence, Teatro Romano di Fiesole

Switzerland:
Monday, 3 June, Zurich, Kongresshaus

Italy:
Wednesday, 5 June, Rome, Auditorium della Conciliazione

Thursday, 6 June, Padua, Gran Teatro Geox

Slovenia:
Saturday, 8 June, Ljubljana, Križanke

Austria:
Sunday, 9 June, Vienna, Stadthalle

Poland:
Tuesday, 11 June, Wroclaw, Hala Stulecia
Wednesday, 12 June, Sopot, Opera Lesna
Friday, 14 June, Zabrze, Dom Muzyki i Tanka

Germany:
Sunday, 16 June, Dresden, Junge Garde
Monday, 17 June, Berlin, Zitadelle Spandau
Wednesday, 19 June, Hamburg, Stadtpark
Friday, 21 June, Gelsenkirchen, Amphitheatre

Belgium:
Saturday, 22 June, Brussels, Forest National

Netherlands:
Monday, 24 June, Amsterdam, Heineken Music Hall

Germany:
Tuesday, 25 June, Frankfurt, Jahrhunderthalle

France:
Thursday, 27 June, Lyon, Théâtre Romains de Fourvière
Saturday, 29 June, Nîmes, Arènes de Nîmes
Sunday, 30 June, Paris, Le Zénith

England:
Tuesday, 2 July, London, The Roundhouse

Denmark:
Friday, 5 July, Roskilde Festival

France:
Sunday, 7 July, Hérouville-St-Clair, Château de Beauregard

Greece:
Tuesday, 9 July, Malakása, Terra Vibe (Rockwave Festival)

At Barcelona's big Primavera Festival, DCD played the prime 9:00 p.m. slot on the 'Ray-Ban' stage, and were followed by Scottish band Camera Obscura, another of the new crop of 4AD artists. Sadly, the Ljubljana show was cancelled so Slovenia wasn't added to DCD's countries played and fans there were left disappointed, but otherwise the European leg ran smoothly. Nicki and I headed out to Lisbon. Arriving the day before the show in the picturesque Portuguese capital, we dropped our bags at the hotel, walked down to the harbour front and immediately bumped into drummer Dan and his then-girlfriend/now-wife Camilla also taking an exploratory stroll. Dan warned us that Brendan had done an all-nighter on the tour bus over from Madrid and was now comatose in the hotel. Sure enough, he wasn't answering his phone and when I eventually got a text message from him in the late afternoon, he confessed to having just woken up. He wanted to pass on meeting for a meal/drinks that night – 'Am not able to bounce back like I used to!' – so we arranged to meet for a meal the following evening as it was a late show. Both meal and show turned out great. Next evening Nicki and I found a Fado bar to get our local music fix, and the following day headed home to wait for the DCD bandwagon to reach London. The show on 2 July was another occasion when I had a sharp pang of regret about not being involved – the Chalk Farm Roundhouse had been such an important part of my musical grounding with all the concerts I attended back in the 1970s that I would have loved to return all those years later to perform. One day perhaps? Louise and Ellie both came, also bringing boyfriends Chris and Josh to see DCD for the first time – suitably impressed, I believe.

DCD 2013 tour part 4:

Chile:
Saturday, 13 July, Santiago, Movistar Arena

It might seem overstated to give a single show the status of a dedicated 'part' of the tour. However, it was on a separate continent and was a significant show to an audience of around ten thousand, albeit in a rather curious big, open-sided metal shed sponsored by a mobile phone company. Brendan came back marvelling at the setting of the Chilean capital, with its spectacular backdrop of the Andes Mountains. Even in what was by now a heavily constricted market, sales of *Anastasis* passed the 150,000 mark and it made the main album charts in several countries, hitting the No. 1 spot in Poland and on *Billboard* Top

World Albums, No. 6 in The Netherlands, 7 in Germany, 11 in Belgium, 13 in both France and Italy, and 46 in the US. The extensive touring also gave rise to DCD's second live album, issued in April 2013 by PIAS. There were a couple of different versions – the vinyl set and double CD versions comprising sixteen tracks (all songs from *Anastasis* plus the live renditions of 'Rakim', 'Lamma Bada', 'Sanvean', 'Nierika', 'The Host of Seraphim', 'The Ubiquitous Mr Lovegrove', 'Dreams Made Flesh', and 'Song to the Siren'), while the standard CD version contained a selection of eleven of these songs.

The possibility of getting a 'TPUC' band on the road came up from time to time, but we knew we'd created a rod for our own back by indulging in such a vast range of contributors and instruments. What we **were** doing, however, was to continue writing and recording. Whereas in the past, when I'd completed a solo album, I would pause creatively and focus entirely on its release and promotion, T didn't let up for a moment. Even before *TPC* was released, we already had a few new songs, and with T driving the project on, we continued accumulating. Much of the time T was way ahead of me. A constant stream of lyrics, themes, and ideas flows out of him, and often he'd have Anne Husick provide the initial melodic shape. Sometimes I'd receive an outline sketch, sometimes an almost fully-formed song, sometimes with vocals (or vocal guide) already added, sometimes not. I added percussion and other instrumentation to varying degrees to give the songs my 'touch'. Songs such as 'Mr Johnson' (an ode to Delta Blues legend Robert Johnson), 'Green', and 'Don Juan's Lament' came about this way, all of which introduced new singers to the Collaboration – Timothy Dark, Sharon Hochma-Hawk, and Shane Chapman, respectively.

We kept a healthy mix going. I wrote a song called 'Drum The River' based on an East Anglian folk tale which I sent to T with basic arrangement and vocal. I created another musical framework for Sara Wendt to work with, out of which came a song called 'Migrators' for which she brought in additional vocalist John Penwarden. I also invited Spyros and Evi to participate, and they contributed pandoura and vocals to a song T initiated around an allegorical reference to the Greek legend of Icarus. It was a fascinating project to work on, constantly veering off in unexpected directions.

Although he couldn't make it himself, Brendan tipped me off that there was to be a launch evening in London on 26 September for a new history of 4AD book by journalist and longtime 4ADophile Martin Aston – *Facing the Other Way*. The 4AD of this retrospective is principally the Ivo-era, only touching on the start of the very different directions the label has subsequently taken, so the evening was always likely to attract the older alumni. The launch was to be held at . . . ha . . . Rough Trade East. I was tempted to return my 'Archie Shepp' album saying 'This doesn't sound like I remember him,' but decided to focus on the matter in hand.

The store was rammed and the evening kicked off with a 'Q & A' on the small stage featuring Vaughan Oliver and Miki Berenyi from Lush, but I was distracted, eyes scanning the crowd trying to recognise people I might not have seen for over twenty years. Once set loose, first I found Wolfgangers Mick Allen and Andrew Gray – Mark Cox had made a big contribution to Aston's research but was out of the country and was, in any case, now estranged from his former bandmates. Next I caught up with Simon Raymonde (sole Cocteaus representative), then embrace-laden reunions with Colin Wallace and Ray Conroy (both surprised and touchingly pleased to see me – those guys had given me my crash course in tour management!), then Xmal drummer Manuela Zwingmann who barely seemed to have changed. I managed to miss Vaughan, who perhaps had to leave early or was maybe hidden too deep in the throng, and Ivo was absent, long since having suffered a nervous breakdown, divorced himself from 4AD and retreated to self-imposed exile in a remote outpost of New Mexico. A shame too that none of the Dif Juz boys appeared, but a nostalgia-soaked night nonetheless.

Though a homage to a label he clearly loves and has intimately followed, Aston's book took a 'warts and all' approach, including exposing a depth of drug culture at 4AD that even Lisa and Brendan had been unaware of. Lisa, in particular, reacted furiously to discovering that Ivo's ill health and abandonment of the label he'd created and nurtured was likely in large part self-inflicted, or at least significantly exacerbated by drugs – a mix of recreational narcotics and unprescribed antidepressants. Both she and Brendan were further appalled to read that, back in 1999, Ivo had sold out for a 'seven figure sum' to Beggars Banquet which, less than two years later, apparently rubber-stamped director Andy Heath's sale of publishing arm Momentum to Universal Music Publishing Group for a great windfall, again without any consultation with the affected artists (which included DCD, Cocteaus, Bauhaus, and other mighty chunks of the 4AD back catalogue).

Brendan had at least brief warning of Ivo's intent. They'd been in touch sporadically about the release of his *Eye of the Hunter* album and when Brendan visited London for the cutting, Ivo had seemed very downbeat, including voicing that he felt Brendan's album sounded 'unfinished'. Then at time of release, Ivo had called to say he was leaving, giving precious little detail, but sounding sad about it, and apologising for the timing and any fallout which would be to the detriment of Brendan's release. But for Lisa, there was not so much as the briefest word from Ivo, and after they'd worked together for over fifteen years and had many heart-to-hearts during that time, Lisa was deeply upset to only find out via the grapevine. According to Brendan, Lisa called Ivo and heftily laid into him for selling out and betraying their trust.

I'm not sure when Lisa actually read the Aston book, or when that call to Ivo was made, but nothing of it was mentioned when I saw her only a couple of weeks after the launch bash. Years later Lisa told me her anger still burned strong over the manner in which first Ivo, then Heath, sold out without warning, and that Beggars Group head Martin Mills was the only one she retained any iota of respect for because at least he'd always been open about the commercial intent with which he managed Beggars. For now though, Lisa was in London to appear at the Barbican Centre with the Britten Sinfonia and Crouch End Festival Chorus in the UK Premiere of *Diaries of Hope* by Polish composer Zbigniew Preisner, a five-movement work for voices, strings, cello, and piano inspired by the diary entries of Polish child victims of the Holocaust. It was a very moving, yet bleak performance given the weighty subject matter, followed by an understandably subdued aftershow, but at least an opportunity for a quick catch-up.

As 2013 came to a close, T found a review of *TPC* posted on the Amazon website which we found quite striking. From the way it closes, you might think it had been 'planted' by us, or one of our promoters, so you'll have to decide whether to accept our word that it is entirely independent and unsolicited:

A brilliant, eclectic album, which warrants as the best new album I've heard since *Apple Venus* by XTC and that came out nearly twenty years ago! I won't labour a track by track review, but would rather sum it up by saying it is THE great West Coast album, that never was and, by that I don't wish to brand *The Painted Caravan* as some sort of retro rehash, struggling to create a shattered dream. As far as I can tell there is no active attempt to slavishly copy any of the great artistes of West Coast Rock like Jefferson Airplane or It's a Beautiful Day, it is just obvious that the West Coast ethos has influenced Peter Ulrich substantially and he has paid his tribute by producing a record that will stand shoulder to shoulder with the best that period could throw up. To refine that view, there are elements of *The Painted Caravan* which are reminiscent of some of the British groups who hitched their wagon to the West Coast horses, like The Incredible String Band and again it would easily rank with the best they had to offer. I cannot sing the praises of this album enough, it should win every award going, but it probably won't, more's the shame. Please give it a chance and pick up one of the extremely cheap copies to be had on Amazon and if you like it spread the word, because this is a record that demands to be heard!

In February 2014, I guested with Daemonia Nymphe again, this time at The Lexington, a well-loved pub on the London music circuit with a large upstairs event space. I watched much of the performance from the audience before being invited on stage for the last few numbers, which gave me a chance to enjoy the show from both perspectives. Although the stage was cramped by DaeNym's entourage and range of instruments, the audience attention was rapt with the vocal trio of Evi, Rey Yusuf, and Tanya Jackson, and sensual dancing of Spanish actress Denise Moreno.

In May, Lisa was back in London, this time performing the *Gladiator* soundtrack live, together with Hans Zimmer and full orchestra and chorus, to a screening of the movie at the Royal Albert Hall. The Ulrich family was out in force for the Saturday night show, and as Lisa was in town for four performances over five days, Nicki and I were able to meet her for lunch a couple of days later which gave us the first opportunity for a long chat for ages. Lisa was in great form, relaxed, hilarious, and enjoying life. As ever, we invited one another to come and stay at respective homes whenever time allowed, but we're still trying to organise that one.

In early July I met up with singer/songwriter I.V. Webb, an American who's lived in London for many years. She'd 'met' T online and contributed vocal parts to 'Tempest' on *TPC* as well as appearing in a video for the same song made for us by artist friend Nathalie Moore. We'd invited I.V. to continue her involvement with TPUC and this time planned that she and I would record together for a more live, connected feel. T had told me she was a big fan of DCD and the early 4AD era, but I was gobsmacked when she told me she'd been in a relationship for many years (after she first arrived in London) with Robin Gibson, the music journalist who gave DCD some of our best early reviews and was a former flatmate of our old bassist Scott, hence how she knew so much detail. Our recording session took place in August at Deep Studios in Shepherds Bush, which I.V. had used before and where she knew engineer Luke Southwell, and we put down the vocals for a T-penned song called 'Beloved Suicide'.

One of our relatively new 'collaborators' in the States was Erin Hill. At T's invitation, she'd already recorded vocal parts for 'Icarus' and 'Drum the River' before stepping into a more prominent role which caused me to check out her background – and I was amazed. Erin had been in the original Broadway casts of *Titanic* and *Cabaret*, a TV regular in Comedy Central's *Chappelle's Show*, appeared in the Tim Robbins movie *Cradle Will Rock*, and as a singer and/or harpist had worked with artists as diverse as Kanye West, Moby, Enya, Cyndi Lauper, Sinead O'Connor, a-ha, Randy Newman, and Martha Wainwright. T had been surprisingly casual about adding TPUC to Erin's CV. Now he sent a largely formed song for me to add percussion which had been written by Erin and featured her lead vocal and her harp as principal instrument. The song was called 'Dark Daddy' and I was immediately drawn in – it was sinister and yet had an airiness to it, an unsettling beauty. I kept the percussion light so as not to anchor it down – just a root drum with tambourine and occasional claves and clicks. Despite its thematic darkness, it felt to me like a song with mainstream appeal, the track with the most obvious commercial potential to come out of TPUC. The central melody with Erin's pure voice was stuck in my head 24/7 and I emailed T to say I felt we should make a video for this song and release it as a single. T took no convincing – he was already having similar thoughts, and amongst his constant networking, he was in touch with a Polish animation company whose work had impressed him called Dodo4Story. It was going to take a significant investment – around three thousand dollars – but we were nearing completion of the next album and launching it with this lead song and a professional video would give us some real impact potential. So we went for it.

While the video was being made, I repeated my trick of hitting T with a final song for the album. The previous year Nicki and I had stayed on the beautiful East African island of Zanzibar. We were woken each morning by a very distinctive birdsong – always exactly the same melodic phrase and perfect rhythm – and I was told by locals it was the song of their native dove, the Swahili name for which is 'njiwa'. I recreated the njiwa's call using an ocarina (a bulbous clay flute) from which I generated a song about the perilous maritime spice-trade route between Zanzibar and its one-time ruler Oman. Without directly copying the style, I also tried to capture an element of the exuberance of the taarab music of Tanzania. I sent my initial arrangement to T, who emailed back 'This is fucking lovely' – I think the most positive reaction I ever had from him!

T determined that we must take the plunge with at least one high-profile live show to launch the next album, and secured TPUC an appearance at the Steampunk World's Fair in May 2015 in Piscataway, New Jersey. T was intrigued by the core concepts of steampunk, the juxtaposition of nineteenth-century engineering with futuristic time travel and exploration, incredible airships flying into the unknown, the kind of realms that have fired the imaginations of writers from Jules Verne and H. G. Wells to Philip Pullman and Scott Westerfeld.

It fitted with the conceptual journey of TPUC through ever further lands and worlds, while in terms of promotions and audience Venn diagrams, there was a healthy overlap between goth/ethereal and steampunk, a potentially responsive sector for us to aim at. Planning got underway, and steampunk imagery started to work its way into the planning of the cover art for the new album.

Fig. 26. Still frame taken from the animated video for TPUC's song 'Dark Daddy' featuring a cartoon Erin Hill and her harp in the eye of the forest. Art & animation by Piotr Piotrowski. Courtesy of Dodo4Story and City Canyons LLC.

A relative on another strand of the 'Ulrich' family, Dee Helmore (née Ulrich), while researching our genealogy, had discovered an extraordinary ancestor – John Gottlieb Ulrich (1798–1875). Dee's fascination with 'JGU' became an obsession, and in 2012 – after years of painstaking research – she self-published a lovingly compiled biography. A skilled maker and repairer of chronometers, JGU had scraped his living on the border of London's City and East End from his basic trade, but devoted the bulk of his time and energy to a lifelong quest to solve the problem of accurate time-keeping at sea, his own recent ancestors having been seafarers in the Danish and British navies. Believing he'd made the breakthrough, JGU tried desperately to have his inventions officially recognised and adopted, drawing him into a protracted and often acrimonious confrontation with the Astronomer Royal and Board of the Admiralty in London. His devotion to his cause, and unshakeable belief in his advancements, led him regularly into financial difficulties, resulting in spells in Debtors'

Prison, court summonses for pawning watches taken in for repair, and even an attempted garrotting on London Bridge in 1868, a report of which made *The Times* newspaper and for which two of his assailants were arrested and 'condemned to the Cat and ten years penal servitude'.

Fig. 27. Trebor taking a break during TPUC rehearsals for a consultation with studio manager 'Cloudy' MacLeod – well, OK, that's Erin and Mike's dog (sadly no longer with us) who became a firm favourite with the entire TPUC crew during the run-up to the Webster Hall show, June 2015. Photo by Erin Hill. Courtesy of City Canyons LLC.

A number of timepieces made by JGU survive him and bear our family name. There's a beautiful chronometer on display in The Clockmakers Museum & Library at the Guildhall in London, and in 1973 London auction house Christies sold for £2,730 a marine chronometer 'signed "invented and made by John Gottlieb Ulrich AD1831"'. The British Museum also has an Ulrich marine chronometer in its collection, with a great steampunk look to it – I applied for permission to reproduce their online photo in the TPUC album booklet, but they wanted an unrealistic fee. Dee came to the rescue, and provided an image of an original JGU clockface bearing the inscription 'ULRICH & C°. 27 CORNHILL' which we could use in our artwork, and it fell neatly into place as T – before I'd mentioned to him anything about JGU's chronometers – proposed the title for the album . . . *Tempus Fugitives*!

Despite reaching an advanced stage with contractual terms, the booking for the Steampunk Fair fell through. It was a blow, but T now had the concept for the TPUC show too far mapped out and wasn't about to give up on the idea. He came bouncing back with news that he'd secured us a booking at Webster Hall, a landmark nineteenth-century venue in Manhattan's Lower East Side whose history is truly the stuff of legend. In the 1950s it hosted Latin greats Tito Puente and Tito Rodriguez before becoming home to the folk movement, with regular performers including Woody Guthrie and Pete Seeger. For a period it became a recording facility for RCA Records because of its great acoustics, and was used by artists including Sinatra, Ray Charles, and Elvis, who recorded 'Hound Dog' there. Bob Dylan made his first ever TV recording at Webster in 1962, and when it housed NY's Ritz Club in the 1980s, U2 and Depeche Mode both played their first US shows there, and it hosted Prince, Eric Clapton, Tina Turner, Guns N' Roses, Sting, BB King . . . the list goes on. And now we were going to add TPUC to the list. Exciting though the prospect was, our safety net had been whisked away – the Steampunk Fair would have provided a ready-made, captive audience, whereas now we'd have to create and draw that audience entirely under our own steam.

Following an introduction from Greg Beron, T had secured a new international release outlet through specialist American label AIS Records run by Kevin Berg. The 'Dark Daddy' video would be launched on YouTube on 1 April 2015, release of *Tempus Fugitives* was scheduled for 21 April, and the Webster Hall show for 20 June. *Tempus Fugitives* comprised another lengthy cast list and weighed in with a substantial fourteen tracks:

Don Juan's Lament
Dark Daddy
Drum the River
King of Fools (The Prisoner)
Mr Johnson
En Bleu
Big Iron Gun
Green
The Lycanthrope

Icarus
Beloved Suicide
Song of All the Prophets
Migrators
Zanzibar (Song of Njiwa)

The band to be assembled for Webster Hall would be all New York–based musicians apart from me, so T could get rehearsals underway and we'd only have to assimilate my roles nearer the date. We agreed to continue with a steampunk 'flavour' as we'd already gone some way down that road and we liked the way the imagery fitted with our concept for TPUC.

I booked flights, and my accommodation came about through a great supporter in Canada, Coral Andrews. Coral had come into our orbit during promotion of *Enter the Mysterium* when a Canadian publicist working with City Canyons circulated a media list in her homeland. Coral has given extensive airplay to both *ETM* and to TPUC material ever since on her internet radio show Coral FM, as well as airing several interviews with me. Coral pointed me to an agency in NYC primarily catering for visiting classical and operatic artists which was able to offer me a short let on a studio apartment on the Upper West Side, just around the corner from the Beacon Theater, which felt like a good omen.

My visa became the epic battle. As the performance would be a 'loss leader' for its promotional value, and I wouldn't earn a fee, I could've taken a chance on a tourist visa. But I couldn't afford any danger of being turned back on arrival in the States, so decided to go for a full work permit visa. The process proved ridiculously complex, involving various agencies and advisers, questionnaires, and submission of a veritable dossier of evidence to prove that, despite me being 'Peter Ulrich', only I could appear as myself in a performance by 'The Peter Ulrich Collaboration' and I could not be replaced by an American performer masquerading as me! After weeks of wranglings, I was told I must obtain a letter from the American Guild of Musical Artists stating they had no objection to me entering the US to perform – no problem, I was informed, provided I stumped up their $500 fee for the pleasure.

Amidst this madness, my mother's health suddenly deteriorated and she was admitted to hospital. The NHS medical team were brilliant and did everything they could for her, but her time had come and she died on 24 March. She lived to ninety-three, had a good life, and died naturally and peacefully. I'd been able to spend a lot of time with her in her later years, and she knew she was much loved, so after the initial shock and upset, I was determined her funeral should be a celebration of her life, a happy occasion. Mum and Dad had lived for many years in a flat overlooking Sussex County Cricket Ground in Hove, and derived enormous pleasure from their shared love of the game, so I arranged the wake after her funeral service in the 'Long Room' at the County Ground and collected for a plaque to Mum and Dad's memory on a bench in the stands. I made 'party bags' for all attendees with memories of my mother – a cricket club mug, a miniature easel (she loved painting), a crossword book (she'd been an ardent cryptic crossword solver), and a model beach hut (my parents spent many happy hours in their real one).

Finally my visa clearance permissions came through from US Homeland Securities, but I now had to get the physical stamp in my passport which meant an entirely fresh application to the US Embassy in London. The earliest appointment I could get was on 7 May, just a week before my scheduled flight to NYC on 14 May, and the 'fast track' visa issue period at the Embassy was . . . seven days. At the appointment, my application was initially rejected because my photographs weren't the right type. By chance (yeah, right) there was a photo studio around the corner where the correct photos could be done immediately for another twenty-five pounds – I joined the conveyor-belt queue from the Embassy. Finally my application was done and now I had the nail-biting wait. On 14 May I was in Central London waiting for the visa collection office to open at 9:00 a.m. Thankfully, my passport was ready, visa installed. I rushed back to Harrow where Nicki was waiting with the car, engine running, my bags in the back, and sped me to London's Heathrow Airport where I just made my flight to JFK, like an episode climax of *Mission Impossible*.

The US Immigration Officer barely glanced in my passport before adding the entry stamp, and a classic yellow NYC taxi sped me over the bridge to Manhattan. The apartment was perfect, with the Hudson River and Pier I Cafe a short walk west, and Upper Broadway with Seventy-Second Street Metro Station a short walk east. I went to the local store for provisions, and for the next five weeks I wasn't so much a tourist as a temporary local resident. It was the weekend of the Steampunk Fair in New Jersey that TPUC had originally been booked to play. Despite our cancelled booking, organiser Jeff Mach was still supportive and arranged for me to make a promotional guest appearance the following night with one of his regular acts, Frenchy and the Punk, who would also join us on the bill at Webster Hall, along with a performance by Erin with her band.

I hadn't been able to carry any instruments from London other than a few small items of hand percussion, so I needed to start accumulating. I found the kind of quirky 'Aladdin's Cave' I love on West Fourth Street called World Music Inn and bought a darabuka and frame drum – darabuka has become my go-to busking instrument when I'm invited to guest, so would head to the Steampunk Fair with me. I was collected by Pat McGowan and Anka Jurena of local band The Long Losts and we headed out to Piscataway, NJ. It wasn't what I'd expected – the kind of bland, soulless out-of-town-off-the-highway hotel used by travelling company reps. But Jeff and his team had dressed the place up and it was alive with amazing costumes and homemade contraptions. Frenchy and the Punk turned out to be Samantha Stephenson (vocals and percussion) and Scott Helland (vocals, guitars, and percussion, as well as on-off associate member of Dinosaur Jr.) who had a stall in the Fair's marketplace selling their CDs and artworks. They're the perfect festival act, being just the two of them with a relatively portable stage set from which they cook up a terrifically vibrant set of punk-cabaret songs delivered with infectious energy, and have unwittingly become darlings of the Steampunk circuit.

I was worried Jeff might've pressed my guest appearance on them, but they couldn't have been more welcoming. I was to join them for a song called 'Dark Carnivale' in which I could feel free to add some lowkey stuff during the verse/chorus sections, but then we'd let rip during a midsection in which all three of us would play percussion. We intended to run it through in soundcheck, but as so often happens at festivals, the soundcheck ended up nothing more than a quick 'line test' (i.e. checking only that microphone and instrument cables are plugged in and working). When I was summoned, it turned out to be a great song with a bit of a North African flavour in the mix, so darabuka was ideal. The audience responded enthusiastically to a former member of Dead Can Dance taking the stage, and Samantha got in a good plug for TPUC's upcoming Webster gig as I took my leave. Among the audience after the show, I met some lovely DCD fans and was able to do some more Webster promo. It also hit home that fate had smiled on us – it would've been a disaster for TPUC to play an event like the Steampunk Fair with our complex stage set and no soundcheck.

The following day I met up with T to head out to Queens and the home of Erin and her husband Mike Nolan. Their basement studio was being used for my inaugural TPUC rehearsal and I was about to meet for the first time a bunch of the people I'd already recorded two albums with. I think we were all a bit apprehensive about this. I was nervous about singing prominent parts for the first time alongside real professional singers, and I think they were unsure if I was going to turn up with some big star complex and be a complete pain in the arse. The rehearsal was with the guitars, pedal steel, harp, bass, keyboards, drums, and singers, which already totalled fourteen of us – the strings and woodwind (another three) would come in on other rehearsals. Mike, a highly accomplished steel player, was also our onstage musical director, and had worked closely with T on arrangements for the live versions of our songs. We went tentatively through a few, and it was all sounding good.

I had a moment of panic when I discovered – possibly as a result of a stonking cold a couple of months earlier – my naturally limited vocal range seemed to have dropped a little and I couldn't hit my own top notes in 'Zanzibar'. Tim, Steph, and Erin, who were singing this one with me, quickly rallied round and we came up with a rearrangement that kept me in my range. They were incredibly supportive and understanding, and it relaxed me completely. Then we came to our first run-through of 'Drum The River' but . . . it sounded all wrong. I stood back from the microphone and listened for a moment. The notes and arrangement seemed right, but the performance was lifeless. Without thinking I called a halt and this group of hugely experienced pro musicians were now all looking at me in anticipation. 'Everyone's playing the right parts,' I said, 'but you're all sitting back on the beat so it's dragging. We have to be on the front foot, driving this along.' I got drummer Ray and bassist Antar underway, pushing the beat, and Sharon offered up an additional hand drum part which made a big difference. Then I brought everyone else back in, urging them to punch it out, and the song was transformed. At the end of the run-through everyone looked at each other and said a collective 'Yeah!' Now they had my confidence and I had theirs, I came out of the rehearsal on a real high.

Next morning I was at the big Sam Ash Music store on W Thirty-Fourth buying a pair of bongos, a cajon, and a set of chimes, and then at Carroll's on W Fifty-Fifth hiring a beautiful tenor steel pan. Mike and Erin produced a wonderful old hammered dulcimer from their vaults, which saved me an extra hire cost, and my stage setup was coming together. A couple of days later, at the invitation of TPUC's Annie Husick, I was at the intriguingly named Otto's Shrunken Head bar on Lower East Side for a live web-radio interview with her friend, host of the *Rew & Who* show, followed by an evening vocals rehearsal at Ultrasound studios, and a couple of days after that, back at Ultrasound to sit in on the first strings rehearsal.

A pressing need was to find somewhere I could watch the Championship Play-Off final back home. My beloved Norwich City had waited until I was safely out of the UK to make the 2015 final and, instead of being at Wembley Stadium on 25 May with my family and Canary opera, I was stranded in a land where 'soccer', although fast gaining traction, was far from being streamed to every sidewalk. A well-known bar on the NYC music scene, the 'Red Lion' on the fringe of Greenwich Village, occasionally showed English football and would be a good omen as our pre-match pub in Norwich was the Red Lion. But, because of the time difference and a three o'clock kick-off back home, I needed to be installed by 9:00 a.m. Amazingly – and I'm grateful to this day – they agreed to open early just for me and hence I found myself, on a warm May morning in a dimly lit bar in downtown Manhattan, wearing my bright yellow home-kit shirt, sinking beers on my own, yelling at the TV screen and treating the barman to my renditions of 'On The Ball City' (Norwich's anthem, and the world's oldest football/soccer song). Despite having lost both home and away to opponents Middlesbrough during the course of the season, we stormed into a 2–0 lead with cracking goals from Cameron Jerome and Nathan Redmond in the first fifteen minutes, a lead we held to the end. We were on our way back to the Premier League, and my phone was jumping with messages from friends and family. At some point in the afternoon, I stumbled happily out of the Red Lion into a dazzling heat haze, and apparently found my way home.

In the following weeks I attended rehearsals, had planning meetings with T, visited Webster Hall with Mike, circulated promo flyers, had a lunch meeting with Jeff Mach, picked up costume accessories from the Gothic Renaissance store, did more interviews, gathered more instruments, planned my stage setup and helped organise the 'merch' stall. All the while I was getting to know the TPUC gang better. They were a truly lovely group of people and everyone seemed to get on – it's very unusual in a group of nearly twenty performers, all established in their own fields, not to get any friction or backbiting, but if there was any, it never reached me. And they all seemed to be really into what we were doing – in large part a tribute to T for bringing us together and managing the complex logistics so well. I went on my own a couple of times to Mike and Erin's in Queens to work on preparations, I went to a solo gig of Annie's at Sidewalk Bar, I had lunch with Sara Wendt in Tribeca, and I went with T to a Steven Wilson gig at the Best Buy Theater on Broadway where TPUC keyboard player Kathy Sheppard got us backstage as Wilson's keyboard player was a friend. Wilson namechecks Dead Can Dance and This Mortal Coil in his song 'Perfect Life' which was in the set.

In between, I took in a lot of New York. Aside of the Manhattan essentials, I went out to Brooklyn, took my classic photo looking up at the bridge from *Dumbo*, rounded the Statue of Liberty on the Staten Island ferry, walked the full length of the High Line, and went to Harlem to see the Apollo Theater. I spent two full days in the incredible 'Met' (Metropolitan Museum of Art), and discovered some less-well-known gems including the time-locked Van Cortland House Museum in the Bronx and the National Museum of the American Indian. I read *Breakfast at Tiffany's* and walked the streets of 'brownstones', and explored Chinatown, Little Italy, and Little Ukraine, where I bought a batch of traditionally decorated Ukrainian flutes as post-show gifts for the band.

Jeff arranged another promo guest appearance for me, this time on 12 June with a Joy Division tribute band called Disorder at QXT's club in New Jersey. I'm wary of tribute acts, but Disorder turned out to be great – they'd thoroughly researched every element of the sounds and faithfully recreated them, and thankfully singer Mike Strollo wasn't trying overly to emulate Ian Curtis. It was a little weird to be joining them on a few numbers with the darabuka, but it fitted surprisingly well, my appearance was warmly received in the packed club, and the band kindly told me I was welcome back any time. On a sparsely populated Metro train home at around 4:00 a.m., I was woken with a start at Times Square station as my carriage suddenly filled with a group of bubbly teenagers who started rapping and breakdancing. As we neared Seventy-Second Street, I gave them a round of applause, in response to which they lined up to high-five me off the train – that felt like a very 'New York' experience.

The following evening found me outside Webster Hall handing out flyers for the TPUC gig, now just a week away. I'd spotted that English bands Embrace and Starsailor were playing, and thought their crowd might find TPUC worth a punt. A guy came out from soundchecking for a cigarette break. We got chatting and he turned out to be Starsailor's bassist James Stelfox, who'd also toured with Jason Pierce's Spiritualized. The next week was final preparations, a photoshoot and dress rehearsal. It had been an epic run-up to a one-off show. The 'day' arrived and there was my name in lights above Webster Hall's entrance. I should've been more nervous – this would be my debut singing lead vocals on a couple of the songs to a live audience. But such was the tight-knit support from 'The Collaborators' that all I felt was excitement. Nicki and Ellie had come over from London, Stan and Patricia up from Mexico City, Coral down from Canada, Jeff was in, Pat and Anka came along, Samantha and Scott were there (to play, and had me guest with them again on 'Dark Carnivale'), and some fans had travelled great distances across the US to boost the locals. T had also brought Logan Myers along, a sound engineer from Engine Room Audio who I'd corresponded with many times during the TPUC recording process but never previously met.

TPUC played a set of a dozen songs taken from both albums, finishing with an extended percussive jam ending to 'Drum the River'. The band was brilliant, the audience reaction great. T had a tear in his eye and had been dancing at the back to 'Zanzibar' along with Natasa and TPUC contributor Alain Rozan. Band and audience members alike came up to hug me, and a friend of Coral's – Elle – maintains to this day it was one of the finest shows she's ever attended. That's some accolade, but it certainly felt like we put on something pretty special that night.

> TPUC's lineup at Webster Hall was:
> Deni Bonet – violin, percussion
> Shane Chapman – vocals, recorder, percussion
> Timothy Dark – vocals, percussion
> Antar Goodwin – bass, percussion
> Erin Hill – vocals, harp, percussion
> Sharon Hochma-Hawk – vocals, percussion
> Anne Husick – guitars, percussion
> Stephanie Linn – vocals, percussion
> Mike Nolan – pedal steel, percussion, musical director
> David Patterson – guitars, mandolin, percussion
> Ray Rizzo – drum kit
> Kathy Sheppard – keyboards, percussion
> Leigh Stuart – cello, percussion
> Peter Ulrich – vocals, percussion, hammered dulcimer, steel pan
> Robert 'Knot' Watkins – guitars, percussion
> Sara Wendt – vocals, percussion
> Keve Wilson – woodwind, percussion

After the show, T circulated a 'Thank You' email to everyone, setting off an extraordinary chain of heartfelt messages which remain very special to me (and, I'm sure, to T). In no time I was on the plane back to London, on my own as Nicki and Ellie had gone west to hire a car and drive the Pacific Coast Highway. I'd dearly have loved to have been starting out on a lengthy tour with that TPUC show, but it wasn't to be.

During my stay in NYC, I received an email from Brendan with the news that he, Fran, and Emma had moved to Brittany – back to Fran's roots. They'd sold their house in Ireland, but he was keeping Quivvy for the time being while he built a studio in a barn on the site of their new house. It further transpired that Robin Guthrie, also having found himself a French wife, had settled not too far away to avail himself of the bucolic Breton life. Brendan had the front to address me as 'you old steampunker' before telling me that he and Robin were planning to meet for a round of golf – imagine!!!

On a far more sombre note, I was aware that Lisa had been suffering some serious health problems, but I didn't know any details. Brendan was very concerned and had told me at one point that her condition was potentially life-threatening. I'd tried emailing Lisa, but heard nothing back, and didn't want to press at such a sensitive time. The news via Brendan now was more positive – a successful operation and, although still very fragile, making good progress. Nevertheless, her throat and mouth were affected and it remained touch and go whether she'd be able to sing again. Life itself is, of course, paramount, but life for Lisa without song . . . ?

Fig. 28. TPUC live at Webster Hall, NYC on 20 June 2015. Left to right: Sharon Hochma-Hawk, me, and Steph Linn to the fore in this particular shot, with Mike Nolan and his fez just visible in the bottom corner. Photo by Melissa Kinski. Courtesy of City Canyons LLC.

Despite being dormant again, DCD's tentacles continued to stretch out. 'Summoning of the Muse' found its way into an episode in series two of US TV legal drama *How to Get Away with Murder* starring Viola Davis, and an episode in the following series would feature 'The Host of Seraphim'.

As ever, T wasn't resting on his laurels and wanted to crack on with new material. I'd mentioned to him in New York that it would be good to write another song with the same approach we'd used for our first ever TPUC song, 'Hanging Man' – that is, he give me a set of lyrics and basic outline, and I take it from there, which we hadn't done throughout *Tempus Fugitives*. He sent me words for 'Artificial Man' and the theme suggested to me that we could make a kind of Steampunk anthem out of this. I set up a mechanical rhythm, adding grand strings, industrial hammers, hisses of steam, and a background repetitive chant, and wrote the vocal melody. T developed the arrangement, with some input from Kingsley Sage, and brought David Steele in to sing it. Work on the final album of what had now been determined would be a trilogy was underway.

In July Nicki and I joined Nicki's sister Debbie and husband Adolfo at the second 'Underneath the Stars' festival in Yorkshire. We'd been to the first one the previous year at Dolf's instigation, and it was wonderful. Organised by the family of folk singer Kate Rusby, it's held on a farm amidst rolling hills and the inaugural lineup had included my festival favourites Tunng, our first opportunity to see young folk singer Maz O'Connor, whose debut album we'd been playing heavily, the happy discovery of Scottish singer/songwriter Rachel Sermanni, and a headliner by Kate herself featuring songs from the lovely *Ghost* album. This year the lineup included what seemed an unlikely scheduling of a solo appearance by Radiohead drummer Phil Selway. I went along intrigued to find on stage with him, playing keyboards and guitars and generally directing proceedings, was Simon Raymonde – I hadn't realised that Selway's solo output was on Simon's label Bella Union (originally set up jointly with Robin Guthrie). Indeed, Selway's music was a bit of a stretch for what was ostensibly a folk festival, and after the first song, one miffed traditionalist in the front row stood up, yelled 'fucking shit' at the stage, and stormed out. Poor Phil looked a bit taken aback, but recomposed himself and I enjoyed the set. Also appearing at UTS 2015 was Galleon Blast featuring on drums the UK radio DJ Mark Radcliffe. His longtime airwaves compatriot Stuart Maconie is one of the few DJs in the UK to have played my music in the past, so I tracked Mark down after the performance and pressed CDs of *The Painted Caravan* and *Tempus Fugitives* into his hand. He promised to give them a listen in the car on the way home, but as far as I know, he never gave any TPUC tracks a public broadcast ... probably still in his 'glove box.'

In October we uploaded a 'Zanzibar' video to YouTube – essentially a phased slide show of some photos I'd taken on the island – and I circulated the news to my email list. A couple of weeks later a surprise reply came through from Lisa saying simply: 'Peter you're a star.' I wrote back immediately asking how she was. She replied that she was still up and down but, incredibly, that she was in New York to do a concert that evening at Carnegie Hall with Balázs Havasi (Hungarian pianist/composer). She ended, 'It's just one show so I decided to risk it, he is so kind to me' – well OK, just one show with a considerate collaborator, but this was at CARNEGIE HALL!! Only Lisa could make such a 'lowkey' comeback. I assume she hadn't mentioned it to her doctor.

It also transpired that Lisa had just added the world of gaming to her burgeoning CV with the launch of *Armello*, a fantasy featuring four animal clans battling to storm their kingdom's castle and seize its throne, for which she'd provided the soundtrack alongside Wolfgang Presser Mick Allen. *Armello* was developed by Australian company League of Geeks, whose core team included a certain Jacek Tuschewski, and while it received a generally warm if not wildly enthusiastic reception from the gaming community, it was highly commended for its graphics and visuals.

I met up with Steve Tyler and his partner Katie Marchant at the Early Music Festival in Greenwich – the first time I'd been. Steve was performing at a 'maker demonstration' for one of the hurdy-gurdy manufacturers, and Katie accompanied him on bagpipes. It drew a good audience in the 'cosy' demo room and proved a lovely intimate performance. We had a wander round the fascinating exhibition afterwards and I picked up a mountain dulcimer from the Early Music Shop – we hadn't featured one of those before in TPUC, and in the end, we never did, but its day will come.

Nicki and I were invited by friends Helen and Chris Moore to a Natacha Atlas gig at the Junction in Cambridge in February where the support was to be Baladi Blues Ensemble. Helen is active in the local belly dance scene and knew the Baladi Blues guys from workshops. Led by Guy Schalom, who has mixed Egyptian Jewish heritage (and is a sometime member of Joglaresa), they comprised an accordionist, saxophonist, and three percussionists. All appeared to be from the lands of their musical heritage apart from one percussionist who was a ginger-haired bloke from Yorkshire. After the gig, I went out to the merch table to buy a CD and found said Yorkshireman on sales duty. He looked at me quizzically and asked, 'Are you Peter Ulrich?' Taken aback, I checked my lapel for a name badge – nothing. Astonishingly, he'd recognised me from a DCD show he attended as a teenager some twenty-five years earlier, which he told me had been a huge inspiration to him. We exchanged contact details. He was Adam Warne but his chosen email persona was 'rhythmic ginger' – hence my above hair reference is affectionate, not rude. We vaguely planned to meet and try out some ideas together, but the chain broke down and a while later I heard from Helen that he'd tragically died following an illness and surgery. Trawling through old files while researching for this book, I discovered a letter from Adam from 1991 – he'd been one of the people who purchased a copy of *Taqaharu's Leaving* directly from me by mail order and I hadn't realised when we met.

Fig. 29. Brendan kilted up for his role in Olivier Mellano's 'NO LAND', performed with the Bagad Cesson-Sévigné. Photo by Dan Ramaen.

Brendan had embraced his new environs and been singing with a thirty-piece Breton Bagad – a traditional pipe and drum band of Brittany – even donning a Breton kilt for the part (there's something about being in northern France that makes him whip his knees out). He collaborated with French composer Olivier Mellano on a work called 'NO LAND', which was performed at several festivals with the Bagad Cesson-Sévigné. In a quite different vein, he was invited to compose and record the theme music for what turned out to be a triumphant bid by the Greek city of Elefsina to be chosen as one of three European Capitals of Culture for 2021. The bid was centred around a contemporary reworking of the mythical Eleusinian Mysteries, in which Elefsina is one of the five holy cities and Persephone one of the key figures. Coincidentally, one of the other cities awarded ECoC 2021 was Novi Sad in Serbia, which just happens to be twinned with Norwich (sorry, had to slip that in).

Frenchy and the Punk were booked to play the 2016 'Asylum' – the UK's main Steampunk festival held each August bank holiday weekend in the historic city of Lincoln. Samantha and Scott invited me to guest on 'Dark Carnivale' again, so I booked in for the weekend. I ended up appearing twice with them – two very different shows. The first on the Saturday night was at the Engine Shed, the main student entertainments venue of Lincoln University, on a bill with French band Victor Sierra who were lovely and turned out to be big DCD fans, plus the in-yer-face The Men That Will Not Be Blamed for Nothing whose front man doubles on vocals and musical saw, and whose drummer Jez Miller reminisced with me about JBs in Dudley. (I later discovered Miller had a stint as a guitarist in Lords of the New Church – but many years after our Marseille incident.) The second was in the historic Assembly Rooms, billed as 'The Steerage Ball', and opened by Captain of the Lost Waves who did a hugely entertaining one-man show, mostly down from the stage, serenading people sat on their laps, dancing on tables and organising an audience kazoo band. F&TP were wonderful as ever and it was great to hook up with them again.

The following month brought a curious new release from English duo the Pet Shop Boys – a bonus track called 'The Dead Can Dance' issued with their single *Say it to Me*. There's no apparent connection with 'DCD', and I think it's a song that remains little known beyond die-hard PSB completists. Its final stanza warns that a single glance from the dancing dead will cause your blood to freeze! At time of writing, DCD has yet to retaliate.

I heard from Lisa in November that she was passing through London and had a free Saturday evening. It coincided with a Norwich away game at Queens Park Rangers, conveniently just a couple of miles from Lisa's hotel, but meant I would be turning up in obligatory canary-yellow and having already consumed a quantity of beer. Lisa considered this a marvellous prospect, and in the end Ellie and Josh came along as they were at the match with me, Nicki met us there, and Lisa invited Astrid, so we had a bit of a party. Lisa was looking well and was much her old self, so we barely touched on the ordeal she'd been through. Her strength was returning and her desire to keep performing burned bright as ever. Apparently she'd been down in Cornwall for a few days, something to do with a film about elephants – I never did find out what that was about. And the following morning she was off again, headed for concerts in Bucharest and Vienna.

Fig. 30. Frenchy and the Punk performing 'Dark Carnivale' at the Asylum Steampunk Fair, Lincoln, UK in August 2016 with a certain guest darabuka player. Left to right: Samantha Stephenson, Scott Helland, and me. Courtesy of Frenchy and the Punk.

Nicki and I decided to finally leave London. With Louise and Ellie independently settled, we had nothing to stop us realising a long-held dream to live in the country, so much of our 2017 became consumed with selling our house and plotting our escape. Lisa was continuing to tour periodically, both solo shows and more *Gladiator* performances with Hans Zimmer, while Brendan was still involved with the Bagad and 'NO LAND', the CD version of which was released towards the end of the year on PIAS. There was no word of any latent fresh DCD activity, but plunderings of the back catalogue continued to pop up in unexpected places, on this occasion courtesy of Fergie, formerly of Black-Eyed Peas, whose track 'Hungry' featured both rapper Rick Ross and a sample from DCD's 'Dawn of the Iconoclast'. 'Hungry' became both opening track and promo single for Fergie's *Double Dutchess* album which topped R&B charts and dented mainstream charts worldwide.

In June 2017, London's Cherry Red label, by now tending to specialise in back catalogues and retrospectives, trawled the archives and released a five-CD box-set compilation titled *Silhouettes & Statues: A Gothic Revolution 1978–86*. It included DCD's 'The Arcane' amongst tracks by artists that read like a rerun of the early chapters of this book: Joy Division, The Cure, The Birthday Party, Rema Rema, Love and Rockets, Flesh for Lulu, Play Dead,

The Legendary Pink Dots, Gene Loves Jezebel, Cocteau Twins, Tones on Tail, and Bauhaus, to name but twelve. As Brendan observed, it was news to us there'd even been a gothic 'revolution', let alone that we played any part in it.

T was flying with material for the final TPUC album and I needed to get all my contributions done before I moved and had to pack up the home studio for an uncertain period. He sent me a sea shanty–style song called 'Pirate Jane' which he and Annie had written, and we agreed that a traditional washboard rhythm would work well. I cursed having passed up several past opportunities to buy an original washboard in antique (or junk) shops when I'd seen them as, inevitably, now I wanted one, I couldn't find one. I ended up buying a 'washboard tie' from Hobgoblin Music's London store – literally a neck-tie made of ridged steel and sold with a pair of metal thimbles so it can be worn and played against the chest. It actually makes for a remarkably ergonomic playing position. I wrote a song called 'Squaring the Circle', for which T brought in a new co-singer, Mira Morningstar. Although Mira's also UK-based, we recorded separately, and I only got to meet her in London after our separate sessions had been completed. The pairing worked well and it was a shame she'd only come into TPUC just as we were finalising material. This would have followed the tradition of me penning the final song for the album, but T also wanted to add a couple of remixes of songs from the beginning of TPUC to bring the project full circle. He chose 'Hanging Man' and 'Love's Skeleton' – the first two songs completed by TPUC nearly a decade earlier.

In October, Nicki and I moved to Norwich, where we rented a house for six months in the city centre while we searched for our dream country home in the hinterland. One of the first items on my must-do list when we arrived in the 'Fine City' was to attend a gig at locally famed club 'The Waterfront'. Checking their upcoming events, I was amazed to find that Mark Lanegan was due to play there in November – I never imagined it would be on his circuit. The Waterfront is an old-fashioned rock/blues den, dark walls, low ceiling, bar in the room, wide stage which (nearly) everyone can get close to, holds about seven hundred, decent sound – all-in-all the perfect place to see Mark and his band. To my joy, they played just about everything off his brilliant *Blues Funeral* album (which just happens to be on the latter-day 4AD) and it undoubtedly qualifies as one of my all-time favourite gigs. Then, as if preordained, a gorgeous whitewashed seventeenth-century farmhouse came available, west of Norwich in the heart of the county of Norfolk and a half-hour drive from the coast. We viewed it twice in the same weekend, agreed to buy it, and in the spring of 2018 – after a delay when access was severed by heavy snows – we moved in. I'd hoped for an outbuilding – an old barn or stable – in which I could build my new studio. It doesn't have that, but it has a big converted attic space which has been commandeered.

May brought the release of an album called *BooCheeMish* by Mystery of the Bulgarian Voices featuring Lisa Gerrard. Some years earlier the Bulgarian state choir, which reached a global audience on 4AD thanks to Peter Murphy and Ivo, had been curiously rebadged with an English translation as if the French version used for the first few albums was too difficult for a world music audience to grasp. The change also saw the choir expand its repertoire to collaborations and performing bespoke works by guest composers. By a stroke of fate, Jules Maxwell was one of three composers invited to submit songs for consideration for a new album. Having joined DCD's live contingent in 2012, he was well aware of the huge influence Les Voix Bulgares had been on Lisa, so turned to her for help with the new material.

Fig. 31. Lisa in action during 'The World of Hans Zimmer' tour in 2018, here seen at the SAP Arena in Mannheim, Germany. Photo by Dita Vollmond.

Following sessions together in Lisa's Gippsland studio, Jules submitted six songs, of which four were accepted for the album, and hence Lisa came via this unexpected route to feature with some of her most important musical mentors. She has subsequently toured with the choir, by now comprising eighteen members ranging in age from twenty-four to seventy-one, of which only the eldest, Elena Bozhkova, featured on the original 4AD-released recordings actually made in the 1970s. In a later interview with *The Guardian* newspaper's Robin Denselow, Lisa recalled how she'd been inspired, after first hearing Les Voix Bulgares, to write 'The Host of Seraphim', but that: 'I nearly destroyed my voice trying to sing like them without proper guidance'.

Now, having mastered the open-throat technique, she was singing with them, touring Europe with them in a somewhat dilapidated old bus, and enjoying their adventures:

> In Germany the ladies excitedly tried to enter what looked like a Tudor pub, because they thought it was where we were staying. Then a policeman with a huge dog came out and said it was a police station they were trying to break into. I love those women.

Jules and DCD percussionist David Kuckhermann were also involved in some of the live performances with Lisa and the choir, and separately Lisa worked with David to create an album largely based around voices and hand percussion, including 'hang' drums – a form of flying-saucer-shaped, hand-played steel pan. *Hiraeth* was released in August 2018 and picked up a Grammy nomination in the Best New Age Album category.

Spyros and Evi had decided to return to Greece. Before leaving there would be a Daemonia Nymphe show at the O2 Academy in Islington on 28 June, and I was invited to guest again. I'd played with them at the Garage, Highbury around three years back and this was their first London show since, as well as their most prestigious yet in the capital. It was also the most ambitious of their shows that I'd participated in, featuring a nine-strong band, dancers, puppetry, swords, fire bowls, and guests – including the wonderful Dessislava Stefanova who leads the London Bulgarian Choir and who, back in her homeland, had once worked as an assistant to Filip Koutev, creator of the first State Radio Choir in Sofia back in the early 1950s! The night also featured the debut performance of Spyros and Evi's teenage son Orestes, playing double bass alongside regular bassist Stephen Street. Despite a few technical issues, the show was rapturously received by a packed audience and several encores gave me the nice personal bonus of playing for considerably longer than expected.

After another lengthy absence, Dead Can Dance rose again. Behind the scenes, Brendan had submerged himself in a couple of years' worth of research. His inspiration came from reading Friedrich Nietzsche's *The Birth of Tragedy from the Spirit of Music* – which describes two forms of cultural thinking – Apollonian (order, measurement, control) and Dionysian (dreamlike, free-spirited, improvisation). When the two work together it creates the best art, and for Brendan this perfectly encapsulated what he and Lisa had strived for in their music through the years. He also explored singing without 'words' to a greater degree than previously, using a computerised database of choral libraries to generate sung syllables in different harmonies that he and Lisa could blend with and create an ensemble effect. Out of this process came a new album which stretched the boundaries of DCD's repertoire yet further.

Ninth studio album *Dionysus* was the first to be recorded at Brendan's Ker Landelle studio in France, was mastered at Abbey Road Studios by Geoff Pesche (formerly of Tape One Studios where DCD's first album was mastered back in 1984), and was released by PIAS on 2 November 2018. Brendan and Lisa dedicated it to the memory of Frank Lovece who'd been a leading light in the Melbourne scene in which they'd met, and from which DCD had been born. Less song-based, but packed with glorious, rich textures and sonic soundscapes, *Dionysus* is presented in two 'acts' and many reviewers used metaphorical references to the epic nature of the music inspired by Greek classicism. Jason Anderson, reviewing for UK magazine *Uncut*, considered that '*Dionysus* is not only one of the most vivid works they've recorded, it's also the most intricately and insistently rhythmic . . . the album bursts with all the unruly energy its subject matter demands,' while the *Pitchfork* review opened with the question: 'Is music now too small for . . . Dead Can Dance?'

In fact, the 'subject matter' of the album had initially been a potential stumbling block to it even seeing the light of day. Brendan later admitted to Glen Johnson that introducing Lisa to the idea of making an album around the Dionysus legend hadn't quite gone to plan:

> She was a bit shocked by the Dionysus myth – but I think I'd mistakenly given her some literature about the Bacchae where all these women started ripping up animals and eating them (laughs). And this drunken, abandoned, wanton god . . . 'I'm not singing an album to Dionysus!' She holds a lot of Christian beliefs and values so it was anathema to her. It was hard to get her fully involved in that one so I did the lion's share of that album. The previous album, *Anastasis*, was much more collaborative and it was more song-orientated anyway, so we worked a lot closer together.

In an interview for *Rolling Stone*, Lisa told Kory Grow that Brendan had broached his ideas for the new album saying: 'Let's not do songs this time; let's

make this the sound of the forest so that we can wake up the beauty inside people to remember nature and the ancient.'

Lisa hints at having initial reservations, but thankfully her trust in Brendan's
vision remained strong enough to carry the project through. Given all that had
gone into the creation of this album, and all I've said before about music 'pi-
geonholing', I couldn't help a wry smile when, some time later, I received a
random marketing email from Amazon suggesting that I might like to try *Dionysus* should I be looking for something in their 'Alternative Rock Store' . . .
you've gotta love an insightful algorithm!

It was announced that DCD would tour again in 2019. Brendan limbered up
with a tour of his own comprising thirty shows through February and March
taking in France, Germany, Netherlands, Belgium, and Switzerland. DCD then
headed out at the end of April to play:

France:
Tuesday, 30 April, Nantes, Le Lieu unique
Wednesday, 1 May, Rennes, Le Liberté

England:
Saturday, 4 May, London, Hammersmith Apollo
Sunday, 5 May, London, Hammersmith Apollo

Belgium:
Tuesday, 7 May, Brussels, Cirque Royal
Wednesday, 8 May, Brussels, Cirque Royal

France:
Friday, 10 May, Paris, Grand Rex
Saturday, 11 May, Paris, Grand Rex

Netherlands:
Monday, 13 May, Utrecht, TivoliVredenburg
Tuesday, 14 May, Utrecht, TivoliVredenburg

Germany:
Thursday, 16 May, Berlin, Tempodrom
Friday, 17 May, Berlin, Tempodrom

Spain:
Monday, 20 May, Barcelona, BARTS
Tuesday, 21 May, Barcelona, BARTS

Portugal:
Thursday, 23 May, Lisbon, Aula Magna
Friday, 24 May, Lisbon, Aula Magna

Italy:
Sunday, 26 May, Milan, Teatro degli Arcimboldi
Monday, 27 May, Milan, Teatro degli Arcimboldi

There was a pause while Lisa snuck in a quick mini-tour with Les Voix Bulgares (I have to still call them that). In their promo for the London show on 6 June, the Queen Elizabeth Hall described Lisa as 'formerly of Dead Can Dance', but ten days later she was restored and DCD continued:

Germany:
Sunday, 16 June, Frankfurt, Alte Oper
Tuesday, 18 June, Bochum, RuhrCongress
Wednesday, 19 June, Bochum, RuhrCongress

Poland:
Friday, 21 June, Warsaw, Arena COS Torwar
Saturday, 22 June, Warsaw, Arena COS Torwar

Czech Republic:
Monday, 24 June, Prague, Kongresové centrum Praha

Hungary:
Wednesday, 26 June, Budapest, Papp László Sportaréna

Serbia:
Friday, 28 June, Belgrade, Sava Centar

Bulgaria:
Sunday, 30 June, Plovdiv, Roman Theatre of Philippopolis

Greece:
Tuesday, 2 July, Thessaloniki, Earth Theatre
Thursday, 4 July, Athens, Odeon of Herodes Atticus

The tour was billed as 'A Celebration – Life & Works 1980–2019' and the set included ten songs/pieces that I'd played during my touring days with DCD, so retro-heaven for me! 'Dance of the Bacchantes' from the new *Dionysus* album featured, along with a cover version of a beautiful song 'Autumn Sun' by French-based band Deleyaman who Brendan had befriended. The first night in London brought the Ulrich family out again. I bumped into both Gary Levermore and I.V. Webb among the audience. As DCD took the stage, I could see the now familiar lineup, with Brendan and Lisa, of Astrid, Jules, Dan, David, and Richard – but there was one more. I had to blink and rub my eyes a couple of times, but it surely was none other than Robert Perry. Brendan had omitted to tell me his kid brother had been restored to the ranks, and I hadn't seen Robbie since the *Spiritchaser* sessions in 1995 – we had an emotional reunion at the aftershow! The following night I spotted comedian Frank Skinner among the audience (who has kindly also been known to give my music an airing on his Absolute Radio show), and backstage found both Kate Arnold, who was with Lisa's cousin, and Jeff Craft, who although no longer organising DCD's tours, had remained in touch with Brendan.

Nicki and I then travelled to catch both shows at Le Grand Rex in Paris, where Brendan reunited me with Jean-Luc Martin who'd promoted our 'Veni Vidi Vici' concert in Fréjus back in 1987, and had joined the latter part of our 1990 US tour, giving poetry readings as DCD's support act. We also met Aret and Beatrice of Deleyaman. Then on to Berlin for both shows at the Tempodrom, where David's girlfriend Milena joined him on stage for a hang duet during his opening act, and backstage we 'met' their new baby. Astrid told us of an opera she was writing and spoke very touchingly of what a great vocal teacher Lisa has been to her. As the tour reached Bulgaria, the show in Plovdiv coincided with Brendan's sixtieth birthday and the old chap was rather touched when Lisa led the audience in serenading him.

Nicki and I had hoped to get out to Greece for one or both the last two shows, but our plans fell through. Jules rubbed it in (not intentionally!) by telling me later of the amazing setting of the final show in particular, performing on the slopes of the Acropolis with the Parthenon looking down behind the audience, and how he'd looked at Brendan and Lisa ahead of him on the stage and been struck by the journey they'd been on from their early days of poverty and hardship to this epic moment. He felt the import of the lyrics to 'Labour of Love' more than ever that night – their clinging to an unshakeable faith in their abilities, anticipating what was to come, and ultimately realising their dreams.

The TPUC album had been 'in the can' for a good while when the stars aligned and Trebor scheduled the release for 3 December 2019 with the title *Final Reflections* and the track listing:

Artificial Man

Lessons of Love
Severely Blessed
Pirate Jane
Nightwalker and Love Witch
Hawk Dreams
Swimming in my Sleep
Squaring the Circle
Love's Skeleton (remixed and remastered)
Hanging Man (remixed and remastered)

The artwork followed an established theme whereby the 'Mysterium' symbol features in all three TPUC album covers/booklets, the cover of *The Painted Caravan* features in the *Tempus Fugitives* cover which, in turn, appears in the *Final Reflections* cover. In the booklet notes, T finally outs himself as a contributing musician to the project, as well as writer and producer. While I tend to get the plaudits for being the front man, T's far greater input and commitment to TPUC cannot be overstated.

Again, very positive reviews came in. *Anti-Pitchfork* called it 'One of the coolest releases of 2019' and others included:

> *Final Reflections* is a very unusual, creative, and conceptually striking work of art, and you should check it out!
> —artpublikamag.com

> Chock full of wondrous tales . . . *Final Reflections* has a dark side as well as a briskly adventurous one, but the meld is perfect.
> —annecarlini.com

> Uniquely creative and compelling . . . connects the dots between cinematic escapism and musicianship . . . an album that makes and breaks its own rules every step of the way.
> —stereostickman.com

And, posting on Amazon, Lisa Tenzin-Dolma gave the verdict from within our established fan base: 'darkly beautiful, evocative, and at times dreamlike . . . *Final Reflections* is a triumph!'

ELEVEN

April 2020. Dead Can Dance were due to kick off a tour of the Americas with a show at The Met in Philadelphia. Nicki and I were booked to go to Peru to see them play at the Gran Teatro Nacional in Lima on 21 May before embarking on a trip that's been sitting patiently on our bucket list for years, taking in Machu Picchu, the Colca Canyon, Lake Titicaca, Cuzco, and the Sacred Valley of the Incas.

Instead, the world was gripped by the contemporary plague of COVID-19. Countries 'locked down', international travel ground to a halt, and DCD's tour – as with pretty much every public event – was cancelled. Our Peruvian adventure went down the pan leaving us, like thousands of others, negotiating a refund and hoping we could reschedule. Of course, such concerns paled into insignificance compared to the terrible loss of life, illness, 'long-COVID' after-effects, and the collapse of so many businesses, losses of jobs and livelihoods. Health workers who'd done such an amazing job, putting their own lives on the line to care for virus victims, were left running on empty for months on end, with some tragically falling victim themselves. Once again nature pulled us up, emphatically reminding us that no matter how technologically advanced we think humanity has become, it can wipe us out at will with disease, flood, famine, earthquake, hurricane, wildfire, and other fearsome weaponry as it has from the earliest dawn.

Attempts to reschedule DCD tours – both of the Americas and Europe – have twice come to grief in the face of COVID's refusal to back down. As I write this concluding chapter, dates have been reset for North America in autumn/fall 2021, and Europe in spring 2022. If the 2021 shows do take place, they will mark the fortieth anniversary of Dead Can Dance's first performance in Australia back in 1981 – an impressive milestone. As and when the tours do happen, they will likely still be an extension of the tour which started in 2019 featuring a retrospective of works from across the DCD back catalogue, though I have been told there is some new material in the offing which might be given an airing.

Also in April 2020, I got news that the final compilation album in the 'John Barleycorn' series of dark British folk compilations was being readied, and received a last-minute invitation to contribute from the Cold Spring label, with literally just a few weeks to provide a final mix of an original song. Inspired by my now bucolic life, I wrote and recorded a song called 'Lammas Dance', a take on the traditional August harvest festival. I brought in TPUC collaborator Kingsley Sage to mix and produce it for me, and received a lovely email from Joanne at Cold Spring saying it was 'stunning'. I was then taken by surprise when asked to forward it to the studio of Martin Bowes for mastering and final compilation. Aside of his mastering services, Martin is the main driving force behind Coventry-based darkwave band Attrition, and hence an old label-mate of mine from Projekt days, as well as being an alumnus of Gary Levermore's Third Mind label, but we hadn't been in touch since promoting the Projekt 200 album back in 2007.

In between writing my new song and the release of the 'folk' compilation to which it was contributed, I came across an interview in the UK's *Observer* newspaper with legendary English singer Shirley Collins in which she's quoted as saying:

> I just hate the misuse of the word 'folk'. Somebody says on Facebook: 'Oh, I sat up in my bedroom and wrote a folk song last night.' Oh no, you didn't! That's not how it works! A folk song has to go on a passage through time, generations and individual people singing it to earn its title of a folk song.

I fully understand this view, and technically I accept that she's absolutely correct. There's also a laudable intent that I support unreservedly in wanting to preserve the traditional, historic repertoires of the ordinary 'folk' who sang on their ships and in their fields, forges, and factories. The problem is one of labelling and comes back again to this issue that the media must be able to categorise music, to put everything in pigeonholes – in order to file it, package it, play it and sell it, to know how to divide it up for audience sectors. So, perhaps we need another word to encapsulate contemporary songs written in a folkish-sort-of-manner, or perhaps we should differentiate between 'folk' and 'folk-style' – or 'neo-folk', a category which has already been coined, but which seems to mean different things to different folk. Whatever the answer, I remain intent on trying to carve myself a little niche in this sector.

Amid the process of providing 'Lammas Dance' to Cold Spring, an email arrived from Trebor to say that Nik Zenkevich of Russian label Infinite Fog was trying to contact me which, it transpired, was with a proposal to release my 1999 album *Pathways And Dawns* for the first time on vinyl. I confess to not having been aware of the label up to this point, but a quick look at their website revealed a well-established back catalogue, including vinyl pressings of Lisa's *Departum* album and *The Trail of Genghis Khan* soundtrack. The prospect of having *P&D* on vinyl after all these years, plus having the cover art in 12" x 12" format, was a big excitement and I quickly agreed terms with Nik. After making a nuisance of myself by having Sam Rosenthal hunt through the Projekt vaults in search of the original masters, I found I had them tucked away at the back of a drawer all along, and was asked by Nik to forward them for remastering to the studio of . . . Martin Bowes! We then found that the original CD cover artwork lost too much definition when enlarged to 12" size, so I tracked down original cover artist Tim O'Donnell, now based in Philadelphia and thankfully still at his drawing board. Tim made a great update for me, very close to the original, but with a reimagined back cover that I particularly love.

This rerelease of *P&D* coincided with a general resurgence in the popularity of vinyl. When I tried to provide UK retail group HMV with the benefit of my wisdom back in 2006, I felt a very lonely voice predicting that there was life yet in physical formats. An HMV store survives in Norwich and has introduced extensive new vinyl racks housing hundreds of albums – a mix of new releases and re-pressings of older classics, often on higher-grade vinyl than the originals. This section of the store seems constantly busy, and their range includes several Dead Can Dance albums and all three This Mortal Coil albums. I was myself inspired to buy new pressings of Pink Floyd's *Dark Side of the Moon* and Van Morrison's *Astral Weeks*, both of which were unaccountably missing from my collection of original 1960s/70s vinyls. And the many great independent vinyl shops, which have clung on through the lean times, are also now benefitting from the upturn in demand. So, I feel vindicated, and people really are prepared to pay for the better audio quality, but nevertheless these vinyl reissues are relatively expensive, and I believe CDs – which offer good audio quality at around half the price of vinyl – still have a future. Digital downloads are reported to be dying – it has really never made sense to pay for poor quality music, even at ninety-nine-cents-a-song, and that realisation is hitting home – so now it looks like being a straight fight between streaming music for free and buying physical formats. Despite the limp protestations of streaming services, most artists earn nothing tangible from them – it can require dozens, if not hundreds of plays to earn a single penny, and then it's not cost effective to make these tiny payments. A backlash is coming – by consumer pressure, by legislation, or by a combination of the two – and my gut feeling is that a natural equilibrium will be arrived at whereby 'consumers' will typically discover new music via streaming, but then purchase the music they love in higher quality physical formats.

Cold Spring used 'Lammas Dance' as their lead promo track for the album *The Forme To The Fyniment Foldes Ful Selden* which, as tradition determined, was released on Lammas Day (1 August). The vinyl *Pathways and Dawns* made its entry to the world on 18 September 2020, with Gary Levermore kindly circulating news of the release to his contact list to support Infinite Fog's promotions, together generating announcements by *Side-Line* (Belgium), *EBM* (Greece), *Black & Blue* (Brazil), plus *Altvenger* and *Maximum Volume Music* in the UK. Nik set up an interview for me with Klemen Breznikar of website 'It's Psychedelic Baby' in which I was asked: 'Looking back, what was the highlight of your time in Dead Can Dance, which songs are you most proud of, and where and when was your most memorable gig?' to which I began my reply: 'Oh wow, what a question (or sequence of questions) . . . I might have to write a book to answer that!'

I had, in fact, just finished writing this book and was in touch with Brendan and Lisa over final amendments, checking facts and dates, and musing over our differing recollections of particular incidents. Brendan and I wrestled with a few uncertain dates in the quest to finally reach a definitive record of every concert ever performed by Dead Can Dance – we know what's included in these pages is very close, but there remains an obstinate handful from early days on which the jury's still only got its foot halfway through the door. And, of course, by the time this book hits the streets, further shows will hopefully have taken place. Lisa was touchingly excited to receive my draft, went through it with a fine-tooth comb, and sent me a string of over twenty emails of comments spread over several days which variously had me laughing or shedding an oversentimental tear.

Lisa had been, and continued to be as industrious as ever. A new collaboration with Polish composer Zbigniew Preisner, this time working with pianist Dominik Wania, gave rise to an album released in late 2019 entitled *Melodies of my Youth*, comprising nine original pieces, two of which were co-composed with Lisa. This was closely followed in January 2020 by the release of her interpretation of the magnificent Górecki Symphony No. 3: 'Symphony of Sorrowful Songs', recorded at the Bulgarian National Radio Studios in Sofia with Yordan Kamdzhalov and The Genesis Orchestra. She then embarked on a collaboration with Jules Maxwell, further developing some of the improvisations they'd initiated during past DCD rehearsals and tours, culminating in an album, *Burn*, released in May 2021.

Brendan had immersed himself in another of his mighty research projects, this time to deeply explore his love of 'Rebetiko' – what I think Shirley Collins might allow me to describe as a melting pot of Greek and Turkish urban 'folk' music, these being working class songs of the tavernas and hash dens from the late nineteenth century to the 1950s which, until the later revivalist period, went largely untranscribed and were passed on solely through performance. Brendan's album, released in November 2020 under the title *Songs of Disenchantment: Music from the Greek Underground* is an amalgamation of his own English translations of lyrics of the ten featured songs, his own arrangements employing a raft of traditional instruments – including three types of bouzouki and the santouri (hammered dulcimer), and his own historical and contextual notes – the first time, he believes, these songs have been available in English language renditions. It brings to mind a snippet from a 2018 interview in which writer Bret Miller describes Brendan as 'the Indiana Jones of musical research'.

Fig. 32. Recording an udu part in my home studio for the Tenzin album *Echoes* in 2021. Photo by Nicola Arundell.

I was in touch again with Lisa Tenzin-Dolma, principally for some advice with regards to book publishing, when she revealed herself to also be a songwriter and sent me demos for an album she was compiling, a kind of memoir in music to be called *Echoes*. The songs were single-track recordings, just voice and acoustic guitar, but had a nice atmosphere to them and brought to my mind some of the elements I always enjoyed in 1970s folk/rock – hints of Fairport Convention and Pentangle. It seems I wasn't alone – she'd uploaded a song to YouTube which garnered a positive response from Fairport/Albion Band guitarist Simon Nicol. I offered a few thoughts on how she might work up the arrangements, and how she might go about getting it properly recorded. Next I heard, she'd enlisted the services of Zac Ware, long-time guitarist in the backing band of Scottish duo The Proclaimers, to engineer and produce her recordings as well as contributing additional guitars (including slide and steel), mandolin, and more. This connection was the result of a chance meeting at an open mic night in her local pub just prior to the UK's first 'COVID-lockdown'. We agreed that I would contribute some percussion, and sundry other quirkiness, and see how things progressed, so I found myself in an unexpected new collaboration project of sorts, and an honorary member of the band Lisa has determined we now comprise – 'Tenzin'.

Having extensively edited and updated my draft for this memoir, I launched myself once more into the perturbing world where creativity is assessed for commercial potential, only this time, instead of having music demos to lay before label heads and A&R execs, it was my first foray into literature on offer to publishers and commissioning editors. The early response was promising, with several major publishing houses requesting a manuscript to read, but I didn't chance upon an editor fully in tune with all the reference points and sufficiently enthused to work it up to publication with me. I decided to target a handful of the smaller, independent, and typically free-spirited publishers on the American West Coast, unbound by the shackles of the literary giants of New York and London. Almost instantly this precipitated exactly the kind of response I'd been hoping for – this from Kate Gale at Red Hen Press in Pasadena, CA who wrote:

> I'm not sure what led you to think of Red Hen, but it's funny, we are a bit of a 4AD family. When we started the press, we had to sell my then boyfriend's car and furniture. Later we got married and raised our kids sitting on the floor listening to Dead Can Dance, This Mortal Coil, Heidi Berry, His Name is Alive, Sandy Denny, Lisa Gerrard, Lisa Germano, Nina Simone, and Lou Reed. That music was

the soundtrack for the founding of the press. We listened to it all the time, every day on every camping trip – those were our vacations. When Lisa Gerrard got famous with *Gladiator*, it was weird because DCD was long part of our cellular structure . . . I'd love to see this.

The rest, as they say, is history, and the result here in your hands. And Kate's right that there was, and is, something weird about the fame that *Gladiator* brought Lisa's way to those of us familiar with the great range of her work over so many years. In recent times, I've seen Lisa crop up as an answer in a general knowledge quiz in a UK national newspaper (the question being: 'Which Australian musician and singer's only Golden Globe was at the 2001 awards when she won alongside composer Hans Zimmer for the score for the film *Gladiator* starring Russell Crowe?'), I've encountered her providing the telephone queue-holding music (with 'Now We Are Free') when I had cause to call my credit card provider, and I've heard her selected (also singing 'Now We Are Free') as a choice on the UK's long-running BBC radio show *Desert Island Discs* – one of the eight favourite records chosen by Sue Biggs, Director General of the Royal Horticultural Society. That certainly does seem weird when I think back to first hearing Lisa's voice rattling the wire window grilles of the Barkantine community hall when all we had was youthful energy and dreams.

One thing's for sure: without my chance meeting with Brendan and Lisa on the Isle of Dogs back in 1982, I wouldn't have been on this amazing musical journey. They are two exceptionally talented artists who it's been an incredible privilege to work with, and who opened my eyes and ears to the enormous possibilities of music. They are also two genuinely wonderful friends who, despite the scale of their own successes, have never faltered in their interest in, and support of, my projects. I am eternally grateful.

∧PPENDIX I

An Introductory Guide To 'World Music'

During the writing of this book, a friend mentioned he'd like to start exploring 'world music' and would appreciate some guidance. I think he anticipated I'd simply suggest a dozen or so artists/titles to check out, but he unwittingly sparked a deluge. As my travels through musics of the world have greatly influenced my compositions, and have run parallel to Dead Can Dance's musical explorations, it feels relevant to offer my musings here, though on an entirely 'take it or leave it' basis. There's nothing scholarly or academic about what follows – it's purely a personal view, but one I hope might lead to some interesting discoveries.

The specific scenario given by my enquirer was that he'd heard some music by Nusrat Fateh Ali Khan, but suspected it had been tailored to attract 'Western' audiences and not representative of its true roots; he was keen to discover some real, traditional music from different parts of the world. This triggered two responses:

(a) It very much depends what you've heard by Nusrat Fateh Ali Khan. In his early life he was trained in the tradition of 'Qawwali' – a devotional music of Sufi Muslims – and became a leading exponent in his native Pakistan. He came to the attention of 'Western' audiences in the early 1980s, was a global star by the turn of the '90s, and was latterly involved in numerous fusion and collaboration projects with many artists who admired his work. Thus, recordings prior to, say, 1985 are likely to feature authentic songs in the Qawwali tradition, while from around 1985 on you might hear varying degrees of 'Western' influences in his recordings, or indeed samples of his voice in works by others. Bear in mind, however, that – unlike the much more contemplative music that accompanies the mystic rituals of the Dervishes, for example – Qawwali performances traditionally incorporate bright melodies played on the harmonium plus rattling rhythms from tabla drums, hand clapping and other percussion, and can build to a frenzied climax – such elements are not falsely incorporated to appeal to a wider audience;

(b) Such has been the development of international communication and travel, it is very difficult to find any culture whose music has not been exposed to influences from other musical cultures and styles. During the entire period in which recording equipment has existed, there is very little known music which has remained in an isolated bubble and preserved in its pure original form.

The closest we can get to original, unadulterated ethnic sounds are 'field recordings' mostly made by musical anthropologists. By their nature, such recordings can be of variable quality, and tend to be more widely used for educational and reference purposes rather than recreational listening or 'entertainment'. However, if you want to investigate this area, the following are a few suggestions:

(i) *Music in the World of Islam.*
I have this as a set of six vinyl LPs released on Tangent Records in 1976 and it features a series of field recordings made across the Middle East and northern Africa in the late 1960s and early 1970s by Jean Jenkins and Poul Rovsing Olsen. A veritable treasure trove of themes and rhythms and a wonderful reference source over the years.

(ii) Recordings of David Fanshawe.
In 1973 David Fanshawe launched *African Sanctus*, at the time a startling and groundbreaking mix of rock band with African choir and rhythms. Today it sounds very dated and is not a hybrid I'd personally recommend. However, in preparation for his composition, Fanshawe made a valuable collection of field recordings which have subsequently appeared in various groupings and formats. The two I have are:

(a) *Music of the Nile*, ARC Music EUCD1793
(b) *Kenya & Tanzania: Witchcraft & Ritual Music*, Elektra Nonesuch LC0286

(iii) *The Secret Museum of Mankind.*
This is a three-volume CD set which I've seen recommended but haven't heard. It's described as a collection of 'ethnic music classics' recorded around the world between 1925–1948 and was released on Yazoo Records

in 2000. This would potentially be a good starting point as it gathers to-gether early field recordings from all across the globe in a single anthology.

(iv) Recordings of Hugh Tracey.
Sharp Wood Productions makes available a selection of the recordings made throughout Africa from the 1920s onwards by Hugh Tracey who accumulated such an enormous collection of field recordings they're reputed to fill over two hundred LPs! Again, I haven't heard these myself, but I understand some of Tracey's field recordings have also been made available more recently by specialist American archive label Dust-to-Digital.

(v) Waorani Waaponi.
A relatively recent set of field recordings, having been made in 1991 and released on CD on the Tumi label in 1994 (TUMI CD043). They feature chants at a Waorani tribal festival deep in Ecuador's Amazonian rainforest. While the quality is very good for a field recording, the chanting is extensively monotonal and repetitive, and the sleeve notes recommend listening in 'silent darkness'.

(vi) Congo – *Pygmy Polyphonies from North Congo.*
This is an even more recent set of field recordings of central African Pygmy tribes performing traditional music without any 'Western adornment', released on the VDE Gallo label. The recordings feature polyphonic vocal chants, and instrumentation including mouth bows, thumb piano, papaya-stalk flute and percussion.

(vii) Master Musicians of Jajouka.
MMoJ is principally a pipe and drum band native to the foothills of the Rif Mountains in Morocco. Although they incorporate some stringed instruments and vocals, their music is largely characterised by the shrill, primal sounds of their 'Pipes of Pan' (entirely different and not to be confused with the 'Pan-Pipes' of the Andes in South America) and their pounding drums. Their music is said to have remained unchanged for over four thousand years and lays claim to being the oldest-known music (as distinct from 'ancient music' which can be speculated about on the basis of instrument remains unearthed by archaeologists). Their music has fascinated 'Western' musicians for generations and there are various modern field-style recordings which have been made and 'produced' by

contemporary recording artists including original Rolling Stones guitarist Brian Jones. The ones I have are:

(a) *The Pipes of Pan at Jajouka*, prod. Brian Jones, 1971, (rereleased on CD in 1995 on Point Music)
(b) *Apocalypse Across the Sky*, prod. Bill Laswell, 1991, Axiom/Island
(c) *Master Musicians of Jajouka*, prod. Talvin Singh, 2000, Point/Universal

I'd recommend starting with the Laswell offering which I would guess stays closest to the authentic sound.

(viii) Gamelan.
Gamelan is a form of music unique to Indonesia – principally the islands of Java and Bali – performed by elaborate orchestras of tuned gongs and xylophones, augmented by gentle percussion. Numerous recordings are available of both traditional and contemporary Gamelan works, but provided you stick to performances by ensembles confined to the use of acknowledged Gamelan components, the sound should be authentic.

(ix) Throat singing.
This is a very distinctive style of vocalisation, of which two quite separate forms have come to global prominence in recent years. Tuvan throat singing is traditional to nomadic horsemen from the regions of Mongolia and Siberia, typically accompanied by primitive stringed instruments and percussion. The recordings I have are by a contemporary group called Huun-Huur-Tu which regularly tours and performs to Western audiences, but there are field recordings in existence – *Melodii Tuvi* for example on the aforementioned Dust-to-Digital label. The Inuk people of the Arctic also have a historic form of throat singing, of which the most prominent contemporary exponent is solo artist Tanya Tagaq. Traditionally, however, it was more typical for Inuk throat singing to be performed by duos or groups, generally women as it had developed as a pastime while men were away on hunting expeditions. It's likely field recordings exist, but I don't know of anything I can recommend.

(x) Recordings of David Attenborough.
A recent and valuable addition comes via a collection of field recordings made by UK 'National Treasure' David Attenborough and released as a two-CD set

in 2018 on Wrasse Records under the title *My Field Recordings from Across the Planet*. Attenborough made the recordings between 1954–63, having been inspired by the collecting and cataloguing of folk musics by American ethnomusicologist Alan Lomax. Extraordinarily, however, Attenborough's recordings were only made as a sideline during his travels for the BBC making nature documentaries. Each time he returned to the UK, he donated his field recordings to the BBC sound library, and there they languished in the BBC vaults until unearthed and compiled into this anthology.

As a general footnote to this section on field recordings, there is a musical offshoot to the well-known 'Rough Guide' series of travel reference books, beloved of 'gap-year' explorers. Like the books, the 'Rough Guide' music albums focus on a specific city, country or region. In order to give a broad understanding of the spectrum of music, the tracks will range from field recordings of traditional folk to modern pop of the specified territory so they are a bit of a mixed bag, but they provide a good starting point for the uninitiated and include a few gems to discover. Some of the packages also contain bonus CDs and, as a way of neatly coming full circle to our starting point, the *Rough Guide to the Music of Afghanistan* (RGNET1237CD) includes, for example, an eight-track bonus CD by the Ahmad Sham Sufi Qawwali Group which you might find an interesting comparison to the recordings you've heard of Nusrat Fateh Ali Khan.

☾

Having provided a few pointers to where you might find authentic recordings of traditional musics in their most original forms, I find much of the music that excites and inspires me doesn't have to be a slave to its origins and can have positively benefitted from broader exposure or even cross-culturalisation. I will therefore, free of such restrictions, indulge myself by recommending a selection of my favourite albums from the forty-odd years I've spent collecting music from around the planet. My choices are presented in a generally random list which may show some semblance of a global circumnavigatory order:

(1) Olatunji! – *Drums of Passion*, Columbia CK8210.
   I'll start here as it was amongst the first music I was introduced to by Brendan Perry. Although recorded in New York (I presume in the late 1960s or early '70s), this album by Nigerian expatriate Babatunde Olatunji encapsulates everything I love about African tribal drumming and chanting. The title

track – 'Jin-Go-Lo-Ba' (Drums of Passion) – was famously covered by supergroup Santana and will be instantly recognisable if you know their Latinated version, but this is the raw original. Thunderous drums, joyous voices and tons of passion – simply brilliant. Be careful, however, to find the original version (comprising eight tracks, starting with 'Akiwowo') and not one of the later spinoffs which also go under the name 'Drums of Passion' and, while not without merit, are not in the same class.

(2) King Sunny Ade and his African Beats – *Juju Music*, Island ILPS9712.
One of my pre-CD-era vinyl collection, so another of my earliest forays into 'world music'. Juju is the infectious blend of jangly electric guitars, rattling percussion (combining drum kit with Latin congas and traditional Nigerian talking drums, rattles, shakers, etc.) and 'call-and-response' vocals which greeted visitors to the steamy nightclubs of Lagos in the 1970s, and of which Sunny Ade was the self-proclaimed 'King'.

(3) Ali Farka Touré and Ry Cooder – *Talking Timbuktu*, World Circuit WCD040.
It's really an impossible task to pick just one of Ali Farka Touré's albums – I love and recommend anything and everything of his. There's an amazing flow of wonderful music that emanates from Mali, where the ebullience of Nigerian music meets the laid-back style of the Saharan desert. Ali Farka Touré was the kind of 'godfather' of Malian music and is greatly missed. Glorious understated rhythms and hypnotic Malian blues guitar riffs. This album with Ry Cooder is, perhaps, a good starting point, though my own introduction came via an earlier album *The River* which might jump the queue if you prefer something a bit more raw, earthy. Or, if serenity's your thing, try *In the Heart of the Moon* on which AFT duets with Toumani Diabate, a master of the kora (African gourd harp) – absolutely beautiful!

(4) Bassekou Kouyaté and Ngonie Ba – *Miri*, Outhere Records OH032.
Malian Kouyaté is an exponent of the ngoni, a kind of rustic banjo with a wood or gourd body and very thin neck. This album, the title of which means dream or contemplation in the Bamana (or Bambara) language, harks back to his rural village upbringing, far from the noise and chaos of Malian capital Bamako.

(5) Amadou and Mariam – *Dimanche a Bamako*, Radio Bemba BBCS772000.

Yup – Mali again! The blind hubby and wife couple from Bamako who seem permanently happily surprised at the joyous response they get (at shows I've attended) to their upbeat, high tempo sounds. This album was produced by French Catalan Manu Chao and incorporates some of his characteristic trademarks to heighten the effect still further. Dancefloor essential.

(6) Catrin Finch and Seckou Keita – *Soar*, Bendigedig/ARC Music BEND12.
Welsh harpist and Senegalese kora player duet on an album inspired by the migrations of the osprey (sea hawk) between Europe and Africa. Beautiful and evocative interplay between harps of two very different traditions. I saw/heard them perform some of this live at the 2019 Cambridge Folk Festival – they have a wonderful connection on stage.

(7) Tinariwen – *Amassakoul*, Independent IRL014.
The Touareg is one of the proud nomadic tribes of the Sahara desert which, during the past couple of decades, has spawned a number of blues guitar bands. Quite how it came about that these people added electric guitars to their camel bags, and where they plugged in and set up to practice amongst the rolling dunes, I couldn't tell you, but the sound of Saharan desert blues is unique and distinctive, and is one of those musics that, if you close your eyes and drift with it, can transport you to its source. Tinariwen were (I believe) the first band from this scene to have an album released for the consumption of 'Western' audiences – *Amassakoul* in 2003 – and this is as good a starting point as any, but if you like this, you will get much of the same from any subsequent Tinariwen album, and similar fare from the likes of Toumast. The recording of the 2003 Festival in the Desert (Independent IRL012) is also worth tracking down, and includes a track by Robert Plant who pitched up that year and joined the party, and who – together with regular collaborator Justin Adams – has subsequently been strongly influenced by the sounds he absorbed from the indigenous performers.

(8) *The Soul of Cape Verde*, LusAfrica 08775-2.
The location of the Cape Verdean islands – off the west coast of Africa, well south of the Canaries – became strategic to the historic trade triangle between Portugal, Angola and Brazil, and consequently the contemporary music of Cape Verde is a blend of those influences. This album is an excellent introduction, including the opening track from the late grand

dame of Verdean music Cesaria Evora who has an extensive catalogue of recordings if you want to explore further.

(9) *Buena Vista Social Club*, World Circuit WCD050.
Probably the most commercially successful 'world music' album of all time, this became ubiquitous on its release in 1997, took its originator Ry Cooder by complete surprise, and transformed a bunch of relatively elderly Cuban bar performers into global stars. Its overexposure as 'muzak' in bars and restaurants has slightly dulled its impact, but nevertheless, it's a fine album and if it's somehow passed you by, make up for lost time.

(10) Machito Orchestra – *!Que Viva Latina!*, Mode Laser 670033/VG671.
I love the 'electricity' generated by a big Latin dance band. Machito and Tito Puente were two of the outstanding bandleaders in this field, and there's a vast catalogue of their recordings. I choose this album by Machito simply because it was the first CD I ever bought and for me it's as good a collection as any I've heard. Those random 'gunshots' or 'machine gun' outbursts on the timbale drums do it for me every time!

(11) The Garifuna Women's Project – *Umalali*, Cumbancha/Stonetree CMB-CD-6.
The Garifuna people of central America – *Belize*, Guatemala, Honduras and Nicaragua – are descendants of shipwrecked African slaves who intermarried with Caribs and Arawaks of the Caribbean coast. Many of their women sing songs as they go about humble, rustic lives, and the folk music of the Garifuna survives and develops in this way. This album is a remarkable collection of recordings of women of all ages who are not 'performers' but who are merely singing the songs that tell the stories and history of their everyday lives, with some sympathetic embellishments from the producers.

(12) Toto La Momposina y Sus Tambores – *La Candela Viva*, Real World CDRW31.
Toto La Momposina is the queen of Colombia's Caribbean coastal sound and this is a fabulous album, released back in 1993 on Peter Gabriel's Real World label. Combining African, Spanish, and Native American influences, her voice soars over the pounding rhythms of her drummers.

(13) Lido Pimienta – *Miss Colombia*, ANTI- 7638-2

Lido Pimienta is actually Canadian, based in Ontario, but her music is very much that of her ancestral roots. The album title is a tongue-firmly-in-cheek jibe inspired by a presentational bloomer at the final of the 2015 Miss Universe contest when the wrong contestant was crowned, but nevertheless, it doesn't belie the album's content. This is something of a hybrid with 'synthpop', but the rhythms and passion are all Colombian.

(14) Río Mira – *Marimba del Pacifico*, Aya Records AYA005CD.
Gorgeous marimba-based sounds from the Pacific coast region that extends across neighbouring Ecuador and Columbia. This is pretty much all done with percussion and voices – very much my 'thing'. Music that will have your body moving whether you want it to or not!

(15) Chancha Vía Circuito – *Amansara*, Wonderwheel WonderCD-23.
Bit of a quirky choice this one, and not everyone's cup of tea. Chancha Vía Circuito is the stage name of Argentinian DJ/producer Pedro Canale and this is a kind of LatAm dub mashup of influences from folk musics across the continent and featuring the thunderous candombe drums of Uruguay. I came across a YouTube video by chance of the track 'Sueño en Paraguay' and was hooked – on both the music and the artwork.

(16) Inti Raymi – *Inca Quena*, Tumi CD047.
Much as I love Simon & Garfunkel, they committed an unforgiveable sin when they ripped 'El Condor Pasa' from its Andean folk roots and stuck the opening line 'I'd rather be a hammer than a nail' on it, inspiring a legion of shopping mall buskers. If your exposure to Andean music ends there, therapy is available in the form of albums such as this. Inti Raymi (named after the Inca sun festival) use only authentic Inca wind instruments such as quenas (notched-end flute) and zamponas (pan-pipes), without any of the stringed instruments which were introduced by the Conquistadors. This particular album was written as the soundtrack to a documentary film *Qeros – the last of the Incas*.

(17) Takashi Hirayasu and Bob Brozman – *Jin Jin/Firefly*, Riverboat TUGCD1020.
The Okinawa Islands in the south of Japan boast their own unique instrument – a form of three-stringed banjo with a soundbox covered in snakeskin (traditionally python). Takashi Hirayasu is a virtuoso of the

'sanshin' and made this collaboration album with globetrotting American guitarist Bob Brozman in 2000.

(18) Jing Ying Soloists – *Like Waves Against the Sand*, Saydisc SDL325.
Another offering from my vinyl vaults, this is quite an obscure collection of Chinese folk songs played on traditional instruments including yang ch'in, er-hu, pi-pa and bamboo flutes. It has a beautiful lightness and freshness about it. It was released in 1981 and, sadly, may be difficult to obtain now.

(19) Les Cosaques du Don – *Chants Russes*, Deutsche Grammophon 439 675-2.
A double CD set of both popular folk and religious chants. Polyphonic singing – sometimes gentle, and at other times with great gusto – by the Don Cossacks group which was founded by refugees faithful to the Tsar after the Russian Revolution. The recordings were made in the 1960s under the direction of Serge Jaroff.

(20) Taraf de Haidouks – *Dumbala Dumba*, Crammed Discs CRAW21.
A band of Romanian gypsies who in the late 1990s were plucked from their local village weddings circuit and thrust under the 'world music' spotlight. Their performances are wild and frenetic, and the speed of playing on the fiddles, cymbalom (enormous hammered dulcimer) and accordions is scarcely believable. I've picked this particular album pretty much at random – if you like it, you can fairly safely buy any of their albums for more of the same.

(21) Le Mystere des Voix Bulgares, 4AD CAD603.
The 1986 original of a series of releases of recordings by the Bulgarian State Radio and Television Female Vocal Choir – folk songs about mundane subjects but performed with astonishing power and purity. The open-throat singing which proved a huge inspiration to Lisa Gerrard and consequently influenced the sound of Dead Can Dance.

(22) Muzsikas – *Blues for Transylvania*, Ryko/Hannibal.
More groovy Balkan sounds to get your feet tapping, this time from Hungary. As with many Muzsikas albums, this one features guest vocals by Marta Sebestyen – the voice of the soundtrack to the film *The English Patient*.

(23) Darko Rundek and Cargo Orkestar – *Ruke*, Piranha CD-PIR1894.
This is essentially Croatian blues, so you could argue it's misplaced here in

a guide to traditional musics of the world. However, there's something very uniquely of its homeland about the way this album sounds which I feel must be drawn up from its Balkan roots. Very earthy, and fabulous use of a brass section.

(24) Cocanha – *Puput*, Pagans PA023.
A female vocal trio from the French side of the Pyrenees Mountains, Cocanha mix traditional local stringed drums and handclaps, with vocal clicks and yelps, and beautiful, insistent harmonies. Highly polished, yet raw and rustic at the same time – a fine combo! If you like this, and feel ready for another French group combining voices and percussion, but with more complex arrangements and more 'Sturm und Drang' (excuse the cross-cultural drift), also check out *La Grande Folie* by sextet San Salvador (MDC026) – this from another mountainous region, the Massif Central.

(25) L'Ham de Foc – *Cor de Porc*, GEMA GMC010.
Steve Tyler introduced me to this Spanish duo whose name apparently translates as 'Fish Hook of Fire'. Together with guest contributors, they create a heady mix where Andalusian and Arabic traditions meet, using a range of traditional folk and early music instruments.

(26) Radio Tarifa – *Rumba Argelina*, World Circuit WCD042.
The concept behind the creation of this contemporary Spanish group is that, if there were a radio station in Tarifa – the most southerly tip of Spain – it would broadcast to a mixed audience of southern Iberians and north Africans. Their music would be a mix of Arabic, Flamenco and medieval traditions, and 'Radio Tarifa' set out to create that music. As far as I know, *Rumba Argelina* was their first album and, for me, it remains the best.

(27) Bellemou Messaoud – *Le Pere du Rai*, World Circuit WCD011.
'Rai' is a traditional music of Algeria which has its roots in groups of women singing in villages and developed to feature solo female singers in urban bars and brothels. In the 1960s, trumpeter Bellemou Messaoud rearranged the style of Rai, transposing traditional female choral parts onto his trumpet, and fronting his band with guest male solo vocalists ('Chebs'). He named his version 'Pop-Rai' and it became the forerunner for the much heavier disco-style Rai which stormed the French club scene and beyond in the 1980s. This is 'feel good' fun, in which tracks typically

start with a slow accordion intro before bursting into a tumbling cascade of brass and percussion.

(28) Rachid Taha – *Made in Medina*, Ark Records ARK21.
Rachid Taha was an Algerian exile in France whose musical heroes were The Clash and whose guitar riffs borrow from the heaviest offerings of Led Zep's Jimmy Page. Add to the mix some oud (Arabic lute) and darabuka (goblet drum) and you get the idea. All music of Algerian root tends to get lazily lumped under the heading 'Rai' in reviews, but Taha's music wasn't Rai (or not as I understand it). He made something very distinct that truly does 'Rock the Casbah'. This is my favourite Taha album, but he is another artist of whom, if you like this, you can safely get pretty much anything else.

(29) Abdel Hadi Halo and the El Gusto Orchestra of Algiers, Honest John HJRCD32.
Originally a mixed ensemble of Muslim and Jewish musicians based in the Algerian capital, the Orchestra broke up in the mid-1960s following Algeria's independence from French rule when most Jews fled the country. The Orchestra didn't perform for some years until 2006, when a relaxation in the fundamentalist rule allowed the Orchestra to reform and record this album, albeit with only the Muslim musicians who had remained in Algeria. Largely by now comprising sexagenarian and septuagenarian members, plus a few younger recruits, the Orchestra seemingly picked up where it left off and recorded this wonderfully exuberant album which amazingly exhibits no obvious tinges of resentment or regret. When the Orchestra subsequently toured in Europe in 2007, there were reportedly some emotional reunions with former Jewish members.

(30) Souad Massi – *Deb*, Wrasse 096.
An Algerian artist in an entirely different hybrid vein is Souad Massi, a female singer/guitarist who combines her home influences with Latin rhythms to fine effect.

(31) Abdel Gadir Salim All-Stars – *The Merdoum Kings Play Songs of Love*, World Circuit WCD024.
This is a particular favourite which I regularly return to. Abdel Gadir Salim is one of the leading lights of Sudanese music. The cover never fails to draw a smile, both for its tongue-in-cheek title – the album was released in the

wake of the international success of the New York/Puerto Rican book (highly recommended), film and album *The Mambo Kings Play Songs of Love* – and for the sparkling grins of Abdel and his 'All-Star' band. These guys get a great groove going.

(32) Ali Hassan Kuban – *From Nubia to Cairo*, Piranha/GEMA PIR3166-CD.
Multi-instrumentalist, singer and bandleader Hassan Kuban was the 'Godfather' of Nubian Music, a twentieth century east African uptempo jazz of the region straddling southern Egypt and northern Sudan. Ripping stuff!

(33) Soliman Gamil – *The Egyptian Music*, Touch TO:7CD.
I found this album on a stall in London's Camden Market many years ago and took a chance on buying it, having never previously heard of it. Happily it turned out to be a gem. Soliman Gamil was a composer who sought to recreate the sounds of ancient Egypt using traditional instruments. He was also a scholar and music journalist. This is an instrumental album resulting from his research and contemplations – I can't vouch for its authenticity, but it's certainly very evocative.

(34) Oum Kalsoum – *The Legend*, Manteca MANTDBL513.
If taking any interest in Arabic music, it is essential to be aware of Oum Kalsoum (alternatively Oum Kalthoum, Umm Kulthum and other variations) who is revered throughout the Middle East, and typically known simply as 'The Lady'. She is widely regarded as the greatest Arabic singer of all time, and was considered 'incomparable' by the opera singer Maria Callas. She had a huge vocal range, was said to be one of only five women in history who has been able to sing every Arabic scale, and had such vocal strength that sound technicians struggled to find microphones and settings that could cope. She was highly 'decorated' in the 1940s by King Farouk, and when Kalsoum died in 1975, more people attempted to attend her funeral than that of Egypt's famed President Nasser five years earlier. There are many collections of Kalsoum's music, and I'm not in any way qualified to advise on their relative merits – suffice to say that the particular collection I've recommended here is one I happened to purchase, is a two-CD set showcasing a selection of her styles, and I believe is still fairly readily available. If you want to delve further, the album *Al Atlal* on the Sono Cairo label comprises a live recording of a

single forty-eight-minute-long song, considered by many aficionados to have been Kalsoum's greatest ever performance.

(35) Musicians of the Nile – *Charcoal Gypsies*, Real World CDRW63.
MotN is a collective of musicians from Upper Egypt which has existed for several decades and whose fluid membership continually evolves. They started to come to the attention of an international audience in the mid-1970s and have subsequently toured the world almost continuously. You can safely start with any of their recorded works, but the one I've named here can save you any deliberations.

(36) Ofra Haza – *Kirya*, East West 9031-76127-2.
Israeli singer Ofra Haza came from the Yemenite Jewish tradition whose instrumentation, scales and rhythms are closely related to the Arabic. Although she sometimes sang in Hebrew and in 1983 represented Israel in the Eurovision Song Contest (!) – in which she came second, making her a big star at home and a recognisable name across Europe – she also enjoyed considerable popularity in Arabic countries across the Middle East. She favoured a commercial, disco-style production, which is in evidence on the album I've selected here, but it suits her music. 'Kirya' is an old Hebrew name for Jerusalem. Haza is the singer Hans Zimmer had originally intended to work with on the *Gladiator* soundtrack. There is also a sampled segment of her vocals in M|A|R|R|S's 'Pump Up The Volume'.

(37) Le Trio Joubran – *AsFar*, World Village WVF479055.
The three Joubran brothers from Palestine are oud (Arabic lute) players who conjure up a bubbling cauldron of mesmeric string sounds. Add to this some great percussion and powerful guest vocals and you have this terrific album in which ancient traditions and contemporary Arabic jazz collide.

(38) Reem Kelani – *Sprinting Gazelle*, Fuse Records CFCD048.
Reem Kelani was born in England to Palestinian parents and so crosses the cultural divide between the countries. This debut album released in 2005 is designed to introduce the music of the land of her parents to an English-speaking audience and so comes with extensive explanatory sleeve notes. Kelani is passionate about Palestine, both culturally and politically, her approach is both scholarly and artistic, and the music is great.

(39) Andre Hajj & Ensemble – *Amaken*, ARC EUCD2219.

This album is subtitled 'Instrumental Music from Lebanon' and features another master oud player, Andre Hajj with his ensemble comprising violin, ney (flute), qanam (zither), double bass and percussion. As with Trio Joubran, there is a fusion of tradition with a contemporary jazz element.

(40) Ghada Shbeir – *Al Muwashahat*, Forward Music.

A much more ethereal and atmospheric side of Arabic music is showcased on this beautiful album by Lebanese female singer Ghada Shbeir. According to the sleeve notes, the Muwashah is a genre of Arabic song that has its roots in tenth-century Andalusia (i.e. during the Arabic reign of that region).

(41) Kudsi & Suleyman Erguner – *OI (Sufi Music of Turkey)*, Silva Screen CMP3005.

The Erguner brothers follow in a family tradition of great exponents of the 'ney' – the haunting Turkish flute – and this album of Sufi devotional music is another fine example of the more meditative, spiritual side of Arabic music.

(42) Vardan Hovanissian and Emre Gültekin – *Karin*, Muziekpublique 10.

Hovanissian plays 'duduk', the traditional flute of Armenia, and is joined on this recording by Belgian/Turkish oud (lute) player Emre Gültekin. The duduk has a naturally plaintive sound, and this is another very atmospheric album with a richness provided by a range of guest musicians and vocalists. Duduk also features in the soundtrack to *Gladiator*, in that instance performed by another master of the duduk, Djivan Gasparyan, whose recordings are also well worth checking out.

(43) Constantinople and Ablaye Cissoko – *Traversées*, Ma Case CONS1811.

A real melting pot – Canadian-based trio inspired by the historic Turkish capital, using setar (Iranian lute), viola da gamba, and Arabic percussion, are joined by US-based Senegalese kora player for a fusion that threatens to suffer from too many ingredients, but actually works beautifully.

(44) Azam Ali – *From Night to the Edge of Day*, Six Degrees 657036-11772.

Described as a 'collection of lullabies from the Middle East', I'm not at all sure this album by US-based Iranian singer Azam Ali would be the ideal backdrop to induce slumber. While Ali dedicates the album to her son Iman (three years old at time of release in 2011) and may well have used a cappella versions of the same songs to somnambulistic effect at home, the arrangements which appear on this album feature some big strings and percussion to glorious effect.

(45) Alim Qasimov – *Love's Deep Ocean*, Network World Music 34411.
Alim Qasimov is a leading exponent of the 'mugham' singing tradition of Azerbaijan and his recordings feature his impassioned vocals accompanied by rhythms on a simple frame drum. As he has developed from local performer to international recording artist he has absorbed influences from Islamic neighbours in Turkey, Iran, and Pakistan – citing Nusrat Fateh Ali Khan as being of particular importance to him. On this album – as with several of his recordings – he is accompanied by his daughter, Ferghana Qasimova.

(46) *Saaz Raag Aur Taal (Music of India)*, Sirocco/CBS SIR-CBS008.
I have to confess to being hopelessly out of my depth when it comes to Indian classical music. I understand that it divides broadly into two categories – the 'Hindustani' of the north and the 'Carnatic' of the south – that it further divides by the 'core concepts' of Shruti, Swara, Alankar, Raga, and Tala, and I know that rhythmically it involves an extraordinarily complex 'language' which must be learnt in depth to fully understand it. Whenever I've sought to delve deeper, I've become overwhelmed, and have concluded that unless you study from a very early age and are immersed and raised in the traditions, you don't stand a chance! I've found this CD to be a useful reference point over the years, comprising a collection of eighteen classical pieces, none of which is overlong. A simple inlay card gives a chart showing the instrumentation, performers, styles and beats of each track, and when opened out is entirely blank as though to confirm that it would be impossible to explain the compositions and performances in the confines of a booklet which would fit in a CD case.

(47) *Sadak* film soundtrack, Super Cassettes India SFCD1/125.
Jumping from my last selection to this is certainly going from one extreme to the other, and less flatteringly might be described as going from the sublime to the ridiculous. However, it's impossible to ignore the impact of the vast 'Bollywood' machine on Indian music and culture. This is an entirely random selection from the thousands of Bollywood soundtracks which follow the formula in much the same way the film plots do, and just happens to be in my CD library because it was given to me. I've never seen

Sadak, but apparently it was the second highest grossing Bollywood film of 1991 and has a plot which borrows from Martin Scorsese's *Taxi Driver*. The music is twee and sugary, but I love it – great rhythms, catchy melodies and big, orchestral production.

(48) *The Mahabharata* film soundtrack, Real World CDRW9.
Another film soundtrack, but there the similarity ends. This is a veritable potpourri. *The Mahabharata* is, of course, the epic Hindu story, originally written in Sanskrit and by some considerable distance the longest poem ever. The film is the 1989 interpretation by English Francophile director Peter Brook, and this soundtrack was composed and performed by musicians from India, Japan, Iran, Turkey, Denmark, and France. Whether or not such treatment of the sacred text sits well with Hindu purists, I don't know, but it is a beautiful album of evocative themes and sounds.

(49) Shye Ben Tzur, Jonny Greenwood and the Rajasthan Express – *Junun*, Nonesuch 7599-79484-7
Contender for unlikeliest collision of cultures in my list – this is Israeli composer Shye Ben Tzur who has based himself in India and specialises in Qawwali (Sufi) devotional music written in Hebrew, Urdu, and Hindi, collaborating with Radiohead guitarist Jonny Greenwood and Rajasthan Express – a traditional Hindustani brass band. The result is this wonderful double CD set, one minute mellow, the next bursting with vitality.

(50) Debashish Bhattacharya and Bob Brozman – *Mahima*, Riverboat TUGCD1029.
Globetrotting serial collaborator Bob Brozman pops up again (see (17) above), this time as a maestro of the Hawaiian slide guitar to jam along with Hindustani slide guitar master Debashish Bhattacharya, accompanied by the latter's sister Sutapa on vocals and brother Subhashis on tabla (drums). The basic structures are taken from classical Indian forms, which have then been improvised around and realised in contemporary song formats.

((

OK, it's a mite contrived, but I've *almost* naturally arrived at a 'Top 50', which I think should be quite sufficient as a starting point, and one from which you'll hopefully be inspired to go on and make your own discoveries.

I'd like to emphasise that this 'guide' barely scratches the surface of 'world music' which, in itself, is a daft category, being so excessively broad. There is a marked emphasis on West African and Arabic musics as I'm particularly drawn to their sounds and rhythms. At the same time, I'm acutely aware that my selections omit numerous entire countries and regions, peoples and cultures, all with rich musical heritages. I've also omitted some of the 'great' names of world music – my Indian selections omit sitarist Ravi Shankar, my Egyptian selections omit master percussionist Hossam Ramzy, my West African selections omit legendary singers/bandleaders Fela Kuti (Nigeria) and Youssou N'Dour (Senegal) and drummer Tony Allen (Nigeria); none of the leading Flamenco guitarists feature, none of the great Portuguese Fado singers is included, and in Latin America I've missed out Brazilian superstars Caetano Veloso and Gilberto Gil, and Argentinian tango maestro Astor Piazzolla. These are all fabulous, and all more than worthy of your attention, but I was looking to generally go a little further off-piste. I've omitted Nusrat Fateh Ali Khan from the '50' only because he was already covered in my introduction. Furthermore, I've deliberately avoided all folk music of the British Isles and of the Celtic lands as this would have needed another entire list. I mean no disrespect to any artist, person, peoples or culture not included – I simply have to impose some parameters and stop somewhere.

The bottom line is that I'm still a beginner myself in exploring the world of music, and am constantly making new discoveries – undoubtedly one of the great joys of life.

APPENDIX II

Discography

ARTIST	SONG TITLE	RELEASE FORMAT	RELEASE TITLE	RELEASE DATE	CATALOGUE NUMBER	RECORD LABEL	ULRICH PERFORMANCE
Dead Can Dance	Instrumental (aka Orion)	BBC radio	John Peel Show	Nov-83			drum machine
Dead Can Dance	Ocean	BBC radio	John Peel Show	Nov-83			hammered dulcimer
Dead Can Dance	Labour of Love	BBC radio	John Peel Show	Nov-83			drum machine
Dead Can Dance	Threshold	BBC radio	John Peel Show	Nov-83			drum kit
Dead Can Dance	The Trial	vinyl album	Dead Can Dance	Feb-84	CAD 404	4AD	drum kit
Dead Can Dance	Fortune	vinyl album	Dead Can Dance	Feb-84	CAD 404	4AD	drum kit
Dead Can Dance	Ocean	vinyl album	Dead Can Dance	Feb-84	CAD 404	4AD	metal percussion
Dead Can Dance	East of Eden	vinyl album	Dead Can Dance	Feb-84	CAD 404	4AD	drum kit
Dead Can Dance	Threshold	vinyl album	Dead Can Dance	Feb-84	CAD 404	4AD	drum kit
Dead Can Dance	A Passage in Time	vinyl album	Dead Can Dance	Feb-84	CAD 404	4AD	drum kit
Dead Can Dance	Wild in the Woods	vinyl album	Dead Can Dance	Feb-84	CAD 404	4AD	drum kit
Dead Can Dance	Carnival of Light	BBC radio	John Peel Show	Jun-84			drum kit
Dead Can Dance	Penumbra	BBC radio	John Peel Show	Jun-84			drum kit
Dead Can Dance	Panacea	BBC radio	John Peel Show	Jun-84			drum kit
Dead Can Dance	Flowers of the Sea	BBC radio	John Peel Show	Jun-84			bongoes
Dead Can Dance	Carnival of Light	vinyl EP	Garden of the Arcane . . .	Oct-84	BAD 408	4AD	drum kit
Dead Can Dance	In Power We Entrust . . .	vinyl EP	Garden of the Arcane . . .	Oct-84	BAD 408	4AD	drum kit
Dead Can Dance	The Arcane	vinyl EP	Garden of the Arcane . . .	Oct-84	BAD 408	4AD	drum kit
Dead Can Dance	Flowers of the Sea	vinyl EP	Garden of the Arcane . . .	Oct-84	BAD 408	4AD	congas

Artist	Title	Format	Album	Date	Catalogue	Label	Credit
Dead Can Dance	The Trial	CD album	Dead Can Dance	1986	CAD 404 CD	4AD	drum kit
Dead Can Dance	Fortune	CD album	Dead Can Dance	1986	CAD 404 CD	4AD	drum kit
Dead Can Dance	Ocean	CD album	Dead Can Dance	1986	CAD 404 CD	4AD	metal percussion
Dead Can Dance	East of Eden	CD album	Dead Can Dance	1986	CAD 404 CD	4AD	drum kit
Dead Can Dance	Threshold	CD album	Dead Can Dance	1986	CAD 404 CD	4AD	drum kit
Dead Can Dance	A Passage in Time	CD album	Dead Can Dance	1986	CAD 404 CD	4AD	drum kit
Dead Can Dance	Wild in the Woods	CD album	Dead Can Dance	1986	CAD 404 CD	4AD	drum kit
Dead Can Dance	Carnival of Light	CD album	Dead Can Dance	1986	CAD 404 CD	4AD	drum kit
Dead Can Dance	In Power We Entrust . . .	CD album	Dead Can Dance	1986	CAD 404 CD	4AD	drum kit
Dead Can Dance	The Arcane	CD album	Dead Can Dance	1986	CAD 404 CD	4AD	drum kit
Dead Can Dance	Flowers of the Sea	CD album	Dead Can Dance	1986	CAD 404 CD	4AD	bongoes
This Mortal Coil	At First, And Then	vinyl album	Filigree and Shadow	Sep-86	DAD609	4AD	drums, perc, ocarina
This Mortal Coil	At First, And Then	CD album	Filigree and Shadow	Sep-86	DAD 609 CD	4AD	drums, perc, ocarina
The Wolfgang Press	The Wedding	vinyl EP	Big Sex	Apr-87	BAD 702	4AD	percussion
The Wolfgang Press	The Wedding	CD EP	Big Sex	Apr-87	BAD 702 CD	4AD	percussion
Dead Can Dance	Dawn of the Iconoclast	vinyl album	Within the Realm of . . .	Sep-87	CAD 705	4AD	timpani & snare
Dead Can Dance	Dawn of the Iconoclast	CD album	Within the Realm of . . .	Sep-87	CAD 705 CD	4AD	timpani & snare
Dead Can Dance	Summoning of the Muse	vinyl album	Within the Realm of . . .	Sep-87	CAD 705	4AD	timpani
Dead Can Dance	Summoning of the Muse	CD album	Within the Realm of . . .	Sep-87	CAD 705 CD	4AD	timpani
P Nooten & M Brook	Time	vinyl album	Sleeps With the Fishes	Oct-87	CAD 710	4AD	bongoes
P Nooten & M Brook	Time	CD album	Sleeps With the Fishes	Oct-87	CAD 710 CD	4AD	bongoes
The Wolfgang Press	Swing Like a Baby	vinyl album	Bird Wood Cage	Nov-88	CAD 810	4AD	percussion

Artist	Title	Format	Release	Catalogue	Date	Label	Role
The Wolfgang Press	Swing Like a Baby	CD album	Bird Wood Cage	CAD 810 CD	Nov-88	4AD	percussion
Peter Ulrich	Taqaharu's Leaving	vinyl single	Taqaharu's Leaving	PTD-001	Mar-90	Cornerstone	voice, drums, sequencing
Peter Ulrich	Evocation	vinyl single	Evocation	PTD-001	Mar-90	Cornerstone	voice, drums, percussion
Dead Can Dance	Nierika	vinyl album	Spiritchaser	CAD 6008	Jun-96	4AD	bass drum
Dead Can Dance	Nierika	CD album	Spiritchaser	CAD 6008 CD	Jun-96	4AD	bass drum
Dead Can Dance	Dedicace Outo	vinyl album	Spiritchaser	CAD 6008	Jun-96	4AD	bass drum
Dead Can Dance	Dedicace Outo	CD album	Spiritchaser	CAD 6008 CD	Jun-96	4AD	bass drum
Dead Can Dance	Sambatiki	CD single	Sambatiki	(promo)	Jun-96	4AD	bass drum
Peter Ulrich	Taqaharu's Leaving	CD album	Pathways and Dawns	PRO95	Sep-99	Projekt	voice, drums, sequencing
Peter Ulrich	Always Dancing	CD album	Pathways and Dawns	PRO95	Sep-99	Projekt	voice, sequencing
Peter Ulrich	Life Amongst the Black…	CD album	Pathways and Dawns	PRO95	Sep-99	Projekt	voice, sequencing
Peter Ulrich	Journey of Discovery	CD album	Pathways and Dawns	PRO95	Sep-99	Projekt	sequencing
Peter Ulrich	Nocturne	CD album	Pathways and Dawns	PRO95	Sep-99	Projekt	voice, sequencing
Peter Ulrich	Evocation	CD album	Pathways and Dawns	PRO95	Sep-99	Projekt	voice, drums, percussion
Peter Ulrich	The Springs of Hope	CD album	Pathways and Dawns	PRO95	Sep-99	Projekt	voice, sequencing
Peter Ulrich	Time and a Word	CD album	Pathways and Dawns	PRO95	Sep-99	Projekt	voice, sequencing
Various Artists	Life Amongst the Black…	CD album	Orphee	PRO102	Aug-00	Projekt	voice, sequencing
Various Artists	Taqaharu's Leaving	CD album	Within This Infinite Ocean	PRO122	2001	Projekt	voice, drums, sequencing
Dead Can Dance	Labour of Love	CD album	1981-1998	DCDBOX1	Nov-01	4AD	drum machine
Dead Can Dance	Ocean	CD album	1981-1998	DCDBOX1	Nov-01	4AD	hammered dulcimer
Dead Can Dance	Orion	CD album	1981-1998	DCDBOX1	Nov-01	4AD	drum machine
Dead Can Dance	Threshold	CD album	1981-1998	DCDBOX1	Nov-01	4AD	drum kit

Artist	Title	Format	Release	Date	Catalog	Label	Instruments
Dead Can Dance	Carnival of Light	CD album	1981-1998	Nov-01	DCDBOX1	4AD	drum kit
Dead Can Dance	In Power We Entrust...	CD album	1981-1998	Nov-01	DCDBOX1	4AD	drum kit
Dead Can Dance	Summoning of the Muse	CD album	1981-1998	Nov-01	DCDBOX1	4AD	timpani
Dead Can Dance	Nierika	CD album	1981-1998	Nov-01	DCDBOX1	4AD	bass drum
Dead Can Dance	Sambatiki	CD album	1981-1998	Nov-01	DCDBOX1	4AD	bass drum
Various Artists	Taqaharu's Leaving	CD album	The Arbitrary Width of...	Oct-02	PRO136	Projekt	voice, drums, sequencing
Dead Can Dance	Carnival of Light	2 CD comp	Wake	May-03	DAD 2303 CD	4AD	drum kit
Dead Can Dance	In Power We Entrust...	2 CD comp	Wake	May-03	DAD 2303 CD	4AD	drum kit
Dead Can Dance	Summoning of the Muse	2 CD comp	Wake	May-03	DAD 2303 CD	4AD	timpani
Dead Can Dance	Nierika	2 CD comp	Wake	May-03	DAD 2303 CD	4AD	bass drum
Various Artists	At Mortlake	CD album	Unquiet Grave Vol. IV	Nov-03	CLP 1298-2	Cleopatra	voice, guitar, sequencing
Peter Ulrich	At Mortlake	CD album	Enter The Mysterium	Mar-05	PUETM-004	City Canyons	voice, guitar, sequencing
Peter Ulrich	The Scryer and the Sh...	CD album	Enter The Mysterium	Mar-05	PUETM-004	City Canyons	voice, perc, dulcimer, seq
Peter Ulrich	Across The Bridge	CD album	Enter The Mysterium	Mar-05	PUETM-004	City Canyons	voice, perc, h/dulcimer
Peter Ulrich	Nothing But the Way	CD album	Enter The Mysterium	Mar-05	PUETM-004	City Canyons	voice, perc, flute, sequen
Peter Ulrich	The Witchbottle of Suffolk	CD album	Enter The Mysterium	Mar-05	PUETM-004	City Canyons	voice, perc, sequencing
Peter Ulrich	The True Cross	CD album	Enter The Mysterium	Mar-05	PUETM-004	City Canyons	voice, perc, sequencing
Peter Ulrich	Kakatak Tamai	CD album	Enter The Mysterium	Mar-05	PUETM-004	City Canyons	voice, drums, perc, seq
Peter Ulrich	Another Day	CD album	Enter The Mysterium	Mar-05	PUETM-004	City Canyons	voice, drums, perc, seq
Peter Ulrich	Through Those Eyes	CD album	Enter The Mysterium	Mar-05	PUETM-004	City Canyons	voice, guitars, perc
Peter Ulrich	Flesh to Flame	CD album	Enter The Mysterium	Mar-05	PUETM-004	City Canyons	voice, h/dulcimer, perc
Peter Ulrich	At Mortlake	SACD album	Enter The Mysterium	Apr-05	MWCD-1016	Music & Words	voice, guitar, sequencing

Artist	Title	Format	Album	Date	Catalogue	Label	Instruments
Peter Ulrich	The Scryer and the Sh…	SACD album	Enter The Mysterium	Apr-05	MWCD-1017	Music & Words	voice, perc, dulcimer, seq
Peter Ulrich	Across The Bridge	SACD album	Enter The Mysterium	Apr-05	MWCD-1018	Music & Words	voice, perc, h/dulcimer
Peter Ulrich	Nothing But the Way	SACD album	Enter The Mysterium	Apr-05	MWCD-1019	Music & Words	voice, perc, flute, sequen
Peter Ulrich	The Witchbottle of Suffolk	SACD album	Enter The Mysterium	Apr-05	MWCD-1020	Music & Words	voice, perc, sequencing
Peter Ulrich	The True Cross	SACD album	Enter The Mysterium	Apr-05	MWCD-1021	Music & Words	voice, perc, sequencing
Peter Ulrich	Kakatak Tamai	SACD album	Enter The Mysterium	Apr-05	MWCD-1022	Music & Words	voice, drums, perc, seq
Peter Ulrich	Another Day	SACD album	Enter The Mysterium	Apr-05	MWCD-1023	Music & Words	voice, drums, perc, seq
Peter Ulrich	Through Those Eyes	SACD album	Enter The Mysterium	Apr-05	MWCD-1024	Music & Words	voice, guitars, perc
Peter Ulrich	Flesh to Flame	SACD album	Enter The Mysterium	Apr-05	MWCD-1025	Music & Words	voice, h/dulcimer, perc
Dead Can Dance	Nierika	CD album	Memento	Oct-05	R2 73264	Rhino/ 4AD	bass drum
Various Artists	Taqaharu's Leaving	3CDretro set	Projekt 200	Aug-07	PRO200	Projekt	voice, drums, sequencing
Various Artists	The Scryer and the Sh…	CD album	John Barleycorn Reborn	Sep-07	CSR84CD	Cold Spring	voice, perc, dulcimer, seq
Dead Can Dance	The Trial	SACD album	Dead Can Dance	Jun-08	SAD 2705 CD	4AD	drum kit
Dead Can Dance	Fortune	SACD album	Dead Can Dance	Jun-08	SAD 2705 CD	4AD	drum kit
Dead Can Dance	Ocean	SACD album	Dead Can Dance	Jun-08	SAD 2705 CD	4AD	metal percussion
Dead Can Dance	East of Eden	SACD album	Dead Can Dance	Jun-08	SAD 2705 CD	4AD	drum kit
Dead Can Dance	Threshold	SACD album	Dead Can Dance	Jun-08	SAD 2705 CD	4AD	drum kit
Dead Can Dance	A Passage in Time	SACD album	Dead Can Dance	Jun-08	SAD 2705 CD	4AD	drum kit
Dead Can Dance	Wild in the Woods	SACD album	Dead Can Dance	Jun-08	SAD 2705 CD	4AD	drum kit
Dead Can Dance	Carnival of Light	SACD EP	Garden of the Arcane…	Jun-08	SAD 2706 CD	4AD	drum kit
Dead Can Dance	In Power We Entrust…	SACD EP	Garden of the Arcane…	Jun-08	SAD 2706 CD	4AD	drum kit

Artist	Song	Format	Release	Date	Catalogue	Label	Credits
Dead Can Dance	The Arcane	SACD EP	Garden of the Arcane . . .	Jun-08	SAD 2706 CD	4AD	drum kit
Dead Can Dance	Flowers of the Sea	SACD EP	Garden of the Arcane . . .	Jun-08	SAD 2706 CD	4AD	bongoes
Dead Can Dance	Dawn of the Iconoclast	SACD album	Within the Realm of . . .	Jun-08	SAD 2708 CD	4AD	timpani & snare
Dead Can Dance	Summoning of the Muse	SACD album	Within the Realm of . . .	Jun-08	SAD 2708 CD	4AD	timpani
Dead Can Dance	Nierika	SACD album	Spiritchaser	Jun-08	SAD 2713 CD	4AD	bass drum
Dead Can Dance	Dedicace Outo	SACD album	Spiritchaser	Jun-08	SAD 2713 CD	4AD	bass drum
Ulrich Collaboration	Hanging Man	digital single	Hanging Man	Apr-09		City Canyons	percussion, sequencing
Piano Magic	March of the Atheists	CD album	Ovations	Oct-09	MMM060	MakeMineMusic	hammered dulcimer
Piano Magic	A Fond Farewell	CD album	Ovations	Oct-09	MMM060	MakeMineMusic	percussion
Piano Magic	La Corbardia de los Tor . . .	CD album	Ovations	Oct-09	MMM060	MakeMineMusic	hammered dulcimer
Ulrich Collaboration	Love's Skeleton	digital single	Love's Skeleton	Feb-10		City Canyons	percussion, sequencing
Ulrich Collaboration	Starship (Golden Eye)	digital single	Starship (Golden Eye)	May-10		City Canyons	percussion, sequencing
Ulrich Collaboration	Drug of War	digital single	Drug of War	Nov-10		City Canyons	perc, sequenc, back vox
Ulrich Collaboration	Children of the Rain	digital single	Children of the Rain	Apr-11		City Canyons	percussion, back vox
Ulrich Collaboration	Dark Lover	digital single	Dark Lover	May-11		City Canyons	percussion, sequencing
Ulrich Collaboration	Pureland	digital single	Pureland	Jun-11		City Canyons	perc, sequenc, back vox
Ulrich Collaboration	Secret Gardener	digital single	Secret Gardener	Jul-11		City Canyons	voice, perc, bass, sequen
This Mortal Coil	At First, And Then	CD album	This Mortal Coil (box set)	Nov-11	TMCBOX1	4AD	drums, perc, ocarina
This Mortal Coil	At First, And Then	CD album	This Mortal Coil (remastr)	Aug-12	CAD3X05CDJ	4AD	drums, perc, ocarina
Ulrich Collaboration	In This or Other Skin	CD album	The Painted Caravan	Mar-13	MSMCD162	Market Square	perc, moon guitar, sequen
Ulrich Collaboration	Pureland	CD album	The Painted Caravan	Mar-13	MSMCD162	Market Square	percussion, chants/vox
Ulrich Collaboration	The Secret Gardener	CD album	The Painted Caravan	Mar-13	MSMCD162	Market Square	voice, perc, bass, sequen

Artist	Title	Format	Release	Date	Catalog	Label	Role
Ulrich Collaboration	Dark Lover	CD album	The Painted Caravan	Mar-13	MSMCD162	Market Square	percussion, sequencing
Ulrich Collaboration	Starship (Golden Eye)	CD album	The Painted Caravan	Mar-13	MSMCD162	Market Square	percussion, sequencing
Ulrich Collaboration	Children of the Rain	CD album	The Painted Caravan	Mar-13	MSMCD162	Market Square	percussion, back vox
Ulrich Collaboration	Drug of War	CD album	The Painted Caravan	Mar-13	MSMCD162	Market Square	perc, sequenc, back vox
Ulrich Collaboration	Hanging Man	CD album	The Painted Caravan	Mar-13	MSMCD162	Market Square	percussion, sequencing
Ulrich Collaboration	Fanfare for the Lost Tribe	CD album	The Painted Caravan	Mar-13	MSMCD162	Market Square	percussion, blown bottles
Ulrich Collaboration	Desert	CD album	The Painted Caravan	Mar-13	MSMCD162	Market Square	percussion, harmonium
Ulrich Collaboration	Love's Skeleton	CD album	The Painted Caravan	Mar-13	MSMCD162	Market Square	percussion, sequencing
Ulrich Collaboration	Tempest	CD album	The Painted Caravan	Mar-13	MSMCD162	Market Square	voice, guitar, h/dulc, perc
Daemonia Nymphe	Psychostasia	CD album	Psychostasia	May-13	PRIK159	Prikosnovenie	darabuka, maracas
Ulrich Collaboration	In This or Other Skin	CD album	The Painted Caravan	Feb-14	AISCD 001	AIS	perc, moon guitar, sequen
Ulrich Collaboration	Pureland	CD album	The Painted Caravan	Feb-14	AISCD 001	AIS	percussion, chants/vox
Ulrich Collaboration	The Secret Gardener	CD album	The Painted Caravan	Feb-14	AISCD 001	AIS	voice, perc, bass, sequen
Ulrich Collaboration	Dark Lover	CD album	The Painted Caravan	Feb-14	AISCD 001	AIS	percussion, sequencing
Ulrich Collaboration	Starship (Golden Eye)	CD album	The Painted Caravan	Feb-14	AISCD 001	AIS	percussion, sequencing
Ulrich Collaboration	Children of the Rain	CD album	The Painted Caravan	Feb-14	AISCD 001	AIS	percussion, back vox
Ulrich Collaboration	Drug of War	CD album	The Painted Caravan	Feb-14	AISCD 001	AIS	perc, sequenc, back vox
Ulrich Collaboration	Hanging Man	CD album	The Painted Caravan	Feb-14	AISCD 001	AIS	percussion, sequencing
Ulrich Collaboration	Fanfare for the Lost Tribe	CD album	The Painted Caravan	Feb-14	AISCD 001	AIS	percussion, blown bottles
Ulrich Collaboration	Desert	CD album	The Painted Caravan	Feb-14	AISCD 001	AIS	percussion, harmonium
Ulrich Collaboration	Love's Skeleton	CD album	The Painted Caravan	Feb-14	AISCD 001	AIS	percussion, sequencing
Ulrich Collaboration	Tempest	CD album	The Painted Caravan	Feb-14	AISCD 001	AIS	voice, guitar, h/dulc, perc

Artist	Title	Format	Album/Project	Date	Catalog	Label	Instruments
Ulrich Collaboration	Don Juan's Lament	CD album	Tempus Fugitives	Apr-15	AISCD 002	AIS	bongoes, cymbals, perc
Ulrich Collaboration	Dark Daddy	CD album	Tempus Fugitives	Apr-15	AISCD 002	AIS	bass drum, tambourine
Ulrich Collaboration	Drum The River	CD album	Tempus Fugitives	Apr-15	AISCD 002	AIS	voice, cahon, bass, perc
Ulrich Collaboration	King of Fools (T/Prisoner)	CD album	Tempus Fugitives	Apr-15	AISCD 002	AIS	bass steel pans, percuss
Ulrich Collaboration	Mr Johnson	CD album	Tempus Fugitives	Apr-15	AISCD 002	AIS	drums, cymbal, steel pan
Ulrich Collaboration	En Bleu	CD album	Tempus Fugitives	Apr-15	AISCD 002	AIS	drums, percussion
Ulrich Collaboration	Big Iron Gun	CD album	Tempus Fugitives	Apr-15	AISCD 002	AIS	drums, percussion
Ulrich Collaboration	Green	CD album	Tempus Fugitives	Apr-15	AISCD 002	AIS	recorders, perc, h/dulcimr
Ulrich Collaboration	The Lycanthrope	CD album	Tempus Fugitives	Apr-15	AISCD 002	AIS	sequencing, perc, recordr
Ulrich Collaboration	Icarus	CD album	Tempus Fugitives	Apr-15	AISCD 002	AIS	drums, percussion
Ulrich Collaboration	Beloved Suicide	CD album	Tempus Fugitives	Apr-15	AISCD 002	AIS	voice, percuss, sequencg
Ulrich Collaboration	Song of All the Prophets	CD album	Tempus Fugitives	Apr-15	AISCD 002	AIS	perc, voice, blown bottles
Ulrich Collaboration	Migrators	CD album	Tempus Fugitives	Apr-15	AISCD 002	AIS	drums, perc, seq, voice
Ulrich Collaboration	Zanzibar (Song of Njiwa)	CD album	Tempus Fugitives	Apr-15	AISCD 002	AIS	voice, djembe, perc, seq
Dead Can Dance	The Trial	vinyl album	Dead Can Dance (remstr)	Jul-16	CAD 3622	4AD	drum kit
Dead Can Dance	Fortune	vinyl album	Dead Can Dance (remstr)	Jul-16	CAD 3622	4AD	drum kit
Dead Can Dance	Ocean	vinyl album	Dead Can Dance (remstr)	Jul-16	CAD 3622	4AD	metal percussion
Dead Can Dance	East of Eden	vinyl album	Dead Can Dance (remstr)	Jul-16	CAD 3622	4AD	drum kit
Dead Can Dance	Threshold	vinyl album	Dead Can Dance (remstr)	Jul-16	CAD 3622	4AD	drum kit
Dead Can Dance	A Passage in Time	vinyl album	Dead Can Dance (remstr)	Jul-16	CAD 3622	4AD	drum kit
Dead Can Dance	Wild in the Woods	vinyl album	Dead Can Dance (remstr)	Jul-16	CAD 3622	4AD	drum kit
Dead Can Dance	Carnival of Light	4 x vinyl set	Garden Arc; Peel Sesn's	Nov-16	DAD 3628	4AD/BBC	drum kit

Artist	Title	Format	Notes	Date	Catalogue	Label	Instrument
Dead Can Dance	In Power We Entrust . . .	4 x vinyl set	Garden Arc; Peel Sesn's	Nov-16	DAD 3628	4AD/BBC	drum kit
Dead Can Dance	The Arcane	4 x vinyl set	Garden Arc; Peel Sesn's	Nov-16	DAD 3628	4AD/BBC	drum kit
Dead Can Dance	Flowers of the Sea	4 x vinyl set	Garden Arc; Peel Sesn's	Nov-16	DAD 3628	4AD/BBC	congas
Dead Can Dance	Instrumental (aka Orion)	4 x vinyl set	Garden Arc; Peel Sesn's	Nov-16	DAD 3628	4AD/BBC	drum machine
Dead Can Dance	Ocean	4 x vinyl set	Garden Arc; Peel Sesn's	Nov-16	DAD 3628	4AD/BBC	hammered dulcimer
Dead Can Dance	Labour of Love	4 x vinyl set	Garden Arc; Peel Sesn's	Nov-16	DAD 3628	4AD/BBC	drum machine
Dead Can Dance	Threshold	4 x vinyl set	Garden Arc; Peel Sesn's	Nov-16	DAD 3628	4AD/BBC	drum kit
Dead Can Dance	Carnival of Light	4 x vinyl set	Garden Arc; Peel Sesn's	Nov-16	DAD 3628	4AD/BBC	drum kit
Dead Can Dance	Penumbra	4 x vinyl set	Garden Arc; Peel Sesn's	Nov-16	DAD 3628	4AD/BBC	drum kit
Dead Can Dance	Panacea	4 x vinyl set	Garden Arc; Peel Sesn's	Nov-16	DAD 3628	4AD/BBC	drum kit
Dead Can Dance	Flowers of the Sea	4 x vinyl set	Garden Arc; Peel Sesn's	Nov-16	DAD 3628	4AD/BBC	bongoes
Dead Can Dance	Dawn of the Iconoclast	vinyl album	Within the Realm (remstr)	Nov-16	CAD 3629	4AD	timpani & snare
Dead Can Dance	Summoning of the Muse	vinyl album	Within the Realm (remstr)	Nov-16	CAD 3629	4AD	timpani
Dead Can Dance	Nierika	vinyl album	Spiritchaser (remaster)	Mar-17	DAD 3637	4AD	bass drum
Dead Can Dance	Dedicace Outo	vinyl album	Spiritchaser (remaster)	Mar-17	DAD 3637	4AD	bass drum
Piano Magic	March of the Atheists	vinyl album	Ovations	May-17	DRL 227-1	Darla	hammered dulcimer
Piano Magic	A Fond Farewell	vinyl album	Ovations	May-17	DRL 227-1	Darla	percussion
Piano Magic	La Corbardia de los Tor . . .	vinyl album	Ovations	May-17	DRL 227-1	Darla	hammered dulcimer
Dead Can Dance	The Arcane	CD Box Set	Silhouettes & Statues	Jun-17	CRCDBOX34	Cherry Red	drum kit
Peter Ulrich	The Scryer and the Sh . . .	vinyl album	John Barleycorn Reborn	Dec-17	BWR047	Burning World	voice, perc, dulcimer, seq
This Mortal Coil	At First, And Then	CD album	This Mortal Coil (remaster)	Dec-18	CAD3X05CDJ	4AD	drums, perc, ocarina
This Mortal Coil	At First, And Then	vinyl album	This Mortal Coil (remastr)	Dec-18	DAD 3X05	4AD	drums, perc, ocarina

Artist	Track	Format	Album	Date	Catalogue	Label	Credits
Ulrich Collaboration	Artificial Man	CD album	Final Reflections	Dec-19	AISCD 003	AIS	drums, perc, seq, voice
Ulrich Collaboration	Lessons of Love	CD album	Final Reflections	Dec-19	AISCD 003	AIS	drums
Ulrich Collaboration	Severely Blessed	CD album	Final Reflections	Dec-19	AISCD 003	AIS	percussion
Ulrich Collaboration	Pirate Jane	CD album	Final Reflections	Dec-19	AISCD 003	AIS	washboard, percussion
Ulrich Collaboration	Nightwalker & Love Witch	CD album	Final Reflections	Dec-19	AISCD 003	AIS	drums, percussion
Ulrich Collaboration	Hawk Dreams	CD album	Final Reflections	Dec-19	AISCD 003	AIS	drums, percussion
Ulrich Collaboration	Swimming in My Sleep	CD album	Final Reflections	Dec-19	AISCD 003	AIS	drums, percussion
Ulrich Collaboration	Squaring the Circle	CD album	Final Reflections	Dec-19	AISCD 003	AIS	voice, perc, sequencing
Ulrich Collaboration	Love's Skeleton (remix)	CD album	Final Reflections	Dec-19	AISCD 003	AIS	percussion, sequencing
Ulrich Collaboration	Hanging Man (remix)	CD album	Final Reflections	Dec-19	AISCD 003	AIS	percussion, sequencing
Peter Ulrich	Lammas Dance	CD album	Forme to the Fynisment . . .	Aug-20	CSR252CD	Cold Spring	voices, perc, recorder, keys
Peter Ulrich	Taqaharu's Leaving	vinyl album	Pathways and Dawns	Sept-20	IF-103LP	Infinite Fog	voice, drums, sequencing
Peter Ulrich	Always Dancing	vinyl album	Pathways and Dawns	Sept-20	IF-103LP	Infinite Fog	voice, sequencing
Peter Ulrich	Life Amongst the Black . . .	vinyl album	Pathways and Dawns	Sept-20	IF-103LP	Infinite Fog	voice, sequencing
Peter Ulrich	Journey of Discovery	vinyl album	Pathways and Dawns	Sept-20	IF-103LP	Infinite Fog	sequencing
Peter Ulrich	Nocturne	vinyl album	Pathways and Dawns	Sept-20	IF-103LP	Infinite Fog	voice, sequencing
Peter Ulrich	Evocation	vinyl album	Pathways and Dawns	Sept-20	IF-103LP	Infinite Fog	voice, drums, percussion
Peter Ulrich	The Springs of Hope	vinyl album	Pathways and Dawns	Sept-20	IF-103LP	Infinite Fog	voice, sequencing
Peter Ulrich	Time and a Word	vinyl album	Pathways and Dawns	Sept-20	IF-103LP	Infinite Fog	voice, sequencing
Tenzin	The Beginning	digital album	Echoes	Oct-21			percussion
Tenzin	Into The World	digital album	Echoes	Oct-21			percussion
Tenzin	Shooting Star	digital album	Echoes	Oct-21			drums, percussion

Artist	Title	Format	Album	Date	Instruments
Tenzin	The Singing Fields	digital album	Echoes	Oct-21	kalimba, drums, perc
Tenzin	T's Something About You	digital album	Echoes	Oct-21	drums, finger cymbals
Tenzin	He Will Be Mine	digital album	Echoes	Oct-21	drums, percussion
Tenzin	Predatory Woman	digital album	Echoes	Oct-21	drums, percussion
Tenzin	Enter My Space	digital album	Echoes	Oct-21	udu, drums
Tenzin	I Believe in You	digital album	Echoes	Oct-21	drums, percussion
Tenzin	Time Stands Still	digital album	Echoes	Oct-21	cymbal, shekere
Tenzin	Tides	digital album	Echoes	Oct-21	maracas, claves
Tenzin	Free	digital album	Echoes	Oct-21	percussion
Tenzin	Trust in Me	digital album	Echoes	Oct-21	slaps, maracas, cymbals

INDEX

BIOGRAPHICAL NOTE

Ulrich grew up in London of the sixties and seventies, absorbing the music scene and teaching himself to play drums. A competent but unexceptional pub-band drummer, he was carving himself a career in theatre publicity when a twist of fate in 1982 landed him the drum stool of a nascent Dead Can Dance alongside Lisa Gerrard and Brendan Perry. Ulrich now proves a compelling writer as his memoir takes us on the incident-packed journey that followed: through the 4AD of the 1980s, managing DCD's international tours, contributing to *This Mortal Coil*, going solo with Perry's huge helping hand, releasing his debut album through the US Projekt label, then heading up a long-running collaboration with producer Trebor Lloyd and a host of artists from the New York scene. Peter Ulrich lives and works in the very centre of Norfolk, UK.